EXPLORING DISTANCE IN LEADER–FOLLOWER RELATIONSHIPS

Leadership: Research and Practice Series
A James MacGregor Burns Academy of Leadership Collaboration

Series Editors

Georgia Sorenson, Ph.D., Research Professor in Leadership Studies, University of Maryland and Founder of the James MacGregor Academy of Leadership and the International Leadership Association.

Ronald E. Riggio, Ph.D., Henry R. Kravis Professor of Leadership and Organizational Psychology and former Director of the Kravis Leadership Institute at Claremont McKenna College.

Michelle C. Bligh and Ronald E. Riggio (Eds.)
Exploring Distance in Leader–Follower Relationships:
When Near is Far and Far is Near

Jon P. Howell
Snapshots of Great Leadership: Pathways for People, Profit, and Planet

EXPLORING DISTANCE IN LEADER–FOLLOWER RELATIONSHIPS

WHEN NEAR IS FAR AND FAR IS NEAR

EDITED BY

Michelle C. Bligh
Claremont Graduate University
Claremont, California, USA

Ronald E. Riggio
Claremont McKenna College
Claremont, California, USA

Routledge
Taylor & Francis Group

NEW YORK AND LONDON

First published 2013
by Routledge
711 Third Avenue, New York, NY 10017

Simultaneously published in the UK
by Routledge
27 Church Road, Hove, East Sussex BN3 2FA

Routledge is an imprint of the Taylor & Francis Group, an informa business

© 2013 Taylor & Francis, LLC

Library of Congress Cataloging in Publication Data
A catalog record for this book has been applied for

ISBN: 978-1-84872-602-4 (hbk)
ISBN: 978-0-203-12063-7 (ebk)

Typeset in Minion
by Keystroke, Station Road, Codsall, Wolverhampton

Printed and bound in the United States of America by
Walsworth Publishing Company, Marceline, MO.

This volume is a result of an ongoing collaboration between the Kravis Leadership Institute and Claremont Graduate University, and is dedicated to those helping leaders and followers to understand and negotiate new meanings of distance in the twenty-first century. Through jointly determined efforts, both leaders and followers can now tackle challenges across vast distances, as technology and increased interconnectedness change our conceptions of what is "near" and what is "far."

Contents

Series Foreword

We live in a world where today is yesterday somewhere in the world, and near can be much more distant than far when it comes to leadership impact.

The science and study of leadership has moved beyond a simple trait X situation analysis and become "curiouser and curiouser" with the introduction of new books such as this one edited by management professor Michelle Bligh and social psychologist Ron Riggio. This work, drilling deeper into the core of the leadership construct, is fresh and rich and provides profound new vistas for insight and consideration.

In this volume, "distance" is conceptualized in a multitude of interesting and provocative ways. The study of physical, geometric, proximal, psychological, and organizational distance in leader–follower relationships has a rich history, from Georg Simmel's to Park's seminal paper on social distance and more recently, Bogardus's work on vertical and horizontal distance. That was then.

This is now. The concept of leadership and distance is front-and-center today, as globalization and virtual groups dominate our social, political, and commercial discourse. Leading from a distance is part and parcel of a leader's job, at the same time that we know that a sense of "closeness" to a leader is critical for engaging employees and building loyalty and commitment.

To give the reader an idea of the variables at hand, take, for example, the management of a presidential campaign. In years past citizens were able to base their perceptions of the candidate mainly on some direct experiences of the leader. Today voters in a presidential campaign have a limited ability to experience the leader first-hand. A campaign is emblematic of a type of temporary work group so common today, yet issues of group trust are salient, even paramount. Yet voters who are distant from the leader must base their perceptions of the leader mainly on image, projection, and message branding. How close or far engenders trust? And what of the ethical use of distance? What is true and what is manufactured?

As this book reveals, even physical distance is confounded by other variables in the leadership mix. For example, teams have been found to exhibit higher performance when a transformational leader is physically close to followers and when a transactional leader is physically distant. And followers of distant leaders may be more prone to degrade or ridicule a distant leader (for instance, after an ethical failure or an error made by the leader) because their experience is projective rather than real. And chapter author, Alice Eagly, adds another dimension when she introduces the impact of gender on these complexities with enlightening strategies for women leaders in any profession.

Anne Duffy and I are especially excited about these new directions in leadership scholarship and practice and about this book in particular. If you're going to fall into a rabbit hole, this book will provide unique knowledge and strategies based on distance, as well as leave you "curiouser and curiouser" about the leadership vistas ahead.

Georgia Sorenson, Ph.D.
Visiting Professor of Leadership Studies
Francis King Carey School of Law, University of Maryland
Series Editor

Ronald E. Riggio, Ph.D.
Henry R. Kravis Professor of Leadership and Organizational Psychology
Claremont McKenna College, Claremont, California
Series Editor

Acknowledgments

We would like to thank the authors for their insights and contributions to both the conference and the development of this volume. We also thank Paul Thomas, who helped organize the conference, as well as Joshua Lewondowski, Sheilesha Willis, and Nickolas Lamel for assisting with editing the volume. Finally, we thank the School of Behavioral and Organizational Sciences at Claremont Graduate University, as well as the Kravis Leadership Institute at Claremont McKenna College, for their support for both the conference and this volume.

SCHOOL OF BEHAVIORAL AND ORGANIZATIONAL SCIENCES

Since the late 1960s, the School of Behavioral and Organizational Sciences (SBOS) at Claremont Graduate University has been a leader in providing graduate education in applied psychological science, and in preparing students to meet the challenges of an increasingly diverse and global community. http://www.cgu.edu/pages/154.asp

CLAREMONT SYMPOSIUM ON APPLIED SOCIAL PSYCHOLOGY

The Claremont Symposium on Applied Social Psychology began in 1986 under the leadership of Dr. Stuart Oskamp. Over the years, the series has examined a broad range of topics crucial to our understanding of human relationships and the building of a healthy, diverse society. http://www.cgu.edu/pages/4513.asp

THE KRAVIS–DE ROULET LEADERSHIP CONFERENCE

The Kravis–de Roulet Leadership Conference began in 1990 with a joint endowment from Henry R. Kravis and the de Roulet family. This funding supports an annual leadership conference on cutting-edge topics in leadership including the finest leadership scholars and presenters. http://www.claremontmckenna.edu/kli/conference/

THE KRAVIS LEADERSHIP INSTITUTE

The mission of the Kravis Leadership Institute at Claremont McKenna College is to be the premier academic center for the promotion and understanding of responsible, innovative leadership and to provide unique opportunities for CMC students to develop as outstanding real world leaders in the public, private and social sectors. http://www.claremont mckenna.edu/kli/

About the Editors

Dr. Michelle C. Bligh is an Associate Professor in the School of Behavioral and Organizational Sciences and the Drucker-Ito School of Management at Claremont Graduate University. Her research interests include charismatic leadership, interpersonal trust, and political and executive leadership. Her work has been published in the *Journal of Applied Psychology, Leadership, Employee Relations, Leadership Quarterly, Applied Psychology: An International Review, Group and Organization Management, Journal of Managerial Psychology,* and *The Journal of Business Ethics,* and she serves on the editorial review boards of *The Leadership Quarterly* and *Leadership.* She was awarded the *Sage Best Paper Award* in *Group and Organization Management* and the *Sage Outstanding Paper Award for Research Methods.* Dr. Bligh has also helped a variety of public and private sector organizations assess and improve their effectiveness in the areas of leadership development, organizational culture, and change management.

Ronald E. Riggio, Ph.D. is the Henry R. Kravis Professor of Leadership and Organizational Psychology and former Director of the Kravis Leadership Institute at Claremont McKenna College. Professor Riggio is the author or editor of over a dozen books, and a hundred book chapters and research articles in the areas of leadership, assessment centers, organizational psychology, and emotional and nonverbal communication. His books include *The Art of Followership, The Practice of Leadership* (Jossey-Bass, 2008, 2007), *Transformational Leadership (Second edition)* co-authored with Bernard M. Bass (Erlbaum, 2006), *Leadership and the Liberal Arts* (2009; co-edited with J. Thomas Wren and Michael Genovese), and *Leadership Studies: The Dialogue of Disciplines* (2012; co-edited with Michael Harvey).

He has served as an organizational consultant to dozens of businesses and nonprofit organizations in the areas of selection, organizational development, and leadership assessment and development.

Most recently, Professor Riggio guest edited a special issue of *The Leadership Quarterly* on "Longitudinal Studies of Leadership Development," co-edited a special issue of *Consulting Psychology Journal* on "Character and

Leadership," and a forthcoming special issue of *Group Processes and Intergroup Relations* on Leadership. He is the leadership blogger for *Psychology Today* magazine, which can be accessed at: http://blogs.psychologytoday.com/blog/cutting-edge-leadership.

About the Contributors

John Antonakis is Professor of Organizational Behavior in the Faculty of Business and Economics of the University of Lausanne, Switzerland. Professor Antonakis's research is currently focused on predictors and outcomes of leadership, leadership development, strategic leadership, social cognition, as well as on causality. He has published over 40 book chapters and articles in journals such as *Science, The Leadership Quarterly, Journal of Management, Journal of Operations Management, Human Relations*, and *Personality and Individual Differences*, among others. He has co-edited two books: *The Nature of Leadership*, and *Being There Even When You Are Not: Leading Through Strategy, Structures, and Systems*. Antonakis is Associate Editor of *The Leadership Quarterly*, and is on the editorial boards of the *Academy of Management Review, Journal of Management, Human Relations, Leadership, Organizational Psychology Review, Organizational Research Methods*, and *Journal of Management Studies*.

Alice H. Eagly is Professor of Psychology and of Management and Organizations, James Padilla Chair of Arts and Sciences, and Faculty Fellow in the Institute for Policy Research, all at Northwestern University. She has also held faculty positions at Michigan State University, University of Massachusetts in Amherst, and Purdue University. She received her Ph.D. in social psychology from the University of Michigan and her undergraduate degree from Radcliffe College of Harvard University. Her research interests include the study of gender, attitudes, prejudice, stereotyping, and leadership. She is the author of several books, numerous articles, chapters in edited books, and reviews. Her most recent book is *Through the Labyrinth: The Truth About How Women Become Leaders*. Eagly has also received several awards for her contributions, most recently the Distinguished Scientific Contribution Award from the American Psychological Association, the Gold Medal Award for Life Achievement in the Science of Psychology, and the Berlin Prize from the American Academy in Berlin. She also received an honorary doctorate from the University of Bern, Switzerland.

Amber M. Gaffney is a Ph.D. student at Claremont Graduate University. Her research focuses on social influence from a social identity and self-categorization perspective. Most of her work examines the conditions under which non-prototypical group members or minority group members can gain influence within their groups and enact social change.

Michael A. Hogg received his Ph.D. from Bristol University and is currently Professor of Social Psychology at Claremont Graduate University, and an Honorary Professor at the University of Kent and the University of Queensland. President-elect of the Society of Experimental Social Psychology, he is a Fellow of numerous associations, including the Association for Psychological Science, the Society for Personality and Social Psychology, the Society for the Psychological Study of Social Issues, and the Society of Experimental Social Psychology. Hogg's research on group processes, intergroup relations, social identity, and self-conception is closely associated with social identity theory. He has 300 scientific publications on these topics, and was the 2010 recipient of the Carol and Ed Diener Award in Social Psychology from the Society for Personality and Social Psychology. He is foundation co-editor of the journal *Group Processes and Intergroup Relations*, and a past associate editor of the *Journal of Experimental Social Psychology*. His current research focuses on influence, leadership, and self-uncertainty.

Edwin P. Hollander authored *Inclusive Leadership* (Routledge, 2009), highlighting his extensive research and theorizing on leader–follower relations. His other books include *Leaders, Groups, and Influence; Leadership Dynamics; Principles and Methods of Social Psychology*, translated into Chinese and Spanish; and the series *Current Perspectives in Social Psychology*. A Distinguished Professor since 1989 on the CUNY doctoral faculty at Baruch College and the Graduate Center, he taught before at Carnegie-Mellon, Washington (St. Louis), and American University (DC). In 1962, he became founding director of the doctoral program in social/organizational psychology at SUNY–Buffalo, and later provost of social sciences there. He earned his Ph.D. in Social Psychology and his M.S. in Psychometrics at Columbia University, with his B.S. in Psychology from Case Western Reserve. He was elected president of APA's General Psychology Division (1), and the Eastern Psychological Association. He served also as Chair of the APA Committee on Psychology in National and

International Affairs. While teaching as a Fulbright Professor for a year at the University of Istanbul, he lectured at academic institutions in seven nations, and has been visiting faculty at Wisconsin, Oxford, the Paris Institute of American Studies, and Harvard.

Philippe Jacquart received his Ph.D. from the University of Lausanne, Switzerland, and is currently a visiting scholar at The Wharton School of the University of Pennsylvania. During his doctorate, he has also been a visiting scholar at the business school of the University of Amsterdam. His primary research focuses on leadership at the upper echelons of organizations. His work has been published in *Leadership Quarterly* and has received the best paper award for 2010. He has also been awarded two fellowships from the Swiss National Science Foundation, and has received a faculty award for his doctoral dissertation.

Surinder S. Kahai is an Associate Professor of MIS at SUNY–Binghamton. He has a program of research spanning over twenty years that attempts to understand what affects performance of distributed or virtual teams. Much of his work has focused on leadership in such teams. Surinder is also working on projects that examine (a) CIO leadership and its effects on IT unit alignment and performance, (b) the use of virtual worlds for virtual team collaboration and leadership development, (c) leadership issues in the implementation of enterprise systems, and (d) online learning. Surinder has authored over forty journal articles, book chapters, and conference papers. His research has appeared in journals including *Decision Sciences, Journal of Applied Psychology, Journal of Management Information Systems, Leadership Quarterly,* and *Personnel Psychology.* He serves on the editorial boards of *Group & Organization Management, IEEE-TEM,* and *International Journal of e-Collaboration.* Surinder often writes on his blog at http://www.leadingvirtually.com.

Ronit Kark has received her Ph.D. from the Hebrew University and is currently a tenured Senior Lecturer in the Social-Organizational Group at the Psychology Department, Bar-Ilan University, Israel. Her research interests include leadership, identity and identification processes, emotions and positive relationships in organizations, and the interplay of gender and leadership in the organizational context. Her work has been published in the *Academy of Management Review, Journal of Applied Psychology,*

Leadership Quarterly, Journal of Organizational Behavior, Organization, and other outlets. She had served on the board of *The Academy of Management Journal* and is currently a member of the editorial boards of *The Leadership Quarterly* and *The International Journal of Management Review.* She received the 2001 Loreal–Rekanati Prize for the Study of Women and Management in Israel in her dissertation work, and her papers were awarded the 2005 ILA (International Leadership Association) best paper award, the CCL (Center for Creative Leadership) Award Finalists for the best article published in *The Leadership Quarterly* for 2007 and the Best Overall Paper Award for the 2011 IAMB (International Academy of Management and Business) conference. Dr. Kark also consults for a variety of public and private sector organizations and NGOs on topics related to her research interests and is involved in social activism in Israel.

Joshua Lewandowski is a doctoral student at Claremont Graduate University whose research involves how distance and virtuality shape organizational processes. Specifically, he studies how spatial distances affect messages of online support and how social distances bias perceptions of team outcomes. His current research includes the validation of a social distance scale, the application of Twitter as a research platform, and the study of virtual environments in understanding performance attributions. He earned his M.A. in Organizational Behavior & Evaluation at Claremont Graduate University and B.A. in Psychology at Rutgers University.

Timothy C. Lisk is a member of the Science team at Evolv On-Demand, a company specializing in data-driven workforce selection. He obtained his Masters from Claremont Graduate University where he is currently a Ph.D. candidate in industrial and organizational psychology in the School of Behavioral and Organizational Sciences. His research interests include leadership in distributed teams, personnel selection for distributed teamwork, and big data machine learning.

David E. Rast is a doctoral candidate in social psychology at Claremont Graduate University. He studies the effects of social identity processes and phenomena with a focus on leadership, influence, and persuasion. He (along with Hogg and Gaffney) was presented with the 2010 SPSP Outstanding Research Award and is currently a pre-doctoral research fellow with the Army Research Institute at Fort Leavenworth, Kansas.

Moran Anisman Razin is a Doctoral Candidate, University President's Program for Exceptional Students, at the Social-Organizational Group at the Psychology Department, Bar-Ilan University, Israel. She has received her B.A. in Psychology and Sociology from Tel Aviv University, Israel. Her research interests include leadership and psychological distance. She also teaches courses on inter-cultural psychology at the Open University.

Rebecca J. Reichard, Ph.D. is currently an assistant professor of organizational behavior at Claremont Graduate University. Her defining area of research interest is the development of leaders, including assessing the effectiveness of current organizational interventions aimed at developing leaders and identifying characteristics of effective leader development initiatives, researching what motivates individuals to want to improve their leadership (i.e., developmental readiness), identifying influential early life experiences that result in adult leader emergence and effectiveness, and lastly, developing and implementing evidence-based strategies to accelerate the development of leaders in organizations. Professor Reichard has published 21 papers in journals such as *Leadership Quarterly, Organizational Behavior and Human Decision Processes, Consulting Psychology Journal,* and *Human Resource Development Journal* and has presented her research over 25 times at national and international conferences on the topics of leader development and organizational behavior.

Shawn A. Serrano is currently a consultant in the area of workforce development and a doctoral student of Organizational Behavior at Claremont Graduate University. His Master's degree is in Organizational Behavior and Evaluation Sciences. His background in Coaching has guided his research interests, as he is interested in improving organizational performance through engagement interventions, leader development, and assessing organizational readiness to change.

Birgit Schyns is Professor at Durham University, UK. She received her Ph.D. from the University of Leipzig, Germany in 2001. Before moving to the UK in 2006 as a Reader in OB at the University of Portsmouth, she lived and worked in the Netherlands from 2002 to 2006. Her research topics include leadership and career development. She has published widely on topics including Leader–Member Exchange, transformational leadership, implicit leadership theories, followers' perception of leadership, as well as employability. Birgit has edited several special issues and two books. She is an associate editor for *European Journal of Work and Organizational Psychology* and *British Journal of Management* and serves on several editorial boards.

Boas Shamir, Ph.D. (London School of Economics and Political Sciences) is a Professor at the Department of Sociology and Anthropology, Hebrew University of Jerusalem, Israel, where he served as Dean of Social Sciences between 2005 and 2009. For the past two years he was Visiting Professor at the Department of Management and Organization, Stern School of Business, New York University. His primary research area is leadership in organizations. He has published on topics such as charismatic and trans-formational leadership, leaders' life stories, social distance and leadership, and followers' roles in the leadership process. His work was published in journals such as the *Academy of Management Review, Academy of Management Journal, Journal of Applied Psychology*, and *Organizations Science*. He is a member of the editorial boards of the *Academy of Management Review, Leadership*, and the *Leadership Quarterly*.

Andrew J. Wefald is an Assistant Professor at Kansas State University in the School of Leadership Studies. He received his Ph.D. in Industrial and Organizational Psychology from Kansas State University. His areas of research include leadership, job attitudes, and personality, focusing on examining and promoting positive organizational leadership. Wefald has published in *Journal of Organizational Behavior, Journal of Psychology: Interdisciplinary & Applied*, and *Journal of Management Inquiry*, among others.

Introduction: When Near is Far and Far is Near

Michelle C. Bligh and Ronald E. Riggio

A human being is part of the whole called by us universe, a part limited in time and space. We experience ourselves, our thoughts and feelings as something separate from the rest. A kind of optical delusion of consciousness. This delusion is a kind of prison for us, restricting us to our personal desires and to affection for a few persons nearest to us.

Albert Einstein, 1954

Scholars and philosophers have long recognized and debated how space, time, and distance fundamentally shape one's notion both of the self and of others. According to Merriam-Webster, use of the word 'distance' dates to the fourteenth century, and five different definitions of the term are provided in the online dictionary.[1] These definitions include (1) a separation in time; (2) the quality or state of being distant, as in spatial remoteness, personal or emotional separation, and difference or disparity; (3) a distant point or region; (4) aesthetic distance and the capacity to observe dispassionately; and (5) discord (now obsolete). In scanning these definitions, it is quickly clear that all of them have marked and fundamental impacts on the practice and study of leadership. At the most basic level, distance shapes how and to what degree we can and do interact with others; at the most complex level, changing notions of distance are literally morphing our relationships and spheres of influence at a rapidly increasing pace. Technology renders some separations of time and space less meaningful, as we analyze the details of fallen dictatorships and changing governments from locations around the globe. Paradoxically, technology modifies and enhances other types of distance as parents and managers alike bemoan their waning influence on followers who increasingly turn to smartphones and social media rather than to immediate leaders for daily guidance.

Given these radical shifts in what distance means for our modern organizations and our relationships with both leaders and followers within and without them, it is perhaps surprising that the domain of leadership has for the most part ignored it altogether. The majority of our theories of leadership implicitly suggest that it does not matter how often, across what distances, and through what media leaders and followers interact. The dual impacts of globalization and technology, however, are forcing us to reevaluate these assumptions. In this volume, we seek to establish the topic of distance as both a new approach to leadership and an important context for leadership that will essentially require a retesting and reevaluation of much of what we now know or think we know. It may be no exaggeration to state that the landscape of organizations is changed forever, as the spectrum of leader–follower relations grows infinitely more complex. Leaders may be radically separated or intimately close to followers physically, socially, and psychologically: indeed, all of these types of "distance" can and do also interact with one another. As a result, leadership scholars and practitioners are beginning to reevaluate the extent to which their theories and practices are impacted by factors such as geographic distance, virtuality, and modality of interaction. Distance, therefore, is not merely an attribute of one particular type of team or organization, but is inherent in all contexts to a greater or lesser degree.

This volume was inspired by these issues. In the following chapters, contributors address these and the myriad of other challenges leaders and followers face as they cope with changes in culture, technology, and the workplace. The jointly convened 24th Annual Claremont Symposium on Applied Social Psychology and 20th Annual Kravis–de Roulet Leadership Conference, held in Claremont on March 6, 2010, examined the breadth of these changes and what models might be adopted and adapted for effective leader–follower relations. This conference brought together scholars in the field of leadership studies to discuss the latest research on interpersonal leader–follower relations. The resulting discussions tackled the impact of distance—physical, interpersonal, and social—on our organizations. The chapters that follow represent some of the major themes that emerged from these discussions, including how to define distance and the ways in which it impacts leadership, exploring a myriad of applications to leadership and leader–follower relationships, and finally what extensions and future challenges distance represents for both leaders and scholars of leadership.

FOUNDATIONS OF DISTANCE

In the first chapter, Joshua Lewandowski and Timothy C. Lisk provide the "foundations of distance" to inform the rest of the volume. Specifically, they review the fundamental questions of what it means to be "distant" and how distance impacts human relations. While over a century of research has attempted to answer these questions, Lewandowski and Lisk provide a basis for understanding the formulation and evolution of distance, as well as its more modern conceptualizations in the context of leadership. They also provide a framework for understanding the general dynamics of distance in defining leader–follower relations. This chapter reviews several major forms of distance, including physical, psychological, and organizational distance, and provides a summative outlook of where distance has been, where it is going, and what areas still lay unexplored for future research. Overall, Lewandowski and Lisk make a compelling argument that, given the prevalence of virtual teams, decentralized structures, and the ubiquity of the online presence of both leaders and followers, what were once clear demarcation lines between "distant" and "not distant" are much hazier in modern organizations.

In the second chapter, Boas Shamir's "Notes on Distance and Leadership" expands on this question of how distance shapes and defines the leader–follower relationship. Building on previous discussions of distance as a characteristic of the *context* in which the leadership relationship exists, Shamir argues that distance can also be viewed as a characteristic of the *leadership relationship itself.* As an attribute of relationships between leaders and other organization members, distance can be viewed as something which is not an external condition given by the leadership context but, at least partially, as something which is *created* by the participants in the leadership relationship, who construct and construe the level of distance between them.

In addition, Shamir outlines some of the potential disadvantages as well as advantages of distance. He notes that distance is frequently viewed as an obstacle to communication and individualized consideration of followers, and as allowing fewer opportunities for leaders to engage in role modeling, guidance, and coaching. However, Shamir also points out that distance offers important benefits as well. Specifically, distance may enable leaders to hide their errors, failures, weaknesses, and vulnerabilities and thus to maintain a more "clean" and positive image in followers' eyes. Distance may thus increase followers' acceptance, as well as enhance the prestige and authority of the leader. Distance also allows leaders to reflect and recharge their batteries, gaining needed perspective and objectivity from the daily realities of organizational life. Furthermore, distance may be needed for the leaders to maintain detachment from daily operational details, obtain a broader perspective on organizational situations, prioritize, think strategically, identify longer-term needs and opportunities, articulate a long-term vision, and make long-term plans. Finally, Shamir notes that some of the effects of leader behavior may actually be enhanced by distance, as well as the autonomy and independence of followers.

EXPLORING THE IMPACT OF DISTANCE ON LEADER–FOLLOWER RELATIONS

The second section of the book builds on these foundations of distance to explore to what extent and in what ways different types of distance impact the study and practice of leadership. In "Leading in a Digital Age: What's Different, Issues Raised, and What We Know," Surinder Kahai outlines the debate between those who argue that effective leadership is the same despite increasing levels of distance and virtuality and those who suggest that the process of leadership changes fundamentally in a "wired" world. He discusses leadership in three IT-mediated contexts: same-place IT-mediated meetings, virtual teams, and complex organizations. Kahai proposes that IT can help a leader become a better "enabler" of adaptive leadership. Building on Shamir's arguments, Kahai argues that technology has both advantages and disadvantages for leaders to increase or decrease perceptions of distance. Specifically, he points out that in some ways technology is increasing distance, such as by introducing anonymity and by letting organizations distribute their workers worldwide, and in other cases it is decreasing distance, such as by bringing like-minded individuals together and by letting organizations tap into resources outside their boundaries. Consequently, the difference that IT can be expected to make for leadership is not likely to be uniform or simple. Further, Kahai points out that it may be precisely due to these complexities in "the difference" that IT is making for leadership that researchers offer seemingly contrasting viewpoints about whether or not leadership is fundamentally changing in a wired world.

In "Engaging Followers at a Distance: Leadership Approaches that Work", Rebecca Reichard, Shawn Serrano and Andrew Wefald discuss how various forms of leader–follower distance moderate the relationship between leadership and employee engagement. Specifically, they point out that leadership functions emphasized in traditional leadership models, including face-to-face interactions, communication, role clarification, team development, and task execution may all be significantly impacted by distance. As such, traditional models may fail to fully explain the relationship between distant leaders and employee engagement. The chapter emphasizes that even when leading from a distance, leaders can influence follower engagement through: (1) designing meaningful and motivating work, (2) supporting and coaching employees, (3) enhancing employees' personal resources (e.g., PsyCap), and (4) facilitating rewarding and supportive co-worker relations. In addition, Reichard and her coauthors provide four practical suggestions for increasing employee engagement in situations of high leader–follower distance.

Birgit Schyns' chapter addresses how distance impacts Leader–Member Exchange theory, one of the most intensely interpersonal theories of leadership. "The Role of Distance in Leader–Member Exchange (LMX)" points out that there is a long tradition of research suggesting that leaders have limited resources, which may jeopardize their efforts to establish and maintain good relationship qualities with all of their followers. Schyns proposes that when leaders are physically distant, it may be particularly difficult to establish and maintain good quality LMX relationships due to the low levels of interaction that can take place. She subsequently outlines arguments for how different types of leaders and different levels of follower needs can exacerbate or mitigate the role of distance on the leader–follower relationship. This suggests that distance may be particularly problematic as it relates to dyadic relationships which are difficult to establish and maintain under distance conditions in which there is little direct and/or intense contact. However, in this chapter, Schyns proposes both leader and follower characteristics that might make it easier to establish and maintain good quality LMX relationships even when leaders are distant.

While these three chapters all deal with how leadership behaviors are influenced by distance, in "The Far Side of Leadership: Rather Difficult to Face," John Antonakis and Philippe Jacquart address the importance of leader–follower distance in the selection of top-level leaders. They explore how distance from the leader can highlight inherent biases in the leadership-selection process that may be rooted in our evolutionary history. Specifically, in high-distance situations, followers have very little information about leaders and may be prone to judge them by basic heuristics of similarity or representativeness. Antonakis and Jacquart provide a great deal of evidence to suggest that leaders who make it to the top may do so *not* because of the skills they possess, but because they "look the role"; in other words, we choose leaders based on how "leaderly" they look, and not based on any real evidence of their leadership ability. Moreover, this biasing effect appears to be accentuated with leader distance.

Antonakis and Jacquart also point out that our evolutionary history may be particularly mismatched to the current milieu of technology and virtuality. In the absence of individuating information about potential leaders, individuals are likely to choose leaders who have qualities that would have been valuable in ancestral times, but do not matter today. While the stereotypical qualities sought may have had some adaptive function for our ancestors, for example, having domain-specific expertise (which historically was correlated with age), or being physically dominant (which historically was associated with height and strength), they are simply irrelevant today in the vast majority of leadership situations. Thus, Antonakis and Jacquart argue that it is now imperative that we develop accurate selection systems and processes to ensure that leader evaluations downplay "outside" characteristics and focus on "inside" characteristics in situations where the distance between leaders and followers is greater.

EMERGING CONCEPTS AND EXTENSIONS OF LEADER–FOLLOWER DISTANCE

The final section of the book addresses new and potentially innovative perspectives on the role of distance in various leadership contexts. In a different take on the notion of distance, Alice Eagly presents the idea of cultural distance in her chapter "Women as Leaders: Paths Through the Labyrinth." She points out that role incongruity for women as leaders follows from the disjunction between the communal qualities believed to be intrinsic to the female sex and the mainly agentic qualities that people believe are required to succeed as a leader. This incongruity takes the form of "cultural distance" between consensually defined concepts of women and leadership, whereas "cultural closeness" exists between men and leadership. Thus, to the many distance concepts invoked in the chapters of this volume, Eagly suggests that cultural distance is equally relevant. She defines this form of distance as the gap between cultural stereotypes that are applied to the same person, in the manner that concepts of women and leaders are applied to women who occupy or attempt to occupy a leadership role. The implications for women of this large cultural distance between "women" and "leaders" are profound, as exemplified by the negative reactions that powerful women often receive: women do not typically impress others as especially qualified for leadership. Even those women who possess objectively excellent qualifications generally have to overcome preconceptions that they are not well equipped to lead. In sum, this argument suggests that cultural distance from leadership prototypes can also impact leader-selection and promotion processes.

In "The Tyranny of Normative Distance: A Social Identity Account of the Exercise of Power by Remote Leaders," David Rast, Amber Gaffney, and Michael Hogg point out that while leaders vary in their social, psychological, and interactional distance from followers at an interpersonal level, on the intragroup level leaders also strive to close the gap between themselves and what is normative for their group and its members. This latter type of distance, which the authors term "normative distance," is defined as the extent to which the leader approximates the group's prototype. In general, a leader close to the group's prototypical position will wield more influence, while a leader remote from the prototype will be less influential. This approach emphasizes the relationship of the leader to the overall group. For example, a given leader may hold a position that embodies the thoughts, feelings, and actions of most of the group; alternatively, the leader may choose to advocate a position that is somewhat or markedly disparate from the majority of the group to incite important changes within the group or organization. Leaders may also utilize followers' uncertainty as a means to counteract the negative impact of being distant from the group's prototype, and thus gain additional influence within the group. Finally, they argue that leaders can strategically manipulate their own distance from the normative group position to maintain or challenge the group's cohesion in their attempts to either represent stability or promote change and innovation.

Moran Razin and Ronit Kark's chapter builds on these themes of change and innovation in a case study of Steve Jobs. In "The Apple does not Fall Far from the Tree: Steve Jobs's Leadership as Simultaneously Distant and Close," they examine the leadership of Apple's 14-year CEO. Jobs was often described as an extraordinary person who was greatly admired both inside and outside of the company. More relevant for the current volume, Jobs used both distance and proximity in his attempt to influence others. While Jobs felt that technology was fundamentally about bringing people closer, Razin and Kark present a compelling argument that Steve Jobs managed to shape people's perceptions of him as a charismatic leader who was simultaneously close and distant. Drawing from theories of leadership and distance in this volume and elsewhere, the chapter explores the notion of leaders "doing distance and proximity," suggesting that Steve Jobs's dual-distance strategy (of eliciting both a sense of distance and a sense of proximity among followers) was a successful leadership strategy which distinguished him from other business leaders and helped to foster the myth of Jobs as an extraordinary and legendary leader.

The final chapter in the volume engages notions of distance in the political arena. In "American Presidential Leadership: Leader Credit, Follower Inclusion, and Obama's Turn," Edwin Hollander examines a case study of US President Barack Obama and follower perceptions of his distance. Hollander notes that the American president has been called the "most personal" of our elected officials, and yet the leader in this role is also perceived to be at a great distance from the public. Specifically, the "majesty" and formality of the presidential office creates perceived social distance from followers and their everyday concerns. Hollander analyzes how both supporters and critics use the notion of "distance" to influence the "power distance gap" between leaders and followers. Specifically, Hollander notes that the physical and psychological distance between a president and his audience is bridged through media transmissions, not just from him but also from others (press secretary, spokespersons) repre-senting the president and including messages sent via the internet. These messages are then interpreted by individuals through their identification with or rejection of the president, and subsequently filtered through their primary groups as social supports. Hollander concludes that to bridge the power–distance gap, it was essential for the passion that President Obama showed in his presidential campaign to be re-expressed in his speeches and other appearances.

MOVING FORWARD

Although Einstein (1954) conceptualized distance as a kind of "prison," restricting us to our personal desires and to affection for those closest to us,[2] the chapters in this volume suggest that technology is beginning to offer some release from this psychic prison. It is now quite possible to develop followers and influence others halfway around the world, while it remains equally likely that the follower in the next cubicle may be oblivious to a leader's sphere of influence. While this volume provides some initial ideas about how distance is altering the study and practice of leadership, we hope its contents will spur the development of new research and theory that explores when and how leadership is transformed through space and time, and in what ways the notion of "distance" creates continuously evolving meanings for the leader–follower relationship.

NOTES

1   Retrieved August 25, 2011 from http://www.merriam-webster.com/dictionary/distance.
2   Retrieved October 11, 2010 from http://open-site.org/Science/Physics/Modern.

Section I

Foundations and Definitions of Distance

1

Foundations of Distance

Joshua Lewandowski and Timothy C. Lisk

> In the case of the stranger, the union of closeness and remoteness involved in every human relationship is patterned in a way that may be succinctly formulated as follows: the distance within this relation indicates that one who is close by is remote, but his strangeness indicates that one who is remote is near.
>
> Georg Simmel, 1908, p. 143

What does it mean to be distant? How does distance govern human relations? Over a century of research has attempted to answer these very questions and uncover the mechanisms that drive the formation and processing of human interactions. The topic of distance spans one hundred years of research and a multitude of disciplines. Therefore, it is not our intention to provide an exhaustive and comprehensive discussion of distance—such a task would fill volumes beyond this chapter. Rather, our intention is to provide a cornerstone for understanding the formation and initial evolution of distance as well as its modern conceptualizations.

Thus, we begin by discussing the foundations of distance: what is it, who conceptualized it, how has it changed, and what effect has it had on how we think about humanity? We provide a brief framework for understanding the general dynamics of distance in defining human relations. Then, we discuss several major forms of distance that encompass a vast array of operationalizations both theoretically and empirically, including physical, psychological, and organizational distance. Last, we provide an outlook regarding where distance has been, where it is going, and what areas still lay unexplored for future researchers.

FOUNDATIONS

Over a hundred years ago, the French sociologist Jean-Gabriel De Tarde first explored the dynamics of social imitation. In Tarde's (1903) *The Laws of Imitation,* distance is explored in terms of class differences, and is strictly defined by the level of imitation between two classes. Several years later the German sociologist Georg Simmel created the notion of "the stranger." Simmel's (1908) *Soziologie* treatise was one of the first examinations of physical *and* metaphorical manifestations of distance, and served as the seed from which the construct grew and developed. More widely known is Robert Park's (1924) popularization of distance in sociology; ironically, less known is that Park studied under Simmel. However, throughout the twentieth century, the curator of distance in both sociology and psychology was Emory Bogardus through his creation of the Bogardus Social Distance Scale (1925a). Bogardus's work launched the notion of distance into sociological and psychological stardom that reverberates even today. Unfortunately, by the time Bogardus's scale was created the distance construct had deviated substantially from Simmel's original manifestation, leaving merely a diluted shell of *The Stranger*'s initial form. Below we briefly trace the initial lineage of distance and describe its historical evolution.

Originally, Simmel conceptualized distance in two forms: geometric and metaphoric. He argued that both forms interact such that "Spatial relations not only are determining conditions of relationships among men, but are also symbolic of those relationships" (1908, p. 143). Simmel used the metaphor of a wandering stranger to represent an individual who is the union of both forms: physically near yet socially far. The stranger is not too far in that he is independent of the group, yet not close enough to become a member. Simmel regards the stranger as a *trader* of society: physically close, interacting frequently, etic in nature, yet made of a different substance from the rest of the society in which he lays embedded. It is this particular "constellation" (Simmel, 1908, p. 145) of near and far elements that define the stranger and ultimately, all human relations. Fundamentally, Simmel's conceptualization of distance rests on the antecedence of physical elements in defining human form and metaphorical relations.

Years later, Simmel's *Stranger* would take on a drastically different form. In Park's (1924) seminal paper on social distance, his opening remarks explicitly expel Simmel's notion of geometric distance. He writes, "The concept of distance, as applied to human, *as distinguished from spatial relations*, has come into use among sociologists" (p. 339; italics added). With those opening words the divergent evolution from Simmel's work began. Park seems to reject the very foundation of *The Stranger* later in this essay when he writes, "the frontier had passed . . . The characteristic prejudice of the frontier was directed not against the stranger, but against the man who acted strangely" (p. 342). Thus, Park defined distance not in terms of spatial distance but in terms of *social* distance, "in an attempt to reduce to something like measurable terms the grades and degrees of intimacy which characterize personal and social relations" (p. 339). In Park's defense, spatial distance was not a primary concern to him. The goal of Park's essay was to highlight the subtle social inequities that arise in democratic society, as opposed to social inequity inherent in a hierarchical social system. He employed social distance as an explanation of racial prejudice to maintain social order and to act as an equalizing force that preserves the status quo. The consequence of Park's manifestation of distance was the opposite of Simmel's: Simmel suggested that spatial relations aid in determining social relations, whereas Park suggested that racial divides or social distances result in spatial separations (Ethington, 1997).

One year after Park's (1924) essay, Emory Bogardus published the first version of the social distance scale (1925b, 1925c). Bogardus maintained Park's definition of distance, focusing on intimacy and understanding between individuals. It was the simplicity and novelty[1] of Bogardus's scale that ignited its use in sociology. Bogardus's scale simply asked participants to mark next to one of seven categories the extent to which they would "willingly admit members of each race" to some social situation. For example, "I would willingly admit members of [race]" to close kinship by marriage (worth 1 point) or to exclude from my country (worth 7 points). This allowed Bogardus to measure the extent to which each participant felt distanced from any given race or class. A limitation, Bogardus admits, is that this scale provides no indication as to *why* a participant harbors a specific sentiment or distance toward a particular race. However, it does allow for a quantification of social separation by calculating a distance index, or as Bogardus entitled it, a social quality index (1925b), which represents the average of the summed distances for a given race. Ultimately, Bogardus's scale provided a novel way to assess an exciting new area of research in sociology.

Emory Bogardus's contributions in the development of social distance extend well beyond his twin 1925 papers in the *Journal of Applied Sociology*. Eventually, distance evolved into a form much different from Simmel's original manifestation, whose content was defined both by its geometric as well as its metaphoric discontinuity. Bogardus later (1927) applied Park's social distance definition toward the then nascent leadership domain. He defined leadership distance using two independent dimensions: vertical and horizontal distance. Vertical distance is defined by differentials in achievement between two individuals, unique from rank or position, although "these social forms help to create or magnify social distances" (p. 174). Horizontal distance is defined as nominal activities of equal social rank. In other words, the horizontal distance between two followers or leaders is greater when the value of their activities is held constant but grows ever more unique in some fashion. Of the two, vertical distance ultimately survived the test of time, becoming the more widely accepted dimension in defining social distance with regard to leadership studies (e.g., Antonakis & Atwater, 2002).

Bogardus (1928) also applied his framework of leadership distance toward a group-level phenomenon which he called occupational distance, or the "degree of sympathetic understanding existing between the members of any two occupations" (p. 73). He applied the exact same scaling technique from his 1925 papers. Rather than asking participants to what extent they would admit members of a race to marry or exclude them from their country, he used occupations such as barber or detective. Bogardus also hypothesized a number of unique interactants regarding occupational distance. For example, he predicted a set amount of variability within each occupation, which he called occupational mobility, or the "tendency of a particular profession to move up and down the scale of prestige" (p. 75). If Simmel and Park are our metaphorical tinder, then Bogardus's insightful essays (1925a, 1925b, 1927, 1928) provided a spark which lit the way for numerous future studies in leadership and distance (e.g., Katz & Kahn, 1978; Shamir, 1995). Unfortunately, that spark would light a fire whose "embers" lay dormant for over fifty years (Antonakis & Atwater, 2002, p. 673).

Bogardus's 1928 essay is obviously not the last paper written on the topic of distance until the 1970s. In fact, numerous efforts were made to advance and modernize Bogardus's Social Distance Scale as advanced statistical methods were born in the early part of the century (for a review see Crano & Lac, 2011). These noble endeavors lie outside the scope of this chapter.

Instead, we aim merely to retrace the initial steps from Simmel's wandering stranger and direct our story into its modern forms and guises.

DISTANCE FRAMEWORK

Distance is conceptualized in a multitude of interesting and provocative ways, all of which guide scientists and practitioners in understanding human relations. Therefore, it may be useful to provide a descriptive framework for thinking about distance and what implications it has for our understanding.

For this mode of thought, we turn back to Simmel's (1908) opening words in *The Stranger* for inspiration. He wrote, "If wandering, considered as a state of detachment from every given point in space, is the conceptual opposite of attachment to any point, then the sociological form of 'the stranger' presents the synthesis, as it were, of both of these properties" (p. 143). Incorporating both Simmel's original construct of distance as well as its more evolved forms from Park and Bogardus, we propose that distance is represented by two functions: the type of *active* discontinuities between two entities and the magnitude of each disconnect. The first function poses the following question: which dimensions of distance assist in describing a given relationship? For example, Antonakis and Atwater (2002) describe several typologies of distant leaders in which three dimensions are active in describing relationships: physical distance, perceived interaction frequency between the leader and follower, and social distance. Namely, they contend that leaders are described as "virtually close" (p. 689) to followers when physical distance and interaction frequency are high but social distance is low. Together, these three dimensions create the "virtually close" leader–follower relationship when they are aligned in the fashion described above.

The second element that describes distance is not only the active dimensions of distance but also the magnitude of the disconnect. Previous research has examined distances of physical space (e.g., Podsakoff, MacKenzie, & Bommer, 1996) and perceived similarity (e.g., Liviatan, Trope, & Liberman, 2008) which indicate that the size of distance along any particular dimension may impact the dynamics of the relationship. For example, Helmreich, Aronson, and LeFan (1970) found that when participants observed a pratfall (or blunder), the reaction to that blunder depended on the perceived similarity between the participant and the confederate. In one case participants were told the confederate was an individual of average stature, and in another the participants were told the confederate was above average. Therefore, the magnitude of the distance |(in this case social distance) affects the interpretation of the event or relationship.

In addition to providing the components that form distant relationships, it is also important to provide several parameters or assumptions that further establish the foundation for how distance functions.

Rummel (1976) proposed three assumptions that guide the description of distant relationships. First, distance assumes some level of commonality between actors. For example, in order to measure the organizational distance between a leader and a follower one must assume each individual belongs to a common organization from which to draw a dimension. Thus, distance is a simultaneous representation of similarity and dissimilarity. Second, distance in and of itself is behaviorally independent; it does not necessarily imply positive or negative affect or outcome. For example, distance may be operationalized as a status differential which may hinder implicit affect between individuals. However, the form of distance is separate from its content (see Ethington, 1997). Last, distance assumes directionality. Distance is thus measured not only by its magnitude but also by its direction in a comparison. For example, one may be interested in perceptions of power in an organization. Although it is important to denote the magnitude of distance between a subordinate and a supervisor, it is equally important to suggest the direction of that distance. It may be the case that a newly hired subordinate reports a large distance toward his/her supervisor in that he or she perceives less power, and a veteran subordinate reports an equal amount of distance from the same supervisor but perceives having more power.

Simmel (1908) posits that the stranger maintains a specific set of characteristics that inherently define him as strange. As we have noted above, the stranger's characteristics are described as such: a low physical distance, yet high social distance in the form of individual dissimilarity or low group prototypicality, and a high level of interaction. The determinant of this arrangement is, as Simmel writes, strangeness and an objective view of the society in which the stranger lives. It is this particular constellation that defines the stranger's relationship to other individuals or groups. More importantly, one can concoct any number of discontinuities between two entities that extend far beyond physical or social distance.

For example, previous research describes a leader who is hierarchically distant (e.g., high vertical distance), infrequent in interactions with their followers, and socially unfamiliar, as susceptible for gaining charismatic attributes (Katz & Kahn, 1978). However, a very different set of active distance dimensions also result in charismatic attributes (Bass, 1990). For example, Shamir (1995) argues that charisma is also present in socially close circumstances, therefore alternative sets of distance dimensions result in an identical outcome. Charisma, like Simmel's (1908) notion of strangeness, is partially a function of a unique set of active distances. In other words, a leader may be regarded as being charismatic in very different circumstances depending on the types of distance that characterize his/her relationship with followers. To provide another example, leaders may be perceived as charismatic if they resemble Katz and Kahn's (1978) definition—hierarchically distant, socially unfamiliar, and infrequent in their interactions with followers. Moreover, leaders may also be regarded as charismatic under very different circumstances. Shamir (1995) suggests that charisma is also prevalent in close (rather than distant) relationships when the leader exhibits low social distance, provides more information about his/her traits and behaviors (i.e., demonstrating prototypical qualities), and exhibits transactional behaviors. Antonakis and Atwater's (2002) typology of distant leadership achieves the same goal, except they limit the varying dimensions of distance to social, physical, and interactive components. Their typology provides a matrix of leadership styles that correspond to different levels of each distance component. Put differently, defining relationships in the form of distances allows researchers to classify the same outcome from various settings (e.g., charismatic leadership in close and distant contexts depends upon specific distances).

It is not the purpose of this chapter to examine every constellation and net result of distance arrays, although a treatise on such a topic would provide information on a much needed gap in distance literature. Instead, this chapter serves to identify and discuss many of the major types of distance that occur between individuals, groups, and organizations, and what effects those distances have in specific circumstances such that later arrays and theories might be developed. Ultimately, the purpose of our proposed framework is to serve as a guide in not only synthesizing the present forms of distance under one mental umbrella (i.e., discontinuity) but also in the creation and incorporation of new and exciting forms that aid in our understanding of what Simmel (1908) referred to as "states of detachment" (p. 143).

FORMS OF DISTANCE

There are as many states of detachment as one can probably imagine. Indeed, various scholars have attempted to construct different forms of distance or create new categorical systems of discontinuity. In order to synthesize previous frameworks into an overarching guide, it may first be helpful to examine several examples of how previous research has attempted to organize the vast distance literature.

As mentioned earlier, Simmel (1908) originally defined distance along one dimension of spatial distance. Bogardus (e.g., 1925a) and Park (1924) later adopted this framework to include not only space but also social distances such as class differentials or racial differences. Poole (1927) introduced yet another type of distance—personal distance—which he added to Bogardus's (1925a) and Park's (1924) social distance construct, resulting in three dimensions in total.

Building on Poole's system, Rummel (1976) posited eleven types of distance which comprise four super-structures: material, psychological, social, and cultural distance. Material distance is composed of physical and personal distance, tapping into the notion of a spatial area around each individual. Psychological distance contains four components: psychological, interests, ideological, and affine distance (defined as a potential or actual closeness between two entities). This construct focuses internally, examining differences in perceptions, beliefs, moods, and goals. Social distance also contains four components: social, status, power, and class differences. These elements generally assess surface-level features such as wealth, authority, education, occupation, and gender. Cultural distance, the final component, is composed of differences in values, norms (also known as normative distance; Rast, Gaffney, & Hogg, this volume), ethics, and law.

Alternatively, Napier and Ferris (1993) describe distance using three dimensions that construct dyadic distance: psychological, structural, and functional. Psychological distance, for example, includes perceived similarity between actors or status differentials. Structural distance includes spatial distances, the span of management, and the opportunity to interact with others. Functional distance generally refers to affect, perceptual congruence, or the quality of relationships (e.g., trust, support, or satisfaction).

From a leader–follower perspective, Antonakis and Atwater (2002) utilize a similar system that consists of social distance, physical distance, and perceived interaction frequency. They use these three dimensions to assemble a matrix that describes leader–follower relationships. For example, a "proximal leader" maintains a low physical distance, and high interaction frequency.

Another framework is proposed by Karakayli (2009), who posits four unique dimensions of only social distance: affective, normative, interactive, and cultural or habitual distance. Using these dimensions, she constructs five constellations that describe human interactions with regard to Simmel's (1908) original stranger metaphor (e.g. the stranger as a competitor or as an ally). She posits that social distance is a multi-dimensional construct that contains elements of emotion, norms and values, the degree to which individuals interact, and the degree to which two groups are similar.

Alternatively, a typology of distance was also conceived by Liberman, Trope, and Stephan (2007) who categorized distance into four components: temporal distance, spatial distance, social distance, and hypotheticality. The main unique component of their framework refers to hypotheticality, which denotes "the distinction between real and imagined objects and between probable and improbable events" (Trope & Liberman, 2010, p. 444). Complicating things further, many of the above identically labeled dimensions (e.g., social distance) are operationalized quite differently depending on the author and the field of research. In general, there is substantial overlap for how scholars have defined distance in which they often include aspects of space, context, and internal references.

Certainly the above lists are not exhaustive dimensions, but they do illuminate the vast forms that distance might take and what relationships it might portray when particular dimensions are activated. In the following sections, we classify the above frameworks into several relevant forms of distance that attempt to encompass many of the unique facets described above; these include physical or spatial distance, psychological distance, and organizational distance. Next, we describe recent findings and advancements in the field, and finally discuss the implications of distance as a whole.

───────────

PHYSICAL DISTANCE

Simmel (1908) first noticed the importance of physical distance in determining human relations. Since then, vast amounts of theoretical work (e.g., Antonakis & Atwater, 2002; for a review on distributed work, see Hinds & Kiesler, 2002) and empirical work (e.g., Podsakoff, MacKenzie, & Bommer, 1996) have been conducted on the topic. Physical distance is generally defined as how far or close any two entities are located to one another at a given point in time or for a particular activity. While this construct may seem intuitive at first, there is a surprising amount of variation of its use in recent literature. Indeed, the interpretation of physical distance research has shifted throughout the latter part of the twentieth century and is often mixed with elements of social distance or interaction frequency (e.g., Howell, Neufeld, & Avolio, 2005; Napier & Ferris, 1993). Recent advances in technological communication have further blurred the line between "present" and "not present." However, Antonakis and Atwater (2002) state explicitly that "social distance and physical distance are distinct" (p. 684) and independent constructs. For example, imagine air traffic controllers who work physically near one another yet may never actually interact (Kirkman & Mathieu, 2005). Additional researchers on the other hand (e.g., Bass, 1998) operationalize physical distance much differently, and argue that dimensions of distance are interrelated (Trope & Liberman, 2010). Here we provide several conceptualizations of physical distance and discuss its consequences.

Keisler and Cummings (2002) provide a similar criticism with regard to shifting definitions of physical distance. Therefore, they define workplace proximity strictly in terms of measured units like inches or miles. Keisler and Cummings dichotomize the effects of physical distance such that individuals are placed either (1) outside direct observation from one another or (2) far enough so that they cannot easily assemble (i.e., miles away). They argue that several phenomena create effects within these two categories: the presence of others, the amount of face-to-face communication, the sharing of social spaces, and opportunities for spontaneous communication. For example, social presence leads to changes in performance when working near others, higher levels of conformity and attention, as well as increased familiarity, which ultimately lead to lower levels of effort when working in group settings. For complex or highly autonomous tasks, physical distance generally leads to higher levels of performance. They conclude that when physical distance is a factor, group performance ultimately depends upon the level of group and individual coordination and group cohesion.

A less strict interpretation of physical distance is provided by Napier and Ferris (1993) who conceptualize physical distance in terms of interaction frequency, spatial distance, or temporal distance between leaders and followers. In order to encompass these three terms, they introduce *structural distance* which includes several types of physical discontinuities such as the organization's physical design, relational distance, task-related distance, and manager's span of control. Physical design includes the actual structure of the work space—for example, the distance from an individual's work area to his or her manager's work area or to the proverbial office "water cooler." Relational distance is generally concerned with non-task-related information exchange or accessibility to others, which is positively related to work satisfaction and performance evaluation reception (Fulk, Brief, & Barr, 1985). Task-related distance (Napier and Ferris refer to this as spatial distance) is the frequency with which leaders and followers interact regarding work-related topics (see Karakayli, 2009). Lastly, Napier and Ferris discuss the span of management as a final component of physical distance, which we discuss at length later in the chapter. Overall, Napier and Ferris conceptualize physical discontinuities at work vastly differently from other scholars.

In general, physical distance is associated with negative effects toward organizational outcomes. In their meta-analysis, Podsakoff, MacKenzie, and Bommer (1996) demonstrate a relatively small negative relationship between spatial distance and organizational criterion variables including role ambiguity, role conflict, in-role performance, altruism, conscientiousness, and civil virtue (however, they fail to define how spatial distance is operationalized). Similarly, Kerr and Jermier (1978) posit that physical distance creates "circumstances in which effective leadership may be impossible" (p. 396), and that distance generally creates a suppression effect with regard to leader effectiveness (Bass, 1998).

Despite the overwhelming negative effect of physical distance in organizational contexts, the advent of the twenty-first century has seen a monumental movement toward *more* physically distant work environments, ushered in by globalization, hypercompetitive markets, and the increasingly fast-paced development of online technology (Cascio & Aguinis, 2011).

Thus, conventional physical distance is evolving to include more subjective phenomena such as perceived physical presence (Short, Williams, & Christie, 1976) and electronic propinquity (i.e., online "nearness", the opportunity to converse, and feelings of closeness; Walthers & Bazarova, 2008). Indeed, many new dimensions of physical discontinuity arise that explain and complicate human relations.

PSYCHOLOGICAL DISTANCE

One of the first major changes of the distance construct was led by Park (1924) in his exposition of distance as a function of understanding and intimacy rather than spatial relations. Park employed social distance as an explanation for racial divides. He observed that formal social tiers are nonexistent in a democracy yet still racism exists. Therefore, prejudice must be based solely on individual differences. Prejudice, however, "is not an aggressive but a conservative force" (p. 344), attempting to maintain social order. Park concluded that distance was the mechanism by which that social order is maintained.

Understanding and intimacy were only some of the first manifestations of psychological and social distance (Park, 1924). Throughout the past century psychological distance has come to encapsulate a variety of discontinuities between actors. However, the expansion of distance has led to an encroachment of physical or objective measures, leading researchers to often combine or confuse the two as identical constructs (Van Boven, Kane, McGraw, & Dale, 2010). In general, psychological distance is concerned with subjective experiences between one actor and the psychological space of another actor. It is often operationalized as perceived differences or similarities in affinity, ideology, interest, mood, motivation, ability, and temperament (for an extended discussion of psychological distance, see Rummel, 1978). The number of possible dimensions along which two individuals define their relationship is, for all intents and purposes, infinite. Therefore, instead of discussing each dimension *in vacuo*, we discuss several newly proposed mechanisms that govern psychological distance, including construal level theory and emotional intensity.

Construal level theory (CLT) is a relatively new phenomenological perspective that attempts to explain the general dynamics of distance (for a review, see Trope & Liberman, 2010). Although not concerned with defining particular dimensions of social distance per se, CLT provides an explanation for how distance functions. Trope, Liberman, and their colleagues define psychological distance as "a subjective experience that something is close or far away from the self, here, and now" (p. 440). It contains four primary dimensions: time, space, social distance, and hypotheticality (i.e., the likelihood of hypothetical outcomes). CLT essentially provides a framework for understanding various dimensions of distance by positing the following points: (a) Humans form mental construals or representations of objects; (b) As the psychological distance from an object increases, higher levels of construal are employed to represent that object because higher levels maintain more stable representations; and (c) Using higher-level construals of objects will in turn bring to mind more distance objects. For example, Trope and Liberman (2010) argue that the more abstract goal of contacting a friend is more stable than the more specific goal of sending that friend an email. A central tenet in CLT is that all forms of distance inherently contain the common point of reference of the perceiver (called a "zero-point" reference), a similar observation to that made by Poole (1927). Therefore, all forms of distance must be interrelated because of the singularity of their origin (cf. Antonakis & Atwater, 2002; Stephan, Liberman, & Trope, 2010).

Indeed, Stephan, Liberman, and Trope (2010) have shown that increasing distance along one dimension also increases distance on others. Trope and Liberman's mechanism of distance is quickly expanding into a number of realms both empirically and theoretically. For example, Shamir's (1995) pivotal essay on charismatic leadership is grounded in CLT, and other works have also addressed issues in perceptions of similarity in judging performance (Liviatan, Trope, & Liberman, 2008), making decisions about an object based on primary or secondary features (Liberman & Trope, 1998), and categorization of the self and external objects (Liberman, Sagristano, & Trope, 2002; Wakslak, Nussbaum, Liberman, & Trope, 2008). Overall, CLT provides a promising new mechanism in explaining the effects of distance in determining the quality of human relations.

A contending thread of research approaches psychological-distance mechanics much differently by positing that distance is governed by emotional intensity rather than nonemotional cognitive representations vis-à-vis construal theory (Van Boven et al., 2010). Indeed, as far back as Bogardus (1925a, 1947), emotional reactions and feelings of closeness have been regarded as important elements among scholars; recent conceptualizations have also included affective distance as its own unique dimension (Karakayali, 2009). Van Boven et al. (2010) regard emotional intensity as a key mechanism governing distance that is independent of "nonemotional experiences such as construal level" (p. 873). Their logic is as follows: (a) Psychological distance—which is defined as a "set of introspectively accessible subjective experiences" (p. 874)—is positively associated with objective distance. In other words, the more you feel something is far away, the further away it probably is. (b) Emotional intensity is negatively associated with objective distance. For example, the closer events are in time the more emotionally intense they are. (c) Emotions (at least partially) direct behavior. (d) Therefore, higher levels of emotional intensity result in lower objective distance and, as a result, lower psychological distance. In other words, when an experience is more emotionally intense it feels psychologically less distant, regardless of its mental representation (i.e., construal level). Van Boven et al. essentially provide a mechanism for determining whether phenomena are perceived as psychologically close or distant regardless of the psychological dimension. However, Wong and Bagozzi (2005) suggest that this affect may be moderated by cultural orientation (strong vs. weak filial piety).

Other scholars have recently reported similar effects with regard to emotional intensity. Across seven studies, Caruso (2010) showed an asymmetric emotional bias toward future rather than negative events, suggesting also that future events seem psychologically closer than objectively equal past events. Similar research found that effort affects perceived temporal distance such that the more effortful an event the larger the perceived time the event takes, "calculated backward from the event deadline to the present" (Jiga-Boy, Clark, & Semin, 2010, p. 1815). The authors also suggest that effort may be linked to both emotional intensity and construal level, providing a bridge between these otherwise separate threads of research. For example, in order to meet a deadline, one might calculate the number of steps required or the number of actions taken to fulfill that deadline; thus, resulting in both a more concrete representation of the effort required as well as higher perceived effort to complete the task. Ultimately, the authors conclude a potential link between the two aforementioned mechanisms that govern psychological distance. Both CLT and emotional intensity serve as important driving forces in explaining how psychological distance functions and aid in unraveling the complexity that is human relation.

ORGANIZATIONAL DISTANCE

Thus far, we have discussed two forms of distance: physical and psychological. Physical distance is addressed in objective units of space and psychological distance is conceptualized as subjective experiences between two entities from the reference point of the actor. Distance is also frequently examined with organizational implications in mind. A common research area relating to distance in organizations is leadership. While organizational distance can be conceptualized at the dyad, group, or organization level, it tends to be examined in dyad relationships between leaders and followers (Atonakis & Atwater, 2002). The related fields of virtual teams, computer-supported cooperative work, and computer-mediated communication often examine elements of distance at the group level. Organizational-level distance tends to be limited to aspects of distance relating to national and regional culture. Here we discuss three forms of organizational distance—dyad, team, and organizational—their practical implications, and recent findings.

Distance in Dyads

Antonakis and Atwater (2002) provide a comprehensive review of dyadic leader–follower relations. In addition to the three components of distance they identified—physical distance, social distance, and interaction frequency—we also include the strength of follower identification (Rast et al., this volume).

Physical distance interacts with leadership behavior in leader–follower relationships. Teams have been found to exhibit higher performance when a transformational leader was physically close to followers and when a transactional leader was physically distant (Howell, Neufeld, & Avolio, 2005). Though at first glance this sounds like a team-level finding, leader distance in this study was categorized as a dichotomy based on the majority of leader–follower dyads within the team. This is a common approach, due in part to the complexities of group-level research and analysis with relatively small samples.

Though physical distance can mute a charismatic leader's message, transformational leadership still holds sway over followers. When physically distant leaders facilitated group discussions around the topic of software piracy, transformational leaders elicited a greater balance of arguments and the greatest change in members' intentions to copy software (Kahai & Avolio, 2008). Transactional identified leaders (as opposed to anonymous leaders) were associated with increased communication frequency. Though transactional leadership facilitated more communication, transformational leadership led to better communication.

Other studies also address social distances between leaders and followers. Social distance is often conceptualized as real or perceived differences in both formal and informal status, rank, authority, or achievement (Bogardus, 1927; Antonakis & Atwater, 2002). In a content analysis of interviews regarding charismatic leaders, Shamir (1995) compared the associations between hierarchically close charismatic leaders with those of hierarchically distant charismatic leaders. Followers were more likely to treat close leaders as individuals, taking into account performance cues and functional expertise. Distant leaders, on the other hand, were more likely to be described in ways that presented them as prototypical representatives of the group. Close leaders also tended to be associated with high energy, dynamism, intelligence, interpersonal skills, sensitivity, physical attractiveness, sense of humor, and originality. With greater physical exposure comes greater personal identification. Indeed, followers expressed increased wishes to identify with a close leader. Distant leaders were no more idealized than close leaders, but they were more often associated with prototypical imagery, rhetorical skills, and vision. Their performance cues also operated at the group level, such that their success was tied less to their individual accomplishments than to the success or failure of the entire group.

Subsequent research supports these findings. Followers of socially close transformational leaders are more likely to emulate role-modeled leadership behavior (Cole, Bruch, & Shamir, 2009). Distant leaders are more strongly linked to a positive emotional climate and are more likely to increase collective efficacy beliefs. Distant leaders, it seems, have an easier time managing their group image. They can more easily broadcast their success and hide their failings with distant followers.

These findings also relate to normative distance, an extension of the social identity theory of leadership (Hogg, 2001; Hogg & van Knippenberg, 2003). Normative distance refers to "the extent to which the leader approximates the group's prototype" (Rast et al., this volume). The more a leader matches the idealized representation of the group, the more influence he or she will tend to exert over the group's members. For a detailed discussion of normative distance, we refer the reader to Chapter 8.

Distance in Teams

There is admittedly no solid demarcation between distance research at the dyad, team, and organization levels. A leader's impact is not felt only in a dyad—indeed, his or her influence affects the entire team. The rapid pace of technological innovation further blurs our attempts to categorize distance in human interactions (Bikson, Treverton, Moini, & Lindstrom, 2008). The constant release of new hardware and software breakthroughs is commonly assumed to create additional distance in work and non-work relationships. Often that perception is correct and the introduction of new technology does create distance. It can reduce the need or justification for face-to-face meetings, create a new set of communication cues which users must learn to interpret, and act as a substitute for functions previously carried out by people. After participating in "telepresence" meetings using Cisco's high-tech, custom-designed meeting rooms, Drake Bennett (2011, p. 55) wrote "I would occasionally experience a fleeting claustrophobia, a sense that the entire world had collapsed into a single, infinitely iterating conference room." However, technology itself is not distant. Machines and software do not inherently create distance unless people design or use them in ways that do. Thus the reverse is true as well—technology can also reduce distance. Referring to the very same Cisco system, Rich Redelfs stated, "You want to look somebody in the eye and say, Do I trust this person enough to write them a multimillion-dollar check? We feel we can do that with telepresence" (Bennett, 2011, p. 54).

The dual role technology plays in interpersonal communication, and assumptions regarding its negative effects, have been investigated in the literature on virtual teams. The notion of virtuality itself, common across research on virtual, distributed, and dispersed teams (also computer-supported cooperative work and various similar names), is very similar to distance. Some aspects of distance, such as physical distance, are explicitly mentioned in the virtual teams literature (e.g., Bell & Kozlowski, 2002). Moreover, one might imagine virtuality as simply a modern "repackaging" of the original manifestations of distance. Often virtual team research identifies a number of critical discontinuities that define online relations, including physical, psychological, or social elements as mentioned throughout this chapter. Online environments merely serve as a new landscape for which to apply the wealth of existing research on distance—both subjective and objective manifestations of it (see Shamir, this volume).

Virtual team research has circled around several primary components exhibited by virtual teams. The most common consist of computer-mediated communication (CMC; Kirkman & Mathieu, 2005), the crossing of boundaries—cultural, temporal, or organizational (Gibson & Gibbs, 2006), and geographic distance (Johnson, Heimann, & O'Neill, 2001; Bell & Kozlowski, 2002). Although the field does not yet agree on what essential element defines virtuality (i.e., whether it be geographic distance, technology, or other components; Locke, 1986; Kirkman & Mathieu, 2005), in general, it is safe to say that all of these components imply increases in distance.

The shift away from traditional, exclusively face-to-face teams has occurred quite rapidly (Morris, 2008), and many researchers now agree that all teams are inherently virtual to some degree (Martins et al., 2004; Griffith, Sawyer, & Neale, 2003; Zigurs, 2003). Put another way, most if not all teams exhibit some degree of distance among at least one of the member dyads. In terms of Atonakis and Atwater's (2002) leadership typologies, it follows that even the most proximal leader (or proximal team member) maintains some distance from other members of the team, whether it be based on physical distance, social distance, or communication frequency.

In many studies, physically distant team leaders and members underperform relative to face-to-face, collocated teams (for a review see Powell et al., 2004). Virtual teams tend to inhibit leadership and develop more defensive rather than constructive interaction styles (Balthazard, Waldman, & Atwater, 2008). Although virtual teams often perform poorly at the start of a task, they can reach equivalent or superior levels of performance, given enough time (Derks, Fischer, & Bos, 2008; Reid, Malinek, Stott, & Evans, 1996).

But distance in teams is not simply a matter of geography. It is now common for teams to communicate through technology even when they are physically collocated. This does not mean the effects of distance are not still felt in other ways. Lojeski, Reilly, and Dominick (2006) proposed a virtual distance construct composed of temporal, spatial, and relational aspects. The "virtual" distance construct applies equally to collocated and geographically dispersed teams and is operationalized as a composite of team member perceptions of their organization and team across the underlying factors. The factors revealed by exploratory factor analysis were interpersonal congruence, social relationships, and technical expertise. Of these, interpersonal congruence (values, status, and interdependence) and social relationships (prior communication and relationships) had the greatest impact on performance outcomes, such that increased distance tended to result in poorer performance.

In a virtual laboratory study, participants in a financial decision-making scenario tended to work with the socially close partner they could see (versus a non-visible partner) to the overall detriment of the group (Fiedler, Haruvy, & Li, 2010). In online volunteering groups, small blogs moderated by a central leader were initially able to accomplish more than larger forum-based groups (Torrey et al., 2008). Over time, as the central leaders abandoned their blogs and the small groups withered away, the larger forum-based groups were able to slowly but surely maintain and build on their progress and have a greater long-term impact on their community. The authors also noted that the long-term groups, which tended to be driven by group consensus rather than strong central leadership, appeared to create subgroups that may have served as outlets for emerging leaders while still maintaining overall group cohesion.

Birnholtz and Finholt (2008) examined facets of social distance (operationalized as perceived similarity) when studying the implementation of a cyber-infrastructure project. During the project implementation, a deteriorating situation stemming from the cultural dissimilarity of the participating teams was addressed by strong leadership. The new leader bridged cultural gaps and leveraged preexisting interpersonal relationships to put the project back on track. One key takeaway was the importance of identifying distance gaps among team cultures before starting a project. Research also suggests that frequent informal communication from the leader helps improve virtual team performance (Cummings, 2008).

Individuals in virtual teams adapt at a slower pace (than those in face-to-face teams) and should communicate early and often to compensate (Walther & Bunz, 2005). In addition to the frequency of interaction, the type of interaction is important in a virtual team. In other words, not all virtual communication is equal. In the past, organizations have taken this communication equality for granted because most communication was face-to-face. Indeed, best practice stipulates that face-to-face communication is important when a team forms (Bradner & Mark, 2008). While this is good advice, it does tend to defeat the purpose of a virtual team. While many teams do have opportunities for some or all members to meet in person, others are not provided such a luxury. Luckily, while technology can obscure an individual while he/she is working, it tends to highlight what that individual is working on (or can easily be configured to do so). Work outputs can therefore serve as a substitute for individual visibility, combating the "out-of-sight, out-of-mind" problem common among distance workers.

One concern pertaining to teams is social loafing. Loafing has been demonstrated to increase in virtual teams (Blascovich, 2008); however technology can reduce or negate its effects. Team *processes* may be obscured in a virtual work environment but team *products* are often more visible and are easier to track (Bradner & Mark, 2008). Organizations such as Best Buy have embraced this phenomenon and shifted to a results-only work environment which seeks to abandon traditional notions of regular hours and work locations in favor of a focus on employee outputs and results.

Obfuscation of a team's processes or products may lead to another form of distance: leader–team perceptual distance. A study of distance that focused on leader–team perceptions of goal accomplishment and constructive conflict found that team performance was higher when leader–team distance was low (Gibson, Cooper, & Conger, 2009). Generally speaking, as the views of the leader and the team aligned, team performance increased. Leader–team distance also served as a stronger predictor of performance than did within-team distance. Leader–team distance on decision-making autonomy showed no significant impact on performance.

Cultural Distance

Distance at the organizational level has received attention across a variety of research streams, though most ultimately relate back to culture. Cultural distance is generally operationalized as the difference between host and home countries across various cultural dimensions, typically Hofstede's (1980) dimensions. The greater the cultural distance between a host country and a home country, the more difficult it is for an organization to conduct its business. For instance, cultural distance predicts the number of expatriates employed in a subsidiary, even after controlling for the age of the subsidiary (Colakoglu & Caligiuri, 2008). As distance increases, organizations have a tendency to send more expatriates, which may compound the organization's initial gap in cultural awareness. Cultural distance also interacts with gender roles among expatriates and their families. Women tend to be more concerned with assignments to high cultural-distance locations when there are children present (Dupuis, Haines, & Saba, 2008). Finally, cultural distance impacts cross-border, business-to-business investing and partnerships. Organizations seeking partnerships within their home country tend to assume higher levels of control when cultural distance between the organization and the foreign partner is low (Lee, Shenkar, & Li, 2008). Conversely, when a foreign company invests in another country with a low cultural distance partner, they tend to seek less control over the partnership.

Cultural distance has been used interchangeably with psychic distance, though recently there have been efforts to distinguish the two concepts (Brewer, 2007; Sousa & Bradley, 2006). Psychic distance shares many cultural aspects with cultural distance, but includes an element of business distance and places a greater emphasis on individual levels of measurement. Business distance in turn refers to the difference in how business is conducted from one location to another, including the political and regulatory environment, predominant language of business, and market structure (Evans & Mavondo, 2002). Cultural distance is typically examined at a large group level, often national, and has been demonstrated to stand apart from psychic distance (Sousa & Bradley, 2006).

IMPLICATIONS AND CONCLUSIONS

The purpose of this chapter was to provide an overview of the historical evolution of the distance construct and to present a number of different perspectives for how distance functions, how it is studied, and its impact in both psychology and sociology. We traced the initial lineage of distance from its early sociological roots and provided an account of the major changes that occurred within the first forty years of its inception. Although an endless number of dimensions characterize human relationships, distance provides a means by which to define our interactions with personal events and with others. Several threads of research have progressed our understanding of distance; some scholars identify new dimensions of distance in order to identify constellations that comprise styles or relationships with others (e.g. Antonakis & Atwater, 2002; Karakayli, 2009), others have developed the mechanics that govern distance through theory and mediating processes (e.g. construal level theory and emotional intensity). Still other scholars have identified distance as a contextual variable that ultimately alters the landscape of psychology (e.g. Shamir, 1995; this volume). Indeed, the ubiquity of humanity's online presence represents a major shift in the context of distance scholarship. For example, organizations are quickly adopting models of virtual teams and decentralized structures in order to compensate for the overwhelming force of distant work and leadership (Cascio & Aguinis, 2011). What were once clear demarcation lines between "distant" and "not distant" are much hazier.

Despite vast strides in understanding how distance functions and defines human relations, distance still remains an elusive construct whose mechanisms are routinely engaged by scholars. As future researchers refine such dimensions, it will become clear how each constellation comprises simultaneously elements of nearness and farness and ultimately defines both internal and external distances. "Although both [nearness and farness] are found to some extent in all relationships, a special proportion and reciprocal tension between them produce the specific form of the relation to the stranger" (Simmel, 1908, p. 149). Simmel's stranger represents merely the first of many collections of distance, but throughout the course of the twentieth century, it did not represent the last. Indeed, much work lies ahead.

NOTE

1   Bogardus coincidentally created the first Guttman scale in constructing the social distance scale. Louis Guttman later used Bogardus's scale as a platform for refining this scaling technique (Ward, 2011).

REFERENCES

Antonakis, J. & Atwater, L. (2002). Leader distance: A review and a proposed theory. *Leadership Quarterly*, 13, 673–704.
Balthazard, P. A., Waldman, D., & Atwater, L. E. (2008). The mediating effects of leadership and interaction style in face-to-face and virtual teams. In S. Weisband (Ed.), *Leadership at a distance: Research in technologically-supported work* (pp. 127–150). New York: Lawrence Erlbaum Associates.

Bass, B. M. (1990). *Bass and Stogdill's handbook of leadership* (3rd ed.). New York: Free Press.

Bass, B. M. (1998). *Transformational leadership: Industrial, military, and educational impact.* Mahwah, NJ: Lawrence Erlbaum Associates.

Bell, B. S. & Kozlowski, S. W. J. (2002). A typology of virtual teams: Implications for effective leadership. *Group & Organization Management*, 27, 14.

Bennett, D. (2011, February 21). I'll have my robots talk to your robots. *Bloomberg Businessweek*, 52–61.

Bikson, T., Treverton, G. F., Moini, J., & Lindstrom, G. (2008). Leadership in international organizations: 21st century challenges. In S. Weisband (Ed.), *Leadership at a distance: Research in technologically-supported work* (pp. 13–30). New York: Lawrence Erlbaum Associates.

Birnholtz, J. P. & Finholt, T. A. (2008). Cultural challenges to leadership in cyber infrastructure development. In S. Weisband (Ed.), *Leadership at a distance: Research in technologically-supported work* (pp. 195–207). New York: Lawrence Erlbaum Associates.

Blascovich, J. L. (2008). Exploring the effect of distance: An experimental investigation of virtual collaboration, social loafing, and group decisions. *Journal of Information Systems*, 22, 27–46.

Bogardus, E. S. (1925a). The occupational attitude. *Journal of Applied Sociology*, 9, 171–176.

Bogardus, E. S. (1925b). Social distance and its origins. *Journal of Applied Sociology*, 9, 216–226.

Bogardus, E. S. (1925c). Measuring social distances. *Journal of Applied Sociology*, 9, 299–308.

Bogardus, E. S. (1927). Leadership and social distance. *Sociology and Social Research*, 12, 173–178.

Bogardus, E. S. (1928). Occupational distance. *Sociology and Social Research*, 13, 73–81.

Bradner, E. & Mark, G. (2008). Designing a tail in two cities: Leaders' perspectives on collocated and distance collaboration. In S. Weisband (Ed.), *Leadership at a distance: Research in technologically-supported work* (pp. 51–69). New York: Lawrence Erlbaum Associates.

Brewer, P. A. (2007). Operationalizing psychic distance: A revised approach. *Journal of International Marketing*, 15, 44–66.

Caruso, E. M. (2010). When the future feels worse than the past: A temporal inconsistency in moral judgment. *Journal of Experimental Psychology: General*, 139, 610–624.

Cascio, W. F. & Aguinis, H. (2011). *Applied psychology in human resource management* (7th ed.). Upper Saddle, NJ: Pearson Prentice Hall.

Colakoglu, S. & Caligiuri, P. (2008). Cultural distance, expatriate staffing and subsidiary performance: The case of US subsidiaries of multinational corporations. *The International Journal of Human Resources Management*, 19, 223–239.

Cole, M. S., Bruch, H., & Shamir, B. (2009). Social distance as a moderator of the effects of transformational leadership: Both neutralizer and enhancer. *Human Relations*, 62, 1697–1733.

Crano, W. D. & Lac, A. (2011). The evolution of research methodologies in social psychology: A historical analysis. In A. W. Kruglanski & W. Stroebe (Eds.), *Handbook of the history of social psychology*. New York: Psychology Press.

Cummings, J. N. (2008). Leading groups from a distance: How to mitigate consequences of geographic dispersion. In S. Weisband (Ed.), *Leadership at a distance: Research in technologically-supported work* (pp. 33–50). New York: Lawrence Erlbaum Associates.

Derks, D., Fischer, A. H., & Bos, A. E. R. (2008). The role of emotion in computer-mediated communication: A review. *Computers in Human Behavior*, 24, 766–785.

Dupuis, M., Haines III, V. Y., & Saba, T. (2008). Gender, family ties, and international mobility: Cultural distance matters. *The International Journal of Human Resource Management*, 19, 274–295.

Ethington, P. J. (1997). The intellectual construction of social distance: Toward a recovery of Georg Simmel's social geometry. *Cyberego: European Journal of Geography*. Retrieved February 27, 2011 from http://cyberego.recues.org/index227.html.

Evans, J. & Mavondo, F. T. (2002). Psychic distance and organizational performance: An empirical examination of international retailing operations. *Journal of International Business Studies, 33*, 515–532.

Fiedler, M., Haruvy, E., & Li, S. X. (2010). Social distance in a virtual world experiment. *Games and Economic Behavior*.

Fulk, J., Brief, A. P., & Barr, S. H. (1985). Trust in supervisor and perceived fairness and accuracy of performance of evaluations. *Journal of Business Research*, 13, 301–313.

Gibson, C. B., Cooper, C. D., & Conger, J. A. (2009). Do you see what we see? The complex effects of perceptual distance between leaders and teams. *Journal of Applied Psychology*, 94, 62–76.

Gibson, C. B. & Gibbs, J. L. (2006). Unpacking the concept of virtuality: The effects of geographic dispersion, electronic dependence, dynamic structure, and national diversity on team innovation. *Administrative Science Quarterly*, 51, 451–495.

Griffith, T. L., Sawyer, J. E., & Neale, M. A. (2003). Virtualness and knowledge in teams: Managing the love triangle in organizations, individuals, and information technology. *MIS Quarterly*, 27, 265–287.

Helmreich, R., Aronson, E., & LeFan, J. (1970). To err is humanizing—sometimes: Effects of self-esteem, competence, and pratfall on interpersonal attraction. *Journal of Personality and Social Psychology*, 2, 259–264.

Hinds, P. & Kiesler, S. (Eds.) (2002) *In Distributed Work*. London: MIT Press.

Hofstede, G. H. (1980). *Culture consequences: International difference in work-related values*. London: Sage Publications.

Hogg, M. A. (2001). A social identity theory of leadership. *Personality and Social Psychology Review*, 5, 184–200.

Hogg, M. A. & van Knippenberg, D. (2003). Social identity and leadership processes in groups. In M. P. Zanna (Ed.), *Advances in experimental social psychology* (pp. 1–52). San Diego: Academic Press.

Howell, J. M., Neufeld, D. J., & Avolio, B. J. (2005). Examining the relationship of leadership and physical distance with business unit performance. *Leadership Quarterly*, 16, 273–285.

Johnson, P., Heimann, V., & O'Neill, K. (2001). The "wonderland" of virtual teams. *Journal of Workplace Learning*, 13, 24–29.

Jiga-Boy, G. M., Clark, A. E., & Semin, G. R. (2010). So much to do, so little time: Effort and perceived temporal distance. *Psychological Science*, 21, 1811–1817.

Kahai, S. S. & Avolio, B. J. (2008). Effects of leadership style and anonymity on the discussion of an ethical issue in an electronic meeting system context. In S. Weisband (Ed.), *Leadership at a distance: Research in technologically-supported work* (pp. 97–125). New York: Lawrence Erlbaum Associates.

Karakayli, N. (2009). Social distance and affective orientations. *Sociological Forum*, 24, 538–562.

Katz, D. & Kahn, R. L. (1978). *The social psychology of organizations*. New York: Wiley.

Keisler, S. & Cummings, J. (2002). What do we know about proximity and distance in work groups? A legacy of research. In Hinds, P. & Kiesler, S. (Eds.), *In distributed work,* (pp. 76–109). London: MIT Press.

Kerr, S. & Jermier, J. M. (1978). Substitutes for leadership their meaning and measurement. *Organizational Behavior and Human Performance,* 22, 375–403.

Kirkman, B. L. & Mathieu, J. E. (2005). The dimensions and antecedents of team virtuality. *Journal of Management,* 31, 700–718.

Lee, S., Shenkar, O. & Li, J. (2008). Cultural distance, investment flow, and control in cross-border cooperation. *Strategic Management Journal,* 29, 1117–1125.

Liberman, N., Sagristano, M., & Trope, Y. (2002). The effect of temporal distance on level of construal. *Journal of Experimental Social Psychology,* 38, 523–535.

Liberman, N. & Trope, Y. (1998). The role of feasibility and desirability considerations in near and distant future decisions: A test of temporal construal theory. *Journal of Personality and Social Psychology,* 75, 5–18.

Liberman, N., Trope, Y., & Stephan, E. (2007). Psychological distance. In A. W. Krunglanski & E. T. Higgins, (Eds.), *Social psychology: Handbook of basic principles* (pp. 353–383). New York: Guildford Press.

Liviatan, I., Trope, Y., & Liberman, N. (2008). The effect of similarity on mental construal. *Journal of Experimental Social Psychology,* 44, 1256–1269.

Lojeski, K. S., Reilly, R., & Dominick, P. (2006). The role of virtual distance in innovation and success. *Proceedings of the 39th Hawaii International Conference on System Sciences.*

Locke, E. A. (1986). Generalizing from laboratory to field: Ecological validity or abstraction of essential elements? In E. A. Locke (Ed.), *Generalizing from laboratory to field setting* (pp. 1–9). Lexington, MA: D. C. Heath.

Martins, L. L., Gilson, L. L., & Maynard, M. T. (2004). Virtual teams: What do we know and where do we go from here? *Journal of Management,* 30, 805–835.

Morris, S. (2008). Virtual team working: Making it happen. *Industrial and Commercial Training,* 40, 129–133.

Napier, B. J. & Ferris, G. R. (1993). Distance in organizations. *Human Resource Management Review,* 3, 321–357.

Park, R. E. (1924) The concept of social distance as applied to the study of racial attitudes and racial relations. *Journal of Applied Sociology,* 8, 339–344.

Podsakoff, P. M., MacKenzie, S. B., & Bommer, W. H. (1996). Meta-analysis of the relationships between Kerr and Jermier's substitutes for leadership and employee job attitudes role perceptions, and performance. *Journal of Applied Psychology,* 81, 380–399.

Poole, W. C. (1927). Distance in sociology. *The American Journal of Sociology,* 33, 94–104.

Powell, A., Piccoli, G., & Ives, B. (2004). Virtual teams: A review of current literature and directions for future research. *The Database for Advances in Information Systems,* 35, 6–36.

Reid, F. J. M., Malinek, V., Stott, C., & Evans, J. S. B. T. (1996). The messaging threshold in computer-mediated communication. *Ergonomics,* 39, 1017.

Rummel, R. J. (1976). *The Conflict Helix: Vol. 2: Understanding conflict and war.* Beverly Hills, CA: Sage.

Shamir, B. (1995). Social distance and charisma: Theoretical notes and an exploratory study. *Leadership Quarterly,* 6, 19–47.

Short, J., Williams, E., & Christie, B. (1976). *The social psychology of telecommunications.* London: Wiley.

Simmel, G. (1908). Soziologie: Untersuchungen uber die formen der vergesellscaftung. Boston: Dunker & Humbolt. Translated by Donald N. Levine.

Sousa, C. M. P. & Bradley, F. (2006). Cultural distance and psychic distance: Two peas in a pod? *Journal of International Marketing*, 14, 49–70.

Stephan, E., Liberman, N., & Trope, Y. (2010). Politeness and social distance: A construal level perspective. *Journal of Personality and Social Psychology*, 98, 268–280.

Tarde, G. (1903). *The Laws of Imitation*. New York: Holt & Company.

Torrey, C., Burke, M., Lee, M., Dey, A., Fussell, S., & Kiesler, S. (2008). Approaches to authority in online disaster relief communities after hurricane Katrina. In S. Weisband (Ed.), *Leadership at a distance: Research in technologically-supported work* (pp. 223–245). New York: Lawrence Erlbaum Associates.

Trope, Y. & Liberman, N. (2010). Construal-level theory of psychological distance. *Psychological Review*, 2, 440–463.

Van Boven, L. (2011, January). Feeling close: The emotional foundation of psychological distance. In L. Van Boven (Chair), *Perspectives on psychological distance's phenomenological foundations*. Symposium conducted at the meeting of the annual Society of Personality and Social Psychology Conference, San Antonio, TX.

Van Boven, L., Kane, J., McGraw, P. A., & Dale, J. (2010). Feeling close: Emotional intensity reduces perceived psychological distance. *Journal of Personality and Social Psychology*, 98, 872–885.

Wakslak, C. J., Nussbaum, S., Liberman. N., & Trope, Y. (2008). Representations of the self in the near and distant future. *Journal of Personality and Social Psychology*, 95, 757–773.

Walther, J. B. & Bazarova, N. (2008). Validation and application of electronic propinquity theory of computer-mediated communication in groups. *Communication Research*, 35, 622–645.

Walther, J. B. & Bunz, U. (2005). The rules of virtual groups: Trust, liking, and performance in computer-mediated communication. *Journal of Communication*, 55, 828–846.

Ward, L. G. (2011). *The Mead Project*. Retrieved February, 27, 2011, from http://www.brocku.ca/MeadProject/inventory5.html.

Wong, N. Y. & Bagozzi, R. P. (2005). Emotional intensity as a function of psychological distance and cultural orientation. *Journal of Business Research*, 58, 533–542.

Zigurs, I. (2003). Leadership in virtual teams: Oxymoron or opportunity? *Organizational Dynamics*, 31, 339.

2

Notes on Distance and Leadership

Boas Shamir

What is distance in leadership relationships? Much of the interest in distance and leadership stems from two sources: First, a growing recognition that the majority of leadership theories have been presented as theories that apply equally to all levels of leadership and this may be a mistake. Thus, transformational leadership theory (Bass & Avolio, 1993), for instance, has been presented as applying equally to the leadership of CEOs and to the leadership of first-line supervisors. Yet the two situations are very different in many respects, one of which is the fact that upper echelon leaders do not have direct contacts with the majority of their followers and the latter do not have direct experiences with the leader. This difference may have significant implications for the nature of the leadership process and for the relationships which develop between leaders and followers. For instance, the reasons for accepting and following a direct leader may be different from the reasons for accepting and following a distant leader.

Second, the interest in leadership and distance has grown as a result of two environmental developments that present leaders with new challenges: On the one hand, globalization has dictated that a growing number of organizational leaders have to lead from a distance, and on the other hand, the development of digital telecommunication technologies has perhaps offered new means by which to lead from a distance.

Both sources of interest have led to the conceptualization of distance as a characteristic of the context in which the leadership relationship exists, and such a conceptualization has dominated the literature on leadership and distance. This view treats distance as emerging from contextual separations between the leader and his/her followers: Geographical or physical separation (working in different offices, cities, or countries); hierarchical separation (leader and followers separated by other layers in the organizational hierarchy); or social separation (e.g., belonging to different cultural or ethnic groups) (Antonakis & Atwater, 2002; Collinson, 2005; Napier & Ferris, 1993; Shamir, 1995; Yagil, 1998). Consequently, the questions that have been asked following this conceptualization concern the effects of such separations on leaders' and followers' perceptions, attitudes, and behaviors, and the implications of these effects for the practice of leadership.

However, distance can also be viewed as a characteristic of the leadership relationship itself. This attribute of the relationship is related to the contextual dimensions of distance but is not fully determined by them. As an attribute of relationships between leaders and other organization members, distance can be viewed as something which is not an external condition given by the leadership context but, at least partially, as something which is created by the participants in the leadership relationship. Leaders can socially construct the relational distance between them and their followers, for instance by hiding their thoughts and emotions and by restricting access to them, and followers may construct the distance by hiding some of their activities from the leaders or by addressing the leaders in a formal language. Both views of distance, the contextual or given distance and the socially constructed distance, are relevant to the study of leadership. Therefore, both will be discussed in this chapter, in which I attempt to highlight some of the major implications of distance for leadership, in the hope of suggesting directions for future research on this topic.

DISTANCE AS THE CONTEXT OF LEADERSHIP

From the point of view of distance as the context of leadership, the most fundamental difference between proximal and distal leadership is that proximal leadership enables the parties to have direct experiences with each other. Considerable efforts have been invested in clarifying the dimensions of contextual distance that are relevant to leadership (e.g., Antonakis & Atwater, 2002) but recent research in cognitive social psychology suggests that the distinction between various dimensions of distance is perhaps less important than the distinction between having a direct experience with an object or a person and not having such direct experience. This is because when an object and/or a person are not experienced directly, they have to be construed by the perceiver.

We have less information about remote entities (people, events, places) on which to base our perceptions of them and attitudes toward them. According to a recent theory of cognitive social psychology—Construal Level Theory (Liberman & Trope, 2008; Liberman, Trope, & Stephan, 2007)—anything that is not present in the direct experience of reality is distal. It may be thought of, constructed, reconstructed, but it cannot be experienced directly. According to this theory, our mental representations of directly experienced people, events or objects are concrete, relatively detailed, relatively unstructured, and contextualized. In contrast, our mental representations of distant people, events or objects are more abstract, schematic, less detailed, and de-contextualized. Many studies conducted under the umbrella of Construal Level Theory (CLT) support these theoretical claims (Liberman & Trope, 2008; Liberman, Trope, & Stephan, 2007). Furthermore, the findings are highly similar across different types of distance: temporal, spatial, and social. Translated to the leader–follower relationship, this means that followers who are close to the leader and experience him or her directly are likely to base their perceptions of the leader, attitudes toward the leader, and responses to the leader mainly on their direct experiences with the leader. Followers who are distant from the leader, whether due to physical separation, minimal direct interactions, hierarchical separation or some other social separation, are likely to base their perceptions of the leader, attitudes toward the leader, and responses to the leader mainly on mental processes of cognitive construal.

Similarly, leaders who are close to their followers are more likely to base their perceptions of the followers, and their attitudes and behaviors toward them mainly on their *experience* with the followers, whereas leaders who are distant from their followers are likely to base their perceptions, attitudes, and behaviors mainly on *mental images* they have created of the followers. In other words, proximal leadership is more experience-based and distal leadership is more image-based. Distal leadership is therefore more likely to be based on attributions, projections, and other construal processes.

This fundamental difference has several implications, some of which have already been highlighted in the literature on distance and leadership. Others, which can be derived from CLT, have received less attention in the leadership literature.

The Basis for Accepting and Following the Leader

According to CLT (Liberman et al., 2007), distant entities are represented in our minds more abstractly. Because irrelevant or inconsistent details are omitted from abstract representations or assimilated into them, abstract representation may be expected to be simpler, less ambiguous, and more prototypical than concrete representations. In other words, abstraction involves moving to a more schematic, simple, and coherent representation of the perceived or evaluated object. Consequently, we can expect differences in the basis on which distant and close leaders are likely to be accepted and followed.

In part, leaders are accepted on the basis of the extent to which they are perceived to match certain mental images or prototypes held by potential followers. Two types of schema or prototypes have been suggested in the literature as bases for accepting leaders. The first type includes general leadership schema, especially prototypes of the ideal leader, which are stored in our heads and activated when we meet a leader or a potential leader (Lord & Maher, 1991). The second type includes group prototypes. According to the social identity theory of leadership (Hogg, 2001) leaders are more likely to be accepted and followed to the extent that they are perceived to be prototypical of the group, namely, the extent to which they are perceived to represent or embody the central characteristics of the group.

When people are presented with an appointed leader or a potential leader they compare the characteristics of that individual to the prototypes of the ideal leader and the ideal group member, and their acceptance of the leader is higher if the individual matches the prototypes. This prototype-matching process is relatively simple since research has shown that followers or potential followers do not engage in a detailed matching process. If they perceive a match between the leader and the prototype on three to four central characteristics, they tend to complete the matching automatically and assume that the person matches the prototype (Lord, Foti, & De Vader, 1984).

Due to their lack of direct experience with the leader, followers of a distant leader are more likely than followers of a proximal leader to base their acceptance and followership on such simple matching. Followers of proximal leaders are more likely to base their acceptance and followership on a more complex and less automatic process which takes into consideration information gathered from direct interactions and experiences (Shamir, 1995). From this point of view, it may be easier to establish a leadership position with distant followers than with proximal followers, because all one has to do in the former case is to offer information that matches a number of central prototypical characteristics, whereas in the latter case the leader has to provide followers with direct experiences to substantiate his or her claim for their followership. However, for a similar reason, it may be easier for distant leaders than for proximal leaders to lose their leadership relationship with others, because in the case of distant leaders the relationship is based on a simplified, schematic image of the leader, which is not grounded in actual followers' experiences and may therefore be vulnerable when the leader fails or behaves in ways that do not fit his or her schematic image. In the case of proximal leaders, the leader's image is likely to be richer and less schematic. Consequently, followers who have accepted the leader on the basis of their direct experiences with him or her may be more immune to the effects of a single failure or a single behavior that seems to deviate from their image of the leader.

Idealization and Vilification of the Leader

Related to the previous point, followers of a distant leader are more likely to idealize or "romanticize" the leader than followers of a proximal leader This point was made by some writers on charisma (e.g., Etzioni, 1975; Katz & Kahn, 1978) who emphasized that charisma (in the original Weberian sense of attributing special qualities and power to the leader) requires distance because followers who experience the leader directly are more likely to observe the leader's weaknesses, vulnerabilities, and errors, and therefore are less likely to construct an image that idealizes or idolizes the leader. A similar point was made by Meindl (1995) in his work on the romance of leadership and the social contagion of charisma. Less attention has been given to the possibility that a similar effect may operate in the opposite direction as well, namely that followers of distant leaders may be more prone to degrade, disparage, even ridicule a distant leader (for instance, after an ethical failure or an error made by the leader) due to the fact that their relationship with the leader is more image-based than experience-based, and therefore they can more easily ignore or forget the leader's positive intentions, efforts, and qualities. Thus distance from the leader may work in two opposing directions. On the one hand, it may hide the leader's weaknesses and errors and result in idealization (even over-idealization) of the leader. On the other hand, once a leader's weakness, error or failure is revealed, it may result in overly negative perceptions of and attitudes toward the leader on the part of distant followers. In contrast, proximal followers, due to their more complex, rich, nuanced, and experience-based image of the leader, may be less likely to idealize the leader but also less likely to reject the leader and develop exaggerated negative perceptions and attitudes toward him or her.

The Use of External Cues

Because distant followers do not have direct experiences on which to base their perceptions of the leader and their attitudes toward the leader, they are more likely than followers of proximal leaders to base their perceptions and attitudes on other cues. One type of cue that is likely to be more important in distant leadership relationships includes performance cues of the sort that do not have to be observed directly (e.g., various indicators of the organization's success or failure such as profits or losses, increase or decrease in stock value). While performance cues affect all leadership relationships, they are likely to have a greater effect in the case of distant leadership due to the relative lack of more directly observable cues about the leader's attributes and behaviors (Shamir, 1995).

Another type of cue that distant followers are more likely to rely on than proximal followers includes information from other external sources—for instance, media reports about the leader. Again, such cues are attended to by all followers, but proximal followers are more likely to integrate them with knowledge gained from direct experience. Therefore, the leadership of a distant leader is more indirect in the sense of being mediated by external sources such as the media. Similarly, followers of distant leaders are more likely than proximal followers to base their relationship with the leader on the leader's reputation and on the leader's life story as conveyed by external sources, such as internal organizational stories and rumors.

Leader Judgment and Evaluation

Research related to CLT shows that people use different criteria for judging distant and proximal entities (Liberman et al., 2007). Basically, they use higher level principles to evaluate distant entities. Because "why" representations are more abstract than "how" representations, the former may be more salient in the evaluation of distant entities and the latter more salient in the evaluation of proximal entities. In other words, desirability considerations are more prominent in evaluation of distant objects and people, and feasibility considerations are more prominent in the evaluation of proximal objects and people. One manifestation of this difference is that individuals are more likely to use moral principles and value-related considerations when judging distant objects or people than when judging proximal objects or people.

The implication for leadership is that followers and potential followers of a distant leader are more likely to judge the leader on the basis of the answers he or she gives to *why* questions and on the basis of criteria of desirability such as principles and values. Followers and potential followers of proximal leaders are more likely to form attitudes toward the leader on the basis of the answers he or she gives to *how* questions, namely on the basis of the feasibility of the leader's suggestions and directions. Followers of a distant leader may accept the leader's influence if he or she provides them with satisfactory answers to their *why* questions and links the organizational mission to their values, thus infusing their work with meaning and instilling a general sense of optimism and confidence. They may not expect the leader to provide them with detailed goals and detailed guidelines about how to achieve these goals.

Followers of a proximal leader, in contrast, may expect to receive feasible goals and operational guidelines from their leader, and their followership of the proximal leader may depend on the extent to which he or she provides such goals and guidelines. This is one of the reasons why an abstract and value-related vision may be more useful or effective when presented by a distant leader and less effective in the case of a proximal leader. Followers may expect and accept a distant leader who presents a lofty vision because they judge distant objects using abstract categories and higher level principles. They may reject such a vision when it comes from a proximal leader because they evaluate proximal objects on the basis of feasibility considerations.

Therefore, to be effective, a proximal leader cannot remain at the level of abstract generalizations and higher level principles and must address the concrete implications of these generalization and principles. In other words, to influence the followers, it may not be sufficient, and may not even be necessary, that he or she convinces the followers that what they are expected to do is right, just or potentially beneficial. He or she must be able to convince them that what they are expected to do is likely to achieve the expected results.

Leader Behaviors that Influence their Followers

The leader behaviors that affect the followers are also likely to differ, at least partially, between close and distant leadership situations. Close leaders can more easily influence their followers by their observable behaviors (Shamir, 1995). For instance, since close leaders are directly observed by followers, we can hypothesize that role modeling, an important influence mechanism, is more important in proximal than in distant leadership situations. In addition, proximal leaders can more easily influence their followers by their behavior towards them. They can train and coach their subordinates more easily, show consideration and support toward them, touch them, hug them, shout at them, and show their satisfaction and dissatisfaction by their non-verbal behavior. Distant leaders, in contrast, have to rely more on oral and written messages and on symbolic behaviors and gestures.

To illustrate, one dimension of transformational leadership is individualized consideration (Bass & Avolio, 1993). Proximal leaders can demonstrate such consideration in their behaviors and interactions with their followers. Distant leaders, in contrast, can only use symbolic gestures to convey their individualized consideration. They can exhibit such symbolic consideration by showing support and encouragement toward one or few members of the organization or the community, making this behavior public knowledge, and hoping that organization members not directly affected will interpret this event as demonstrating a more general individually considerate style (e.g., a politician who kisses babies during a campaign, or a CEO who extends support to a needy employee and the story of this support is made public by his or her aides through various formal and informal internal communication channels).

However, from the point of view of the leader's followers, there is likely to be a difference between learning about a symbolic gesture of the leader and actually experiencing his or her individualized consideration. Individualized consideration in transformational leadership theory includes recognizing the needs and abilities of each member of the group and tailoring the leadership approach to these needs and abilities, for instance, by delegating responsibility for certain tasks to each individual according to his or her abilities and needs. Such consideration is difficult if not impossible to show from a distance.

The Level of Leadership

The example of individualized consideration raises a more general point. Leadership is a multilevel phenomenon. Leaders have relationships with the groups or organizations they lead but also with individual members of the group or organization. It follows from our discussion above that distant leadership is more likely to focus on the collective level and operate at that level (Chun et al., 2010). The distant leader is likely to address his or her behaviors toward the entire group, and the followers (perhaps at least to some extent) are likely to perceive the leader, interpret him or her, and respond to him or her, as a group. Proximal leadership, in contrast, includes the possibility that, in addition to the collective level, leaders and their followers will develop dyadic relationships that vary within the group.

Almost by definition, a distant leadership relationship cannot be a dyadic relationship and therefore dyadic level leadership theories like LMX (Graen & Uhl-Bien, 1995) apply primarily to proximal leaders. A top-level leader can develop dyadic relationships with his or her aides and with members of the management team, but it is impossible for such a leader to develop dyadic relationships with more than a handful of other organizational members. The implication of this is that distant leadership is likely to be more homogeneous, whereas in proximal leadership heterogeneous relationships may be developed between leaders and their followers (Chun et al., 2010). Indeed, there are indications that distant leaders are less likely to be sensitive to differences among followers, and more likely to stereotype them and treat them in a uniform manner. In this regard, it is important to note that distance affects the perceptions and attitudes of leaders no less than it affects those of the followers, and therefore the distant leader's view of the followers is also likely to be more schematic and simplified than that of the proximal leader.

Dissimilarity as a Dimension of Distance

When discussing distance in terms of contextual influence on the leadership relationship, we commonly think about spatial or geographical separation, low frequency of interactions between leaders and their followers, and hierarchical distance between them (Antonakis & Atwater, 2002; Yagil, 1998). However, as argued by Napier and Ferris (1993), actual and perceived differences between leaders and followers create a psychological distance between them. This point is reinforced by Construal Level Theory (Liberman & Trope, 2008) and related studies which show that dissimilarity is an important dimension of distance, which affects social perceptions and relations in a manner similar to the effects of other types of distance. The implication of these findings is that leaders and followers may be distant from each other even when they have direct experiences with each other. While dissimilarity may not be seen as a dimension of the leadership context, it is nevertheless often a feature of circumstances external to the leadership relationship. For instance, demographic differences on dimensions such as age, gender, race, ethnic origin or culture, may create distance between leaders and followers. Thus some of the difficulties of leading across cultures or leading diverse groups or groups that are different from the leader in terms of ethnic or cultural background (Offermann, in press) may stem not only from communication problems or different cultural values and norms to which these difficulties are commonly attributed, but also from the distance which is created by the dissimilarity between the leader and his or her followers.

Dissimilarity, however, is not only given by circumstances like age, gender, and ethnic or cultural circumstances. To some extent it is also socially constructed by the leaders and the followers. Note, for instance, how many leaders, being aware of the potential difficulty that dissimilarity of cultural, ethnic or socio-economic background introduces to their relationship with their followers, often try to compensate for this difficulty. They attempt to de-emphasize their dissimilarity on the above-mentioned dimensions and emphasize dimensions of similarity with followers, sometimes artificially. For instance, when Jesse Jackson wanted to appeal to a broad audience of underprivileged groups, many of whom were not black, he emphasized his own hardships and suffering during his childhood and youth. He did so to convince the potential followers that while he may be dissimilar to them on the dimension of color, in a more important respect he is similar to them and can therefore be trusted (Shamir, House, & Arthur, 1994). There is evidence that he exaggerated his own hardship to achieve this aim (House, 1988).

Such examples highlight the need, suggested in the introduction and in the final part of this chapter, to move beyond viewing distance only as a feature of the context of leadership relationships, and also explore the ways be which leaders (and sometimes followers) try to influence the perceived distance between them. Perhaps this example also suggests that the need to emphasize similarity in order to reduce perceived distance may be more acute in the case of distant leaders than in the case of proximal leaders, because in many cases the latter are more likely to be similar to their followers in their background (e.g. in the case of first line supervisors) and because their weaknesses and human frailty are more exposed to the followers, thus establishing some ground for perceived similarity.

Distance, Power, and Status

Distance is closely related to power and status. First, power and status differences are often among the most salient dissimilarities between leaders and followers and hence of the social distance between them. The moment a leadership relationship is created by appointment, election, or social construction, a hierarchy is created in the social group, even if it is not expressed in formal ranks or titles. However, in addition to that, power, status, and distance mutually reinforce each other: power and status differences create distance, and physical or interactional distance create power and status differences (Collinson, 2005). Distance may increase power and status due to its potential effects on idealization of the leader and the illusion of the leader's superiority discussed above. More generally, one of the findings of CLT-related research is that distance creates distance, and physical and temporal distances between parties tend to increase social distance between them (Liberman et al., 2007).

Power and status differences increase distance for several more specific reasons. First, power and status often reduce the accessibility of the leader to his or her followers, thus reducing the frequency of the interactions between them (Collinson, 2005). For instance, powerful and high status people tend to employ gatekeepers who make it more difficult to interact with the leader. Second, powerful and high status people tend to engage in higher level construal and to use obscure and less accessible language (Magee, Milliken, & Lurie, 2010; Smith & Trope, 2006). According to CLT and related studies, the relationship between distance and abstraction is bi-directional. Not only do we construe distant entities as more abstract, but we also perceive people who use abstract terms as more distant (Liberman et al., 2007).

Third, other people (followers, peers) tend to change their behavior in the presence of powerful or high status people, either due to their dependence on the powerful or out of respect for high power or high status individuals who are perceived to be superior (Magee & Galinsky, 2008). Thus power and status differences may reinforce followers' illusion of the leader's superiority. Consequently, the behavior of followers is likely to be more restricted, polite, and guarded, thus reinforcing the social distance between them and their leaders.

Fourth, research shows that powerful and high status individuals feel more independent of others, and therefore more distinct and separated from them. Since followers are less powerful and therefore less independent, this introduces another dimension of dissimilarity, and therefore of distance, between leaders and followers. Furthermore, research has shown that powerful people wish to maintain their distance from their less powerful and lower status colleagues. For instance, in an early experiment (Kipnis, 1972), participants were asked to play the role of managers and interact in writing with unseen subordinates. One group of participants was given power by the experimenter (ability to reward and punish their subordinates) and the other group was not given such power. At the end of the experiment, the participants who played the manager role were asked whether they would like to meet their unseen subordinates face to face. The vast majority of those who were given power chose not to meet their subordinates, whereas the majority of the participants who were not given power expressed an interest in meeting them. Thus power, as a dimension of dissimilarity and therefore of social distance, tends to reinforce itself because powerful people tend to wish to minimize their relationships with the less powerful and their sense of independence enables them to act in accordance with their wish.

Distance and Authenticity

Much attention has been given in recent years in the leadership literature to the concept of authentic leadership (Gardner et al., 2005; Luthans & Avolio, 2003; Shamir & Eilam, 2005). There are several definitions of this concept, but basically authentic leaders are those whose goals represent their deeply held values and whose behaviors express their self-concepts, values, and beliefs. It is assumed that authenticity is one of the dimensions on which followers evaluate their leaders and on which they base their trust in the leader and their willingness to follow him or her. Therefore, followers constantly look for evidence for the authenticity or lack of authenticity of their leader or potential leader.

From our point of view in this chapter, it can be hypothesized that because distant leadership is based more on images and attributions and proximal leadership more on direct experiences and observations, followers of proximal leaders are likely to have more "authenticity cues" at their disposal than followers of distant leaders. Authenticity is based, in part, on transparency, and transparency is based on visibility. Proximal leaders are more visible to followers than distant leaders. The followers can more easily judge not only the leaders' espoused values and goals but also the extent to which their behavior is consistent with those values and goals. Proximal followers can also observe more easily the leader's emotions as well as his or her body language. Furthermore, since they have more information about the leader, they have more evidence or data on which to perform judgments of the leader's consistency between values, goals, and behaviors.

Distant followers have to rely on indirect sources of information such as the leader's life stories or on observing the leader from afar or via communication channels that sometimes have a ceremonial nature, such as speeches, video messages, or photo opportunities. Therefore, the authenticity judgments of distant followers are more prone to be based on what sociologists call "staged authenticity" (MacCannell, 1973) whereas those of proximal followers are more likely to be based on what we can call (for lack of a better term) "authentic authenticity."

THE DISADVANTAGES AND ADVANTAGES OF DISTANCE

Commonly, the distance between leaders and their followers is viewed primarily as an obstacle. As mentioned above, it is associated with more restricted communication (mainly one-way communication) and fewer opportunities for leaders to engage in role modeling and guidance, coaching, and supporting their followers. Distant leaders may also have difficulty in recognizing the unique characteristics, abilities, and needs of their individual followers and may tend to stereotype them and treat them accordingly. Distant followers are likely to base their attitudes and reactions to the leader on the leader's image and less on his or her actual attributes and behaviors, thus making authentic leadership more difficult in distal situations. In addition, distant leaders may be perceived as detached and aloof from reality, which may lead to cynical reactions from their followers and sometimes even resistance to the leaders' initiatives or directions (Collinson, 2005). We should note, however, that distance may be advantageous to both leaders and their followers.

From the leaders' point of view, distance may enable them to hide their errors, failures, weaknesses, and vulnerabilities and thus to maintain a more "clean" and positive image in the followers' eyes. This may increase their acceptance and their authority. As Charles de Gaulle put it: "Authority doesn't work without prestige or prestige without distance." However in addition to this self-serving advantage, distance may also provide leaders with functional advantages that may serve the organization or community they lead. A degree of distance enables leaders to reflect and recharge their batteries. Furthermore, distance may be needed for the leaders to maintain detachment from daily operational details, obtain a broader perspective on organizational situations (what Heifetz & Linsky (2002) call "getting on the balcony"), distinguish between important and less important matters, think strategically, identify longer-term needs and opportunities, articulate a long-term vision, and make long-term plans.

In addition, some of the effects of leader behavior may actually be enhanced by distance. In a recent paper (Cole, Bruch, & Shamir, 2009), the authors suggested and demonstrated that whereas certain effects of leadership behaviors on followers may be neutralized or reduced by hierarchical distance between leaders and followers, other effects of the same behaviors may be enhanced. For instance, they found that the relationship between transformational leadership behaviors and followers' emulation of the leader was negatively related to followers' hierarchical distance from their leader. However, the effects of transformational leadership behaviors on collective efficacy and the positive emotional tone in the group were actually enhanced by hierarchical distance: the more distant the leader, the stronger the relationship between his or her transformational leadership behaviors and follower outcomes. The reasons for these findings are not entirely clear, but they support the possibility that distance (in this case hierarchical distance) may be advantageous. These findings even raise the possibility that some leader behaviors (e.g., the articulation and presentation of a vision, which was mentioned earlier in this chapter) may be more strongly associated with all positive effects when they come from a distance.

From the followers' point of view, distance from the leader often provides them with more autonomy, which is not only protective but may also increase their engagement and intrinsic motivation. Distance may also enable followers to create back regions not accessible to the leader and to construct alternative identities and sub-cultures, thus expressing their individuality and their allegiance to other collectivities besides the organization (Collinson, 2005). Thus, despite many complaints about the detachment and aloofness of distant leaders, it is not clear that followers would always prefer their leaders to be closer to them.

It should also be noticed that the fact that distant entities have to be construed means that distance not only enables leaders to control their images more easily but it also gives followers greater latitude in construing the same images. Construal of distant entities involves a choice of which aspects of the perceived entity to maintain, highlight, and organize the image around. While followers of distant leaders may have fewer opportunities than followers of proximal leaders to influence the leadership relationship through direct communication with the leader and reactions to the leader, they may have more opportunity to play an active role in the leadership process (Shamir et al., 2007) by crafting the images they construe of their leaders.

Perhaps we can gain some insight about what followers want from observing the way the image of God was constructed in major religions. On the one hand, God is constructed in Judaism, Christianity, and Islam as the ultimate distant and abstract entity. He or she has no face and no shape, is as far as possible, and cannot be associated with any location. On the other hand, God is also constructed as an ultimate close entity, present in every room, every conversation, and inside the heart of every person. In other words, people constructed their God in a form which is both as distant as possible and as close as possible. Perhaps there is some indication in this dualistic image of followers' somewhat paradoxical desire to have a leader who is both distant and close at the same time.

THE CONSTRUCTION OF DISTANCE BY LEADERS AND FOLLOWERS

As argued in the introduction to this chapter, distance does not necessarily have to be viewed in terms of spatial, hierarchical, or other factors that create a separation between leaders and their followers. Distance can also be viewed as an attribute of the leadership relationship. Close leadership relationships can be characterized by a high level of openness, transparency and honesty, rich two-way communication, de-emphasized hierarchy, egalitarianism, and flexibility. They are also characterized by a higher level of intimacy between the leader and his or her followers and in some cases by friendship between the two parties. Distant relationships are more formal, rigid, controlled, less open, and less egalitarian. Viewed from this perspective, distance is not something that is fully given by the situation, but rather something that is also produced by the parties to the relationships. Leaders and their followers can transcend the contextual constraints of physical, hierarchical or social distance and develop closer relationships between them, if they wish to do so. Similarly they can also increase the relational distance by their behaviors. Below are some examples of leader and follower behaviors that may increase or decrease the relational distance between them.

Leaders can increase distance in several ways: They can limit follower accessibility to them, reduce the frequency of interactions with followers, limit the interactions to task-related matters, and use formal and abstract language. For instance, in the Israeli Defense Forces (IDF) the recruits are usually 18 years old and their commanders are only one or two years older. Often the commanders have no educational or social advantages in comparison to their soldiers. Under such a situation, the commanders may not have sufficient "natural" authority, and therefore they maintain distance, at least in the first phases of the leadership relationship. Soldiers are not allowed to address their commanders freely, and have to use the Hebrew Equivalent to "Sir" whenever they speak to the commander, usually at the commander's initiative. The commanders limit their communication with soldiers to task-related matters and refrain from any personal and social conversation, despite the fact that they have many things in common with their soldiers.

In doing so, they follow Charles de Gaulle's above-mentioned dictum. They artificially increase distance to gain or maintain authority. (Interestingly the word used for distance in the IDF is the German word "distanz.") This example shows how even leaders who are very close to their followers physically, very similar to them socially, and interact with them on a daily basis can become distant leaders in some respects.

In a similar vein, leaders can decrease the distance between themselves and their followers. The first thing distant leaders can do is increase their presence and enable distant followers to have direct interactions with them and thus experience them directly. This is achieved through leading by walking around and talking to people, visiting work sites frequently, and engaging in conversations with distant followers.

A well-known example of a top-level leader who deliberately adopted this approach is Herb Kelleher, the former Chairman and CEO of Southwest Airlines, who used to visit many locations, bring pizzas to mechanics at 3 a.m., sit and eat with them, take lower-level employees to a bar for a drink, work with flight crews in the air, etc. He knew the names of many lower-level employees, and many of them felt they knew him. His approach was deliberately informal, which exemplifies several other ways by which leaders can reduce distance. He did not use abstract or high-level language. He attended employees' parties and fully participated in them in ways that demonstrated that he did not take himself too seriously.

Another example, representing a different approach to reduction of distance through personal presence, is Jack Welch of General Electric (GE), who on a regular basis used to allocate a considerable part of his time with physically and hierarchically distant lower-level managers in retreats devoted to training and discussions of improvements in company operations. In these retreats he also participated in some of the social activities with the lower-level managers. Of course, for the vast majority of the hundreds of thousands of GE employees, Welch remained a distant leader, but an important stratum of the organization experienced him as a proximal leader as well.

Simply sharing personal information is also likely to reduce distance in most situations. In the above-mentioned IDF example, there comes a time in the life of every squad or platoon, usually after several months of training, when the commanders deliberately engage in a ritual known as "breaking distance." They simply come to the soldiers' tents or barracks, sit with them, share some personal details, and discuss with the soldiers issues of common interest such as the sport teams they follow, the rock bands they admire, etc.

Leaders can also decrease distance by involving distant followers in discussions and decisions. Participation connotes equality and equality connotes reduction of social distance. Of course, the more leadership is shared (Pearce & Conger, 2003), the less the leadership relationship is characterized by distance. As discussed in other chapters of this volume, digital communication technologies enable leaders to engage in more participative and shared leadership even from a physical distance. Leaders can also use these technologies and other means of communication to expose themselves more fully even when they are not physically present, for instance, by telling stories that expose some of their vulnerabilities, thus reducing the distance created by spatial or hierarchical separation.

It should be noted, however, that over-reliance on technological means of communication may increase distance. A recent example was provided in the war between Israel and Hizbulla in Lebanon in 2006. The Israeli army had emphasized for many years the physical presence of commanders in the field among their soldiers. However, following other armies (Shamir & Ben-Ari, 1999), the IDF has developed and adopted telecommunication technologies that enable commanders to control their troops from a command car or a command room which is located at some distance from the battlefield. This method of command was used for the first time in Lebanon in 2006. Following the war, this method of leadership was among the main factors cited by many sources as responsible for the relatively poor performance of the Israeli forces in that war and the term "plasma screen leadership" became a symbol for ineffective military leaderships in both military and civilian circles.

As indicated in various parts of this chapter, followers can also construct the distance between themselves and their leaders. They can create back regions inaccessible to leaders, share information with the leader only selectively, and maintain only a formal and restricted communication with the leader. It is more difficult for followers to decrease the distance with their leaders, as the privilege of making a relationship closer (e.g. using first names, expanding the topics of conversation) is usually restricted to the higher-status parties in a relationship.

However, followers may and often do decrease distance in a more internal and psychological manner. Psychological distance is not limited to the cognitive psychology term, namely to the lack of direct experience with an entity and the need to engage in cognitive construal processes. There is another dimension of psychological distance, which is perhaps no less important in leadership relations. This is distance from the self.

A person may work in the same room with his or her leader, observe him or her for many hours each day, and interact with him or her frequently, and yet feel very distant from the leader. On the other hand, a person may feel very close to a leader whom he or she has never seen or heard, someone in a faraway country or even a fictional character. In other words, people have the faculty of identification with others, including their leaders, and this faculty can transcend any distance. Leaders may have several ways by which they can increase followers' identification with them, but ultimately it is the followers who determine the objects of their identification and the strength of their identification. As a large inscription on a New York post office declares: "Closeness has nothing to do with distance."

In this chapter, I have tried to explore some of the possible relationships between distance and leadership. My purpose was to suggest directions in which the discussion and research on distance and leadership can be expanded. I have viewed the relationship between distance and leadership as bi-directional. That is, following the extant literature, I have viewed distance (e.g., spatial or hierarchical separation between leaders and followers) as a dimension of the context of leadership, which affects leaders' and followers' behaviors and the relationships between leaders and followers. However, I have suggested, in addition, that we should pay attention to the fact that distance is to some extent socially constructed and created by the behaviors of leaders and followers.

In discussing distance as a feature of the context, I have emphasized the common feature of all types of contextual distance, namely the difference between proximal leadership, which is primarily based on direct inter-actions and experiences between leaders and followers, and distal leader-ship, which is largely based on constructed and construed images of each other. I have examined the possible implications of this difference for followers' reasons to accept a leader and follow him or her and I have identified some leader behaviors that are likely to be more effective from a distance, and other leader behaviors that are likely to more effective in the case of proximal leadership. I have also suggested that, in addition to spatial, hierarchical and interactional distances, which are commonly discussed in the literature, dissimilarity between leaders and followers can be viewed as a dimension of distance. In this regard, I have particularly emphasized the potential effects of the power differentiation between leaders and followers as a dimension of distance.

In the latter part of the chapter, I focused on distance as socially constructed. I first discussed some of the advantages and disadvantages of distance for leaders and followers, and then suggested some behaviors by which leaders and followers can increase or decrease the distance between them. In these sections, I have tried to show that distance is only partially fixed or given by the situation. By their behaviors, leaders and followers can increase or decrease both the actual distance between them (e.g. the frequency of their interactions) and the felt or experienced distance, which, from a relational point of view, can be seen as a central dimension on which leadership relationships vary.

As I suggested in the introduction, the current interest in distance and leadership is primarily driven by two developments: globalization and the development of advanced telecommunication technologies. These developments are certainly crucial and their implications are discussed in other chapters in this volume. The current chapter attempts to provide a broader theoretical perspective from which to examine these implications. From this perspective, globalization may be only one of the possible causes of increased distance between leaders and followers, and telecommunication technologies may be only one of the possible means by which this distance can be traversed.

REFERENCES

Antonakis, J. & Atwater, L. (2002). Leader distance: A review and a proposed theory. *Leadership Quarterly*, 13, 673–704.

Bass, B. M. & Avolio, B. J. (Eds.) (1993). *Improving organizational effectiveness through transformational leadership*. Thousand Oaks, CA: Sage.

Cole, M. S., Bruch, H., & Shamir, B. (2009). Social distance as a moderator of transformational leadership effects: Both a neutralizer and an enhancer. *Human Relations*, 62, 1697–1733.

Collinson, D. (2005). Questions of distance. *Leadership*, 1, 235–250.

Chun, J. U., Yammarino, F. J., Dionne, S. D., Sosik, J. J., & Moon, H. K. (2010). Leadership across hierarchical levels: Multiple levels of management and multiple levels of analysis. *Leadership Quarterly*, 20, 689–707.

Etzioni, A. (1975). *A comparative analysis of complex organizations* (Rev. ed.). New York: Free Press.

Gardner, W. L., Avolio, B. J., Luthans, F., May, D., & Walumbwa, F. (2005). Can you see the real me? A self-based model of authentic leader and follower development. *Leadership Quarterly*, 16, 343–372.

Graen, G. B. & Uhl–Bien, M. (1995). Relationship-based approach to leadership: Development of leader-member-exchange (LMX) theory over 25 years: Applying a multi-level multi-domain perspective. *Leadership Quarterly*, 6, 219–247.

Heifetz, R. A. & Linsky, M. (2002). A survival guide for leaders. *Harvard Business Review*, 80 (6), 65–74.

Hogg, M. A. (2001). A social identity theory of leadership. *Personality and Social Psychology Review*, 5, 184–200.

House, E. R. (1988). *Jesse Jackson and the politics of charisma*. Boulder, CO: Westview Press.

Katz, D. & Kahn, R.L. (1978). *The social psychology of organizations*. New York: Wiley.

Kipnis, D. (1972). Does power corrupt? *Journal of Personality and Social Psychology*, 24, 33–41.

Lee, F. & Tiedens, L. Z. (2001). Who's being served: Self-serving attributions in social hierarchies. *Organizational Behavior and Human Decision Processes*, 84, 254–287.

Liberman, N. & Trope (2008). The psychology of transcending the here and now. *Science*, 322, 1201–1205.

Liberman, N., Trope, Y., & Stephan, E. (2007). Psychological distance. In Higgins, E. T. & Kruglansky A. W. (Eds.), *Social psychology: A handbook of basic principles*. New York: Guliford, pp. 353–381.

Lord, R. G., Foti, R. J., & De Vader, D. L. (1984). A test of cognitive categorization theory: Internal structure, information processing and leadership perceptions. *Organizational Behavior and Human Performance*, 34, 343–378.

Lord, R. G. & Maher, K. J. (1991). *Leadership and information processing*. Boston: Routledge.

Luthans, F. & Avolio, B. J. (2003). Authentic leadership: A positive developmental approach. In Cameron, K. S., Duttion, J. E., & Quinn, R. E. (Eds.), *Positive organizational scholarship*. San Francisco: Berrett-Koehler, pp. 261–258.

MacCannell, D. (1973). Staged authenticity: Arrangements of social space in tourist settings. *American Journal of Sociology*, 79, 589–603.

Magee, J. C. & Galinsky, A. D. (2008). Social hierarchy: The self-reinforcing nature of power and status. *Academy of Management Annals*, 2, 351–398.

Magee, J. C., Milliken, F. J., & Lurie, A. R. (2010). Power differences in the construal of a crisis: The immediate aftermath of September 11, 2001. *Personality and Social Psychology Bulletin*, 36, 3, 354–370.

Meindl, J. R. (1990). On leadership: An alternative to the conventional wisdom. In B. M. Staw & L. L. Cummings (Eds.), *Research in Organizational Behavior*, Vol. 12, pp. 159–203. Greenwich, CT: JAI Press.

Meindl, J. (1995). The romance of leadership as a follower-centric theory: A social construction approach. *Leadership Quarterly*, 6, 329–341.

Napier, B. J. & Ferris, G. R. (1993). Distance in organizations. *Human Resource Management Review*, 3, 321–357.

Offermann, L. R. (In press). Relational leadership, relational demography: Developing high quality relationships between diverse leaders and followers. In M. Uhl-Bien and S. Ospina (Eds.), *Advancing relational leadership theory: A conversation among perspectives*. Stamford, CT: Information Age Publishing.

Pearce, C. L. & Conger, J. A. (2003). *Shared leadership: Reframing the hows and whys of leadership*. Thousand Oaks, CA: Sage.

Shamir, B. (1995). Social distance and charisma: Theoretical notes and an exploratory study. *Leadership Quarterly*, 6(1), 19–47.

Shamir, B., Arthur, M. B., & House, R. J. (1994). The rhetoric of charismatic leadership: A theoretical extension, a case study and implications for research. *Leadership Quarterly*, 5(1), 25–42.

Shamir, B. & Ben-Ari, E. (1999). Leadership in an open army: Civilian connections, inter-organizational frameworks, and changes in military leadership. In J. G. Hunt, G. E. Dodge & L. Wong (Eds.), *Out-of-the-box leadership: Transforming the 21st century army and other top-performing organizations.* Stamford, CT: JAI Press, pp. 15–40.

Shamir, B. & Eilam, G. (2005). What's your story? Toward a life-story approach to authentic leadership. *Leadership Quarterly,* 16, 395–418.

Shamir, B., Pillai, R., Bligh, M., & Uhl-Bien, M. (2007). *Follower-centered perspectives on leadership: A tribute to J. R. Meindl.* Stamford, CT: Information Age Publishing.

Smith, P. & Trope, Y. (2006). You focus on the forest when you're in charge of the trees: The effect of power priming on information processing. *Journal of Personality and Social Psychology,* 90, 578–596.

Yagil, D. (1998). Charismatic leadership and organizational hierarchy: Attribution of charisma to close and distant leaders. *Leadership Quarterly,* 9, 161–176.

Section II

The Impact of Distance on Leader–Follower Relations

3

Leading in a Digital Age: What's Different, Issues Raised, and What We Know

Surinder S. Kahai

Information technology (IT) is rapidly changing the context for leadership. Due to the growth and ubiquity of both traditional computer-mediated communication systems (e.g., email, instant messaging, and video-conferencing) and new Web 2.0-based social media (e.g., blogs, wikis, Twitter, Facebook, and YouTube), leaders today touch a worldwide audience, which not only includes immediate and remote workers but also other stakeholders such as customers and the general population. Unlike in the past, the communication with these stakeholders is two-way; these stakeholders often provide almost immediate feedback and are engaging in a dialog with business leaders via a variety of internet-based media. As a consequence of this two-way dialog, hierarchies that separated the leaders from various stakeholders are becoming less relevant and organizations are becoming flatter. Additionally, leaders are now in charge of workers who are increasingly communicating via electronic media and are engaged in virtual work.

Leadership in this new context demands new understanding and new skills in addition to old understanding and skills. Most organizational leaders have yet to understand what this new context is and what it means for leadership. In this chapter, I focus on the following aspects. I first adopt a broad view of leadership to argue that several aspects of leadership, such as those dealing with leader–follower interaction and relationship development, are likely to change because of the new context. I then describe the new 'digital' context for leadership by highlighting what is novel relative to the traditional context for leadership. Subsequently, I present existing research that indicates how information technology that defines the new context makes a difference for leadership. I also provide ideas for future research on leadership in a digital world.

DOES LEADERSHIP CHANGE IN A WIRED WORLD?

While it is widely recognized that the environment in which leaders operate today has changed due to proliferation of IT, there is less agreement on what the changes mean for leadership. Some scholars assert that what constitutes effective leadership has not changed. According to Sutton (2010), leaders in the midst of a computer revolution today have to be competent, caring, and benevolent much like the leaders in the pre-industrial age. Similarly, Champy (2010) asserts that leadership requires relationships and personal engagement and technology does nothing to alter this requirement in leaders.

Another set of scholars have suggested that leaders may be unable to display certain leadership behaviors or influence their followers when their communication is mediated by IT. For instance, Purvanova and Bono (2009) argue that transformational leadership may occur to a lower extent in virtual teams, which are teams whose members collaborate via communication technology rather than face-to-face contact because of different work locations and/or different work hours:

> Because electronic communication tends to be lacking in visual and auditory cues—the main carriers of emotional communication—transformational behaviors that are emotional in nature may occur less frequently in virtual teams.
>
> (Purvanova & Bono, 2009)

Den Hartog, Keegan, and Verburg (2007) take Purvanova and Bono's point one step further and question whether leadership behaviors, even if they occur, would be efficacious in virtual work settings:

> One can ask whether the impact of managers' leadership styles is diluted by the virtual or temporary nature of interaction and the ambiguous, frequently changing reporting relationships often associated with more flexible, virtual work.
>
> (Den Hartog, Keegan, & Verburg, 2007, p. 61)

Kahai, Sosik, and Avolio (2004), too, question whether leaders would be able to influence followers in an IT-mediated context where IT can substitute for a leader or neutralize a leader's influence. While focusing on teams supported by a Group Support System (GSS), an IT tool designed to facilitate teamwork and team decision-making, they ask whether participative leadership would be able to influence participation in a GSS context. Specifically, they explore whether this context may substitute for a leader by already providing opportunities for greater participation, or whether a GSS would neutralize a directive leader's influence by conflicting with the directive style.

Avolio and Kahai (2003) take a different view and suggest that the introduction of advanced IT changes the leadership systems in organizations. They argue that IT alters the patterns of how information is acquired, stored, interpreted, and disseminated. Since information is an important basis of power, IT is likely to alter how people are influenced and how decisions are made in organizations, thereby changing expectations for effective leadership in organizations. Leaders, for instance, would need to be aware that multiple stakeholders, such as employees, customers, and investors, are more powerful now because of their unprecedented access to information and media and their ability to form influential collectives via the internet. Those leaders who are able to take advantage of this shifting power base would be more effective.

There are also some scholars who point to new possibilities for leadership effectiveness in the digital age. In a study of leadership in virtual worlds (i.e., 3D digital spaces that simulate physical spaces with inhabitants), Reeves et al. (2008) challenge the notion that leadership is either inborn or acquired through training by suggesting that features of the technology used by a virtual team per se can help an individual become a better virtual team leader. Specifically, their work suggests that technology that tracks individual performance, implements a non-monetary reward system, and makes team member capabilities, performance, and compensation transparent may help a leader motivate performance. Such technology may help by letting the leader give rewards during or immediately after performance and by creating a perception of fairness. Furthermore, the transparency of information about how the team is performing and team members' capabilities and performance can help a leader choose or modify a strategy in real-time as well as select those who are most suitable for a particular task and define their roles accordingly.

This chapter considers the different and seemingly contradictory viewpoints described above to be valid but in need of reconciliation. One way in which the different assertions can be reconciled is by viewing them as referring to different but combinable aspects of the same phenomenon—leadership—much like the different parts of the same elephant described by seven blind men. Yammarino, Dansereau, and Kennedy's (2001) integrative model of leadership is useful for highlighting the aspects of the leadership phenomenon that different scholars refer to when they argue whether leadership is changing due to proliferation of IT. Yammarino et al. identify five areas that have been important to leadership scholars. The first area, fundamental human processes, covers psychological and related processes that enable the formation of relationships people think of as leadership. These processes serve as basic foundations without which leadership would not be possible. They cover cognitive and emotional processes, attraction between individuals, the norms, values, and culture of collectives, and, finally, communication. The second area, leadership core processes, are behaviors or qualities displayed to exercise leadership. They include charisma, transformational leadership, empowerment, providing task and relationship functions to groups, and supervision and management. The third area, leadership outcomes (hereafter referred to as leadership tactics), covers the ways in which the leadership core processes are put together. Examples of such tactics include team building, delegation, and participation in decision-making. The fourth area, second-level leadership outcomes, refers to the immediate outcomes of leadership core processes and includes variables such as performance, satisfaction, absenteeism, engagement of followers, and leader–follower relationships. The last area, substitutes for leadership, covers leadership enhancers, neutralizers, and replacements.

Scholars who argue that leadership does not change with the spread of IT tend to focus on a leader's behaviors or qualities and second-level leadership outcomes in Yammarino et al.'s (2003) model. These scholars accurately assert that in an IT-dominated environment it is still relevant for leaders to display behaviors or qualities such as benevolence, competence, and caring (Sutton, 2010), and they still need to seek outcomes like high level of follower engagement and high-quality leader–follower relationships (Champy, 2010). However, these scholars take a narrow view of leadership and don't focus on other areas within Yammario et al.'s model. For instance, they fail to acknowledge that leaders would need to pay attention to how mediation by IT changes the fundamental human processes that enable them to come across as displaying certain qualities and behaviors and relate to their followers. They also don't realize that certain leadership behaviors or qualities and the tactics for displaying them would become even more relevant and, therefore, would need to be scaled up, while others would need to be toned down in an IT-dominated context (compared to the traditional context) in order to overcome challenges and benefit from opportunities offered by new ways of connecting and accomplishing work. One could also argue that scholars who don't see leadership as changing with the spread of IT miss the point that in a context where IT is prevalent, the source of leadership may be shifting from individuals to emergent and dynamic interaction among many stakeholders (Uhl-Bien, Marion, & McKelvey, 2007).

On the other hand, scholars who assert that leadership (including its development) changes in a "wired" world are typically focusing on how the fundamental human processes that enable leaders and followers to relate to each other are changing with IT. They argue that IT is not an inert communication medium that does nothing to human cognition and emotions or to the norms, values, and culture of collectives and the communication within them. Using ideas from perspectives such as the Adaptive Structuration Theory (DeSanctis & Poole, 1994), they assert that IT shapes human cognition and emotions, as well as the norms, values, culture, and communication within collectives and is, in turn, shaped by them (see, for example, Avolio, Kahai, & Dodge, 2000).

Scholars who question whether leadership would be relevant in an IT-dominated environment tend to focus on the neutralizers and substitutes of leadership. These scholars view the fundamental human processes as changing in a digital world and are concerned about what these changes mean for leadership core processes. Specifically, they question whether leaders will be able to display behaviors that are charismatic, empowering, and transformational or even supervisory and whether the displayed leadership behaviors will have any impact when leader–follower interactions are mediated by technology, which has the potential to neutralize or substitute for the behaviors of leaders. Scholars who point to new possibilities for leadership effectiveness in the digital age are focusing on IT acting as an enhancer of leadership.

The position taken by this chapter is that many aspects of leadership are changing due to IT. While the need for many leader behaviors or qualities such as benevolence, competence, and caring don't change, and leaders still need to seek outcomes like high level of follower engagement and high-quality leader–follower relationships, how the leaders get to a point where they are seen as displaying appropriate behaviors and qualities and are able to get an optimum level of outcomes is changing because IT is creating a new context for leadership. In order to determine how leadership might change with proliferation of IT, I next describe the new context for leadership created by technology.

THE NEW CONTEXT FOR LEADERSHIP

As Avolio and Kahai (2003) have argued, the proliferation of inexpensive, compact, and highly-interconnected IT is leading to new situations by creating new patterns of who has access to information and how information is acquired, stored, interpreted, and disseminated. From the viewpoint of Yammarino et al.'s model (2003), the proliferation of IT is changing communication and psychological processes; at a simple level, the media we use in communication and who can communicate what, with whom, and when are changing, as is the processing of the information that we send or receive. All these changes can influence the emergence, incidence, and reinforcement of leadership. The changes in the context for leadership can also be interpreted from the perspective of "distance." In order to be able to connect these changes in the context for leadership to distance, I employ an expanded version of the view of distance in organizations offered by Napier and Ferris (1993).

Napier and Ferris (p. 326) focus on the dyadic distance between a leader and a follower and conceptualize it as "a multidimensional construct that describes the psychological, structural, and functional separation, disparity, or discord between a supervisor and a subordinate." Psychological distance refers to the psychological effects of actual and perceived demographic, status, cultural, and value differences in a dyad. Structural distance includes those aspects of distance that are brought about by the physical distance or arrangement that characterizes a dyadic relationship as well as those that arise due to organizational and supervision structure. It is considered to be conceptually similar to the notion of propinquity or nearness in place or time, which affects the potential for and the type of interaction in a dyad (also see Walther & Bazarova, 2008). Structural distance is expected to be indicated by the physical design of the workplace, opportunity to interact (social contact or accessibility), spatial distance (task contact), and the span of management of the supervisor. Functional distance is described as "the degree of closeness and quality of the functional working relationship between the supervisor and subordinate" (Napier & Ferris, 1993, p. 337). The indicators of functional distance include affect (trust, liking, support, etc.), perceptual congruence or understanding, latitude or the degree of a subordinate's influence and discretion, and relationship quality. Functional distance is expected to result partially from psychological and structural distance.

When applying the notions of distance offered by Napier and Ferris (1993), I don't apply them just to the distance between a supervisor and a subordinate but to any dyad or relationship that is of relevance to a leader or an organization (e.g., a dyad defined by a politician and a fan or the relationship defined by an organization with its customer). I also go beyond the three notions of distance offered by Napier and Ferris (1993) to describe how the new context for leadership can be related to distance. I employ two additional notions of distance: opacity and attributional distance. Opacity refers to the gap or the distance between what people understand about leaders or organizations and the reality related to them. Attributional distance refers to the distance between the actual actions of a leader or an organization and what is attributed to the leader or organization. While opacity and attributional distance seem to be related, there is a critical difference between them. Opacity implies lack of some information. Attributional distance, on the other hand, implies distortion of reality or distortion of information already acquired or stored.

The following are some specific changes brought about by IT that are defining the new context for leadership.

Greater Incidence of Electronic Communication

It is not surprising that with greater access to technology, the convenience it offers, and increasing pressures to reduce travel expenses, organizational communication is shifting to electronic media (e.g., see Markus, 1994; Sarbaugh-Thompson & Feldman, 1998; Vance, 2009). This shift is also being fueled by the increasing appearance of members of Generation Y or millennials (those born during the 1980s and 1990s) in the workplace. Millennials are known for their proclivity to interact via media such as

Facebook, MySpace, Twitter, and SMS (Jones & Fox, 2009). But while this shift to electronic communication is speeding up communication and is enabling greater connectivity among people, it is also bringing in unintended consequences, many of which can impact leadership.

Among the unintended consequences of the shift to electronic communication is the introduction of structural distance due to reductions in social contact. In a study of changes over a period of two years soon after the introduction of email in an academic unit of a university, Sarbaugh-Thompson and Feldman (1998) found that while email communication increased, the overall communication declined. Moreover, most of the decline involved greetings or unplanned casual conversations, which are valuable for facilitating work and social cohesiveness in an organization (Sarbaugh-Thompson & Feldman, 1998). While the decline in social communication can be partly attributed to the loss of nonverbal cues and the accompanying attenuation in the conveyance of positive emotions and tone in electronic communication (Kahai & Cooper, 1999), it may also be due to inaccurate perceptions of what one is communicating. Specifically, senders of electronic messages suffer from egocentrism and don't appreciate that their audience cannot perceive the emotions or tone that they are trying to communicate (Kruger, Epley, Parker, & Ng, 2005). The challenge in conveying emotions and tone in electronic communication is further compounded by receivers seeing positive messages as less positive and negative messages as more negative than intended by the sender (Byron, 2008).

The shift to electronic communication may also introduce structural distance by reducing the accessibility of those one is in a meeting with. At a large service organization that had recently introduced email, Markus (1994) observed another unintended and socially negative consequence. She found that email users often turned away from those they were meeting face-to-face to read their emails whenever they were alerted to a new email in their inbox. Today, we see this "depersonalizing" behavior when cellphone users text or email while they are meeting someone face-to-face.

Another set of unintended consequences of the shift to electronic communication is due to such communication introducing functional distance, and thus affecting the quality of relationships among organizational members. The digital nature of communication via electronic channels makes it easy to store, duplicate, forward, and manipulate the message. This too is leading to several unintended and oftentimes negative consequences for both the workplace and leadership (Avolio & Kahai, 2003). For instance,

Markus (1994) observed that the ability to store email messages led to compulsive documentation and aggressive accountability games. Such behaviors can make it challenging for a leader to create a work climate based on trust and understanding.

Due to the ease with which electronic communication can be duplicated and preserved, it becomes indelible for all practical purposes. Once someone sends an email or posts a message online, it is practically impossible to remove it. Even if the creator of the email or message tries to delete it, a copy of the original is likely to be retained in the recipient's mailbox or a server somewhere for backup, archival, or caching purposes. This indelible nature of our electronic communication is introducing functional distance and making it difficult to forget past missteps and exercise an important organizational virtue: forgiveness (Rosen, 2010). Forgiveness is important because of its positive effect on organizational performance (Cameron, 2003).

When the effects of electronic communication described above occur over a period of time, they can damage social relationships and cohesiveness within an organizational entity (team, department, business unit, or the whole organization). The leader of an entity in such a state can face challenges in rallying followers and helping them march ahead as a single unit towards the entity's goals. The leader may also face greater demands on her or his time as followers increasingly turn to her or him for social support. The leader would need to be aware of how the increasing shift to electronic communication can alter the development of social relationships. Armed with this knowledge, the leader can use this knowledge to encourage and model behaviors that prevent or repair the damage to social relationships. The indelible nature of electronic communication also puts pressure on leaders to make sure that they are discreet in their electronic communication. New companies are making it their business to aggregate what an individual posts in online public forums and make that information available to those interested in that individual's background check (Preston, 2011). Leaders who are not discreet may find that the record of their communication is used against them in instances such as when they are looking for a new job or are seeking public office.

There are many other unintended consequences of the shift to electronic communication. These are presented below.

Greater Transparency and Openness

More and more of what happens in organizations and what their leaders or others do is becoming widely available to outsiders because someone ends up posting that information on the internet. This is true not only for online happenings but for offline happenings as well. Thus, leaders are less able to control the opacity or the distance between what their stakeholders understand about them or their organizations and reality. The Wikileaks and Cryptome websites[1] are a couple of examples of whistleblower sites that are making leaders and organizations more transparent. During 2010, the US Government experienced the increased transparency enabled by the internet when Wikileaks leaked nearly a hundred thousand secret US military documents related to its offensive in Afghanistan (Schmitt, 2010). In June 2008, NBC News was unable to keep the news of Tim Russert's death a secret until it contacted and informed Russert's family. The news of Russert's death was already circulating the internet via Twitter and Wikipedia (http://www.wikipedia.org) long before NBC's announcement on television (Cohen, 2008). Similarly, when President Obama offhandedly called Kanye West a "jackass" after the latter's inappropriate interruption of MTV Video Music Awards in September 2009, his remarks were recorded and posted on the internet by someone who overheard the conversation (Gold, 2009). Obviously, such transparency puts pressure on leaders to be careful about their actions and also makes it difficult for them to recover from mishaps.

The increased transparency brought about by the internet also makes it challenging for leaders to prevent sensitive information from getting leaked out. The US was unable to keep its special operation to go after Osama bin Laden in Abbotabad, Pakistan, completely secret from the world when its helicopters reached Abbotabad in the early hours of May 2, 2011 (Stevenson, 2011). Mr. Sohaib Athar, an IT consultant from Abbotabad, inadvertently tweeted the US operation on Osama bin Laden's compound: "Helicopter hovering above Abbottabad at 1AM (is a rare event)." A couple of tweets later, he added: "A huge window shaking bang here . . . I hope it's not the start of something nasty."

The increased transparency is not only due to someone posting sensitive information on the widely available internet, it is also resulting from the ease with which electronic communication can be forwarded to others or disclosed inadvertently. The forwarding and inadvertent disclosure of electronic communication has caused trouble for leaders and organizations in the past. Cerner's CEO Neal Patterson was a victim of forwarding. After he sent an email to his managers expressing annoyance with what he saw as Cerner's declining work ethic, his email was widely forwarded to Cerner's employees and eventually made its way to Yahoo message boards. When investors read the message, they concluded that Cerner was in trouble and brought down Cerner's stock 29 percent (Murphy, 2006). The case of US Congressman Anthony Weiner illustrates how easy it is for leaders to make an inadvertent disclosure when they communicate electronically. The Congressman, who communicated regularly via Twitter with his followers, inadvertently started a message containing a link to a lewd photo of his with an '@' instead of the 'd' that would have made the message private and sent it to a selected follower only (Crovitz, 2011). Due to this mistake, the Congressman's message became available to the public and the Congressman had to resign in the wake of public outcry that followed the inadvertent disclosure.

Another way in which the shift to electronic communication is increasing transparency is by providing visibility into the state of interaction within a workgroup. For instance, productivity tools available within Google Apps (e.g., word processing, making spreadsheets, drawing, making presentation slides, survey forms, and wiki) provide visibility into who has contributed what and when. In situations where the relationship between individual effort and output is imperfect, such meta information can provide insights into individual members' efforts and play a critical role in how they are perceived by others (see Burgoon et al., 2002; O'Sullivan, 2000). Consider, for example, a team of individuals attempting to document their work-related knowledge in a wiki. When team members find that one of the members contributed a short page while others contributed significantly longer pages, they may find from the revision history provided by the wiki that the individual in question spent a significantly greater amount of time than others to write the page. Instead of concluding that the individual in question is a slacker or is resisting the documentation of knowledge, which is what they would have likely concluded if all they could see was the short page, they may conclude that the knowledge of this individual does not lend itself well to documentation and become more considerate when assessing her or his future contributions. On the other hand, if team members find out from the wiki's revision history that, in addition to contributing very little knowledge, the effort made by one or more individuals was short of the expected level, the development of trust within the team can suffer (Piccoli & Ives, 2003), thereby making it challenging for a leader to help the team work together towards its goals.

Rapid and Widespread Dissemination of Information

Once information becomes available today, it spreads rapidly and widely via IT. IT reduces barriers in the way of spreading information created by structural distance. Aided by IT, information spreads rapidly and widely as if physical distance did not matter. This rapid and widespread dissemination of information is leading to a change in the level and direction of influence. Partly because of their simultaneity, reactions to a piece of information that has spread rapidly and widely may become a significant force and may end up with leaders being forced out of their positions or making involuntary changes in their organizations. This is illustrated by what happened when, in April 2007, Don Imus referred to Rutgers women's basketball team as "nappy-headed ho's" on his "Imus in the Morning Show" (Barnes, Steel, & McBride, 2007). Among the relatively few people who tuned into the show on April 4, 2007, the day on which Don Imus made his comment, was a blogger for liberal watchdog organization Media Matters for America. The blogger posted a video of the comment on the organization's website and informed the media about it via an email blast to several hundred reporters. The media did not react immediately but the blog post made its way to millions of PC screens and the wider public began to complain to the show's broadcaster, MSNBC. MSNBC apologized for the comment but the apology only made the story explode. Subsequently, the media and civil rights leaders got into the act of criticizing Imus's comment and companies started talking about pulling their advertising from MSNBC. Eventually, within eight days after the comment, both MSNBC and CBS (which carried the show on radio) cancelled the show.

Manipulation of Communication

The incident of Shirley Sherrod, a former US Agriculture Department official who was removed from her job on the basis of a doctored video[2] posted on the internet, illustrates another peril of the shift to electronic communication: organizational leaders and the public can now be easily misled to judge others inaccurately and take uninformed action. It is not very challenging to take an electronic record of someone's communication and doctor it to create a distance between what was actually communicated and what is attributed to that person. In fact, leaders themselves may be misrepresented when someone doctors an electronic record of their communication. Therefore, leaders have an additional task on their hands today—the task of scanning the internet and monitoring how they are presented online.

Ability to Overcome Geographical Separation and Virtualize Organizations

IT is enabling individuals and organizations to connect and work together despite geographical distance or separation. One consequence of this ability is the increasing virtualization of organizations (Ahuja & Carley, 1999). In the past, organizations were mono-cultural and top-down. They had clear boundaries, and clear lines of authority ran through them. Job definitions were constant for a significant period of time. Organizations bought the raw materials or finished items they used in manufacturing from others, but the knowledge-work was done in-house. Today's organizations, however, are different. They tend to differ from the above picture of past organizations in one or more ways. For instance, Amazon is not just one company but a collection of many companies operating with one front-end under the Amazon name. When we order an iPhone from Apple, the fulfillment of this order involves many geographically distributed, but tightly connected companies besides Apple.

IT makes it possible for an organization to overcome geographical distance and partner with suppliers, customers, and even competitors all over the world and improve its efficiency and the quality of goods or services produced without significantly increasing coordination costs. This has led to the creation of networked and distributed organizations with no clear boundaries that indicate where one organization ends and another begins. Accordingly, lines of authority are difficult to draw in such organizations. Moreover, since the network linkages are never constant, the work one has to do is constantly changing. The organizations of today are partnering or collaborating with others not only for manufacturing but also for services and knowledge-work.

In this new context for organizations, leadership cannot be the same as before. Both leadership in organizations and leadership of organizations has to change. For instance, research is indicating that leadership in virtual teams that are formed to enable collaboration in virtual organizations is different from face-to-face teams in traditional organizations. Specifically, while the leadership behaviors found to be effective in face-to-face teams are still relevant for virtual teams, virtual team leaders need to do more in virtual teams (Huang, Kahai, & Jestice, 2010). An example of something that a leader may need to do in virtual teams but which may not be very critical in traditional teams is being proactive in providing task details. In traditional teams, it is possible for team members to use impromptu meetings to gather missing task details. Such impromptu meetings are not possible in virtual teams and to ensure timely and effective task execution, a virtual team leader would need to flesh out and clarify task details early on.

Likewise, leaders of virtual organizations have to make changes in order to increase their workers' willingness and ability to engage in virtual work. Specifically, the structure and culture of an organization may have to be changed to make collaboration across geographical, temporal, cultural, and organizational boundaries a way of life for its workers. For instance, new performance measures and rewards that emphasize collaboration may have to be instituted. Proper technology and training may have to be provided to workers to facilitate their collaboration. Since worker roles will be changing constantly and also threatened, leaders will have to figure out ways to create meaning for their workers and keep them motivated despite role ambiguity and the lack of job security.

The Rise of Social Networks

Today's IT offers unprecedented connectivity which makes it very easy for people and organizations to overcome structural distance and create social networks for various purposes that include communication, coordinated action, or association with an idea, cause, or interest. Several social media applications, such as Facebook, Twitter, and LinkedIn, are designed primarily as platforms that facilitate the formation of networks and communication within them. Even IT tools outside of the social media arena, such as email, instant messaging, and SMS on cellphones, can be harnessed to form networks easily and quickly. SMS on cellphones, for instance, is often used to form a network and organize a flash or a smart mob.

The rise of social networks is partly facilitated by self-selection of individuals into a network. In Twitter, for instance, one becomes a part of an organization's or another individual's network by simply following them. One can also become a part of a network with unknown others who share an interest or are psychologically close by using a common hashtag in a Twitter message. For example, people joined President Barack Obama's Twitter Town Hall meeting[3] in July 2011 by using the hashtag #AskObama.[4] The use of this hashtag allowed them to see the tweets of others who attended the meeting and communicate with them. In the case of some social media, self-selection into a network is even easier than in the examples provided above; it takes place by default without any explicit action by any individual for joining a network. For instance, whenever someone bookmarks a site using Delicious, a social bookmarking site, that individual automatically becomes a part of the network of everyone who has bookmarked that site on Delicious.

Leaders now have significant opportunities for deriving benefits from IT-enabled networks. If used appropriately, IT-enabled networks can be a very efficient and effective way for overcoming structural and psychological distance and connecting with followers in order to improve relationships with them and bridge any functional distance. IT-enabled networks tend to be efficient because of the low cost and instantaneous nature of digital communication. They tend to be effective because of their wide reach and their ability to reach an audience that has typically selected itself to be a part of the network due to the idea it represents. As a presidential candidate, Barack Obama harnessed these features of IT-enabled networks to connect directly with the electorate and raise a record amount of campaign funds.[5] When the producers of USA Networks television show, *White Collar*, changed the show's main title sequence in the summer of 2011 and found out that it was a hit with some fans, and a miss with others, they quickly used their Facebook Fan page[6] in July 2011 to invite the fans to a poll on whether they should revert to the old sequence or keep the new one. Leaders at SAP, an IT technology company, monitor employee activity on networks enabled by social media within the company to gauge if their message is reaching the employees (Starke, 2011).

From a social network perspective, leadership is viewed as building social capital in the network (Balkundi & Kilduff, 2006). One of the opportunities that leaders now have with social media at their disposal is the ability to use this media for building social capital. Serena Software, a company of about 800 geographically dispersed employees, adopted Facebook to overcome geographical separation and build social capital by improving the quality of workplace interaction (Weston, 2009). The company claimed that the use of Facebook led to relationships that would not have existed otherwise and yielded both tactical and strategic benefits. The company's culture changed with the acquisition of new networking skills by its employees. What we see in the case of Serena Software is an example of how leaders could utilize social media to overcome structural distance within an organization and reduce both the psychological distance and the functional distance experienced by its workers.

The social network perspective on leadership also suggests that, in order to be effective, leaders need to be able to develop an accurate view of social relationships in the network they belong to (Balkundi & Kilduff, 2006). By developing an accurate view, leaders are able to forge successful coalitions that help the organization achieve its goals. When social media are used for networking within an organization, they provide visibility into the network and communication activities of those one is connected to and, in some cases (e.g., with Twitter), even further. Thus, by deploying social media, leaders also have the opportunity to develop a more accurate view of their network and increase their effectiveness.

Leaders may also find that they are not the only ones who stand to benefit from IT-enabled networks. It is possible for virtually anyone who has an idea with mass appeal and access to the internet to spark the formation of a network that rises against leaders. For example, the availability of Facebook, Twitter, and email to a significant number of disgruntled youth in Egypt enabled a group of activists to form a network of protesters against President Hosni Mubarak and his government (Sutter, 2011). This network enabled the activists to coordinate powerful gatherings of protesters in the streets during an 18-day revolution, which initially forced President Mubarak to make concessions by dismissing his government and then eventually forcing him out of office in February 2011. It is not only political leaders who should be concerned about protest networks forming against them on the internet. Even business leaders are likely to face pressures via IT-enabled networks. In June 2011, the makers of cottage cheese in Israel had to relent and reduce their prices after Israeli citizens, who were upset about rising prices of cottage cheese, got together on Facebook to support a boycott on cheese purchases (Levinson, 2011).

Leaders are also challenged by the rise of IT-enabled social networks in another way. The visibility offered by IT-based networks may tempt leaders to take unethical actions. As I indicated above, social media provide visibility into the activities of others in the network. When leaders are able to learn via social media about what is on the minds of others, they may be tempted to take punitive action against those who oppose them or their ideas.

Leaders' temptations to behave unethically may also arise due to the relative anonymity or opacity created by IT-enabled social networks. Unlike in situations where social networks are formed on the basis of knowing someone, in situations where the social networks are formed on the basis of an idea, cause, or interest (e.g., as when a Twitter hashtag is used to form a network or when one is a part of an online discussion board focusing on a particular topic), one pays less attention to who is behind a user name and focuses more on the ideas being exchanged. In such situations, leaders may be tempted by their relative anonymity to fake their identity and take advantage of others in the network. In the midst of uprisings against authorities in the Middle East in February 2011, authorities in Sudan pretended to be activists and invited protesters via Facebook and instant messaging to gather in a specific area of Khartoum (Crovitz, 2011). When the protesters arrived, they were arrested. The case of Whole Foods CEO, John Mackey, serves as another example here. For a period of about eight years up to August 2006, the CEO used the pseudonym Rahodeb, an anagram of his wife's name—Deborah—to post numerous messages on Yahoo Finance's bulletin board (Kesmodel & Wilke, 2007). In these posts, he touted his company's stock and even criticized the strategy and management of a publicly traded competitor, Wild Oats Markets, that his company eventually purchased.

Constant Contact

In the past, a leader's influence was largely restricted to face-to-face meetings and to occasional messages via print media, such as newsletters, or broadcast media, such as radio or TV, in the case of political leaders. Today, communication from near and distant leaders takes place via electronic media that allows one to be always on and is, therefore, more frequent. Since successive communications are nearer in time, the structural distance between leaders and their followers is shortening. Leaders and their followers are more accessible to each other than before. Teachers, for instance, reach out to students not only during the class meeting but also in between class meetings via chat, email, Twitter, Facebook, and other online-learning technologies. Leaders who have not adapted to this new context face increasing pressure to adopt the new media and communicate more frequently. Those who adopt the new media will have to figure out the effective temporal rhythms that define the regularity at which they will communicate, the purposes of different communication instances, and which media among the new and old ones at their disposal they will use in each instance (Maznevski & Chudoba, 2000). The inability to figure out effective temporal rhythms may cause excessive stress, burnout, and productivity loss for a leader (Tarafdar, Tu, Ragunathan, & Ragunathan, 2007). Leaders expected to stay in constant contact via technology may also find they are spending more time managing technology and less time managing people (Becker, 2009).

Summary

The above discussion of a new context for leadership illustrates the new environment in which leaders are operating today. The shift to electronic communication, the widespread availability and mobility of communication tools, and the ease with which one can reach and network with others are transforming the various forms of distance experienced in organizations and, consequently, changing the nature of influence in organizations. To examine how influence is changing in organizations, I discuss next the issues, findings, and future research related to leadership in three situations affected by IT.

ISSUES, FINDINGS, AND QUESTIONS FOR LEADERSHIP IN NEW IT-MEDIATED CONTEXTS

In this section, I discuss leadership in three IT-mediated situations: same-place IT-mediated meetings, virtual teams, and complex organizations. These three IT-mediated situations correspond to how IT networks have evolved over time with respect to distance. The initial IT networks (late 1980s and early 1990s) were local area networks that spanned a limited physical distance, such as a room or the floor of a building. During this era, IT was employed to support same-place meetings. With the rise of the internet during the mid-1990s, IT networks were no longer local—they enabled organizations to connect with others all over the world. Organizations used this opportunity to tap into human resources beyond their local areas and create virtual teams, which employed the connectivity enabled by the internet, to carry out organizational work. During the years following the turn of the century, compression of another kind of distance—power distance—took place on the internet. The rise of tools such as blogs, wikis (e.g., Wikipedia), media sharing sites (e.g., YouTube, Flickr), and social networking sites (e.g., Facebook, Twitter) enabled the common man to contribute and participate actively on the internet. No longer did the capability to make a difference on the internet lie only with organizations. This shift corresponded with a dramatic rise in the complexity faced by organizations. Organizations not only have to coordinate their worldwide network of human resources and suppliers, they now have to deal with external stakeholders, such as customers, who are using their increased power to influence an organization in unpredictable ways.

In the following sections, I discuss each of the three IT-mediated situations I presented above and the leadership issues that they give rise to. I also present research that shows how IT is making a difference for leadership. I conclude the discussion of leadership in each situation by presenting ideas or questions for future research.

Leadership in Same-Place IT-Mediated Meetings

Over time, meetings have become more frequent (Rogelberg, Scott, & Kello, 2007). This is partly due to flatter organizational structure and greater employee empowerment. Meetings become a vehicle of choice for tapping valuable information for process improvements and innovations from workers. However, meetings are often unproductive for a variety of reasons: they may lack structure, a few individuals may dominate, attendees may have inhibitions about providing input, or minutes may not be kept. As a result, meetings can be an unsatisfying experience for many. IT-based Group Support Systems (GSS) have been offered to reduce the barriers to effective meetings and make them more productive. GSS may do so by anonymizing input, providing structure, enabling parallel communication, and creating a record (Nunamaker, Dennis, Valacich, Vogel, & George, 1991). Since meeting participants conduct a significant part of their communication by typing their input into the GSS, such systems introduce opacity or distance among participants by reducing the communication of non-verbal cues. Even though participants may compensate for lack of relational cues by employing emoticons and verbal equivalents (e.g., "lol") or by taking more time to develop relationships (Walther, 1995), they cannot compensate for all functions of non-verbal cues, such as turn-taking, regulating the flow of conversation, providing immediate feedback, and conveying subtle meaning when communicating electronically. If individual inputs are made anonymous by the GSS, additional opacity or distance may be introduced by the separation of input from who is providing it and by the shifting of attention away from individual identities (Kahai, Avolio, & Sosik, 1998).

Since GSS create a level playing field and provide or facilitate some of the functions typically provided by a leader (e.g., creating a participative environment, providing a structure, showing consideration), questions can be raised about whether leaders would be able to exercise any influence and whether they provide any value beyond what is provided by a GSS in such situations (e.g., Kahai, Sosik, & Avolio, 2004; Lim, Raman, & Wei, 1994). At the same time, arguments can also be made that certain GSS features, such as anonymity, might enhance the effects of certain kinds of leadership, such as transformational leadership, by creating an environment that facilitates the effects of that leadership (Sosik, Kahai, & Avolio, 1998). Fortunately, there have been some studies that shed light on these and other issues about leadership in GSS-supported, same-place meetings. These studies, which have been conducted in laboratory settings, can be divided on the basis of whether or not they manipulated leadership behavior and they differ in terms of what we can learn from them. Studies that did not manipulate leadership behavior inform us about the emergence of leadership and whether the absence or presence of an elected or designated leader makes a difference in group process and/or outcomes. These studies do not inform us about the effects of specific types or styles of leadership behaviors (e.g., participative versus directive, transformational versus transactional). Consequently, one is unable to derive practical recommendations for what leaders should do when they are leading same-place meetings that are mediated by technology. On the other hand, studies that manipulated leadership behaviors provide information about the effects of specific types of leadership behaviors and enable the generation of practical recommendations.

Findings of Studies that Did Not Manipulate Leadership Behavior

Many laboratory studies of leadership in GSS-supported, same-place meetings employed assigned or elected leaders without systematically manipulating the behaviors shown by these leaders (e.g., Barkhi, Jacob, Pipino, & Pirkul, 1998; George, Easton, Nunamaker, & Northcraft, 1990; Harmon, Schneer, & Hoffman, 1995; Hiltz, Johnson, & Turoff, 1991; Ho & Raman, 1991; Kim, Hiltz, & Turoff, 2002; Lim et al., 1994; Wickham & Walther, 2007). These studies made important contributions by indicating the following:

- Leaders are able to exercise influence and make a difference in computer-mediated groups. For instance, Lim et al. found that in leaderless groups, the GSS tended to promote equality of influence attempts but in groups with an elected leader the GSS did not stop the leader from exercising a greater degree of influence than others. Hiltz et al. found that the presence of a leader was associated with higher decision quality in GSS-supported groups.
- More than one leader can emerge in computer-mediated groups. Wickham and Walther found that more than one leader can emerge in computer-mediated groups, simply because there are many different roles to fill.
- The presence of a leader in computer-mediated groups can interact with the features of technology to influence group process and outcomes. For example, Hiltz et al. found that in the presence of statistical feedback, assigned leadership reduced the level of agreement in the group. The researchers suggested that the statistical feedback feature may have served as a surrogate leader by suggesting a course of action, thereby conflicting with the designated leader.

Findings of Studies that Manipulated Leadership Behavior

In laboratory studies that manipulated leadership (e.g., Hoyt & Blascovich, 2003; Kahai & Avolio, 2006; Kahai, Sosik, & Avolio, 1997, 2003, 2004; Sosik, Avolio, & Kahai, 1997, 1998; Sosik et al., 1998; Sosik, Kahai, & Avolio, 1999; Tan, Wei, & Lee-Partridge, 1999), researchers trained confederates or a group member to display leadership behaviors in a certain style, e.g., as a participative, directive, instrumental, transformational, or transactional leader, over a short period of time (e.g., 20 minutes). While each of the above leadership styles has been found to have a main effect on group process and outcomes, various contextual factors, including the nature of task (e.g., task structure, task interdependence), operating conditions (e.g., rewards and facilitation), and anonymity (a technology feature) have also been found to interact with these leadership styles to influence group process and outcomes. The following are some of the salient findings related to the interaction between leadership styles and anonymity:

- Anonymity may make it easier for a transformational leader to make a group focus on the collective by taking attention away from individual identities. It may also make the effect of contingent rewarding by a transactional leader less potent by rendering the recognition provided by the leader as impersonal. In a study involving a cognitive conflict task, Kahai et al. (2003) found that anonymity enhanced the effects of transformational versus transactional leadership on solution originality, group efficacy, and satisfaction with the task. They also found that transformational leadership helped overcome social loafing that occurred when individual input was anonymous and was pooled for group rewards.
- Anonymity may also substitute for transformational leadership's emphasis on being flexible in how we approach or frame a situation. In one study involving an idea generation task, Sosik et al. (1998) found that though transformational leadership promoted idea flexibility in the identified condition, it did not do so in the anonymous condition.
- How anonymity influences the effects of transformational leadership may depend on the nature of the task. Sosik et al. (1997) observed that the effect of transformational versus transactional leadership on group potency diminished in the presence of anonymity for an idea generation task, which is a low interdependence task, but it increased in the presence of anonymity for a report writing task, which is a high interdependence task.
- Taken together, results seem to suggest that while anonymity may substitute for transformational leadership during an idea generation task, it may enhance the transformational leader's effect for a task requiring a group to integrate its work or resolve conflicting viewpoints.

Given that many researchers (e.g., Den Hartog et al., 2007; Purvanova & Bono, 2009) wonder whether certain leadership styles, such as transformational leadership, would be able to affect group processes and outcomes in computer-mediated settings due to the absence of non-verbal cues, it is interesting to note that the manipulated leadership styles, including transformational leadership, affected group processes and outcomes in computer-mediated settings. It is also interesting to note that the effects occurred despite relatively weak manipulations. The manipulations can be considered as weak because the leaders were not members of their groups and were merely there to facilitate the group process. Additionally, they had no credibility established from prior interactions and interacted for only a short period of time (e.g., 20 minutes).

Questions for Future Research

Within the studies that manipulated leadership behavior, focus on how leadership behaviors might interact with the features of technology use was either absent or limited to variation in anonymity, which is just one of many features of technologies providing support for same-place meetings. Other features of technology that supports same-place meetings include providing structure, enabling parallel communication, and creating a record of communication. An interesting avenue for future research would be to determine how these features might interact with different types of leadership behaviors.

Another interesting avenue would be to examine how the proliferation of cell phones and smart phones is affecting leadership in same-place settings by enabling back-channel communication, or communication that is secondary to but occurring simultaneously with the main communication. The relevance of back-channel communication to leadership was illustrated recently when a Florida senator was found receiving questions on his Blackberry from a lobbyist in the audience to ask insurance regulators during a committee meeting (Gomes, 2010). While this incident raises questions about the ethics of the leader involved, it also stimulates new thinking and new questions about how technology might alter leadership and its effects in same-place settings. The following are some questions that arise:

- How does back-channel communication influence the emergence of a leader? An individual receiving information from outside sources via back-channels may be more likely to emerge as a leader by appearing smarter than others.

- What is the effect of back-channel communication within a group on a leader's performance? Back-channel communication may improve a leader's performance by creating a way for the leader to receive feedback privately without looking bad and change her or his strategy on the fly.
- Does back-channel communication during a same-place meeting give rise to "clique"-like behavior when group members with similar interests are "instant messaging" each other to interpret and to respond to what the leader or others may be saying?
- How does back-channel communication alter the balance of power between the leader and the rest of the group? Back-channel communication may allow followers to bypass a leader who is not inviting discussion on a topic.
- What is the effect of back-channel communication within a group on the level of engagement within the group? A leader may be able to improve engagement during meetings by enabling those present to discuss and elaborate on the points being presented. The idea that back-channel communication may lead to higher engagement is finding support in the case of television viewing. Earlier trends suggested that the internet is taking away the audience from television (Nie, Simpser, Stepanikova, & Zheng, 2005). However, TV viewing during recent years has only gone up apparently because people are watching TV and communicating via social media with their friends and family about what they are seeing on TV at the same time (Stelter, 2010). An experiment to improve engagement with back-channel communication is already underway at Purdue University. The university is making Hotseat technology (http://www.itap.purdue.edu/tlt/hotseat/) available to faculty and students to enable collaborative "micro-discussions" in and out of the classroom.
- What are the types of same-place meeting situations for which back-channel communication is likely to be beneficial? What are the situations for which it is likely to be distracting?
- What leader behaviors and characteristics are most suited to the effectiveness of back-channel communication? It appears that in order to enable effective back-channel communication, a leader would need to provide an initial structure, be IT literate, be a quick processor of information, and be willing to give up control.

Leadership in Virtual Teams

Virtual teams are teams of individuals who collaborate via communication technology rather than face-to-face contact because of different work locations and/or different work hours (Schweitzer & Duxbury, 2010). The notion of team virtualness does not represent a discrete state of teams; instead, it represents a continuum such that some teams are more virtual than others (Schweitzer & Duxbury, 2010). The use of virtual teams in organizations is increasing and this trend is expected to continue in the near future (Petrook, 2008; "Virtual teams," 2008) because virtual teams offer access to the most appropriate, diverse, and less expensive talent. Additionally, as companies face increasing cost pressures, they are using virtual teams to reduce travel. Cisco, for instance, reduced annual travel costs per employee from $7900 to $3400 by using remote collaboration tools (Vance, 2009).

But virtual teams are not without challenges. They may create conflicting demands, role ambiguity, and ambiguity about performance criteria because of having both a co-located as well as a remote leader (Den Hartog et al., 2007). Due to the absence of visible tangible dimensions of organizations (e.g., offices and co-located employees), common norms and expectations, and opportunities for "water-cooler" conversations, virtual teams may suffer from low cohesion, lack of identification, and low trust (Den Hartog et al., 2007; Wiesenfeld, Raghuram, & Garud, 2001). Communication tends to be constrained in a virtual team because of the need to type, which creates confusion about the team's status at any point in time and increases task ambiguity (Huang et al., 2010). Team and task also become less salient to members due to dispersion (Huang et al., 2010).

The above challenges create expectations for virtual team leaders to play a more robust "process facilitation" role than established practices for face-to-face teams (Huang et al., 2010). For instance, a leader would have to pay greater attention to providing a shared sense of purpose and meaning and creating shared values among team members (Shamir, 1999). However, some researchers have raised doubts about leaders being able to have an impact in virtual team settings. For example, Den Hartog et al. (2007) question whether team members can identify with or trust a leader who is leading via electronic channels and whether temporary leaders feel motivated to create shared meaning and values. To make their arguments, they cite the work of Keegan and Den Hartog (2004) who found that (a) transformational leadership increased commitment and motivation and

(b) individualized consideration reduced stress in traditional project teams but not in temporary project teams. Earlier, Howell and Hall-Merenda (1999) had found that while transformational leadership improved performance of proximate followers, it had a negative relationship with the performance of distant followers.

Recent studies of leadership in virtual teams, however, present a more positive picture of the impact of leaders in virtual teams and are covered next. More importantly, they suggest that features of the technology being used by a virtual team and the situation in which virtual teams operate alter the effects of leaders.

Findings of Recent Studies on Leadership in Virtual Teams

Purvanova and Bono (2009) conducted a laboratory study comparing transformational leadership in virtual and face-to-face teams. They argued that virtual teams create a situation of uncertainty and ambiguity in which a transformational leader can have a strong impact by providing a social context, a structure, and a sense of predictability and certainty. They also argued that leaders are not likely to display the same level of transformational behaviors across virtual and face-to-face teams because of communication constraints in virtual teams. The authors found that the effect of transformational leadership on performance was stronger in virtual teams than in face-to-face teams. They also found that an individual leader's behavior in the virtual team cannot be predicted by that same leader's behavior in the face-to-face team. Specifically, they found that while the frequencies and ratings of "composite" transformational leadership displayed by any particular leader were generally similar across virtual and face-to-face teams, the frequencies and ratings of intellectual stimulation and individualized consideration displayed were significantly or marginally different across the two types of teams.

Joshi, Lazarova, and Liao (2009) carried out a field study in which they examined the effects of inspirational leadership and team member dispersion on commitment, trust, and team performance. The authors expected that inspirational leadership would lead to greater commitment and trust. They defined inspirational leadership as leadership that communicates a compelling vision, energizes the team, and expresses confidence in the team's ability to achieve that vision. The authors also expected that the effect of inspirational leadership on commitment and trust would increase with dispersion of team members. The authors used ideas from the Social Identity Model of Deindividuation Effects (SIDE) to support this expectation. According to SIDE, the dispersion of team members and lack of face-to-face contact in virtual teams causes team members to pay less attention to individual differences and become more sensitive to cues that emphasize the team and its social identity (Lea & Spears, 1991). When team members are more sensitive to cues that emphasize the team and its social identity, leadership behaviors (such as inspirational leadership behaviors) that provide such cues (e.g., by highlighting the identity and the vision of the collective) are likely to have a stronger impact. The authors also argued that with dispersion, interpersonal bonding would be more challenging, thereby creating greater room for inspirational leadership to have an impact on trust formation. Consistent with their expectations, the authors found that inspirational leadership led to greater commitment to the team and trust, which in turn led to team performance. Additionally, this effect of inspirational leadership on commitment and trust became stronger with increased dispersion of team members.

Huang et al. (2010) studied the interaction effects between leadership styles and media richness on task cohesion and cooperative climate in virtual teams performing a decision-making task. They found that transactional leadership improved task cohesion of the team whereas transformational leadership improved its cooperative climate which, in turn, led to higher task cohesion. However, these leadership effects depended on media richness, defined as the ability of a medium to enable the development of a shared understanding within a given time period (Daft & Lengel, 1986). Specifically, leadership effects occurred only when media richness was low. The authors argued that lower media richness creates a challenge for a virtual team; when media richness is lacking, the facilitation offered by transactional and transformational leaders is helpful for building task cohesion and cooperative climate whereas when media richness is high, task cohesion and cooperative climate may result without facilitation, thereby reducing the relevance of these leadership styles. According to the authors, transactional leadership may promote task cohesion via goal clarification and contingent rewarding; when team members have clarity on the expected effort and how it would lead to rewards, then in order to receive the rewards, they will be motivated to commit themselves to the team's task and help the team reach its goals.

Transformational leadership may facilitate a cooperative climate by (a) championing teamwork, (b) helping members identify with the team, and (c) creating an environment in which team members feel that it is safe to offer intellectual input with their unique perspectives.

In a field study of virtual teams in a large technology company, Kahai, Sosik, and Avolio (2010) examined the effects of transformational leadership and the nature of media on collaboration quality and team performance. Collaboration quality was conceptualized as being reflected in learning within the team, coordination of effort within the team, commitment of team members towards team goals, and positivity in team interaction. The authors hypothesized and found support for the idea that transformational leadership and the nature of media will interact to affect collaboration quality. They argued that in teams that relied on text-based electronic channels (e.g., email, discussion board, and chat) to a greater extent, the effect of transformational leadership on collaboration quality would be greater because the use of text-based electronic channels reduces attention to individual differences, and team members become more sensitive to a transformational leader's messages related to the team's vision, its identity, and its ability for collective work. The authors also found that collaboration quality improved team performance and group efficacy.

Motivated by the finding of past studies (summarized above) that contextual factors that increase the salience of individual differences in virtual teams might dilute a transformational leader's attempts to foster social identity and collaborative teamwork, Kahai, Huang, and Jestice (2010) investigated whether the use of a virtual world moderates a transformational leader's impact. A virtual world is a computer-based 3-D environment in which users interact via avatars, or digital representations of themselves. Virtual worlds are being increasingly used for virtual team collaboration (Kahai, Carroll, & Jestice, 2007). When a virtual world is employed by a virtual team to collaborate, its visual channel may dilute a transformational leader's efforts to promote collaboration by increasing the salience of individual differences among team members. A laboratory study supported the expected interaction effect of leadership style (transactional versus transformational) and medium (instant messaging versus virtual world) on feedback positivity, an indicator of the quality of collaboration within a team. For groups supported by instant messaging, transformational leadership led to greater feedback positivity than transactional leadership, whereas for groups supported by a virtual world, there was little difference in feedback positivity under transactional and transformational leadership.

In sum, the above studies provide support for the following ideas about leadership impacts in virtual teams.

- Virtual teams present challenges in that they lack a social context and structure and increase the uncertainty and ambiguity of team members. When these challenges increase, leadership behaviors that help overcome them have a stronger impact.
- Distance, reflected in the dispersion of team members (structural distance), the lack of face-to-face or visual contact (opacity), or the use of text-based electronic channels in virtual teams (opacity), causes team members to pay less attention to individual differences and become more sensitive to cues that emphasize the team and its social identity. When team members are more sensitive to cues that emphasize the team and its social identity, leadership behaviors that provide such cues have a stronger impact.

Questions for Future Research

We have only begun to scratch the surface in terms of studying the effects of leadership in virtual teams. The limited research on virtual team leadership research reviewed here indicates that technology and other contextual variables peculiar to virtual teams may moderate both the occurrence and effects of leadership. Consequently, what we know from leadership in face-to-face teams may not simply transfer over to virtual teams. Additional research is needed to enhance our limited knowledge of virtual team leadership and help virtual team leaders. Directions for future research include the following:

1. Examining how technology features and contextual factors interact with leadership to influence team interactions and outcomes in virtual teams. Such an examination would be significant due to the presence of diverse ethnic, national, and organizational backgrounds, the complexity and confusion of communication, and the variety of temporal and spatial virtual work arrangements possible in virtual teams. While examining the interaction of leadership with technology features and contextual factors, researchers should study not only the

effects of different styles of leadership (e.g., transactional and transformational) but also of specific leadership behaviors (e.g., goal clarification and individualized consideration) that make up different leadership styles. Such an examination would lead to the development of more specific and useful guidelines for virtual team leadership. Researchers should also examine the effects of combining different levels of specific transactional and transformational behaviors. Another aspect of leadership, besides leadership style, that deserves attention is individual versus collective leadership.

2. In the past research on virtual team leadership, technology has been generally assumed to have an invariable set of properties, such as filtering out communication cues, which then lead to fixed effects. Alternate views of technology, such as Adaptive Structuration Theory (DeSanctis & Poole, 1994) and Social Information Processing Theory (Walther, 1992) allow for effects of technology to change over time, either because how the technology is interpreted and used changes over time or simply because time gives users sufficient opportunity to express what they want to, albeit slowly due to technology's limited bandwidth. Future research should look at how leadership in virtual teams might impact the emergence of new interpretations of technology. It should also look at how the effects of virtual team leadership might be altered over time with changes in the interpretation of technology or with users having sufficient time to be expressive.

3. Extending laboratory studies of virtual team leadership to the field. While laboratory studies are useful for identifying technology and contextual factors that deserve additional attention, field studies are needed to accurately capture the complexities faced by virtual teams.

4. Training virtual team leaders. This is another area characterized by limited research. In fact leadership training is a little studied area even for traditional teams. As Fiedler puts it, "we know very little about the processes in leadership and managerial training that contribute to organizational performance" (1996, p. 244). Thus, it is critical to systematically study the effect of leadership training on leadership development, team functioning, and team performance in virtual teams. Such a study would not only address a significant research gap, it would also inform team coaches and organizational leaders about how appropriate leadership behaviors can be developed in virtual teams.

5. Using virtual worlds for leadership development. Limited evidence from studies of virtual worlds indicates that they may be useful for bringing about behavioral change in the real world. Specifically, behaviors with one's avatar in a virtual world have been observed to transfer over to the real world—creating an effect termed as the Proteus effect (Yee & Bailenson, 2007). The Proteus effect has its basis in self-perception theory, which states that the behaviors one observes of oneself cause that person to change her or his attitudes (Bem, 1967). These changed attitudes are then thought to affect subsequent behaviors. The Proteus effect raises the question of whether leadership behaviors expressed with one's avatar in a virtual world make one more likely to display those behaviors in the real world. Limited evidence from Reeves et al.'s (2008) study of leaders in a multiplayer virtual world game "World of Warcraft" seems to suggest that this may be the case. As described earlier in this paper, the authors found that features of the game helped individuals, some of whom were not even seeking a leadership role, become better leaders. More importantly, several IBM managers with experience in multiplayer online games indicated that being a game leader had improved their real-world leadership capabilities. Current leadership development programs tend to be expensive because they are often delivered face-to-face. If virtual worlds are shown to be useful for leadership development, they can prove to be a boon to organizations today who are facing unprecedented leadership challenges as well as pressures to bring down costs.

Leadership in Complex Systems

Organizations are increasingly becoming more knowledge-oriented, with manufacturing and production of tangible goods becoming less important than the production of knowledge and innovation. A recent IBM study of more than 1500 CEOs worldwide ("Capitalizing on complexity," 2010) indicates that in order to be effective in this knowledge era, organizations are stepping out of their organizational boundaries to get the knowledge they need from external stakeholders. Consequently, economic activities that were normally carried out under one roof or within one organization are now spread worldwide and make up a complex, highly interconnected network. The external stakeholders, especially customers and key influencers, are using their increased connectivity to network and influence an organization in unpredictable ways. Organizations are also engaging their internal stakeholders in new ways designed to make them (the organizations) more adaptive to emerging challenges and opportunities. They are encouraging the development of social networks that criss-cross hierarchical levels and departmental boundaries and help the organization overcome information-processing limitations imposed by formal hierarchies and departments (e.g., see Thompson (2006) for a description of how several US Intelligence agencies employed social media to create social networks that they expected to facilitate information sharing and processing across departmental boundaries). Additionally, new virtual and boundaryless entities such as Wikipedia and numerous open source software projects, are emerging to carry out, *pro bono*, activities that were previously normally paid for.

The new organizations of today resemble what scholars refer to as complex systems. Uhl-Bien et al. describe complex systems by contrasting them with complicated systems:

> complex adaptive systems are different from systems that are merely complicated. If a system can be described in terms of its individual constituents (even if there are a huge number of constituents), it is merely complicated; if the interactions among the constituents of the system, and the interaction between the system and its environment, are of such a nature that the system as a whole cannot be fully understood simply by analyzing its components, it is complex.
>
> (Uhl-Bien et al., 2007, p. 302)

Complex systems are unlike bureaucratic systems. In complex systems, centralized authorities cannot plan and coordinate the problem-solving efforts of complex systems because in such systems, problem solving emerges from the messy and imperfect information flows and processing that occur via many interconnected agents. According to Uhl-Bien et al. (2007), such systems not only alter the requirements for effective leadership but they also necessitate a change in how we view leadership. Leadership in complex systems does not rest just with individuals or with those in positions of authority; it also rests in the interaction among the system's agents.

Uhl-Bien et al. (2007) envision three types of leadership in complex systems: administrative leadership, adaptive leadership, and enabling leadership. Administrative leadership refers to actions by individuals in formal managerial roles to plan and coordinate organizational activities. Unlike administrative (and even enabling leadership), adaptive leadership does not rest within a person. It refers to the emergent and dynamic interplay among heterogeneous agents (people. ideas, etc.) in the system that give rise to new patterns of behavior or new modes of operating and enable the system to adapt, learn, and produce creative outcomes. This emergent and dynamic interplay is viewed as leadership because of the organizational changes it leads to. Enabling leadership promotes conditions that enable the emergent, interactive dynamic and manages the entanglement between adaptive leadership and administrative leadership.

What difference is IT making for administrative, adaptive, and enabling leadership in complex systems? Research at the intersection of IT and leadership has only addressed, although to a very limited extent, how IT may impact administrative and enabling leadership in complex systems. In the following sections, I look at the relationship of IT to leadership in complex systems and offer questions for future research.

IT and Administrative Leadership

Complex systems are characterized by distributed workforce and outsourcing of organizational activities. In complex systems, same-place meetings are still relevant, although less than in the past. As indicated earlier, such meetings are characterized by increasing availability and use of IT. Since the topics of leadership in virtual teams and leadership in same-place IT-mediated meetings reviewed earlier pertained to administrative leadership (i.e., leadership aimed at structuring tasks, planning, building vision, aligning interests, and acquiring resources to achieve goals), past research as well as questions for future research on those topics are likely to be relevant for administrative leadership in complex systems too. Hence, no separate coverage of IT and administrative leadership in complex systems is provided here.

IT and Adaptive Leadership

The increasing prevalence and use of IT is affecting both the context and mechanisms that enable the emergent and dynamic interplay leading to adaptive leadership. Uhl-Bien et al. (2007) describe context as structural, organizational, ideational, and behavioral features that define the ambiance within which complex dynamics occur and give them a certain character. The context is made up of the network of interactions among agents (people, ideas, etc.), complex patterns of conflicting constraints, patterns of tension, interdependent relationships, rules of action, direct/indirect feedback, and rapidly changing environmental demands. Mechanisms are the dynamic behaviors that occur within a complex system. They are special interactions among an assembly of parts that produce an effect not inherent in any one of them (Hernes, 1998). Mechanisms include resonance and aggregation of ideas, catalytic behaviors, generation of both dynamically stable and unstable behavior, dissipation and phase transitions, nonlinear change, information flow and pattern formation, and accreting nodes (Uhl-Bien et al., 2007). IT is affecting both the context and mechanisms that lead to adaptive leadership in numerous ways.[7]

The new Web 2.0-based social media (e.g., blogs, Twitter, wikis, Facebook) as well as some traditional online media (e.g., email, discussion boards, and instant messaging) facilitate the development of new networks that connect individuals and groups with asymmetrical preferences (knowledge, skills, beliefs, etc). According to Uhl-Bien et al. (2007), it is the clash of ideas from such individuals and groups that leads to adaptive leadership. Adaptive leadership results when individuals and groups with dissimilar knowledge, skills, and beliefs debate conflicting perceptions of an issue and generate a new understanding of that issue. The new social media also make it very easy for the membership and agenda of the network to change in response to shifting events and priorities. Thus, by imparting flexibility to the network, they help the interactions within the network stay adaptive. Another way in which IT is affecting the context that leads to adaptive leadership is by enabling digitization and almost instantaneous delivery of many products and services. This trend is prompting rapid changes in consumer expectations and preferences, thereby creating more asymmetry in preferences and increasing the potential for creative clashes. By enabling more activities to be outsourced, IT networks are also leading to a greater level of interdependence among individuals, groups, and organizations worldwide. With greater interdependence, there is greater incentive for entities in the network to interact and pit their ideas against one another to create new knowledge and enable adaptation.

IT is also changing the mechanisms that may lead to adaptive leadership. IT is clearly affecting the resonance and aggregation of behaviors, such as when Twitter aggregates people's reactions to an idea or an event when they use a common hashtag (e.g., the hashtag #TonyCurtis was used by Twitter users reacting to Tony Curtis's death in September 2010). By providing new and instantaneous channels of communication that connect people worldwide almost on the fly, IT is also changing the speed and patterns of information flows as I had described earlier in the section "The New Context for Leadership." IT is changing the formation of accreting nodes, or ideas that rapidly expand in importance, as we often see in the spread of viral videos or messages.

IT may go beyond affecting the context and mechanisms that enable adaptive leadership. It may become part of the emergent and dynamic interaction that characterizes complex systems and produces adaptive leadership. It may do so by becoming an agent in an interaction with its own preferences (skills, information, and viewpoints) that influences other agents. For instance, consider Google. Like a human agent, Google can translate a passage for us from one language to another. It may even suggest a certain piece of information when we use it to research a topic that we may be discussing with others. Google may also influence our interactions on the internet as a kind of control. Specifically, since Google keeps a history of our search and our other interactions on the internet, our awareness of how much that history might reveal about us in case it falls into wrong hands can influence our behavior on the internet.

IT may not only become a part of the emergent and dynamic interaction in a complex system, it may also be influenced by it. Today's IT is modular and it can be combined in different ways leading to new ways in which agents in a complex system interact with one another (Pentland & Feldman, 2007). To support their interaction, agents in a complex system may combine modular IT components in innovative ways to create IT-based solutions that help the system adapt and learn. Another way in which IT may be influenced is by its use. The use of IT during interaction among agents in a complex system may change its quality (and hence its usefulness and role in future interactions and the adaptive leadership that emerges from those interactions) via the addition of the interaction's history. For instance, when the users of a wiki collaborate on a task, the task-related information that they add improves the wiki's quality and usefulness by preventing the "reinvention of the wheel" when a similar task occurs again.

In summary, adaptive leadership in a complex system does not rest within a person. It is the product of dynamic interaction among heterogeneous agents within the system, some of whom may not even be human. IT has the potential to influence adaptive leadership by (a) affecting the context (or the ambiance) within which adaptive leadership occurs and the mechanisms (or the dynamic patterns) that produce adaptive leadership and (b) becoming a part of the emergent and dynamic interaction that creates adaptive leadership. IT may also be influenced by the interaction that creates adaptive leadership. However, how IT influences adaptive leadership and is influenced by it has not been studied systematically by researchers so far. Consequently, future research should address how IT is both affecting and is affected by adaptive leadership in complex systems. Specific questions that future research should examine are provided later.

IT and Enabling Leadership

Uhl-Bien et al. (2007) describe the roles of enabling leadership as: (a) enabling conditions that catalyze adaptive leadership and (b) managing the entanglement between administrative and adaptive leadership. Catalyzing adaptive leadership involves fostering interaction, fostering interdependence, and injecting tension that motivates and coordinates the emergent and dynamic interaction. Managing the entanglement between administrative and adaptive leadership includes managing the organizational conditions in which adaptive leadership exists, and helping disseminate innovative products of adaptive leadership upward and through the formal structure within an organization.

What difference does IT make for enabling leadership in a complex system? Specifically, can IT in some way help a leader become a better "enabler" of adaptive leadership? Would an enabling leader need to act differently in an IT-dominated context? IT can play a critical role in helping a leader foster interaction, a critical ingredient for emergence in a complex system. IT provides many tools, such as mailing lists, instant messaging, discussion forums, blogs, wikis, and social networking tools, that leaders can implement to foster interaction and enable emergence. Thompson (2006) gives the following example of how Intellipedia, a wiki used by US Intelligence agencies, enabled adaptive leadership to emerge in the Fall of 2006 by letting remotely located agents interact:

> the usefulness of Intellipedia proved itself just a couple of months ago, when a small two-seater plane crashed into a Manhattan building. An analyst

created a page within 20 minutes, and over the next two hours it was edited 80 times by employees of nine different spy agencies, as news trickled out. Together, they rapidly concluded the crash was not a terrorist act.

(Thompson, 2006)

A leader's responsibility in unleashing IT's potential for interaction, in most cases, is not just simply ordering the installation of such tools and turning them on. Leaders need to ensure that an organization's members adopt IT in their work and use it appropriately. Chatterjee, Grewal, and Sambamurthy (2002) found that senior leadership can increase IT assimilation by creating appropriate norms and values regarding the adoption and use of IT. To create appropriate norms and values, leaders have structures of signification (those that give meaning and serve as cognitive guides), legitimization (those that legitimize behavior), and domination (those that regulate behavior) at their disposal. To manipulate structures of signification, leaders can offer a vision for the organization and how IT fits into that vision. To influence the structures of legitimization, leaders may discuss opportunities and risks that accompany the application of IT. By believing in IT, participating in IT strategy and projects, and using IT, leaders can be role models and send signals that legitimize their followers' participation in IT projects and adoption of IT. To manipulate structures of domination, leaders may create appropriate mandates and policies regarding IT adoption and use.

To unleash IT's potential for interaction, leaders may need to make complementary changes that require senior leadership attention (Hitt & Brynolfsson, 1997). These may include changes in leadership, incentive systems, location of decision-making authority, culture, and learning orientation within an organization. If IT and the various complementary factors are misaligned, IT investments may provide little or no gain (Hitt & Brynolfsson, 1997). For instance, in order to ensure the success of IT tools designed to foster interaction and teamwork, leaders may need to create an open and participative environment in which followers feel comfortable sharing information and providing valuable input (Tarmizi, de Vreede, & Zigurs, 2007). This was seen in the implementation of Intellipedia, which was described earlier. During Intellipedia's implementation, organizational leaders in the US Intelligence agencies encouraged change from a "need to know" culture, one in which information was shared with someone only if it was clear that the latter needed to know what was contained in the information, to a "need to share" culture, one in which it was important to share information (Thompson, 2006). This complementary change in information sharing culture was thought to be critical for ensuring the success of Intellipedia.

In summary, IT can make a difference for enabling leadership by providing channels and tools that foster interaction. To ensure that the IT that is deployed leads to increased interaction, leaders would need to play a special enabling role by being involved in IT's adoption and use and making complementary changes. It should be noted that these ideas about the enabling role of leaders with respect to IT were based on research involving older IT. IT development since the beginning of this century is much more representative of IT that is transforming the fabric of organizations, and increasing complexity and additional research is needed to better understand the enabling role of leaders with respect to newer IT (Zammuto, Griffith, Majchrzak, Dougherty, & Faraj, 2007).

Questions for Future Research

Keeping in mind the need to include newer IT in future research related to leadership and IT in complex systems, questions that may be offered for future research are presented below. Note that the focus of the following questions in on adaptive and enabling leadership; those related to leadership in same-place IT-mediated settings and leadership in virtual teams are likely to be relevant to administrative leadership as well and are not repeated here. The questions for future research presented below also pertain to and include questions about leadership related to IT-based social networks. This is because social networks can be thought of as complex systems (Benhan-Hutchins & Clancy, 2010; Hamilton, Milne, Walker, Burger, & Brown, 2007). Viewing IT-based social networks as complex systems is particularly appropriate because they contain a large number of highly interconnected and constantly changing nodes which make the networks quite unpredictable (Nekovee, Moreno, Bianconi, & Marsili, 2007).

1. How is IT affecting the context and mechanisms that enable adaptive leadership in complex systems?
2. How is IT becoming a part of the emergent and dynamic interaction that creates adaptive leadership in complex systems?

3. How is IT influenced by the interaction within a complex system?
4. What IT-related leadership actions or behaviors are likely to enable the interaction, interdependence, and tension required for adaptability, learning, and creativity in complex systems?
5. What IT-related leadership actions or behaviors are better at managing the entanglement between adaptive and administrative structures in complex systems?
6. What IT-related leadership actions or behaviors are better at facilitating the integration of creative outcomes into the formal structure in complex systems?
7. How is the rise of IT-enabled social networks influencing leadership integrity? Given the potential for social networks to put pressure on leaders to behave with integrity by making their actions more transparent as well as the potential for leaders to hide under fake identities, under what conditions are the social networks leading to greater or lower levels of integrity in leaders?

CONCLUDING REMARKS

IT is affecting distance for leaders in a variety of ways. In some ways it is increasing distance, such as by introducing anonymity and by letting organizations distribute their workers worldwide, and in other cases it is decreasing distance, such as by bringing like-minded individuals together and by letting organizations tap into resources outside their boundaries. Consequently, the difference that IT can be expected to make for leadership is not likely to be uniform or simple. It may be due to the complexity in these differences that researchers offer seemingly contrasting viewpoints about whether or not leadership is changing due to IT. In this chapter, I first argued that the different viewpoints of scholars are reconcilable. Subsequently, I discussed how IT is altering the context for leadership and the ways in which IT is affecting leadership. I examined leadership in same-place IT mediated meetings, leadership in virtual teams, and leadership in complex systems.

The discussion on leadership in same-place IT-mediated meetings suggests that features of technology, such as anonymity, are likely to interact with leadership to influence meeting process and outcomes. Moreover, effects of the interaction between technology features and leadership may depend on contextual variables, such as the nature of a group's task. There is need for additional research on leadership in same-place IT-mediated meetings. The proliferation of smart phones is creating interesting and new questions about leadership in same-place settings by enabling back-channel communication.

The discussion on leadership in virtual teams suggests that when uncertainty and ambiguity increase in virtual teams, leadership behaviors that help overcome them have a stronger impact. Furthermore, it appears that distance can be made into a leader's friend in virtual teams. Research suggests that the distance introduced by the dispersion of team members, the lack of face-to-face or visual contact, or the use of text-based electronic channels, may be making team members pay less attention to individual differences and become more sensitive to cues that emphasize the team and its social identity. When team members are more sensitive to cues that emphasize the team and its social identity, leadership behaviors that provide such cues are likely to have a stronger impact. There are still many unexplored questions about leadership in virtual teams, including those of using virtual worlds for leadership development.

Perhaps the most unexplored area at the IT–leadership intersection is that which pertains to the difference that IT is making for leadership in complex systems. While research on leadership in same-place IT-mediated meetings and virtual teams reviewed in this chapter is likely to be relevant to administrative leadership in complex systems, there is little that we know about how IT is affecting adaptive and enabling leadership, despite IT's potential to affect these types of leadership. Related to adaptive leadership, IT has the potential to (a) affect the context and mechanisms that enable adaptive leadership, (b) become a part of the emergent and dynamic interaction that creates adaptive leadership, and (c) be influenced by the interaction among agents in a complex system. In the case of enabling leadership, IT can make a difference for enabling leadership by providing channels and tools that foster interaction.

The discussions in this chapter clearly suggest that opening up the technology black box helps one discover new insights into how the digital age is affecting leadership. They also point to the attention that leaders need to pay to IT. In addition to becoming familiar with IT use, leaders need to pay attention to how IT features can alter the effects of their qualities or behaviors. Leaders also need to understand that as IT accelerates the shift to complex systems, they need to play more of a facilitator role and focus on creating conditions that enable other sources of leadership to emerge.

NOTES

1   Wikileaks: http://www.wikileaks.org; Cryptome: http://www.cryptome.org.
2   http://www.youtube.com/watch?v=t_xCeItxbQY.
3   http://askobama.twitter.com/.
4   Tweets that used #AskObama hashtag: http://topsy.com/s?q=%23AskObama&window =a.
5   See how Barack Obama leveraged social networking to raise funds as a candidate at http://stuff.xplane.com/obama/XPLANED_Obama_Fundraising.pdf.
6   http://www.facebook.com/whitecollar.
7   Uhl-Bein et al.'s (2007) use of the term "context" is narrower than how I use it previously in the section titled "New Context For Leadership." In that section, I have used context to refer to not only the ambiance within which complex dynamics occur but also to the dynamic behaviors themselves.

REFERENCES

Ahuja, M. K. & Carley, K. M. (1999). Network structure in virtual organizations. *Organization Science,* 10(6), 741–757.

Avolio, B. J., & Kahai, S. S. (2003). Adding the "E" to e-leadership: How it may impact your leadership. *Organizational Dynamics,* 31(4), 325–338.

Avolio, B. J., Kahai, S. S., & Dodge, G. (2000). E-leading in organizations and its implications for theory, research and practice. *Leadership Quarterly,* 11(4), 615–668.

Balkundi, P. & Kilduff, M. (2006). The ties that lead: A social network approach to leadership. *Leadership Quarterly,* 17(4), 419–439.

Barkhi, R., Jacob, V. S., Pipino, L., & Pirkul, H. (1998). A study of the effect of communication channel and authority on group decision processes and outcomes. *Decision Support Systems,* 23(3), 205–226.

Barnes, B., Steel, E., & McBride, S. (2007, April 13). Behind the fall of Imus:, A digital brush fire. *The Wall Street Journal.* Retrieved from http://online.wsj.com/public/article/ SB117641076468168180-7y8vXi_eMhvWtEoPiK397ZUoIBc_20070513.html.

Becker, L. (2009). *The impact of organizational information overload on leaders: Making knowledge work productive in the 21st century.* Available from ProQuest Dissertations and Theses database. (UMI No. 3363308).

Bem, D. J. (1967). Self-perception: An alternative interpretation of cognitive dissonance phenomena. *Psychological Review,* 74(3), 183–200.

Benham-Hutchins, M. & Clancy, T. R. (2010). Social networks as embedded complex adaptive systems. *The Journal of Nursing Administration,* 40(9), 352–356.

Burgoon, J. K., Bonito, J. A., Ramirez, A, Jr., Dunbar, N. E., Kam, K., & Fischer, J. (2002). Testing the interactivity principle: Effects of mediation, propinquity, and verbal and nonverbal modalities of interpersonal interaction. *Journal of Communication*, 52, 657–677.

Byron, K. (2008). Carrying too heavy a load? The communication and miscommunication of emotion by email. *Academy of Management Review*, 33(2), 309–327.

Cameron, K. S. (2003). Organizational virtuousness and performance. In K. S. Cameron, J. E. Dutton, & R. E. Quinn (Eds.), *Positive Organizational Scholarship*, (pp. 48–65). San Francisco: Berrett-Koehler.

Capitalizing on complexity (May 2010). Retrieved from ftp://public.dhe.ibm.com/common/ssi/pm/xb/n/gbe03297gben/GBE03297GBEN.PDF.

Champy, J. (2010, May 4). Does leadership change in a web 2.0 world? *HBR Blog Network*. Retrieved from http://blogs.hbr.org/imagining-the-future-of-leadership/2010/05/does-leadership-change-in-a-we.html.

Chatterjee, D., Grewal, R., & Sambamurthy, V. (2002). Shaping up for e-commerce: institutional enablers of the organizational assimilation of web technologies. *MIS Quarterly*, 26(2), 65–89.

Cohen, N. (2008, June 23). Delaying news in the era of the internet. *The New York Times*. Retrieved from http://www.nytimes.com/2008/06/23/business/media/23link.html.

Crovitz, L. G. (2011, February 7). Opinion: The technology of counterrevolution. *The Wall Street Journal*. Retrieved from http://online.wsj.com/article/SB10001424052748704709304576124573160468928.html.

Crovitz, L. G. (2011, June 13). Opinion: The internet lets it all hang out. *The Wall Street Journal*. Retrieved from http://online.wsj.com/article/SB10001424052702304259304576377522779707418.html.

Daft, R. L., & Lengel, R. H. (1986). Organizational information requirements, media richness and structural design. *Management Science*, 32(5), 554–571.

Den Hartog, D. N., Keegana, A. E., & Verburg, R. M. (2007). Limits to leadership in virtual contexts. *eJov*, 9, 54–63.

DeSanctis, G. & Poole, M. S. (1994). Capturing the complexity in advanced technology use: Adaptive structuration theory. *Organization Science*, 5(2), 121–147.

Fiedler, F. E. (1996). Research on leadership selection and training: One view of the future. *Administrative Science Quarterly*, 41(2), 241–250.

George, J. F., Easton, G. K., Nunamaker Jr, J. F., & Northcraft, G. B. (1990). A study of collaborative group work with and without computer-based support. *Information Systems Research*, 1(4), 394–415.

Gold, M. (2009, September 16). Obama, Kanye West and trouble with Twitter. *Los Angeles Times*. Retrieved from http://articles.latimes.com/2009/sep/16/entertainment/et-abc-twitter16.

Gomes, T. (2010, February 14). Do smart phones thwart public records laws? *NPR Around the Nation*. Retrieved from http://www.npr.org/templates/story/story.php?storyId=123573568.

Hamilton, M. J., Milne, B. T., Walker, R. S., Burger, O., & Brown, J. H. (2007). The complex structure of hunter–gatherer social networks, *Proc. R. Soc. B*, 274(1622), 2195–2203.

Harmon, J., Schneer, J. A., & Hoffman, L. R. (1995). Electronic meetings and established decision groups: Audioconferencing effects on performance and structural stability. *Organizational Behavior and Human Decision Processes*, 61(2), 138–147.

Hernes, G. (1998). Real virtuality. In P. Hedström & R. Swedberg (Eds.), *Social Mechanisms: An Analytical Approach to Social Theory* (pp. 74–101). Cambridge: Cambridge University Press.

Hiltz, S. R., Johnson, K., & Turoff, M. (1991). Group decision support: The effects of designated human leaders and statistical feedback in computerized conferences. *Journal of Management Information Systems*, 8(2), 81–108.

Hitt, L. M., & Brynjolfsson, E. (1997). Information technology and internal firm organization: Aan exploratory analysis. *Journal of Management Information Systems*, 14(2), 81–101.

Ho, T. H., & Raman, K. S. (1991). The effect of GDSS and elected leadership on small group meetings. *Journal of Management Information Systems*, 8(2), 109–133.

Howell, J. M. & Hall-Merenda, K. E. (1999). The ties that bind: The impact of leader-- member exchange, transformational and transactional leadership, and distance on predicting follower performance. *Journal of Applied Psychology*, 84(5), 680–694.

Hoyt, C. L. & Blascovich, J. (2003). Transformational and transactional leadership in virtual and physical environments. *Small Group Research*, 34(6), 678.

Huang, R., Kahai, S., & Jestice, R. (2010). The contingent effects of leadership on team collaboration in virtual teams. *Computers in Human Behavior*, 26(5), 1098–1110.

Jones, S. & Fox, S. (2009, January 28). *Generations online in 2009.* Retrieved from http://www.pewinternet.org/Reports/2009/Generations-Online-in-2009.aspx.

Joshi, A., Lazarova, M. B., & Liao, H. (2009). Getting everyone on board: The role of inspirational leadership in geographically dispersed teams. *Organization Science*, 20(1), 240–252.

Kahai, S. S. & Avolio, B. J. (2006). Leadership style, anonymity, and the discussion of an ethical issue in an electronic context. *International Journal of e-Collaboration*, 2(2), 1–26.

Kahai, S. S. & Cooper, R. B. (1999). The effect of computer-mediated communication on agreement and acceptance. *Journal of Management Information Systems*, 16(1), 165–188.

Kahai, S. S., Avolio, B. J., & Sosik, J. J. (1998). Effects of source and participant anonymity and difference in initial opinions in an EMS context. *Decision Sciences*, 29(2), 427–458.

Kahai, S. S., Huang, R., & Jestice, R. (2010). How virtual worlds moderate the effects of leadership on feedback positivity and performance in virtual teams. Unpublished manuscript.

Kahai, S. S., Sosik, J. J., & Avolio, B. J. (1997). Effects of leadership style and problem structure on work group process and outcomes in an electronic meeting system environment. *Personnel Psychology*, 50(1), 121–146.

Kahai, S. S., Sosik, J. J., & Avolio, B. J. (2004). Effects of participative and directive leadership in electronic groups. *Group & Organization Management*, 29(1), 67–105.

Kahai, S. S., Sosik, J. J., & Avolio, B. J. (2010). The effects of transformational leadership and media on collaboration quality and performance in virtual teams. Unpublished manuscript.

Kahai, S. S., Sosik, J. J., & Avolio, B.J. (2003). Effects of leadership style, anonymity, and rewards in an electronic meeting system environment. *Leadership Quarterly*, 14(4–5), 499–524..

Kahai, S. S., Carroll, E., & Jestice, R. (2007) Team collaboration in virtual worlds. *The DATA BASE for Advances in Information Systems*, 38(4), 61–68.

Keegan, A. E. & Den Hartog, D. N. (2004). Transformational leadership in a project-based environment: A comparative study of the leadership styles of project managers and line managers. *International Journal of Project Management*, 22(8), 609–617.

Kesmodel, D. & Wilke, J. R. (2007, July 12). Whole Foods is hot, Wild Oats a dud—so said "Rahodeb." *The Wall Street Journal.* Retrieved from http://online.wsj.com/article/SB118418782959963745.html.

Kim, Y., Hiltz, S. R., & Turoff, M. (2002). Coordination structures and system restrictiveness in distributed group support systems. *Group Decision and Negotiation*, 11(5), 379–404.

Kruger, J., Epley, N., Parker, J., & Ng, Z. (2005). Egocentrism over e-mail: Can we communicate as well as we think? *Journal of Personality and Social Psychology*, 89(6), 925–936.

Lea, M. & Spears, R. (1991) Computer-mediated communication, deindividuation and group decision-making. *International Journal of Man Machine Studies*, 34(2), 283–301.

Levinson, C. (2011, July 1). Israeli Facebook campaign keeps lid on cheese prices. *The Wall Street Journal*. Retrieved from http://online.wsj.com/article/SB1000142405270230 4584004576417543687962906.html.

Lim, L., Raman, K. S., & Wei, K. (1994). Interacting effects of GDSS and leadership. *Decision Support Systems*, 12(3), 199–211.

Markus, M. L. (1994). Finding a happy medium: Explaining the negative effects of electronic communication on social life at work. *ACM Transactions on Information Systems (TOIS)*, 12(2), 119–149.

Maznevski, M. L. & Chudoba, K. M. (2000). Bridging space over time: Global virtual team dynamics and effectiveness. *Organization Science*, 11(5), 473–492.

Murphy, R. M. (2006, April 27). Zero to $1 Billion. *CNN Money.com*. Retrieved from http://money.cnn.com/2006/04/26/smbusiness/zerocover_fsbbillion_fsb/.

Napier, B. J., & Ferris, G. R. (1993). Distance in organizations. *Human Resource Management Review*, 3(4), 321–357.

Nekovee, M., Moreno, Y., Bianconi, G., & Marsili, M. (2007). Theory of rumour spreading in complex social networks. *Physica A: Statistical Mechanics and its Applications*, 374(1).

Nie, N. H., Simpser, A., Stepanikova, I., & Zheng, L. (2005). Ten years after the birth of the internet, how do Americans use the internet in their daily lives. *Stanford Center for the Quantitative Study of Society*, available at: http://www.stanford.edu/group/siqss/research/time_study_files/ProjectReport2005.pdf (accessed September 13, 2010).

Nunamaker, J. F., Dennis, A. R., Valacich, J. S., Vogel, D., & George, J. F. (1991). Electronic meeting systems. *Communications of the ACM*, 34(7), 40–61.

O'Sullivan, P. B. (2000). What you don't know won't hurt me: Impression management function of communication channels in relationships. *Human Communication Research*, 26, 403–431.

Pentland, B. T. & Feldman, M. S. (2007). Narrative networks: Patterns of technology and organization. *Organization Science*, 18(5), 781–795.

Petrook, M. (2008, March 13). *Britain in business: The world of work in 2018*. Retrieved from http://www.managers.org.uk/news/britain-business-world-work-2018.

Piccoli, G. & Ives, B. (2003). Trust and the unintended effects of behavior control in virtual teams. *MIS Quarterly*, 27(3), 365–395.

Preston, J. (2011, July 20). Start-up handles social media background checks. *The New York Times*. Retrieved from http://www.nytimes.com/2011/07/21/technology/social-media-history-becomes-a-new-job-hurdle.html.

Purvanova, R. K. & Bono, J. E. (2009). Transformational leadership in context: Face-to-face and virtual teams. *Leadership Quarterly*, 20(3), 343–357.

Reeves, B., Malone, T. W., & O Driscoll, T. (2008). Leadership's online labs. *Harvard Business Review*, 86(5), 58–66.

Rogelberg, S. G., Scott, C., & Kello, J. (2007). The science and fiction of meetings. *MIT Sloan Management Review*, 48(2), 18–21.

Rosen, J. (2010, July 19). The web means the end of forgetting. *The New York Times*. Retrieved from http://www.nytimes.com/2010/07/25/magazine/25privacy-t2.html.

Sarbaugh-Thompson, M. & Feldman, M. S. (1998). Electronic mail and organizational communication: Does saying " hi" really matter? *Organization Science*, 9(6), 685–698.

Schmitt, E. (2010, July 25). In disclosing secret documents, WikiLeaks seeks "transparency." *The New York Times*. Retrieved from http://www.nytimes.com/2010/07/26/world/26wiki.html.

Schweitzer, L. & Duxbury, L. (2010). Conceptualizing and measuring the virtuality of teams. *Information Systems Journal*, 20(3), 267–295.

Shamir, B. (1999). Leadership in boundaryless organizations: Disposable or indispensable? *European Journal of Work and Organizational Psychology*, 8(1), 49–71.

Sosik, J. J., Avolio, B. J., & Kahai, S. S. (1997). Effects of leadership style and anonymity on group potency and effectiveness in a group decision support system environment. *Journal of Applied Psychology*, 82(1), 89–103.

Sosik, J. J., Avolio, B. J., & Kahai, S. S. (1998). Inspiring group creativity: Comparing anonymous and identified electronic brainstorming. *Small Group Research*, 29(1), 3–31.

Sosik, J. J., Kahai, S. S., & Avolio, B. J. (1998). Transformational leadership and dimensions of creativity: Motivating idea generation in computer-mediated groups. *Creativity Research Journal*, 11(2), 111–121.

Sosik, J.J., Kahai, S.S., &. Avolio, B. J (1999). Leadership style, anonymity, and creativity in group decision support systems: The mediating role of optimal flow. *Journal of Creative Behavior*, 33(4), 1–30.

Starke, M. (2011, June 3). CEOs and the social media monster. *MarcusStarke.com*. Retrieved from http://marcusstarke.com/leadership/ceos-and-the-social-media-monster.

Stelter, B. (2010, February 23). Water-cooler effect: Internet can be TV's friend. *The New York Times*. Retrieved from http://www.nytimes.com/2010/02/24/business/media/24cooler.html.

Stevenson, R. (2011, May 2). Sohaib Athar captures Osama bin Laden raid on Twitter. *The Huffington Post*. Retrieved from http://www.huffingtonpost.com/2011/05/02/osama-bin-laden-raid-twitter-sohaib-athar_n_856187.html.

Sutter, J. (2011, February 21). The faces of Egypt's "Revolution 2.0." *CNN*. Retrieved from http://www.cnn.com/2011/TECH/innovation/02/21/egypt.internet.revolution/index.html.

Sutton, R. (2010, June 9). What every new generation of bosses has to learn. *HBR Blog Network*. Retrieved from http://blogs.hbr.org/cs/2010/06/good_bosses_have_a_passion_for.html.

Tan, B. C. Y., Wei, K. K., & Lee-Partridge, J. E. (1999). Effects of facilitation and leadership on meeting outcomes in a group support system environment. *European Journal of Information Systems*, 8(4), 233–246.

Tarafdar, M., Tu, Q., Ragunathan, B., & Ragunathan, T. (2007). The impact of technostress on role stress and productivity. *Journal of Management Information Systems*, 24(1), 301–328.

Tarmizi, H., de Vreede, G. J., & Zigurs, I. (2007). Leadership challenges in communities of practice: Ssupporting facilitators via design and technology. *International Journal of e-Collaboration*, 3(1), 18–39.

Thompson, C. (2006, December 3). Open-source spying. *The New York Times*. Retrieved from http://www.nytimes.com/2006/12/03/magazine/03intelligence.html.

Uhl-Bien, M., Marion, R., & McKelvey, B. (2007). Complexity leadership theory: Shifting leadership from the industrial age to the knowledge era. *The Leadership Quarterly,* 18(4), 298–318.

Vance, A. (2009, February 5). Travel goes the way of the dodo at Cisco. *The New York Times.* Retrieved from http://bits.blogs.nytimes.com/2009/02/05/travel-goes-the-way-of-the-dodo-at-cisco/.

Virtual teams now a reality. (2008, September 4). Retrieved from http://www.i4cp.com/news/2008/09/04/virtual-teams-now-a-reality.

Walther, J. B. & Bazarova, N. N. (2008). Validation and application of electronic propinquity theory to computer-mediated communication in groups. *Communication Research,* 35(5), 622–645.

Walther, J. B. (1992). Interpersonal effects in computer-mediated interaction: A relational perspective. *Communication Research,* 19(1), 52–90.

Walther, J. B. (1995). Relational aspects of computer-mediated communication: Experimental observations over time. *Organization Science,* 6(2), 186–203.

Weston, R. (2009, March 19). Should Facebook be your company's intranet? *Information Week.* Retrieved from http://www.informationweek.com/news/215901035.

Wickham, K. R. & Walther, J. B. (2007). Perceived behaviors of emergent and assigned leaders in virtual groups. *International Journal of e-Collaboration,* 3(1), 1–17.

Wiesenfeld, B. M., Raghuram, S., & Garud, R. (2001). Organizational identification among virtual workers: The role of need for affiliation and perceived work-based social support. *Journal of Management,* 27(2), 213–229.

Yammarino, F. J., Dansereau, F., & Kennedy, C. J. (2001). A multiple-level multidimensional approach to leadership: Viewing leadership through an elephant's eye. *Organizational Dynamics,* 29(3), 149–163.

Yee, N., & Bailenson, J. (2007). The Proteus effect: The effect of transformed self-representation on behavior. *Human Communication Research,* 33(3), 271–290.

Zammuto, R. F., Griffith, T. L., Majchrzak, A., Dougherty, D. J., & Faraj, S. (2007). Information technology and the changing fabric of organization. *Organization Science,* 18(5), 749–762.

4

Engaging Followers at a Distance: Leadership Approaches that Work

Rebecca J. Reichard, Shawn A. Serrano,
and Andrew J. Wefald

Today's workforce is changing at a rapid pace. Organizations have become flatter and more collaborative, employee access to rewards has become increasingly complex, businesses are operating in a global marketplace, and teams are operating in virtual environments (Rousseau, 1997). While creating opportunities for employee growth and development (e.g., working from home, taking on an overseas assignment), such changes may also produce an array of unintended consequences. One such consequence is the change in the nature of interaction between leaders and their followers. More specifically, rapid business growth, "going global," and virtual teams create leader–follower "distance;" this, in turn, changes the way leaders influence followers' behaviors and outcomes including employee engagement. The purpose of this chapter is threefold: (1) to provide an integrative review of the academic literature for the key constructs of employee engagement and leader–follower distance; (2) to discuss how various forms of leader–follower distance moderate the relationship between leadership and employee engagement; and (3) to provide practical suggestions that distant leaders can implement to increase employee engagement in today's dynamic workplace.

DEFINING ENGAGEMENT

While there are a number of competing definitions of employee engagement (e.g., Macey & Schneider, 2008; Wefald, Reichard, & Serrano, 2011), we agree with Bakker and Demerouti (2008) that there is more overlap than disparity; and, moreover, that employee engagement has an *energy* and an *involvement* component. We summarize the various conceptualizations of employee engagement in Table 4.1 and describe them below.

Energy

The energy component of work engagement may be best characterized by Kahn's (1990) original conceptualization of engagement and Shirom's (2003) vigor. Kahn (1990) asserts that for one to fully deploy the self into a work role or task, he or she must invest physical, cognitive, and emotional energy. Shirom (2003) provides a more expansive view of this work, presenting the construct of vigor. According to Shirom, vigor represents a positive affective response to one's job and work environment and includes three interconnected elements: physical strength, emotional energy, and cognitive liveliness. Vigor, as defined by Shirom (2006), relates only to energetic resources, thus its power in helping us to understand the energy component of engagement.

Involvement

By redefining burnout as an erosion of employee engagement, Maslach and her colleagues assert the second component of the definition: *involvement* (Maslach & Leiter, 1997; Maslach, Leiter & Schaufeli, 2001). Given their proposition that engagement is the positive antithesis to burnout, being engaged requires employees to display high levels of on-the-job involvement

TABLE 4.1

Summary of Conceptualizations of Employee Engagement

Theorist/Study	Energy	Involvement
Kahn (1990) May et al. (2004)	• Physical energy • Cognitive energy • Emotional energy	
Maslach and Leiter (1997)	• Energy	• Involvement
Schaufeli et al. (2002) / Bakker et al. (2008) / Xanthopoulou et al. (2007)	• Vigor	• Dedication • Absorption
Shirom (2003)	• Physical strength • Emotional energy • Cognitive liveliness	

in addition to high levels of energy. Building on this perspective, Schaufeli, Salanova, Gonzalez-Roma, and Bakker (2002) suggest that work engagement requires remarkable dedication and intense absorption. Specifically, *dedication* refers to "a sense of significance, enthusiasm, inspiration, pride, and challenge" (p. 74); while *absorption* is characterized by "being fully concentrated and deeply engrossed in one's work, whereby time passes quickly and one has difficulties with detaching oneself from work" (pp. 74–75). Though absorption appears to transcend the boundaries of *involvement* and *energy*, given its close resemblance to cognitive liveliness and energy, we have grouped it here because it more clearly describes an intense level of task involvement. Taken together, engaged employees fully invest themselves into their work by demonstrating high levels of physical, cognitive, and emotional energy as well as high levels of involvement such that they are fully absorbed in their work tasks.

ENGAGEMENT AND WORK OUTCOMES

Employee engagement has been empirically linked to important work outcomes at both the unit level and the individual level of the organization through a series of research studies. Perhaps the strongest empirical demonstration of the importance of employee engagement was a meta-analysis of nearly 8,000 business units and 36 companies. In this study, Harter, Schmidt, and Hayes (2002) found engagement to be positively related to business-unit performance as well as customer satisfaction, customer loyalty, profitability, productivity, reduced turnover, and safety. In other research, Xanthopoulou, Bakker, Demerouti, and Schaufeli (2009) found that day-level employee engagement was positively associated with higher financial returns; and Salanova, Agut, and Peiro (2005) found employee engagement produced a more effective service climate, which resulted in increased customer-rated employee performance and increased customer loyalty. Based on longitudinal data across multiple US industries, Halbesleben and Wheeler (2008) found a strong link between employee engagement and in-role performance. Schaufeli et al. (2006) demonstrated a similar performance link in terms of increased in-role performance, and also showed that engaged employees are higher extra-role performers. Further, empirical evidence at the individual level of analysis has shown a positive relationship between engagement and organizational commitment (Hallberg & Schaufeli, 2006; Llorens, Bakker, Schaufeli, & Salanova, 2007) and a negative relationship between engagement and turnover intentions (Hallberg & Schaufeli, 2006; Schaufeli & Bakker, 2004) as well as relationships between engagement and constructs related to physical well-being such as health problems, somatic complaints, and psychosomatic health (Christian & Slaughter, 2007). Finally, in a recent study, Wefald, Reichard, and Serrano (2011) demonstrated that employee engagement serves as a mediator between personality traits (e.g., extraversion) and leadership. They also found that engagement relates to the important work outcomes of job satisfaction, organizational commitment, and turnover intentions. In sum, a large body of empirical research has demonstrated the importance of engagement at work.

Unfortunately, the majority of workers are not engaged on the job. Specifically, the Gallup Organization has reported that roughly 20% of US workers are disengaged, 54% are not engaged or are neutral about their work, and only 26% are actively engaged (Fleming, Coffman, & Harter, 2005). Other firms have reported similar results (Towers Perrin, 2003; BlessingWhite, 2008). Indicating the financial impact of such high levels of disengagement, Gallup estimates that this lack of employee engagement is costing US companies between $250 and $350 billion annually (Rath & Conchie, 2009). In sum, not only is engagement a nice benefit for employees in that they are using their physical, cognitive, and emotional energy maximally, but higher levels of employee engagement may positively benefit the organization's bottom line.

LEADERSHIP AND ENGAGEMENT

Having explored the benefits of an engaged workforce and considering the lack of employee engagement on the job, we next examine one of its primary precursors with an eye toward finding leverage points to increase it in today's modern organizational landscape. Schaufeli and Salanova (2007) suggest that leadership may be the most important factor influencing employee engagement. In general, leadership refers to a process of influence between two or more group members toward a common organizational goal (Northouse, 2007). However, there are several models and theories of leadership such as *charismatic leadership* (Conger & Kanungo, 1988), which focuses on a leader's ability to influence followers through the formulation and articulation of inspirational vision; *transformational leadership* (Avolio, Bass, Walumbwa, & Zhu, 2004), which focuses on the leader behaviors of idealized influence, inspirational motivation, intellectual stimulation, and individualized consideration; *leader–member exchange* (Graen & Uhl-Bien, 1995; Gerstner & Day, 1997), which focuses on the quality of the relationship between leader and followers; and *transactional leadership* (Bass, 1985), which is based on leader–follower exchanges, clarifying and setting goals and direction paired with contingent reinforcement upon goal completion. All of these forms of leadership may impact employee engagement and will be referred to throughout this chapter.

Decades of research on the topic of leadership have demonstrated that leadership has a significant impact on work outcomes and job attitudes, including employee engagement. In a meta-analysis of 200 independent studies based on over 13,000 participants, Avolio and his colleagues found that leadership interventions—based on the forms of leadership described above—increased the likelihood of positive affective, behavioral, and cognitive work outcomes by 28% (based on utility analysis; Avolio, Reichard, Hannah, Walumbwa, & Chan, 2009). More specifically, prior research has linked leadership with employee engagement. Shirom (2003) has suggested that having leaders who encourage employees to think creatively is an antecedent to vigor, a specific form of work engagement. Job resources— such as rewards, autonomy, and efficacy—have been shown to be an antecedent of engagement, and for some jobs, those resources can be influenced by a group's leader (Christian & Slaughter, 2007). A more recent study by Zhu, Avolio, and Walumbwa (2007) found a significant positive direct relationship between transformational leadership and engagement. Given the accumulated knowledge of scientific research, it is clear that leadership does impact important employee outcomes, including engagement.

However, traditional leadership models, which we described above, emphasize face-to-face interactions and may fail to fully explain the relationship between distant leaders and employee engagement (Zigurs, 2003). For example, Zaccaro and Bader (2003) pointed out that leadership functions such as communication, role clarification, team development, and task execution differed in virtual teams when mediated through technology—a clear case of leader–follower distance. In addition, virtual leaders provide feedback, encouragement, rewards, and motivation differently than face-to-face leaders (Avolio, Walumbwa, & Webber, 2009). Therefore, a deeper understanding of the relationship between distant leaders and follower engagement is needed to keep up with the changing world of work.

DEFINING DISTANCE

Originally, Napier and Ferris (1993) conceptualized three types of leader–follower distance: psychological, structural, and functional. First, leader–follower *psychological* distance includes demographic distance, power distance, perceived similarity, and values similarity. *Structural* distance, on the other hand, includes both physical distance and distance based on the organizational and supervision structure; it boils down to the amount of interaction between the leader and follower. Finally, *functional* leader–follower distance draws from Leader–Member Exchange theory (LMX). It depends on the follower being a part of the in-group rather than the out-group (e.g., Graen & Uhl-Bein, 1995), seeing eye-to-eye with his or her leader, and being provided a higher degree of autonomy within the work role. Building on this framework, Antonakis and Atwater (2002) conceptualized leader–follower distance similarly as not only *physical* distance (e.g., the leader is in New York while the followers are in Los Angeles), but also *perceived social distance* (i.e., high status and power differential), and *perceived interaction frequency* (i.e., frequent vs. infrequent contact). Culture, gender, and level within the organization can also influence leader–follower distance, and in turn employee engagement.

THE DISTANCE DILEMMA: FUNCTIONAL, FUTILE, OR INEVITABLE?

Historically, a high degree of leader–follower distance was thought to be essential for leaders to maintain follower influence and respect (Bogardus, 1927). Early research supported this perspective. For example, Katz and

Kahn (1978) argued *psychological* distance to be a necessary precursor for charismatic leadership. The old adage "a leader is only as good as his strongest fault" makes sense of this perspective by illustrating that leaders are often judged based on daily decisions and character. Shamir (1995) provided empirical support for this argument in showing that "close" charismatic leaders were judged based on their daily interactions with followers. As such they were required to set examples of personal excellence and observable qualities that reinforced the reason(s) for their appointment as a group's leader. *Distant* charismatic leaders were expected to display a different set of qualities (e.g., vision, performance, image-building and symbolic role modeling) to maintain their charismatic influence. Leader–follower distance can, thus, be useful in maintaining the allure and influence of the charismatic leader resulting in strong influence and arguably, employee engagement.

Beyond maintaining a charismatic influence without having to live up to unreasonable standards (Shamir, 1995), leader–follower distance can produce organizational benefits. First, it is more adaptive with today's changing work environment. For example, it is not uncommon for a leader to reside in a different location than his or her followers (physical distance). Second, particularly in large companies, it is near impossible for a leader to personally reduce social distance (e.g., getting to know everyone). Third, and finally, psychological distance may be functional when leaders are forced to make difficult organizational decisions, such as layoffs or other large-scale organizational changes that may negatively impact employees.

However, leader–follower distance can also be dysfunctional, possibly due to the changing nature of the workforce and its environment. Collinson (2005) conducted a case study of two organizations demonstrating the potential negative effects of distance in two ways: (1) diminishing trust and (2) the construction of countercultures. Employees perceived their distant leader(s) to be too far removed from daily operations, thus leading them to question the leader's ability to make strategic decisions about daily operations. This lack of trust also led them to question what was going on behind the scenes. For example, when a high level manager took an international trip for business, employees questioned its necessity. Further, they questioned the legitimacy of the stated reason of "business," and wondered if it was an excuse for the executive to get away or simply travel at the company's expense. Following their suspicions, they began to act against the company culture by utilizing workplace time, space, and materials for their own personal use. Through comparison with a second organization with distant leaders, critical observation, and in-depth interviews with employees, Collinson concluded that this mistrust and workplace deviance could have been avoided had the leadership team narrowed the distance gap by being more communicative and transparent.

Although distance can potentially produce positive or negative impact in the work environment, we maintain the perspective that it is inevitable in today's workplace, and at times can be functional. For example, physical distance is not only common, but can also be functional if a skilled team member lives in a different geographic location than his or her leader, allowing the team member more autonomy and responsibility. In addition, Meindl's (1995) work on the romance of leadership demonstrates that social distance is inevitable such that some followers perceive leaders (especially high-level executives) as socially distant and inaccessible. While inevitable, adept leaders can learn to utilize such social distance functionally by maintaining a consistent, clear public image and direction enabling followers to have positive perceptions and attributions of the leader which inspire trust and motivation. Finally, given the vast array of leadership responsibilities, it is unrealistic to think that all leaders will have the time to maintain high levels of interaction frequency with all followers (e.g., in groups and out groups in LMX; Graen & Uhl-Bien, 1995). For these reasons, it is imperative that leaders understand the various impacts of distance on followers, how to mitigate its negative effects, and how to leverage its benefits. In particular, distant leaders need to know how to influence employee behavior and attitudes, such as levels of employee engagement.

HOW CAN DISTANT LEADERS IMPACT EMPLOYEE ENGAGEMENT?

Understanding how individuals become engaged is the next step in producing employees who fully deploy themselves in their respective work. Such a task becomes especially challenging for distant leaders. As in the case of conceptualizing engagement, prior researchers have proposed specific paths for engaging employees (see Table 4.2). Some of these paths overlap, while some are unique and specific to conditions of leader–follower

TABLE 4.2

Summary of Leadership Antecedents to Employee Engagement

Theorist / Study	Meaningful and Motivating Work	Supporting and Coaching Employees	Enhancing Employees' Personal Resources	Facilitating Rewarding and Supportive Co-worker Relationships
Kahn (1990) May et al. (2004)	• Job characteristics • Job enrichment • Work role fit	• Supportive supervisors	• Lack of participation in outside activities	• Rewarding co-worker relationships
Maslach and Leiter (1997)	• Sustainable workload • Feeling of choice and control • Meaningfulness and valued work	• Appropriate recognition and reward • Fairness and justice		• Supportive work community
Schaufeli et al. (2002) / Bakker et al. (2008) / Xanthopoulou et al. (2007)	• Job control • Information • Job resources	• Feedback • Supervisory coaching	• Self-efficacy • Organizational based self-esteem • Optimism	• Social support • Social climate • Innovative climate
Shirom (2003)	• Task autonomy • Significance • Feedback • Identity • Skill	• Participation in decision making • Access to rewards		• Social support from others • Group cohesion

distance. A thorough examination of the literature has led us to identify four categories into which the majority of paths can be classified: (1) designing meaningful and motivating work, (2) supporting and coaching employees, (3) enhancing employees' personal resources, and (4) facilitating rewarding and supportive co-worker relations. Distant leaders can have an impact on employee engagement through each of these four categories.

Designing Meaningful and Motivating Work

In general, employees find their work meaningful when they feel that they are receiving a return on their invested energies (Kahn, 1990). They need to feel that their work is worthwhile, useful, and valued by the organization; the work must be impactful. Meaningful and motivating work can be achieved in at least two ways: (1) developing a compelling vision and (2) redesigning work.

To ensure that employees can recognize the impact of their work, distant leaders should *develop a compelling vision* for the organization and explicitly tie that vision to their followers' everyday activities to create meaning and purpose for the work being completed. Such vision also fosters additional antecedents to engagement including improved follower motivation (Conger, Kanungo, & Menon, 2000; Sosik, Kahai, & Avolio, 1999), improved leader–follower interactions (especially needed for socially distant leaders and those with low interaction frequency), improved satisfaction within teams (Dumdum, Lowe, & Avolio, 2002), and improved perceptions of leadership effectiveness (Awamleh & Gardner, 1999). To render optimal results, this vision should also be tied into the company's rewards system.

While it may seem difficult to find meaning and purpose in specific jobs and functions that on the surface seem trivial (e.g., making carpet, telemarketing), structurally distant leaders who are able to do so are likely to increase employee engagement. Take the example of Ray Anderson, CEO of Interface, the world's largest commercial carpet manufacturer. It may seem difficult to link carpet manufacturing to a meaningful vision, but that is just what Anderson did for his employees when he set the company goal of complete environmental sustainability by 2020. It appears that Interface employees have become more engaged in their work by developing innovative products (e.g., carpets made from recycled materials) and manufacturing processes (e.g., zero waste production methods) which are increasing sales and profits. Setting the organizational or unit vision is a task that may be delivered even more effectively by leaders who are structurally distant (e.g., high perceived social distance) given their attributed power (Meindl, 1995) and perhaps charisma (Shamir, 1995), as previously discussed.

Distant leaders can further increase the motivating potential of work by *redesigning work to increase work role clarity, increasing autonomy/job control, and allowing easy access to necessary resources.* Leaders need to first ensure that employees are in the right job for them. If an employee is highly introverted yet is placed in a sales role, then there is a misfit between the person and the job, inevitably resulting in lower employee engagement. As such, leaders need to provide employees with a clear understanding of the role they are to fill. When employees know what to do, they are more likely to be engaged in doing it. Specifically, leaders who are physically distant may have difficulty providing role clarity to the employee if the work is not directly observed. As such, distant leaders can use "leader substitutes" (Howell et al., 1990; Kerr & Jermier, 1978) such as refined and valid selection methods to find the right "fit" (May, Gilson, & Harter, 2004), clear job descriptions providing detailed information on each follower's responsibilities, and empowerment to groups of followers to redesign work into clusters of responsibilities that make more sense and capitalize on followers' strengths. Such employee empowerment (Conger & Kanungo, 1988; Spreitzer, 1995) and task autonomy (Shirom, 2006) provide followers a needed sense of choice and control over their work (Maslach & Leiter, 1997; Schaufeli et al., 2002; Bakker & Demerouti, 2008). Under conditions of leader–follower distance when the leader cannot be there to look over the followers' shoulders (e.g., physical distance), high levels of follower empowerment and autonomy are inevitable and useful for employee engagement.

However, employees cannot function at high levels without access to essential job resources. Since leaders most likely have control of resources and resource distribution and since confidence in one's resources (e.g., means efficacy) has been found to result in follower performance (Walumbwa, Avolio, & Zhu, 2008), distant leaders need to ensure that their employees have the necessary resources available to easily complete the job. Employees following leaders with a large perceived social distance and low perceived interaction frequency may be hesitant to ask for organizational/job resources such as role clarification/feedback, rewards, etc. In these instances, it is up to the leader to initiate the provision of such resources. This can be done by developing formal organizational processes for requesting resources such as weekly "resource" meetings, explicit job descriptions based on thorough analysis of the employee's job, and regular performance evaluation sessions. In summary, to ensure employee engagement, followers must feel that their work is significant and meaningful, identify with it, have an appropriate level of skill to successfully fulfill their roles, and receive appropriate levels of feedback and job resources (Shirom, 2006).

Supporting and Coaching Employees

Distant leaders may enhance employee engagement by providing support and coaching. Empirical research by Zhu et al. (2009) supports this assertion, given that these authors found that the individualized consideration aspect of transformational leadership was strongly and positively linked to employee-level engagement. Individualized consideration refers to leaders paying special attention to each individual follower's needs for achievement and growth by acting as a coach or mentor (Bass & Riggio, 2006). As a result, followers are developed to successively higher levels of potential through the increase of "human capital," or the knowledge, skills, and abilities necessary to complete one's job.

This leadership function is likely to become especially challenging under the various conditions of leader–follower distance. In the Zhu et al. (2009) study described above, a distance variable was not included in the statistical analyses. However, Purvanova and Bono (2009) found that followers' ratings of their leaders' individualized consideration were lower for virtual than for face-to-face leaders. In addition to physical distance, when there is a high level of perceived social distance and low level of perceived interaction frequency, it may become especially challenging for leaders to demonstrate individualized consideration. Thus, it is essential when leading at a distance for leaders to find a way to "get to know" each employee individually (Zhu et al., 2009) and support each employee's growth and development to attain maximal levels of engagement. For example, Disney organizes social events and company softball games which encourage employees, including distant leaders, to get to know one another.

Other ways to show support include giving appropriate feedback (Schaufeli et al., 2002; Shirom, 2006; Bakker et al., 2008), allowing employees to participate in relevant decision making (Shirom, 2006), providing access and clear paths to rewards, recognizing employee accomplishments (Maslach & Leiter, 1997; Shirom, 2006), and providing coaching in specific areas (Schaufeli et al., 2002; Bakker et al., 2008; Xanthopoulou et al., 2009). At a minimum, distant leaders can make this a regular practice in a formal performance review. During this review, leaders can use strategies such as reviewing employees' credentials and talking with them to identify areas of strength, weakness, and interest. When interacting with employees, leaders should take some time to get to know each employee individually before jumping into the task at hand. A leader should not be afraid to share information about himself or herself first to set the tone and build trust (Avolio & Reichard, 2008). After all, building leader–follower trust has been shown to set the stage for employees to engage (Macey & Schneider, 2008). Based on this preliminary work, leaders should implement tailored development plans for each employee, which include both work and training opportunities as well as a regular follow-up on progress. Leaders should make every attempt to tailor and personalize work assignments so that employees can grow and benefit the most. This is especially important when leading at a distance because observing personal artifacts (e.g., family photos) and overhearing water cooler conversations where leaders may learn more about the employee are unlikely.

Enhancing Employees' Personal Resources

Several studies have demonstrated a positive relationship between personal resources—defined as individual views of the self that are generally related to resiliency and one's sense of ability to have control and impact in his/her environment successfully (Hobfoll, Johnson, Ennis, & Jackson, 2003)—and employee engagement. Such resources are equally important to job resources such as autonomy, job control, access to rewards and information, and the like (Llorens, Schaufeli, Bakker, & Salanova, 2007; Xanthopoulou, Bakker, Demerouti, & Schaufeli, 2007). Xanthopoulou et al. (2007) found three personal resources (self-efficacy, organizational-based self-esteem, and optimism) to predict engagement. They concluded that job resources activate personal resources which lead employees to feel more in control of their environment, thus more likely to take a sense of pride and find more meaning in their work. A two-year longitudinal study replicated and expanded these results to conclude that personal resources, job resources, and work engagement form a dynamic cycle (Xanthopoulou, Bakker, Demerouti, & Schaufeli, 2009). For example, a self-efficacious employee may be more likely to seek out opportunities for professional development, thus resulting in higher levels of engagement. Likewise an engaged employee may feel more self-efficacious due to increased opportunities for professional development. Distant leaders can select team members with high levels of personal resources as well as provide the environmental conditions where personal resources can be built on. For example, leaders with low interaction frequency can assign increasingly challenging tasks to followers. By taking on smaller challenges first, employees can develop a strong sense of self-efficacy (Bandura, 1997). Moreover, distant leaders should ensure that employees have the necessary resources to accomplish the job at hand by putting mechanisms in place to give them control over requisitions.

One specific personal resource that distant leaders can help followers to develop is positive psychological capital, or PsyCap. PsyCap has been conceptually identified by Luthans and colleagues (Luthans, 2002; Luthans & Youssef, 2004; Luthans, Youssef & Avolio, 2007) as consisting of the four positive psychological resources of hope, optimism, efficacy, and resilience, and when combined, reflect a higher-order construct that represents an individual's motivational propensity and perseverance toward goals. In a meta-analysis of 48 PsyCap studies, Avey, Reichard, Luthans, and Mhatre (2011) found that PsyCap positively correlated with multiple measures of performance as well as organizational citizenship behaviors and organizational commitment. Furthermore, Gooty, Gavin, Johnson, Frazier, and Snow (2009) found that followers' perceptions of transformational leadership predicted followers' level of PsyCap. Zhu et al. (2009) recommended that for leaders to produce an engaged workforce, they should work to increase employees' individual levels of self-efficacy or confidence, one component of PsyCap. Furthermore, Papalexandris and Galanaki (2009) found that CEOs need to be good mentors (e.g., focus on developing follower confidence, amongst other things) in order to effectively produce highly engaged employees. Taken together, distant leaders who enhance followers' personal resources or PsyCap will yield higher levels of employee engagement.

Prior research has demonstrated that personal resources such as PsyCap can be developed (Luthans, Avey, & Patera, 2008; Luthans et al., in press); and that these strategies can be translated into leading at a distance. To increase efficacy, or a sense of mastery and control, distant leaders should set up incrementally more challenging tasks for employees to master. Related to coaching as discussed above, these tasks should be tailored to the employee's area of interest/development and the leader should provide frequent and specific feedback on employee performance. In instances where there is highly perceived social distance, feedback from the leader can be especially impactful due to the leader's high status and power. To increase hope, leaders should discuss challenging and specific goals with the employees and ensure that they generate multiple pathways to goal attainment. To increase optimism, leaders should mold employees' attributions of success or failure of a specific task to be internal and stable for success and external and temporary for failures. Again, attributions or explanations may be especially effective when the leader is at a highly perceived social distance due to the high status and power he/she maintains. Finally, to build resilience, leaders can help employees build assets they will need to help them succeed and avoid risk factors (e.g., a person–job fit mismatch).

Facilitating Rewarding and Supportive Co-Worker Relations

A final method for developing an engaged workforce at a distance entails building a supportive work community (Maslach & Leiter, 1997). To fully engage in a task or role, employees need to feel that their work environment is safe enough for them to be able show their true selves, openly express opinions, and make mistakes without fear of reprisal (Kahn, 1990; May et al., 2004). This requires building a culture of trust (Macey, Schneider, Barbera, & Young, 2009), which can and should be developed by all types of distant leaders. For example, distant leaders (e.g., top management) of BP Texas City Refinery have developed such a culture by developing formal policies for employees to report safety issues without fear of reprisal, even if it reflects poor knowledge, skills, or conduct on the part of the employee (Macey et al., 2009).

The work environment also needs to foster group cohesion and support from co-workers (Shirom, 2006). In a sample of 85 teams in the Royal Dutch military, Bakker, van Emmerik, and Euwema (2006) found engagement to be contagious amongst work teams. Specifically, they found team-level engagement to be related to individual-level engagement, team-level engagement to be negatively related to individual-level burnout, and team-level burnout to be negatively related to individual-level engagement. Together, these results suggest a contagion effect of engagement; thus, developing such relationships is a key strategy for distant leaders to implement. This can be done by developing a positive social climate (Schaufeli et al., 2002; Shirom, 2006; Bakker et al., 2008). Leaders can do so in their work units by displaying relational behaviors such as open communication, encouraging collaboration, and cultivating trust to produce employee vigor (Carmeli, Ben-Hador, Waldman, & Rupp, 2009). Specifically, Carmeli et al. (2009) found that when leaders display these types of relational behaviors, it produces bonding social capital (i.e., the group becomes cohesive) which leads to increased levels of employee vigor. Thus, it is recommended that leaders focus on building team cohesiveness through leader relational behaviors.

This task may become more challenging when leading at a distance. For example, when leading at a physical distance, it is important that leaders go beyond one-on-one interactions with employees and model relational behaviors when interacting with the group as a whole. This could be accomplished by having virtual social gatherings or even just holding weekly unit meetings. This becomes an even more difficult challenge when the whole team is virtual, as opposed to just the leader. When this is the case, the leader should orchestrate in-person meetings to kick-off projects and provide activities or time for employees working virtually to interact in person. When operating under high perceived social distance, leaders should link co-workers together on work projects which will be mutually beneficial for them. For example, the leader may set up a peer mentoring or step-ahead mentoring program which links similar individuals through frequent meetings or contact.

PRACTICAL SOLUTIONS FOR DISTANT LEADERS

To reiterate, distant leaders can influence follower engagement through: (1) designing meaningful and motivating work, (2) supporting and coaching employees, (3) enhancing employees' personal resources (e.g., PsyCap), and (4) facilitating rewarding and supportive co-worker relations. Though these tasks may seem challenging for any leader to implement, they become even more difficult when leading at a distance. In this final section, we elaborate on the four overarching categories to provide specific strategies by which the various types of distant leaders can enhance employee engagement.

Physically Distant Leaders

Mitigating the effects of physical distance is similar to overcoming the negative effects of virtual teams. Each suggestion provided below is designed to apply primarily to physically distant *immediate supervisors*, not leaders who are physically distant due to their position like a company CEO (e.g., structurally distant), which will be discussed in a section below.

1. *Physically distant leaders should get to know their team members professionally.* Zhu et al. (2009) suggest that leaders should truly understand what their employees' capabilities are. First and foremost, leaders should ensure that their perceptions of employee KSAs (knowledge, skills, and abilities) match up with the respective employee's perception of his or her own talents. In doing so, leaders can avoid the Golem effect—low leader expectations rendering low follower performance—by assigning tasks tailored to each follower's level of competence and developmental needs. Second, physically distant leaders should know what their employees' future professional goals are and how they plan to get there. This will create a greater sense of leader support facilitating greater levels of engagement, while simultaneously setting the stage for employee involvement.

2. *Physically distant leaders should involve employees in decision making.* The most important aspect of involving employees in decision making is relevance (Shirom, 2006). Each decision must impact the work role and/or task of the employee being involved. Since physically distant leaders are likely not "in the trenches" with their followers, involving them in relevant decision making can actually prove to be beneficial to both parties. The leader gains local information as followers may have a different perspective on certain issues that a physically distant leader does not; thus, the follower becomes more engaged. For example, The Boeing Company employs this strategy by allowing employees to improve the processes in their immediate control (Proctor, 2004). In doing so, employees feel a greater sense of involvement, thus they become more open and ready to fully deploy their entire selves on the job (Britt, 1999; Shirom, 2006).

3. *Physically distant leadership should get people involved in projects that they find interesting.* The precursor to this suggestion is that leaders first get to know their employees' interests and talents. Following a

thorough knowledge of employee KSAs, physically distant leaders can take their level of support a step further by involving followers in desired projects. This provides employees with an opportunity to shine while simultaneously gaining new skills; after all, most employees enjoy a certain degree of challenge. In addition, putting the right talent on the right project provides meaningful and motivating work for employees (May et al., 2004). Google provides an excellent example of how this can be implemented by distant leaders of all types through the use of "20 percent time." This policy allows engineers to use 20 percent of their time working on projects they are truly passionate about, thus ensuring maximum creativity and engagement.

Perceived Socially Distant Leaders

Although socially distant leaders are generally characterized as holding high status and power differential in relation to the follower(s), at times, physically distant immediate supervisors may also be perceived in this manner. In such cases, we suggest a careful blend of suggestions to reduce physical distance (above) and the suggestions below. Also, we offer a diversity of solutions in this section as we understand that social distance can, at times, be functional (e.g. in the case of CEOs of larger companies). Solutions 1 and 4 (below) can be used to reduce social distance whereas 2 and 3 can be used to engage followers while maintaining it.

1. *Perceived socially distant leaders should create a culture of engagement.* While perhaps the most powerful solution suggested thus far, creating a culture of engagement is likely the most time-intensive solution. This solution is most relevant to leaders under conditions of highly perceived social distance because it is typically the function of upper management to craft the organizational strategy and structure which drive organizational culture. Drawing on the work of Corace (2007) and Zhu et al. (2009), an engaged culture consists of the following: (1) a trusting environment in which employees are allowed appropriate amounts of job autonomy and relevant decisions are allowed to be made by those at all levels of the organization; (2) a sense of direction for employees, consisting of not only daily direction but a specific, articulated direction of where the organization as a whole is headed;

(3) a steady flow of organizational information provided on a regular basis (e.g., as simple as an employee newsletter or even an internal website); and finally (4) open communication without reprisal to build psychological safety, collaboration, and reward in accordance with job expectations.

2. *Perceived socially distant leaders should (re)design jobs for engagement.* Since leaders have various roles (e.g., strategizing and planning, external business, etc.), socially distant leaders may often be those who do not have the time to interact with employees (i.e., those with a low interaction frequency, as discussed below). However, this does not mean that this type of leader cannot have an impact on employee engagement. Using techniques such as job redesign, rotation, and enlargement, these leaders inform employees that they are valued without having to reduce social distance or interact more frequently. Thus, employees are constantly being encouraged to learn and find work that is personally and professionally meaningful. In becoming more acquainted with the resources needed to perform various jobs, employees are likely to feel that they and their respective work are valued (Schaufeli & Salanova, 2007). If carefully planned and implemented, job (re)design, rotation, and enlargement can assist distant leaders in developing an engaged workforce.

3. *Perceived socially distant leaders should ensure a good person–job fit.* According to Britt (1999) the job must be relevant to one's occupational training to identify his or her work; Kahn (1992) suggests that there must be an appropriate work role fit to produce meaningfulness at work; and Shirom (2006) suggests that job significance is a way to increase employee vigor. It is well supported that ensuring a good person–job fit will prove to be an effective way for socially distant leaders (e.g., those designing work roles, such as HR professionals or mid-level management) to increase employee engagement. Nigel Martin, VP of Harrah's Entertainment, states that the company employs this strategy by hiring people who are likely to thrive in the business environment in which they will operate (Macey et al., 2009). For example, highly customer service oriented individuals are often hired as front desk staff.

4. *Perceived socially distant leaders should craft employee development plans that include information about resources.* Though this can act as a stand-alone suggestion to reduce social distance, it is best coupled

with "getting to know your employees professionally" (see reducing physical distance, suggestion 1). Talking with an employee to develop a career plan can be a powerful means to increase employee engagement (Schaufeli & Salanova, 2008). By taking the time to do so, leaders show support and develop relationships that decrease the perception of social distance. Encouraging followers to develop professional goals and the strategies and resources needed to attain them is the key to ensuring a deeper level of engagement. One creative example of this solution is seen with CEO Bill Zollars of Yellow Roadways in his campaign to turn the company around. Zollars worked with unions to allow employees to set their own goals for on-time pickups and delivery, as well as breakage (i.e., not delivering broken items). In doing so, he was able to ensure that employees deployed themselves on the job to a higher degree, thus transforming Yellow Roadways from one of *Fortune Magazine's* "Least Admired Companies" in 1997 to one of their "Most Admired Companies" in 2003. In addition, union staff began to see him as a man who always keeps his promises.

Leaders with Low Perceived Interaction Frequency

It is not uncommon for leaders to find their time split between leading (e.g., giving direction to their team) and task-focused work (e.g., meeting with a client to secure an important contract). Often it just seems that there is too much to do, so involvement with employees suffers as securing new business simply appears to be a "higher priority." Such situations may result in low interaction frequency between leaders and followers, thus adding yet another challenge to the engagement puzzle. For such scenarios, the following solutions for leaders can be used to produce employee engagement.

1. *Leaders with low perceived interaction frequency should provide regular (job-relevant) training.* Training is one way in which leaders with low interaction frequency can increase employee engagement while making the most of their time with staff. Training offers a number of benefits that can lead to highly engaged employees. First and foremost, job-relevant training enhances personal resources such as employees' base of knowledge, skills, and abilities. Second, it provides

opportunities for job enrichment which leads to more meaning-fulness on the job. Third, it can act as a form of reward. Fourth and finally, training enhances perceptions of a supportive work community by enhancing co-worker relationships and demonstrating perceived organizational support. In designing training, leaders should focus on building job-relevant skills and self-efficacy beliefs; doing so renders a positive spiral toward increasing engagement (Schaufeli & Salanova, 2008). As such, distant leaders who have fewer interactions with followers can implement employee training to increase work engagement without being present. Training serves as an organizational structure which substitutes for the absent leader (Kerr & Jermier, 1978; Howell et al., 1990).

2. *Leaders with low perceived interaction frequency should utilize the power of self-managed teams.* Self-managed teams decentralize the normal bureaucratic chain of command and place the power of decision making into the hands of team members. It becomes the responsibility of team members to come up with governing rules (e.g., timelines, social conduct), the logistics of daily operations, and intra-team behavioral norms. It is the official leader's responsibility to provide the vision by which the team is to develop these collective norms, rules, and values and to ensure that they are being implemented in an appropriate manner. By nature, self-managed teams allow official (distant) leaders to maintain low interaction frequency while continuing to ensure the engagement of each member. The potential for increased levels of engagement comes from a number of sources, including: job expansion (as each team member is taking on leadership roles), a supportive work community (as peers govern one another), group cohesion, full participation in decision making, and task autonomy (as the team is given the autonomy to define the flow of daily work).

3. *Leaders with low perceived interaction frequency should initiate formal and frequent updates of "what's going on" in their business unit.* Leaders who frequently interact with employees have the luxury of receiving updates at meetings and water cooler conversations that low interaction frequency leaders do not. Therefore, we suggest that an update process be formalized, for example, by sending a weekly email or a regular newsletter containing updates that are relevant to your business unit or team. Customizing a weekly update can demonstrate the

leader's support to their employees and ensure that they read what is relevant to them, thereby producing involvement. Leaders can send out unit-wide regular emails, post a blog on the company intranet, and encourage employees to respond or comment directly to the leader. Since increased communication has been shown to increase engagement in the field (Corace, 2007), this suggestion is critical for leaders with lower interaction frequency.

CONCLUSION

Leadership is not an easy undertaking, especially when faced with the challenge of leader–follower distance produced by today's dynamic workplace. Physical and social distance, as well as interaction frequency between leaders and followers becomes increasingly complex as business practice moves to a global, virtual, and more collaborative environment. Impacting important work behaviors and attitudes such as employee engagement becomes increasingly complex under such conditions. For this purpose, we have provided a review of the leader–follower distance literature supplemented by previous theory and research on employee engagement represented by the two components of *energy* and *involvement*. Furthermore, we emphasized the antecedents of employee engagement and provided four leverage points whereby distant leaders can increase employee engagement. Finally, we provided specific strategies and caveats for leading under specific types of distance. In the new world of work, effective leadership is essential in order for today's employees to have fully engaged and productive lives.

BIBLIOGRAPHY

Antonakis, J. & Atwater, L. (2002). Leader distance: A review and proposed theory. *Leadership Quarterly*, 13, 673–704.

Avey, J. B., Reichard, R. J., Luthans, F., & Mhatre, K. H. (2011). Meta-analysis of the impact of positive psychological capital on employee attitudes, behaviors and performance. *Human Resources Development Quarterly*, 22(2), 127–152.

Avolio, B. J. & Reichard, R. J. (2008). The rise of authentic followership. In R. E. Riggio, I. Chaleff, & J. Lipman-Blumen (Eds.), *The art of followership* (pp. 325–337). San Francisco: Jossey-Bass.

Avolio, B. J. (1999). *Full leadership development.* London: Sage.

Avolio, B. J., Bass, B. M., Walumbwa, F. O., & Zhu, W. (2004). *Multifactor leadership questionnaire: Manual and sampler test.* Redwood City, CA: Mind Garden.

Avolio, B. J., Reichard, R. J., Hannah, S. T., Walumbwa, F.O., & Chan, A. (2009). A meta-analytic review of leadership impact research: Experimental and quasi-experimental studies. *Leadership Quarterly,* 20, 764–784.

Avolio, B. J., Walumbwa, F. O., & Webber, T. J. (2009). Leadership: Current theories, research, and future directions. *Annual Review of Psychology,* 60, 421–449.

Awamleh, R. & Gardner, W. L. (1999). Perceptions of leader charisma and effectiveness: The effects of vision content, delivery, and organizational performance. *Leadership Quarterly,* 10, 345–373.

Bakker, A. & Demerouti, E. (2008). Towards a model of work engagement. *Career Development International,* 13(3), 209–223.

Bakker, A. B., van Emmerik, H., & Euwema, M. C. (2006). Crossover of burnout and engagement in work teams. *Work and Occupations,* 33(4), 464–489.

Bakker, A., Hakanen, J., Demerouti, E., & Xanthopoulou, D. (2007). Job resources boost work engagement, particularly when job demands are high. *Journal of Educational Psychology,* 99(2), 274–284.

Bakker, A., Schaufeli, W., Leiter, M., & Taris, T. (2008). Work engagement: An emerging concept in occupational health psychology. *Work & Stress,* 22(3), 187–200.

Bandura, A. (1997). *Self-efficacy: The exercise of control.* New York: Freeman.

Bass, B. M. & Riggio, R. E. (2006). *Transformational leadership* (2nd ed.). Mahwah, NJ: Lawrence Erlbaum.

Bass, B. M. (1985). *Leadership and performance beyond expectations.* New York: Free Press.

BlessingWhite. (2008). *The state of employment engagement—2008: North American overview* [White Paper]. Princeton, NJ: Author.

Bogardus, E. S. (1927). Leadership and social distance. *Sociology and Social Research,* 12, 173–178.

Britt, T. & Bliese, P. (2003). Testing the stress-buffering effects of self-engagement among soldiers on a military operation. *Journal of Personality,* 71(2), 245–265.

Britt, T. (1999). Engaging the self in the field: Testing the triangle model of responsibility. *Personality and Social Psychology Bulletin,* 25(6), 696–706.

Carmeli, A., Ben-Hador, B., Waldman, D., & Rupp, D. (2009). How leaders cultivate social capital and nurture employee vigor: Implications for job performance. *Journal of Applied Psychology,* 94(6), 1553–1561.

Christian, M. S. & Slaughter, J. E. (2007). Work engagement: A meta-analytic review and directions for research in an emerging area. Paper presented at the sixty-seventh annual meeting of the Academy of Management, Philadelphia.

Collinson, D. L. (2005). Questions of distance. *Leadership,* 1(2), 235–250.

Conger, J. A. & Kanungo, R. N. (1988). The empowerment process: Integrating theory and practice. *Academy of Management Review,* 13(3), 471–482.

Conger, J. A. & Kanungo, R. N. (1987). Toward a behavioral theory of charismatic leadership in organizational settings. *Academy of Management Review,* 12(4), 637–647.

Conger, J. A., Kanungo, R. N., & Menon, S. T. (2000). Charismatic leadership and follower effects. *Journal of Organizational Behavior,* 21(7), p. 747.

Corace, C. (2007). Engagement—Enrolling the quiet majority. *Organization Development Journal,* 25(2), 171–175.

Csikszentmihalyi, M. (1990). *Flow: The psychology of optimal experience.* New York: Harper.

Dumdum, U. R., Lowe, K. B., & Avolio, B. J. (2002). A meta-analysis of transformational and transactional leadership correlates of effectiveness and satisfaction: An update and extension. In B. J.Avolio & F. J. Yammarino (Eds.), *Transformational and charismatic leadership: The road ahead* (pp. 35–66). Amsterdam: JAI.

Fleming, J. H., Coffman, C., & Harter, J. K. (2005). Manage your human sigma. *Harvard Business Review*, 83(7/8), 106–114.

Gerstner, C. R. & Day, D. V. (1997). Meta-analytic review of leader–member exchange theory: Correlates and construct issues. *Journal of Applied Psychology*, 82, 827–844.

Gooty, J., Gavin, M., Johnson, P. D., Frazier, M. L., & Snow, D. B. (2009). In the eyes of the beholder: Transformational leadership, positive psychological capital, and performance. *Journal of Leadership and Organizational Studies*, 15(4), 353–367.

Graen, G. B. & Uhl-Bien, M. (1995). Relationship-based approach to leadership: Development of leader–member exchange (LMX) theory of leadership over 25 years—applying a multilevel and multidomain perspective. *Leadership Quarterly*, 6, 219–247.

Hakanen, J., Bakker, A., & Schaufeli, W. (2006). Burnout and work engagement among teachers. *Journal of School Psychology*, 43(6), 495–513.

Halbesleben, J. & Wheeler, A. (2008). The relative roles of engagement and embeddedness in predicting job performance and intention to leave. *Work & Stress*, 22(3), 242–256.

Hallberg, U. E. & Schaufeli, W. B. (2006). "Same same" but different? Can work engagement be discriminated from job involvement and organizational commitment? *European Psychologist*, 11(2), 119–127.

Harter, J. K., Schmidt, F. L., & Hayes T. L. (2002). Business-unit-level relationship between employee satisfaction, employee engagement, and business outcomes: A meta-analysis. *Journal of Applied Psychology*, 87(2), 268–279.

Hobfoll, S. E. (1989). Conservation of resources: A new attempt at conceptualizing stress. *American Psychologist*, 44, 513–524.

Hobfoll, S. E. (1998). *The psychology and philosophy of stress, culture, and community*. New York: Plenum.

Hobfoll, S., Johnson, R., Ennis, N., & Jackson, A. (2003). Resource loss, resource gain, and emotional outcomes among inner city women. *Journal of Personality and Social Psychology*, 84(3), 632–643.

Howell, J. P., Bowen, D. E., Dorfman, P. W., & Kerr, S. (1990). Substitutes for leadership: Effective alternatives to ineffective leadership. *Organization Dynamics*, 19(1), 21–38.

Kahn, W. (1990). Psychological conditions of personal engagement and disengagement at work. *Academy of Management Journal*, 33(4), 692–724.

Kahn, W. A. (1992). To be fully there: Psychological presence at work. *Human Relations*, 45, 321–349.

Katz, D. & Kahn, R. L. (1978). *The social psychology of organizations*. New York: Wiley.

Kerr, S. & Jermier, J. M. (1978). Substitutes for leadership: Their meaning and measurement. *Organizational Behavior and Human Performance*, 22(3), 375–403.

Llorens, S., Schaufeli, W., Bakker, A., & Salanova, M. (2007). Does a positive gain spiral of resources, efficacy beliefs and engagement exist? *Computers in Human Behavior*, 23(1), 825–841.

Luthans, F. (2002). The need for and meaning of positive organizational behavior. *Journal of Organizational Behavior*, 23, 695–706.

Luthans, F. & Youssef, C. M. (2004). Human, social, and now positive psychological capital management. *Organizational Dynamics*, 33, 143–160.

Luthans, F., Avey, J. B., & Patera, J. L. (2008). Experimental analysis of a web-based training intervention to develop psychological capital. *Academy of Management Learning and Education*, 7, 209–221.

Luthans, F., Avey, J. B., Avolio, B. J., & Peterson, S. J. (in press). Impact of a micro-training intervention on psychological capital development and performance. *Human Resource Development Quarterly*.

Luthans, F., Youssef, C. M., & Avolio, B. J. (2007). *Psychological capital*. New York: Oxford University Press.

Macey, W. H., Schneider, B., Barbera, K. M., & Young, S. A. (2009). *Employee engagement: Tools for analysis, practice, and competitive advantage*. Wiley-Blackwell.

Macey, W. H. & Schneider, B. (2008). The meaning of employee engagement. *Industrial and Organizational Psychology*, 1, 1–30.

Maslach, C. & Leiter, M. (2008). Early predictors of job burnout and engagement. *Journal of Applied Psychology*, 93(3), 498–512.

Maslach, C. & Leiter, M. (1997). *The truth about burnout: How organizations cause personal stress and what to do about it*. San Francisco: Jossey-Bass.

Maslach, C., Leiter, M., & Schaufeli, W. (2001). Job burnout. *Annual Review of Psychology*, 52, 397–422.

Mauno, S., Kinnunen, U., & Ruokolainen, M. (2007). Job demands and resources as antecedents of work engagement: A longitudinal study. *Journal of Vocational Behavior*, 70(1), 149–171.

May, D., Gilson, R., & Harter, L. (2004). The psychological conditions of meaningfulness, safety and availability and the engagement of the human spirit at work. *Journal of Occupational and Organizational Psychology*, 77(1), 11–37.

Meindl, J. R. (1995). The romance of leadership as a follower-centric theory: A social constructionist approach. *Leadership Quarterly*, 6, 329–341.

Napier, B. J. & Ferris, G. R. (1993). Distance in organizations. *Human Resource Management Review*, 3(4), 321–357.

Northouse, Peter, G. (2007). *Leadership: Theory and Practice*. (4th Ed.). Thousand Oaks, CA: Sage.

Papalexandris, N. & Galanaki, E. (2009). Leadership's impact on employee engagement: Differences among entrepreneurs and professional CEOs. *Leadership & Organization Development Journal*, 30(4), 365–385.

Proctor, P. (2004). Shared destiny. *Boeing Frontiers Online*. Retrieved January 21, 2011 from: www.boeing.com/news/frontiers/archive/2004/february/cover.

Purvanova, R. K. & Bono, J. E. (2009). Transformational leadership in context: Face-to-face and virtual teams. *Leadership Quarterly*, 20(3), 343–357.

Rath, T. & Conchie, B. (2009). *Strengths-based leadership: Great leaders, teams, and why people follow*. New York: Gallup Press.

Rousseau, D. (1997). Organizational behavior in the new organizational era. *Annual Review of Psychology*, 48, 515–546.

Saks, A. (2006). Antecedents and consequences of employee engagement. *Journal of Managerial Psychology*, 21(7), 600–619.

Salanova, M., Agut, S., & Peiro, J. M. (2005). Linking organizational resources and work engagement to employee performance and customer loyalty: The mediation of service climate. *Journal of Applied Psychology*, 90, 1217–1227.

Schaufeli, W. & Bakker, A. (2004). Job demands, job resources, and their relationship with burnout and engagement: A multi-sample study. *Journal of Organizational Behavior*, 25(3), 293–315.

Schaufeli, W. B. & Salanova, M. (2007). Work engagement: An emerging psychological concept and its implications for organizations. In Gilliland, S. W., Steiner, D. D., & Skarlicki, D. P. (Eds.), *Research in social issues in management (Volume 5): Managing social and ethical issues in organizations* (pp. 135–177). Greenwich, CT: Information Age Publishers.

Schaufeli, W. B., Taris, T. W., & Bakker, A. B. (2006) Dr. Jekyll and Mr. Hyde: On the differences between work engagement and workaholism. In R. J. Burke (Ed.), *Research companion to working time and work addiction* (pp. 193–217). Northampton, MA: Edward Elgar.

Schaufeli, W., Salanova, M., González–Romá, V., & Bakker, A. (2002). The measurement of engagement and burnout: A two-sample confirmatory factor analytic approach. *Journal of Happiness Studies*, 3(1), 71–92.

Schlenker, B., Britt, T., Pennington, J., Murphy, R., & Doherty, K. (1994). The triangle model of responsibility. *Psychological Review*, 101(4), 632–652.

Shamir, B. (1995). Social distance and charisma: Theoretical notes and an exploratory study. *Leadership Quarterly*, 6, 19–47.

Shirom, A. (2003). Feeling vigorous at work? The construct of vigor and the study of positive affect in organizations. In D. Ganster & P. L. Perrewe (Eds.), *Research in organizational stress and well-being*. (Vol. 3, pp. 135–165). Greenwich, CN: JAI Press.

Shirom, A. (2006). Explaining vigor: On the antecedents and consequences of vigor as a positive affect at work. In C. L. Cooper & D. Nelson (Eds.), *Organizational behavior: Accentuating the positive at work*. Thousand Oaks, CA: Sage.

Sosik, J. J., Kahai, S. S., & Avolio, B. J. (1999). Leadership style, anonymity, and creativity in group decision support systems: The mediating role of optimal flow. *Journal of Creative Behavior*, 33(4), 227–256.

Spreitzer, G. M. (1995). Psychological empowerment in the workplace: Dimensions, measurement, and validation. *Academy of Management Journal*, 38(5), 1442–1465.

Terry, P. C., Carron, A. V., Pink, M. J., Lane, A. M., Jones, G. J. W., & Hall, M. P. (2000). Perceptions of group cohesion and mood in sport teams. *Group Dynamics*, 4, 244–253.

Towers Perrin. (2003). *2003 Towers Perrin global engagement workforce study* [White Paper]. Stamford, CT: Author.

Walumbwa, F. O., Avolio, B. J., & Zhu, W. (2008). How transformational leadership weaves its influence on individual job performance: The role of identification and efficacy beliefs. *Personnel Psychology*, 61, 793–825.

Wefald, A., Reichard, R. J., & Serrano, S. A. (2011). Fitting engagement into a nomological network: An examination of the antecedents and outcomes of work engagement. *Journal of Leadership and Organizational Studies*, 18(4), 522–537.

Xanthopoulou, D., Bakker, A., Demerouti, E., & Schaufeli, W. (2007). The role of personal resources in the job demands-resources model. *International Journal of Stress Management*, 14(2), 121–141.

Xanthopoulou, D., Bakker, A., Demerouti, E., & Schaufeli, W. (2009). Reciprocal relationships between job resources, personal resources, and work engagement. *Journal of Vocational Behavior*, 74(3), 235–244.

Zaccaro, S. J., & Bader, P. (2003). E-leadership and the challenges of leading E-teams: Minimizing the bad and maximizing the good. *Organizational Dynamics*, 31, 377–387.

Zhu, W., Avolio, B. J., & Walumbwa, F. O. (2007, April). *The effect of transformational leadership on follower work engagement: Moderating role of follower characteristics.*

Poster session presented at the annual meeting of the Society for Industrial and Organizational Psychology, New York.

Zhu, W., Avolio, B., & Walumbwa, F. (2009). Moderating role of follower characteristics with transformational leadership and follower work engagement. *Group & Organization Management*, 34(5), 590–619.

Zigurs, I. (2003). Leadership in virtual teams: Oxymoron or opportunity? *Organizational Dynamics*, 31, 339–351.

5

The Role of Distance in Leader–Member Exchange (LMX)

Birgit Schyns

Given the positive outcomes of a good relationship quality between leader and follower (Leader–Member Exchange, LMX; e.g., Graen & Uhl-Bien, 1995), a question that is often asked is how many good quality relationships one leader can establish and maintain (e.g. Schyns, Maslyn, & Weibler, 2010). As early as 1975, Dansereau, Graen, and Haga pointed out that leaders have limited resources, which may jeopardize their efforts to establish and maintain good relationship qualities with all their followers. This means that in large spans of control leaders might find it difficult to have a good relationship quality with all their followers. While in LMX research, span of control is considered relatively often (e.g., Cogliser & Schriesheim, 2000), one could argue, based on considerations concerning leader distance in general (Antonakis & Atwater, 2002; Napier & Ferris, 1993), that it is only one of many indicators of distance between leaders and followers. This leads to the question, whether not only in large spans of control, but generally when a leader is distant, establishing and maintaining Leader–Member Exchange relationships can be difficult. Nevertheless, given that span of control is relatively well researched in the context of LMX, it will be used in this chapter as the main basis for drawing conclusions about the effects of leader distance in LMX relationships.

Specifically, this chapter will address the question as to whether, depending on their personality, some leaders may find it easier or more difficult to establish and maintain a large number of Leader–Member Exchange relationships. At the same time, I will discuss whether or not followers with a particular personality structure may perceive more LMX than others. Thus, when followers of a similar LMX-conducive personality structure make up a group, more LMX might be reported even in larger groups. This contribution aims to shed light on the research question: How does leader distance, and specifically span of control as an indicator of leader distance affect LMX relationships and what role do leader and follower personality play in the relationship between leader distance and LMX?

The chapter will begin by defining Leader–Member Exchange and leader distance. Subsequently, I will discuss the relationship between LMX and leader distance before turning to leader and follower personality as possible moderators of the relationship between LMX and leader distance.

DEFINING LEADER–MEMBER EXCHANGE AND LEADER DISTANCE

A Brief Introduction to Leader–Member Exchange

The idea of vertical dyad linkage (VDL, later leading to the development of Leader–Member Exchange) was introduced by Dansereau et al. (1975). Dansereau et al. found that leaders have different relationships with each of their followers, making leadership a dyadic rather than a group process. At the time this was a rather revolutionary finding as most leadership approaches prior to this study concentrated on leader traits or behavior towards their followers as a group. Different evaluations of the same leader by different followers were treated as measurement error rather than a reflection of real differences. In contrast, VDL acknowledged real differences in the interaction between leaders and members.

Later developments of this approach, such as the Leader–Member Exchange approach, highlight the relationship quality between a leader and each of his or her followers (e.g., Graen & Uhl-Bien, 1995). Here, the dyadic interactions between leader and follower are in the focus. However, actual behavior of leader and followers are less important than the relationship they establish with each other. Although the approach is based on exchange, what is exchanged is still in discussion (e.g., Sullivan, Mitchell, & Uhl-Bien, 2003; Van Breukelen, Schyns, & LeBlanc, 2006).

Still, attempts have been made to describe Leader–Member Exchange relationships along different dimensions, shedding light on the exchange process. The conceptualization of LMX by Graen and Uhl-Bien (1995), which is probably the most influential conceptualization (cf., Gerstner &

Day, 1997, on the use of the instrument recommended by Graen & Uhl-Bien based on this conceptualization), defines LMX as one dimension that has underlying but closely intertwined facets (i.e., respect, trust, and mutual obligation). Based on social role theory, Dienesch and Liden (1986) proposed a three-dimensional approach to LMX. The dimensions they suggested were: affect (a friend-like relationship), loyalty (the assumption that one party of the dyad would defend the other party in front of others), and contribution (to the group goals). Based on interviews, Liden and Maslyn (1998) added a fourth dimension, professional respect (in how far one party finds the other party competent in their job). Similar to the one-dimensional approach, all four dimensions are assessed from a leader's as well as a follower's perspective to describe their mutual relationship.

More recently, Berneth, Armenakis, Feild, Giles, and Walker (2007) introduced the idea of Leader–Member social exchange, bringing LMX back to the original idea of Blau's exchange theory and basing LMX on aspects such as reciprocity, voluntary actions, and motivation by returns.

Independent of how LMX is operationalized, ideally, both leader and follower evaluations of their mutual relationships should agree on a high level and all followers of the same leader should concur in their positive assessment of their respective relationships with their leader. This idea has been introduced into the literature as Leader–Member Excellence (Schyns & Day, 2010). Empirically, however, meta-analyses show that the correlation between leader and follower ratings of their relationship is relatively low ($r = .29$; Gerstner & Day, 1997; $r = .37$; Sin, Nahrgang & Morgeson, 2009). Equally, consensus among followers of the same leader is often not very high (Hofmann, Morgeson, & Gerras, 2003). Achieving what Schyns and Day call Leader–Member Excellence is likely to be even more difficult when the leader is distant, as distance may impact on the knowledge that leader and follower have about each other, thus influencing agreement. Consensus among followers is equally likely to be an issue in large groups as followers may hold different views of their leader depending on different sets of knowledge about him or her.

Leader Distance

Leader distance can be defined along different dimensions such as psychological, structural, and functional distance (Napier & Ferris, 1993). Examples of psychological distance are power distance or similarity;

examples of structural distance are opportunities to interact or span of control; and examples of functional distance are affect and relationship quality (Napier & Ferris, 1993).

Antonakis and Atwater (2002) define leader distance along three dimensions, namely, leader–follower physical distance, perceived social distance, and perceived interaction frequency. Physical distance refers to how far away from each other leader and follower work. For example, remote workers may be located at different work places than their leaders. Social distance is similar to Napier and Ferris's psychological distance and one indicator is status differences. Finally, interaction frequency is simply the amount of interaction leader and follower have in their work.

The reason why distance is relevant in the leader context is the effect it has on the perception of leaders. As Shamir (1995) argues, the perception of close versus distant leaders is based on different processes: Whereas in the perception of close leaders, actual leader behaviour is the basis of perception, in the perception of distant leaders, attribution processes are much more important. Using the example of charismatic leadership, Shamir argues that the charisma of close and distant leaders is different in the eyes of the followers. For example, distant leaders might be perceived in a more idealized way than close leaders.

Schyns, Maslyn, and Weibler (2010) recently transferred these considerations into the area of LMX, using span as one indicator of distance. Their considerations will be outlined in more detail below.

LEADER–MEMBER EXCHANGE AND LEADER DISTANCE

Individual, Dyadic and Group Level Leader–Member Exchange and Leader Distance

As mentioned above, one of the aspects of leader distance that has been researched in the context of LMX is span of control. Establishing and maintaining LMX relationships requires resources, such as time (e.g., Dansereau et al., 1975; Schriesheim, Castro, & Yammarino, 2000). It has been argued that leaders do not have enough resources to establish and maintain LMX relationships with large groups of followers (e.g., Cogliser & Schriesheim, 2000; Cogliser, Schriesheim, Scandura, & Gardner, 2009).

Considering that communication with each follower individually on a regular is a basis to establish and maintain a relationship with that follower, one can easily imagine the problem this proposes to leaders of large groups—a simple lack of time to be able to accomplish this goal. Therefore, the relationship between span of control and LMX is expected to be negative. A recent meta-analysis examining the relationship between span of control and LMX over ten studies found an overall relationship of $r = -.08$ (95% confidence interval: $-.04$ to $-.11$), indicating the expected negative relationship (Schyns & Blank, 2010). Thus, in large spans of control, LMX can be expected to be lower than in small spans of control, though the effect size is only small. Schyns and Blank (2010) report some initial findings that the relationship between span of control and LMX is stronger within a certain range of span of control, thus hinting at a "cut-off" value where a larger span of control has no more negative effects on LMX.

Although these results take into account only one aspect of distance, that is, span of control, similar effects can be assumed for other aspects of leader distance. For example, when leaders are physically distant, it may be equally difficult to establish and maintain good quality LMX relationship due to the low levels of interaction that can take place.

Proposition 1: Leader distance and LMX quality are negatively related.

These results related to span of control and LMX function on a dyadic level. However, span of control will likely influence not only individual-level LMX but also group-level LMX, such as the agreement between leader and follower on their mutual relationship and the consensus among followers regarding their relationship with their leader.

Agreement. As leaders and followers evaluate the same relationship, one could assume that the correlation between their assessments is rather high. However, as outlined above, that is not the case. Several reasons could be responsible for this relatively low relationship and some of them are more relevant in large spans of control and other types of distance. For example, the validity of leader evaluations when having to fill in assessment for many followers is likely to go down. This may be due to tiredness or lack of motivation to fill in the same questions over and over again for different followers. In general, it has been pointed out that leaders' LMX measures are less reliable (Gerstner & Day, 1997).

In addition, when leaders are distant—for example, in large spans of control—leaders and followers may simply not know each other well enough to be able to correctly evaluate their relationship. Thus, we can expect that in high leader distance situations, the agreement between leaders and followers regarding their LMX relationship will be lower than in closer relationships.

Proposition 2: Leader distance and leader–member agreement regarding LMX are negatively related.

Consensus. LMX is based on the idea that leaders and their individual followers have dyadic relationships and that these differ within a group (Graen & Uhl-Bien, 1995). Thus, a lack of consensus among followers with respect to their relationship with their leader was the basis of the develop-ment of this approach and consensus is not necessarily expected (Schyns & Day, 2010). However, different scholars have argued that lack of consensus (or differentiation; Cogliser et al., 2009; Henderson, Liden, Glibkowski, & Chaudhry, 2009; Schyns, 2006) is negatively related to follower attitudes and performance, making it worth considering how to achieve consensus in a group with respect to LMX.

In many leader distance situations, LMX consensus seems difficult to achieve. In large spans of control, leaders will not have the resources to uphold good relationship qualities with all followers (cf., Dansereau et al., 1975). When interaction frequency is low and/or leaders are physically distant, followers may have different pieces of information about the leader and some may be closer to him or her than others, again leading to different evaluations of the same leader. In an attempt to overcome the problem of LMX in large spans of control, it has been suggested that in large spans of control, leaders should target some followers when they cannot maintain good LMX qualities with all followers (Liden, Erdogan, Wayne, & Sparrowe, 2006). However, this will contribute to a lower consensus in LMX among followers.

Proposition 3: Leader distance and consensus among followers regarding LMX are negatively related.

So far LMX was discussed as a unified construct. However, as mentioned above, dimensions of LMX can be differentiated (Dienesch & Liden, 1986; Liden & Maslyn, 1998). Particularly reviewing the mixed results of prior studies on LMX and span of control and the relatively small relationship between span of control and LMX, one can speculate whether looking at the different dimensions of LMX as introduced by Liden and Maslyn (1998) is a fruitful approach to further investigate LMX in leader distance situations. The question is whether span of control or other indicators of distance affect different dimensions of LMX differently. The following section will outline this idea further.

Leader–Member Exchange Dimensions and Leader Distance

Recently, Schyns et al. (2010) argued that span of control influences dimensions of LMX differently. Looking at the different dimensions of LMX introduced by Liden and Maslyn (1998), they argued that some dimensions need more direct re-enforcement than others. For example, in order to develop an affective relationship, leader and member need to be in frequent contact and know each other well. This is unlikely to be the case in large spans of control or in cases where leaders are physically distant. Professional respect, on the other hand, does not need direct contact. Even distant leaders can be acknowledged to be good in their job without the follower actually perceiving this distant leader's performance (Shamir, 1995). Although Schyns et al. (2010) argued that loyalty would also work from a distance, recent empirical results contradict this idea (Schyns, Maslyn, & van Veldhoven, in press). Distant leaders and followers might not feel obliged to be loyal to each other, on the one hand, and, on the other hand, they may have too little opportunity to observe the other party being loyal to feel the need for reciprocity.

Proposition 4: Leader distance affects LMX dimensions differently: While some dimensions are not affected by leader distance, others are negatively related to leader distance.

Summary and Outlook

LMX relationships differ in groups and it seems that in large groups or when leaders are distant, LMX quality tends to be lower. Distance affects individual relationships as well as the agreement between leader and follower on their relationship but likely also the whole group, in that mean group LMX and consensus among followers are lower in large spans of control. Potentially, the relationship between span of control and LMX differs depending on which LMX dimension is in the focus. The question

I want to focus on now is whether or not leaders can influence this relationship. Or, to put it differently, are some leaders capable of establishing and maintaining more high quality LMX relationships than others?

LEADER PERSONALITY

In the following, I will argue that some leaders may find it easier to establish and maintain a large number of good quality relationships than others. Specifically, I will examine the role of leader personality in the relationship between leader distance and LMX. However, having argued that the perception of distant leaders as opposed to close leaders is based on attribution rather than behavioral observation (cf., Shamir, 1995), an important point to keep in mind when discussing leader personality in the context of distance and LMX, is that leader characteristics are subject to similar attribution processes as is leader perception. That means that when discussing leader characteristics, we have to keep in mind that there are two perspectives involved: On the one hand, actual leader characteristics might make it easier for the leader to establish and maintain relationships. On the other hand, attribution processes are relevant in so far as followers attribute characteristics to leaders that go hand in hand with LMX attributions. In the next part of the contribution, I will discuss actual leader characteristics. Subsequently, I will outline some considerations regarding the processes involved in the perception of the personality of leaders, especially when they are not very close. I start by discussing broad personality characteristics, that is, the "Big Five." I will then turn to self-efficacy as one aspect of leader success. Finally, I will consider attachment style as an important aspect of how relationships are built.

Big Five

Schyns et al. (in press) suggest that in terms of leader personality, describing leaders along the Big Five can reveal a personality pattern that is conducive to establishing and maintaining LMX relationships. Specifically, they discuss that extraversion and agreeableness are relevant in the context of work relationships. Leaders who are extraverted and, thus, find it easy to communicate with others and approach others will bring these characteristics to the workplace and will be able to establish and maintain a larger number of relationships than introvert leaders. Similarly, agreeable leaders will find it easier to establish and maintain many good quality LMX relationships. As Bernerth, Armenakis, Feild, Giles, and Walker (2007) put it, "In social exchange, such caring and fundamentally altruistic supervisors should foster both feelings and actions of repayment, ultimately developing closer supervisor–subordinate relationships" (p. 618). While these characteristics in general play an important role in LMX relationships, they also make it easier for distant leaders to engage in LMX relationships: For example, extraverted and agreeable people seem to be able to have more social ties than others (cf., Totterdell, Holman, & Hukin, 2008; Wu, Foo, & Turban, 2008), leading me to assume that leaders with this personality pattern find it easier to lead larger groups and still have a good relationship quality with their followers. I therefore assume:

Proposition 5: Leaders' extraversion and agreeableness moderates the relationship between leader distance and LMX. For leaders higher in extraversion and agreeableness, the relationship will be higher than for those lower in extraversion and agreeableness.

In addition to these general personality traits, more specific work-relevant and relationship-relevant leader characteristics are assumed to impact on the leader distance–LMX relationship. First, self-efficacy will be reviewed and then attachment styles will be considered.

Occupational/Leadership Self-Efficacy

Self-efficacy is defined as the "conviction that one can successfully execute the behaviour required to produce certain outcomes" (Bandura, 1977, p. 193). In the context of work, several domain-specific types of self-efficacy have been introduced, such as career self-efficacy (confidence to be able to address educational requirement; e.g., Betz, 2007), occupational self-efficacy (relating to the confidence one has to be able to handle one's job; Schyns & Collani, 2002) or leadership self-efficacy ("the level of confidence in the knowledge, skills, and abilities associated with leading others"; Hannah, Avolio, Luthans, & Harms, 2008, p. 669). In general, self-efficacy has been shown to be related to work-related performance (Stajkovic & Luthans, 1998), probably as people higher in self-efficacy approach more challenging tasks and persist longer in the face of obstacles than people low in self-efficacy (Multon, Brown, & Lent, 1991), and find it easier to approach new and challenging tasks (e.g., Sexton & Tuckman, 1991). With respect to LMX relationships, I assume that leaders who are more confident about their job—that is, those who have a higher occupational self-efficacy belief—will find it easier to uphold good LMX relationships. There are two reasons behind this assumption: (a) Being confident in their job frees up leaders' resources to communicate with followers, thus, allowing leaders to invest more time and resources in establishing and maintaining good quality relationships; (b) Communication and building relationships with followers is a core part of a leader's job. It is therefore difficult to imagine that leaders who are not confident about this aspect of their job will report high self-efficacy. As self-efficacy is related to success, we can define high-quality LMX here as (part of) a leader's success and thus expect self-efficacy to be positively related to LMX. Empirically, our assumption is supported by prior research on social ties: Johnson, Van Vianen, De Pater, and Klein (2003) found a relationship between core self-evaluations (including general self-efficacy) and the number of social ties of expatriates. Thus, high self-efficacy should be related to higher LMX. At the same time, as indicated above, high self-efficacy is a resource that helps the leader to make more time and space to communicate with more followers. Therefore, I assume that the higher a leader's self-efficacy the more positive LMX relationship he or she can uphold. Consequently, there is a moderating effect of self-efficacy on the relationship between span of control and LMX.

Proposition 6: Leaders' occupational self-efficacy moderates the relationship between leader distance and LMX. For leaders low in occupational self-efficacy the relationship between leader distance and LMX will be negative.

More specific to LMX is the question of how attachment styles impact on LMX relationships, especially from a distance.

Attachment Style

Individuals differ in how easy they find it to establish and maintain stable relationships. This is called attachment style. Prior research has differentiated three different types of attachment style, namely, avoidant, anxious, and secure attachment styles (Ainsworth, Blehar, Waters, & Wall, 1978; Hazan & Shaver, 1987). With respect to leadership, Keller and Cacioppe (2001) reviewed the impact attachment has on manager–follower relationships. They pose that avoidant managers are likely to be inattentive, manipulative, and provide little interpersonal support to subordinates (Keller & Cacioppe, 2001). Anxious leaders, on the other hand, may be attentive to followers as a means of creating dependence, though still not trusting in their competence (Keller & Cacioppe, 2001). Finally, secure leaders "may positively approach their leadership role and express more certainty of their ability to perform well in that role" (Keller & Cacioppe, 2001, p. 72). It is easy to assume that attachment style thus has direct effect on LMX relationships, as avoidant and anxious leaders will find it difficult to establish stable relationships with followers at all. However, in distance situations, for example, when a large span of control can serve as an "excuse" not to engage with all followers, this problem may be aggravated: Avoidant leaders may use the situation to withdraw even more and create more distance, thus, leading to low quality LMX relationships with their followers. Anxious leaders may find it difficult to manage closeness, especially when they manage large groups (and, thus, have many relationships to be concerned about), ultimately leading to those leaders not being able to establish good LMX relationships with many followers. Secure leaders, on the other hand, should find it easier to have (many) stable relationships even in a distance situation, as they do not avoid or worry about relationships, but feel secure about their ability to connect to others.

Proposition 7: Leaders' attachment style moderates the relationship between leader distance and LMX. For anxious and avoidant leaders the relationship between leader distance and LMX will be negative.

Summary and Outlook

Assuming that in leader distance situations establishing and maintaining good quality relationships is difficult, this part of the chapter reviewed how far different leader characteristics might be conducive to good quality relationships from a distance. I argued that some of the big five, notably, agreeableness and extraversion, as well as self-efficacy and attachment styles could be vital for LMX in leader distance situations.

Having argued above that LMX agreement between leader and follower is difficult to achieve in leader distance, I would not assume any effect of leader personality on this aspect of LMX. Unless, maybe, a leader is better in self-monitoring (Snyder, 1987), there is no reason to assume that leader personality influences the agreement between leaders and followers regarding their relationship. Leader personality may, however, be relevant when it comes to follower consensus regarding LMX. Especially, when personality traits are strong and salient, followers may agree more on what the leader is like and, consequently, also agree more with regard to their evaluation of their relationship with that leader. However, given that LMX is often assessed from a follower's point of view and Shamir's (1995) argument that in leader distance, attribution is often the basis of leader evaluation, in the following, I will review some follower characteristics that might be relevant for these attribution processes.

FOLLOWER ATTRIBUTION OF LEADER CHARACTERISTICS IN DISTANCE SITUATIONS

Big Five

Research into personality often looks at the role of distance in how others are perceived. Similar to the above-outlined discussion around perception/ attribution and leader distance, the assumption is that when people know each other well (i.e., are close rather than distant), the correlation between the self-rating of a target person and how others rate that person regarding his or her personality will be higher than for people who know each other less well. Indeed that is the case (Watson, Hubbard, & Wiese, 2000). Interestingly, however, in some cases the correlation between observer Big Five and "target" Big Five are substantial. That means that the observer "sees" his or her own characteristics in the other. This is called "assumed similarity" (Cronbach, 1955). Thus, when a person is not very familiar with another person, the perception of that person may be based less on actual personality characteristics but rather on attributed personality characteristics which are based on the perceiver's own personality.

Therefore, one could argue that rather than actual leader characteristics moderating the relationship between leader distance and LMX, what is relevant—at least for follower-rated LMX—are follower attributions of characteristics to leaders (see also Felfe & Schyns, 2010, for a similar argument regarding the perception of transformational leadership). Based on the results outlined above in terms of assumed similarity, this should be especially the case when followers know the leader very little. Leader distance does not only imply not knowing the leader in terms of one's relationship with that leader but also in terms of his or her actual personality, making attribution of characteristics likely. Therefore, I assume:

Proposition 8: Follower-attributed leader extraversion and agreeableness moderates the relationship between leader distance and LMX. For leaders who are attributed higher levels of extraversion and agreeableness, the relationship will be higher than for those lower in extraversion and agreeableness.

Indeed, prior research has shown that follower characteristics are important in predicting different perceptions of leader charisma (Schyns & Sanders, 2007). Therefore, one could take the above argument one step further: Given that the above proposition is based on assumed similarity, one could argue that, ultimately, it is followers' personality that is relevant to the perception of LMX in large spans of control. Thus, I assume:

Proposition 9: Follower extraversion and agreeableness moderates the relationship between leader distance and LMX. For followers higher in extraversion and agreeableness, the relationship will be higher than for those lower in extraversion and agreeableness.

Follower Needs

Given that leader distance is conducive to attribution processes, it is interesting to regard the other side of the leadership equation in more detail, that is, followers. While—as discussed above—some of the leader characteristics involved in the leader distance-LMX relationship may be more attributed than real and may be based on assumed similarity, some follower characteristics should be discussed independently of their relationship to the perception of leader characteristics. For example, Schyns, Kroon, and Moors (2008) argued that followers' needs might influence the perception of LMX. The argument is that followers who feel a stronger need for relationship at work, simply "see" a better relationship quality with their leader. Similar to the argument above that perception/attribution effects are stronger in leader distance, one can assume that the effect of follower needs on LMX is more pronounced in distant leadership. In this case, followers' perception of their relationship cannot be disconfirmed by regular interaction with their leader.

Especially relevant are followers' needs related to leadership, such as "need for leadership" (De Vries, 1997; De Vries, Roe, & Taillieu, 1999; De Vries, Roe, & Taillieu, 2002). The idea of need for leadership has been introduced by de Vries (1997). He argues that followers differ in how far they perceive leaders as necessary for their group processes. Schyns et al. (2008) argue that need for leadership is relevant in the perception of LMX as followers high in need for leadership tend to perceive good quality LMX relationships in order to fulfil their needs. Indeed, they found an (albeit small) effect of need for leadership on the perception of LMX. With respect to leader distance, two assumptions could be made as to the influence of need for leadership on LMX: First, one could assume that a high need for leadership contributes to the attribution process underlying the perception of LMX from a distance so that high need for leadership would increase LMX from a distance. However, need for leadership could also decrease LMX from a distance as the actual need remains constantly frustrated by a distant leader. Thus, while assuming a moderating effect of need for leadership on the relationship between leader distance and LMX, the direction of the effect remains subject to exploratory testing.

Proposition 10: Follower need for leadership moderates the relationship between leader distance and LMX.

Follower Similarity and Consensus in Leader–Member Exchange

Follower characteristics as discussed here can vary within a group reporting to the same leader. This may be labelled deep level diversity. As opposed to surface level diversity, which describes differences in salient demographic characteristics such as gender and age, deep level diversity refers to differences in values or personality (Harrison, Price, & Bell, 1998). Hiller and Day (2003) argue for the importance of deep level diversity in LMX. This could be related to social identity theory. As Hogg, Martin, Epitropaki, Mankad, Svensson, and Weeden (2005) point out, the focus of LMX on dyadic relationships has neglected the group context (though this is not so much the case anymore in recent LMX research, see above). Hogg et al. argue that depending on how strong the group identity is, dyadic LMX may be more or less effective: When group identity is low, dyadic LMX might be useful, but it is not useful when there is a strong group identity. In this case,

LMX should be directed to the group. Coming back to deep level diversity, one could argue that groups that consists of similar members would have a stronger group identity and thus overall, report more consensus in LMX, than groups with a weak group identity, where there is more disparity in LMX relationships.

Thinking about assumed similarity again supports this notion: one could argue that similar followers are more likely to perceive the leader in a similar way, thus, leading to more consensus among them regarding LMX. The larger the group, however, the less likely it is that all members are similar and, indeed, subgroups may develop that are similar within but different from other subgroups, leading to a more diverse view of LMX.

Proposition 11: Similar followers show higher consensus with respect to LMX in leader distance situations than diverse followers do.

Summary

Having discussed leader characteristics that are relevant for the leader distance-LMX relationship, in this part I argued that due to attribution processes, follower characteristics and their similarity within a group are relevant for the perception of LMX relationships. I discussed the Big Five and the need for leadership but easily other characteristics could be discussed, such as follower attachment style (for a discussion on how attachment style influences the perception of transformational leadership see Hansbrough, in press).

GENERAL DISCUSSION

LMX is related to many positive concepts in the organizational practice (for an overview see Martin, Thomas, Topakas, & Epitropaki, 2010) and, therefore, it is an important question to consider how good quality LMX relationship can be upheld under different conditions. Particularly for LMX, distance can be problematic as it relates to dyadic relationships which are difficult to establish and maintain under distance conditions, such as little direct contact. However, in this chapter, I discussed leader and follower characteristics that might make it easier to establish and maintain good-quality LMX relationships even when leaders are distant.

These considerations have several implications. First, on an organizational level, it may be important to consider how leader distance can be reduced. Large spans of control and remote work may seem useful solutions to tight organizational budgets but may backfire when LMX relationships are negatively affected. However, some LMX dimensions may be easier to uphold than others, therefore organizations could try and focus on these dimensions in distance situations. For example, while communicating affect may not work, emphasizing leaders' knowledge and competence to foster professional respect is a good approach to foster LMX in distance situations. However, Henttonen and Blomqvist (2005) found that communication styles can help to develop trust in distant (virtual) teams. This seems to imply that communication can also affect the LMX dimension of affect in distant relationships. Thus, further research into the perception of LMX in distance situations may inform communication and impression management of leaders. Second, where leader distance cannot be avoided, organizations should carefully select or train leaders to facilitate good quality relationships.

In this chapter, I looked at the relationship between span of control and LMX from a linear point of view. However, especially in large groups, subgroups with informal leaders may emerge. LMX may still be high in those groups but the "L" in this case would not be the formal leader of the group but rather the informal leader. However, organizations and groups can benefit from such emergent leadership as these sub-group LMX relationships still contribute positively to followers' attitudes and behaviours.

ACKNOWLEDGMENTS

Many colleagues have contributed to the discussion around span of control, leader–member exchange and leader personality. My thanks to John Antonakis, Hartmut Blank, David Day, John Maslyn, Ron Riggio, Marc van Veldhoven, and Juergen Weibler for many fruitful discussions. Thanks to Robin Martin and the anonymous reviewer for the helpful comments on a prior version of this chapter.

REFERENCES

Ainsworth, M. D. S., Blehar, M., Waters, E., & Walls., S., (1978). *Patterns of attachment.* Hillsdale, NJ: Erlbaum.

Antonakis, J. & Atwater, L. (2002). Leaders distance: A review and a proposed theory. *Leadership Quarterly, 13,* 673–704.

Bandura, A. (1977). Self-efficacy: Toward a unifying theory of behavioral change. *Psychological Review, 84,* 191–215.

Berneth, J. B., Armenakis, A. A., Feild, H. S., Giles, W. F, & Walker, H. J. (2007). Leader–member social exchange (LMSX): Development and validation of a scale. *Journal of Organizational Behavior, 28,* 979–1003.

Betz, N. E. (2007). Career self-efficacy: Exemplary recent research and emerging directions. *Journal of Career Assessment, 15,* 403–422.

Cogliser, C. C. & Schriesheim, C. A. (2000). Exploring work unit context and leader–member exchange: A multi-level perspective. *Journal of Organizational Behavior, 21,* 487–511.

Cogliser, C. C., Schriesheim, C. A., Scandura, T. A., & Gardner, W. L. (2009). Balancing leader and follower perceptions of leader–member exchange: Relationships with performance and work attitudes. *Leadership Quarterly, 20,* 452–465.

Cronbach, L. J. (1955). Processes affecting scores on "understanding of other" and "assumed similarity". *Psychological Bulletin, 52,* 177–193.

Dansereau, F., Graen, G., & Haga, W. (1975). A vertical dyad linkage approach to leadership within formal organizations – A longitudinal investigation of the role making process. *Organizational Behavior and Human Performance, 13,* 46–78.

De Vries, R. E. (1997). Need for leadership: A solution to empirical problems in situational theories of leadership. Catholic University of Brabant: Unpublished dissertation.

De Vries, R. E., Roe, R. A., & Taillieu, T. C. B. (1999). On charisma and need for leadership. *European Journal of Work and Organizational Psychology, 8* (1), 109–133.

De Vries, R. E., Roe, R. A., & Taillieu, T. C. B. (2002). Need for leadership as a moderator of the relationships between leadership and individual outcomes. *Leadership Quarterly, 13,* 121–137.

Dienesch, R. M. & Liden, R. C. (1986). Leader–member exchange model of leadership: A critique and further development. *Academy of Management Review, 11,* 618–634.

Felfe, J. & Schyns, B. (2010). Followers' personality and the perception of transformational leadership: Further evidence for the similarity hypothesis. *British Journal of Management, 21,* 393 – 410.

Gerstner, C. R. & Day, D. V. (1997). Meta-analytic review of leader–member exchange theory: Correlates and construct issues. *Journal of Applied Psychology, 82,* 827–844.

Graen, G. B. & Uhl-Bien, M. (1995). Development of leader–member exchange (LMX) theory of leadership over 25 years: Applying a multi-level multi-domain perspective. *Leadership Quarterly, 6,* 219–247.

Hannah, S. T., Avolio, B. J., Luthans, F., & Harms, P. D. (2008). Leadership efficacy: Review and future directions. *Leadership Quarterly, 19,* 669–692.

Hansbrough, T. K. (in press). The construction of a transformational leader: Follower attachment and leadership perceptions. *Journal of Applied Social Psychology.*

Harrison, D. A., Price, K. H., & Bell, M. P. (1998). Beyond relationasl demography: Time and the effects of surface- and deep-level diversity on work group cohesion. *Academy of Management Journal, 41,* 96–107.

Hazan, C. & Shaver, P. R. (1987). Romantic love conceptualized as an attachment process. *Journal of Personality and Social Psychology,* 52, 511–524.

Henderson, D. J., Liden, R. C., Glibkowski, B. C., & Chaudhry, A. (2009). LMX differentiation: A multilevel review and examination of its antecedents and outcomes. *Leadership Quarterly,* 20, 517–534.

Henttonen, K. & Blomqvist, K. (2005). Managing distance in a global virtual team: The evolution of trust through technology-mediated relational communication. *Strategic Change,* 14, 107–119.

Hiller, N. J. & Day, D. V. (2003). LMX and teamwork: The challenges and opportunities of diversity. In G. B. Graen (Ed.), *Dealing with diversity, LMX leadership: The Series* (Vol. I, pp. 29–57). Greenwich, CT: Information Age Publishing.

Hofmann, D. A., Morgeson, F. P., & Gerras, S. J. (2003). Climate as a moderator of the relationship between Leader–Member Exchange and content specific citizenship: Safety climate as an exemplar. *Journal of Applied Psychology,* 88, 170–178.

Hogg, M. A., Martin, R., Epitropaki, O., Mankad, A., Svensson, A., & Weeden, K. (2005). Effective leadership in salient groups: Revisiting Leader–Member Exchange theory from the perspective of the social identity theory of leadership. *Personality and Social Psychology Bulletin,* 31, 991–1004.

Johnson, E. C., van Vianen, A. E. M., de Pater, I. E., & Klein, M. R. (2003). Expatriate social ties: Personality antecedents and consequences of adjustment. *International Journal of Selection and Assessment,* 11, 277–288.

Keller, T. & Cacioppe, R. (2001). Leader–follower attachments: Understanding parental images at work. *Leadership & Organizational Development Journal,* 22, 70–75.

Liden, R. C. & Maslyn, J. M. (1998). Multidimensionality of leader–member exchange: An empirical assessment through scale development. *Journal of Management,* 24, 43–72.

Liden, R. C., Erdogan, B., Wayne, S. J., & Sparrowe, R. T. (2006). Leader–member exchange, differentiation, and task interdependence: Implications for individual and group performance. *Journal of Organizational Behavior,* 27, 723–746.

Martin, R., Thomas, G., Topakas, A., & Epitropaki, O. (2010). A review of leader–member exchange research: Future prospects and directions. *International Review of Industrial and Organizational Psychology,* 25.

Multon, K. D., Brown, S. D., & Lent, R. D. (1991). Relation of self-efficacy beliefs to academic outcomes: A meta-analytic investigation. *Journal of Counseling Psychology,* 38, 30–38.

Napier, B. J. & Ferris, G. R. (1993). Distance in organizations. *Human Resource Management Review,* 3, 321–357.

Schriesheim, C. A., Castro, S. L., & Yammarino, F. J. (2000). Investigating contingencies: An examination of the impact of span of supervision and upward controllingness on Leader–Member Exchange using traditional and multivariate within- and between-entities analysis. *Journal of Applied Psychology,* 85, 659–677.

Schyns, B. (2006). Are group consensus in LMX and shared work values related to organizational outcomes? *Small Group Research,* 37, 20–35.

Schyns, B. & Blank, H. (2010). The limits of interactional leadership: The relationship between Leader–Member Exchange and span of control. In T. Rigotti, S. Korek, & K. Otto (Eds.), *Gesund mit und ohne Arbeit* (pp. 305–315). Lengerich: Pabst Science Publishers.

Schyns, B. & Collani, G. Vv. (2002). A new occupational self-efficacy scale and its relation to personality constructs and organisational variables. *European Journal of Work and Organizational Psychology*, 11, 219–241.

Schyns, B. & Day, D. (2010). Relationship-based leadership: Issues of consensus, agreement, and context. *European Journal of Work and Organizational Psychology*, 19, 1–29.

Schyns, B. & Sanders, K. (2007). In the eyes of the beholder: Personality and the perception of leadership. *Journal of Applied Social Psychology*, 37, 2345–2363.

Schyns, B., Felfe, J., & Blank, H. (2007). Is charisma hyper-romanticism? Empirical evidence from new data and a meta-analysis. *Applied Psychology: An International Review*, 56, 505–527.

Schyns, B., Kroon, B., & Moors, G. (2008). Follower characteristics and the perception of Leader–Member Exchange. *Journal of Managerial Psychology*, 23, 772–788.

Schyns, B., Maslyn, J. M., & Weibler, J. (2010). Understanding the relationship between span of control and subordinate consensus in leader–member exchange. *European Journal of Work and Organizational Psychology*, 19, 388–406.

Schyns, B., Maslyn. J. M., & van Veldhoven, M. J. P. M. (in press). Can some leaders have a good relationship with many followers? The role of personality in the relationship between leader–member exchange and span of control. *Leadership and Organization Development Journal*.

Sexton, T. L. & Tuckman, B. W. (1991). Self-beliefs and behavior: The role of self-efficacy and outcome expectation of time. *Personality and Individual Differences*, 12, 725–736.

Shamir, B. (1995). Social distance and charisma: Theoretical notes and an exploratory study. *Leadership Quarterly*, 6, 19–47.

Sin, H.-P., Nahrgang, J. D., & Morgeson, F. P. (2009). Understanding why they don't see eye-to-eye: An examination of leader–member exchange (LMX) agreement. *Journal of Applied Psychology*, 94, 1048–1057.

Snyder, M. (1987). *Public appearances/private realities: The psychology of self-monitoring*. New York: W. H. Freeman & Company.

Stajkovic, A. D. & Luthans, F. (1998). Self-efficacy and work-related performance: A meta-analysis. *Psychological Bulletin*, 124, 240–261.

Sullivan, D. M., Mitchell, M. S., & Uhl-Bien, M. (2003). The new conduct of business: How LMX can help capitalize on cultural diversity. In G. B. Graen (Ed.), *Dealing with diversity, LMX leadership: The Series* (Vol. I, pp. 183–218). Greenwich, CT: Information Age Publishing.

Totterdell, P., Holman, D., & Hukin, A. (2008). Social networkers: Measuring and examining individual differences in propensity to connect with others. *Social Networks*, 30, 283–296.

Vvan Breukelen, W., Schyns, B., & LeBlanc, P. (2006). Leader–Member Exchange theory and research: Accomplishments and future challenges. *Leadership*, 2, 295–316.

Watson, D., Hubbard, B., & Wiese, D. (2000). Self-other agreement in personality and affectivity: The role of acquaintanceship, trait visibility, and assumed similarity. *Journal of Personality and Social Psychology*, 78, 546–558.

Wu, P.-C., Foo, M.-D., & Turban, D. B. (2008). The role of personality in relationship closeness, developer assistance, and career success. *Journal of Vocational Behavior*, 73, 440–448.

6

The Far Side of Leadership: Rather Difficult to Face

John Antonakis and Philippe Jacquart

Following the line that Gary Larson's *Far Side* comics took, we present a surrealistic, though serious view of the "far side" of leadership. We highlight the foibles and follies of the leadership-influencing process, explaining how distance from the leader can produce effects that might seem particularly irrational though which may have some evolutionary explanations (Van Vugt, 2010, 2012). In a way, we present an explanation for the "nice-from-far but far-from-nice" phenomenon.

We put the far side at the core of the leadership legitimization process to explore how *leader distance* affects the leader's ability to influence others. Bogardus (1927) was the first to discuss it, proposing that leaders must be socially distant from followers, suggesting that because of "the extent that leadership rests on sheer prestige, it is easily punctured by intimacy" (p. 127). It may seem that we take an "anti-leadership" stance, given the punchline of our chapter, which is: Leaders who make it to the top may do so, not because of the skills they possess but because they "look the role," and this biasing effect appears to be accentuated with leader distance. How, precisely, does leadership work from a distance? If leaders obtain legitimacy merely by maintaining a distance, is leadership—particulary at the upper echelons where leaders are shielded from followers—just about props and smokescreens or does it actually impact the organization?

Although our chapter takes a leader-distance twist, we will also show that leaders actually have an important effect on organizational outcomes. The fact that leaders are selected for reasons other than the competence they possess to do their jobs brings to fore another problem, that of leader selection; however, it certainly does not nullify the fact that leaders can have good and bad effects on organizations. It all depends on how competent and influential the leaders actually are. Put bluntly, a dumb, extraverted leader who looks competent will not be as effective as a smart extraverted leader who looks competent.

In this chapter, we begin by first explaining leadership and the leader distance phenomenon. We then review some evidence indicating that in distant situations (e.g., political elections), followers seem to inordinately rely on specious factors when it comes to selecting a leader. Next, we discuss the ascription-actuality theory of leadership (Antonakis, 2011), which provides an integrative explanation for these findings, and also to the question of why leadership actually matters. Finally, we review some of the traits which are thought to matter for leadership effectiveness (but might not) and some traits that actually matter for effectiveness. We conclude by presenting an evolutionary explanation as to why, when we select leaders, we may rely on factors which actually do not matter at all.

DISTANCE IN LEADERSHIP

Leadership can be exercised close-up, impacting followers and teams directly; this is the type of leadership that most leadership scholars, particularly those who come from a psychology background, study. However, leadership can also work from far away, whether cascading through an organization via subordinate leaders or organizational structures, or through influencing distant followers directly (e.g., voters) via the media or other channels (Antonakis & Atwater, 2002; Antonakis & Hooijberg, 2007; Jacquart & Antonakis, 2012; Shamir, 1995). Insofar as organizational scholarship is concerned, research on the leadership-at-a-distance phenomenon is relatively scarce, and most of the research on leadership has focused on supervisory, or face-to-face leadership (Antonakis & Atwater, 2002; Hunt, 1991; Waldman & Yammarino, 1999). Of course, leadership is required at all levels of organizations (Minkes, Small, & Chatterjee, 1999), yet it is the top-level, "distant" leadership—that is, leadership *of* organizations (Hunt, 1991)—which might matter most for organizational outcomes (Antonakis & House, 2012). The close–distant continuum is important to address because leader distance determines how leader influence is exercised and the level of analysis at which the impact of leadership will lie (Antonakis & Atwater, 2002; Hunt, 1991; Waldman & Yammarino, 1999).

At the upper echelons of organizations, leaders determine the strategy and thus influence the outcomes of their organizations (Hambrick & Mason, 1984); be it a large multinational firm or even a whole country, there is evidence to suggest that leadership matters (Bertrand & Schoar, 2003; Chen, Kirkman, & Kanfer, 2007; Flynn & Staw, 2004; House, Spangler, & Woycke, 1991; Jones & Olken, 2005; Judge & Piccolo, 2004). Top-level leaders' influence on organizational outcomes is even greater in situations where managerial discretion is large (Finkelstein & Hambrick, 1990; Hambrick & Finkelstein, 1987); indeed, as job autonomy increases, so too does the impact of personal characteristics on managerial outcomes (Barrick & Mount, 1993).

Leaders also impact organizational outcomes through shaping values and culture. Organizational culture originates, in part, from the founders' values; these values influence the selection process in such a way that employees with beliefs, values, and assumptions congruent to those of the organization will be sought (Schein, 1990). The culture then becomes self-reinforcing (Schneider, 1987). Finally, top-level leaders also create culture by setting expected standards of behavior through role modeling (Sashkin, 2004; Schein, 1990). Supported by reward and control systems, the values and culture of the organization channel the leaders' strategic vision across organizational levels, and thus ultimately influence performance both at individual and organizational levels (Antonakis & Hooijberg, 2007; Hooijberg, Hunt, Antonakis, Boal, & Lane, 2007; Waldman & Yammarino, 1999).

Shamir (1995) was the first to provide an integrative perspective of the role of distance in the charismatic leadership process; contributions have been made by others as well (Bogardus, 1927, 1928; Katz & Kahn, 1978; Napier & Ferris, 1993; Park, 1924; Yagil, 1998). Although conceptualized in different ways, feeling distant from a leader can be attributed to three types of distances: physical, social, and interaction frequency (Antonakis & Atwater, 2002). One of the aspects which characterizes the leadership of organizations is a high leader–follower distance on all three dimensions of distance (i.e., "Class 3 leaders," following the Antonakis–Atwater model). Top-level leaders are usually physically distant from most of their followers. Interactions between top-level leaders and followers are often rare or may never occur. Finally, social distance (i.e., status and rank differences) between top-level leaders and followers is usually high too.

One way in which leader–follower distance affects the leadership process is that in high distance situations, followers have very little information about leaders and may be prone to judge them by similarity or representativeness. Tversky and Kahneman (1974) have shown that when making judgments under uncertainty, individuals tend to seek attributes that are thought to be representative of a category; even when just a couple of these attributes are found, the category is triggered (Cantor & Mischel, 1977) and the individual will be classifed according to prototypical indicators of the category. Future judgments regarding the target will remain anchored there even if the observer encounters disconfirming information (cf. Nickerson, 1998).

This information scarcity is akin to what Plato evoked in his allegory of the ship captain in *The Republic*. Plato compared the state to a ship; the governor (captain) of the ship represents the ruler of the state, and the crew its citizens. According to Plato, the crew neither has the knowledge nor the technical expertise to select a competent leader and thus they will choose a captain who may be "taller and stronger than any of the crew, but he is a little deaf and has a similar infirmity in sight, and his knowledge of navigation is not much better" (Plato & Jowett, 1901). Similarly to the crew of the ship, citizens of a state lack the knowledge and expertise to vote competently and thus rely on superficial factors when selecting a leader; consequently states are bound to be oftentimes ruled by incompetent, but "tall" and "strong" leaders. Plato certainly has history on this side on this point (and we leave it up to readers to think of salient examples!).

One wonders to what extent Plato's rather gloomy prediction would be prevalent in modern democracies and organizations. Given the abundance of information which prevails in modern societies, is it reasonable to assume that professionals and motivated individuals—company board members, personnel selectors, followers, or voters—are relatively unbiased by irrelevant factors when selecting leaders? Multinational firms pay large sums of money to specialized recruitment firms to ensure that the best executives possible are proposed for a post. We would like to think that those who select leaders do so on the basis of the leaders' competence and influencing skills and not on irrelevant factors like their looks, their sex, or their height.

We would also like to believe that in politics voters pay attention to the issues, the voting history of candidates (and their parties), the values that they are willing to defend, the previous performance of candidates, their constancy and integrity, and so forth. Yet, political candidates and their parties still spend huge sums of money in campaigns to seduce voters, particularly via media outlets like television, and pay particular attention to managing and marketing the image of their candidates. For instance, in early 2008, campaign costs for the 2008 US Congress and presidential elections neared $2 billion (Oliphant, 2008). Unfortunately, recent research shows that voters, particularly those who are not well informed, are inordinately influenced by candidate image instead of substance as a direct result of television viewing (Lenz & Lawson, 2009). We discuss this phenomenon in detail next, as well as provide a test of Plato's allegory with the boat captain (Antonakis & Dalgas, 2009).

Facing Leadership from a Distance

At this point, we have suggested that distance can affect leadership processes like leader emergence; however, how strong is the evidence? Alexander Todorov and his colleagues ran some very interesting experiments in the context of US Congressional and Senate elections (Todorov, Mandisodza, Goren, & Hall, 2005). Their reasoning was the following: Given that physical appearance is probably the most rapidly available (and probably first) information about candidates, and given our innate propensity to rely on our initial impressions to form judgments, could it be that judgments we make about candidates on the basis on their appearance affect electoral outcomes? In other words, do we base one of our most, if not *the most*, important civic decisions, in part, on appearances?

In order to test this proposition, Todorov et al. (2005) presented naive participants with pairs of faces. Each participant was presented with the faces of the winner and the runner-up of one of the races from the 2000, 2002, and 2004 US Congressional or Senate elections. With no other information about the candidates, the participants were asked to rate the candidates on competence and six other traits (i.e., leadership, intelligence, honesty, trustworthiness, likability, and charisma). Lo and behold, Todorov and his colleagues found that individual-level inferences of competences correctly predicted about 70% of the races! Moreover, these inferences of competence also positively correlated with margin of victory ($r = .44$).[1]

These results were equally valid even when participants were exposed to candidates' faces for only one second! In fact, researchers have found that inference of competence (and of other specific traits) does not change as a function of time constraints—even when participants are exposed to pictures for as little as one tenth of a second (Willis & Todorov, 2006). These results seem quite robust. Indeed, Todorov et al. (2005) found that inferences of competence predicted electoral outcomes even when controlling for all of the other trait-based judgments participants had made about the candidates. Actually, inferred competence was the only significant predictor in the model.

The astonishing findings of Todorov et al. (2005) have been replicated in a series of studies (e.g., Antonakis & Dalgas, 2009; Lawson, Lenz, Baker, & Myers, 2010; Poutvaara, Jordahl, & Berggren, 2009; Rule et al., 2010a, 2010b). These studies have generalized the original findings to other cultures and to other age cohorts, and have ruled out some competing explanations (i.e., the effects of baby-facedness, media familiarity, incumbency, and the ability to infer competence from appearance). For instance, it has been argued that the extent to which political candidates' faces share characteristics of a baby's face is what is truly driving the results. Zebrowitz and Montepare (2005) have suggested that the more that candidates have "a round face, large eyes, small nose, high forehead, and small chin" (Poutvaara et al., 2009, p. 1132) the less they will be perceived as being competent; thus, it is plausible that baby-facedness can explain the Todorov et al. findings. This alternate explanation has been ruled out by a study conducted by Poutvaara and colleagues (2009). Whereas baby-faced individuals were indeed perceived as less competent, baby-facedness was unrelated to electoral outcomes (or positively related, depending on the sample of candidates).

Another plausible explanation regarding the association between judgments based on the appearance of candidates and electoral outcomes has to do with prior exposure to these very candidates through the media (Olivola & Todorov, 2010), even though the participants may not have recognized the candidates. Indeed, the design of the Todorov et al. (2005) study does not rule out the possibility that these results are driven by media familiarity with the politicians. Although participants in the Todorov et al. study were asked whether or not they recognized the face of the politicians they were rating (i.e., judgments based on politicians that participants recognized were excluded from the analyses), it is nevertheless possible that they had been exposed to these faces in the media and that they were simply picking the faces of the politicians who were more recognizable (and thus better known); this bias could be due to availability or familiarly effects (Park & Lessig, 1981; Tversky & Kahneman, 1974). By virtue of holding office, election winners are more likely to appear in the media; also, having a large budget would guarantee more exposure in the media (and a higher probability of success). Therefore, participants would be more familiar with the faces of election winners and thus, more likely to select them.

Studies conducted in cross-cultural settings rule out this possible "familiarity effect." In these studies, participants from one country were asked to select between faces of politicians who had been running for office in another country (Antonakis & Dalgas, 2009; Lawson et al., 2010; Poutvaara et al., 2009; Rule et al., 2010a, 2010b). The design of these studies makes it very unlikely that the participants would have been previously exposed to the faces they were asked to rate. For example, Antonakis and Dalgas (2009) found that inferences of competence (including intelligence and leadership) made by Swiss participants predicted the outcome of French parliamentary elections better than chance—that is, with an accuracy rate of 72% at the individual level—and that inferences of competence correlated significantly with margin of victory; also, participants were college students who rated election outcomes of politicians in another country that occurred while they were in their early teens (thus, it is highly unlikely that the students had been exposed to those politicians). Similarly, Poutvaara et al. (2009) found that judgments of competence by non-Finnish participants predicted the outcomes of Finnish parliamentary and municipal elections better than chance.

Highlighting further how the leader-distance phenomenon may affect leader outcomes, two related studies, led by Nicolas Rule, also suggest that the association between judgments from exposure to politicians' faces and election outcomes can be generalized across cultures (Rule et al., 2010a, 2010b). In a first study, Rule and colleagues (2010a) asked Japanese and American participants to make judgments about Japanese and American politicians. Participants from both cultures made similar trait inferences from the exposure to the politicians' faces; consistent with the Todorov et al. (2005) findings, these trait inferences predicted the actual vote share of the candidates. One difference was found, however, between Japanese and American participants: they did not rely on the same traits to predict electoral success. In other words, whereas participants from both cultures agreed about what the candidates were like, they did not agree on which of the candidates' characteristics mattered the most. Consequently, participants were able to predict which candidates would win in their own culture but not in the other. Given that Japanese and Americans come from very distinct genes pools with substantially different facial characteristics, this result is not that surprising.

In a second study, Rule and colleagues (2010b) used functional magnetic resonance imaging (fMRI) to further investigate the findings from this first study. Similarly to the first study (Rule et al., 2010a), Japanese and American participants were asked to make voting judgments about political candidates from both cultures; however, this time the researchers used fMRI to examine the neural activity of participants. Interestingly, the researchers found that participants' voting decisions about candidates from both cultures were reflected in the amygdala's response, thus providing some preliminary support to the proposition that there might be a common neural basis underlying electoral choices across cultures.

Making it More Difficult to Face

The above results are intriguing; however, are they a real effect due to evolutionary mechanisms that have equipped us to deal with judgment under uncertainty (i.e., at a distance) or is it all an artifact (or a confound) of some other process? We answer this question in the following sections.

It is possible that the effect of competence on election outcomes is confounded with that of familiarity due to incumbency (e.g., Gelman & King, 1990) or other factors (e.g., advertising budget). It is also possible that incumbents looked more competent in the first place; thus incumbency, rather than competence, might explain why participants tend to select the faces of election winners rather than runner-ups. This possibility seems to be ruled out, however, by Antonakis and Dalgas (2009). In this study, the researchers "stacked the deck" against themselves by only using election races in which the incumbent lost. Therefore, the fact that participants selected the election winner better than chance cannot be explained by an incumbency advantage.

The study by Antonakis and Dalgas (2009) is also novel in another regard and their replication of the Todorov et al. (2005) findings had a twist. Instead of recruiting only adult participants to take part in their study, they also recruited children ($n = 681$) between the ages of 5 and 13 to take part. After having played a simulation in which they had to sail a boat from Troy to Ithaca, the children were presented with the same pairs of faces from the French parliamentary elections and were asked to choose whom they would rather have as the captain of their boat (Plato would have had a field day were he alive today!). The children correctly predicted 71% of the races! Note that an additional sample of adults ($n = 160$, mean age 30) also took part in the same game which helped verify that changing the format of the experiment did not introduce a confound. This additional sample of adults also allowed researchers to show that the predictive accuracy of participants did not depend on age. Furthermore, children's predictions regarding the pairs of faces followed the same patterns as did those of the adults (i.e., both children and adults collectively "hit" and "missed" on the same pairs). Note also that Antonakis and Dalgas (2009) controlled for the fixed-effect of pairs of faces.

These intriguing findings also address another potential confound. If actual competence can be inferred from appearance in distant leader–follower relationships, one could argue that participants are selecting not only the candidates who appear to be the most competent, but those who actually are; that is, competent individuals have something in their face that signals their competency. After repeated exposure to politicians who have different performance success, voters learn to associate facial competence with actual competence. However, this explanation is problematic, because if voters were able to detect competency, then all elected politicians would be highly competent (which does not appear consistently to be the case). This explanation is also very unlikely, given that Antonakis and Dalgas used small children as participants. Children have very little experience regarding leadership and in this regard their behavioral choices are closer to "nature," which suggests that individuals might be hard-wired with face-processing templates (Antonakis & Dalgas, 2009; Slater & Quinn, 2001).

To get an idea of how easy it is to guess the winners, we include sample pairs of faces from the Antonakis–Dalgas (2009) study (see Figure 6.1). If you would like to test yourself to see whether you can correctly identify the winner in each race, compare your answers with the actual electoral results presented in the endnotes.[2] Before you do so, keep in mind that the chances of correctly selecting the winner in all five races is about 3 out of 100 (i.e., 0.5^5).

So where does all this leave us? It seems that in distance situations followers over-rely on facial appearance when deciding how to cast their votes. Does that mean that we are forever doomed to selecting competent-looking but possibly incompetent leaders? Perhaps; however, individuals should be able to show some Bayesian updating as they receive more information on candidates. That is, the initial classification can be corrected, although it is usually not corrected enough (cf. Gilbert, Pelham, & Krull, 1988; Jones & Harris, 1967); in fact, recent experimental evidence shows

FIGURE 6.1
Examples of
pairs of faces
used by
Antonakis and
Dalgas (2009).

Pair no. 1

Pair no. 2

Pair no. 3

Pair no. 4

Pair no. 5

that individuals can sway observers by using effective leader influence tactics (i.e., charisma) beyond face effects. For example, pre- and post-training speeches are ranked differently by observers, beyond the fixed-effects of leaders (Antonakis, Fenley, & Liechti, 2011); that is, a person who looks incompetent can still overcome an initial (bad) classification by using effective communication strategies, provided of course that they have the opportunity to demonstrate these strategies.

We will now present a theory, the actuality-ascription theory of leadership (Antonakis, 2011), that provides a theoretical framework in which to interpret these findings. We will also present some evidence derived from predictive models of voting behavior which supports the actuality-ascription theory of leadership.

THE ACTUALITY-ASCRIPTION TRAIT THEORY OF LEADERSHIP

Antonakis (2011) recently proposed an actuality-ascription trait theory of leadership to link observable and latent traits in differential ways to leadership outcomes. This theory provides a framework to understand why simple things like candidates' facial appearance predicts electoral outcomes; it also explains why, despite this biasing mechanism, other leader traits actually predict performance more accurately (and, ironically, independently of whether leaders were selected on those traits). The actuality-ascription trait theory of leadership proposes two routes to leader legitimization (see Figure 6.2): It distinguishes between: (a) traits the leader possesses and which matter for leadership, and (b) those which the leader possesses and which are thought to matter for leadership but may not directly matter (though they might matter in an indirect way, as in the case of physical height, as we discuss below).

The first route, which is the actuality route, is a longer route. If the leader *actually* possesses traits which are predictive of leader effectiveness, these will positively affect organization outcomes and, to the extent that these outcomes are observable, the leader will be legitimized and accorded status (i.e., seen as a prototypical leader). The second route, which is the ascription route, can be thought of as a shortcut. This is the route which is likely to prevail in distant situations. It is a more subtle and sinister route, one which may not lead followers and the organization to the desired

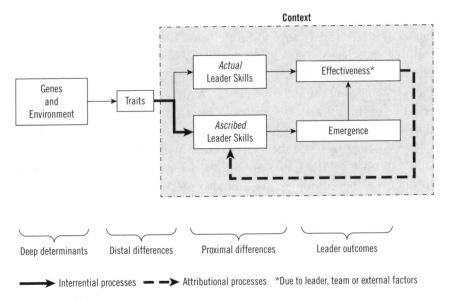

FIGURE 6.2
The actuality-ascription trait theory of leadership (adapted from Antonakis 2011).

destination because the leader might not have the traits that are essential for success. This route stems from traits which are *ascribed* (i.e., imputed) to the leader and which are thought to matter for effective leadership because the leader appears to possess them (i.e., those which are representative of the leader stereotype; Lord, Foti, & De Vader, 1984; Tversky & Kahneman, 1974)—whether this is the case or not. That is, because an individual may look competent, they will be ascribed competence (e.g., intelligence) and emerge as a leader, irrespective of whether they are competent or not.

Consequently, whereas the ascribed route will usually lead to leader emergence, it will only lead to leader effectiveness if the leader possesses traits that actually matter for leadership effectiveness. Furthermore, it is also possible that certain traits, which do not objectively matter for leadership (e.g., height), affect both the leader and followers indirectly. That is, a leader might be more self-confident and/or treated with greater respect to the extent that they are tall, thus gaining credibility and influence; given these conditions, the leader may well become more effective, at least by being able to federate followers around a goal (cf. Judge & Cable, 2004). Furthermore, it is important to note that traits that matter (e.g., intelligence) are not necessarily the traits on which leaders are selected for some leadership positions; and traits on which leaders are selected (e.g., facial appearance) are not necessarily those that matter!

Intelligence is a good example of an important predictor of leader effectiveness (we will discuss this point later); however, it does not always matter for leader emergence—at least, this is what data on US presidents suggests. Note also that, as concerns leadership in general, a meta-analysis indicated that although objectively measured intelligence correlated with objectively measured effectiveness (.35), it only correlated .18 with perceived effectiveness and .25 with perceived emergence (Judge, Colbert, & Ilies, 2004).

Back to US presidents: Imagine you had data on the intelligence of US presidents and on presidential outcomes. If presidents were selected on their intelligence, we would observe range restriction on the measures of presidential intelligence; in other words, there will be very little variance in intelligence because all presidents would be above a certain threshold, for example, above the average IQ of US college graduates, which is approximately 112–120 (Longman, Saklofske, & Fung, 2007; Simonton, 2006). Without variance on intelligence, there cannot be any covariance between intelligence and other variables, and thus intelligence will not correlate with other measures. Dean Simonton has extensively studied individual differences of US presidents and the effect of these individual differences on presidential outcomes (e.g., Simonton, 1988, 2002, 2006). Figure 6.3 presents measures of intellectual brilliance (converted to estimates of general intelligence) and presidential greatness for all US presidents from George Washington to George W. Bush (Simonton, 2002). As is evident from this figure, there is variance on intelligence and there is a significant correlation between intelligence and presidential greatness; this relationship thus indicates that US presidents have been selected on factors other than intelligence (and a fair number of presidents had an IQ lower than average college graduates!). Important to note is that this relationship is not tainted by common-methods variance issues because the independent and dependent variables are gathered from different sources (see Antonakis, Bendahan, Jacquart, & Lalive, 2010).

Two important take-home points to note: (a) US presidents are not selected on intelligence, (b) intelligence matters for leadership effectiveness. If intelligence is so important at the US presidency, just as it is in other performance domains, particularly as job complexity increases (Salgado, Anderson, Moscoso, Bertua, & de Fruyt, 2003; Salgado et al., 2003; Schmidt

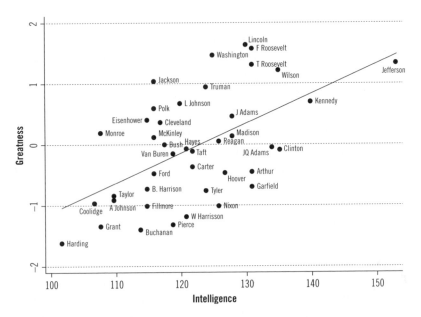

FIGURE 6.3

Correlation between intelligence and greatness amongst US presidents.

Note: Data is Simonton (2002). $r(41) = .55$, $p = .0002$. When disattenuated for measurement error (i.e., assuming a reliability of about .80) using errors-in-variables regression (Draper & Smith, 1998) the standardized coefficient is .69.

& Hunter, 1996), why is it then that US presidents are not selected on intelligence? One possible explanation is that differences in intelligence between candidates are not readily observable (e.g., less intelligent presidential candidates may still appear more intelligent than they actually are through carefully staged appearances). Also, it is possible that voters have a fallacious understanding of the nature of the relationship between presidential intelligence and effectiveness. Highly intelligent candidates are perhaps perceived as aloof, living in a detached world and out of touch with average voters.

In order to understand why the traits on which leaders are selected are not necessarily those that matter, it is important to understand the processes (a) through which traits determine leader emergence, and (b) by which followers use these traits to make inferences about leaders.

Some Not-So-Farfetched Ideas on Judging Leaders

With distance comes reduced information richness. In situations of limited information, individuals are able to make sense of others and of the world at large by using implicit theories (i.e., stereotypes) to "fill in the blanks" and to make rapid and effortless judgments (Fiske, 1995). Concepts (i.e., schemas) are organized around different attributes and the relationships between other concepts and these attributes (Fiske & Taylor, 1991, p. 89). In situations of uncertainty, surprisingly accurate judgments can be made using these schemas (Ambady & Rosenthal, 1992). Individuals also rely on schemas to classify others and can do so using slivers of information that are thought to be representative of a given schema. For instance, individuals develop implicit theories of leadership (Lord et al., 1984) which are triggered by specific attributes of the leadership stereotype or by effects which are considered to be causally related to these attributes. Indicators (i.e., stereotypical proxies) of what naive observers believe are indicative of leadership are associated with leader effectiveness through repeated observations. These associations may be valid. However, at times, it is possible that individuals perceive what have been labeled "illusory correlations" (Tversky & Kahneman, 1974), in other words, spurious associations. For instance, being taller, being a man, being handsome, or perhaps being older, may be stereotypical proxies of a leader. However, whether a tall, handsome, older man is an effective leader will depend on factors which are not readily observable, such as this person's intelligence and personality.

Inferential and Attributional Processes

How do individuals ascribe leadership traits to others? In a recent paper, we have proposed that there are two cognitive processes: attributional and inferential processes (Jacquart & Antonakis, 2012). Although the terms "attributions" and "inferences" are often used interchangeably, they refer to distinct psychological mechanisms (Erickson & Krull, 1999). Inferences are concerned with determining the nature of something (i.e., determining the characteristics of a perceived target), while attributions are mechanisms through which the cause of an outcome is sought (i.e., the cause of a perceived effect is determined). One can *infer* the extent to which another individual is aggressive from the an individual's facial structure (Carré, McCormick, & Mondloch, 2009). One can *attribute* organizational performance to effective leadership, even when performance cannot be traced back to the leader (Weber, Camerer, Rottenstreich, & Knez, 2001)— a phenomenon which readily prevails in the business community (Chen & Meindl, 1991; Rosenzweig, 2007). The ascription route, which we previously discussed, encompasses both these inferential and attributional processes. The ascription route springs from factors that are often specious and this route is likely to be preponderant in situations where leader–follower distance is large. Two paradigms of leadership research—the romance of leadership paradigm and the performance cue paradigm— are particularly important in discussing the role of attributions in the leadership process:

1. Scholars from the "romance of leadership school" have proposed that leadership is mostly an attributional process in which observers attempt to make sense of organizational outcomes by attributing them to leadership (see Calder, 1977; Pfeffer, 1977). This perspective therefore suggests that in some situations followers are susceptible to a romantic view of leaders and leadership, a view in which leaders receive unwarranted credit (or blame) for organizational outcomes (Meindl & Ehrlich, 1987). The proponents of the romance of leadership were correct to propose that observers causally attribute organizational outcomes to leadership (see, e.g., Weber et al., 2001); however, they did not consider how this process chiefly matters in distant situations (Antonakis & Cacciatore, 2003). Also, contemporary leadership research has demonstrated that leadership does in fact matter for individual and organizational outcomes (e.g., Bass, Avolio, Jung, & Berson, 2003; Dionne, Yammarino, Atwater, & James, 2002), and hardline perspectives that suggest that leadership is but a social construction and that it does not matter (e.g., Gemmill & Oakley, 1992; Lieberson & O'Connor, 1972; Salancik & Pfeffer, 1977) appear to be waning (Antonakis, Cianciolo, & Sternberg, 2004; Day & Antonakis, 2012; Lowe & Gardner, 2001).

2. Numerous studies have shown that performance cues (i.e., knowledge of organizational outcomes) influence ratings of leader behaviors and consequently ratings of leadership (e.g., Lord, Binning, Rush, & Thomas, 1978). Weber and colleagues (2001) have argued that the context in which performance cues operate should influence the extent to which observers rely on these cues to form judgments. More

specifically, the more a leader can be observed directly (i.e., in low distance situations), the less observers should rely on performance cues to infer leader behaviors. Antonakis and Cacciatore (2003) specifically tested this proposition using an experimental design. In this study, participants were presented with a vignette description of a leader in which the amount of individuating information about the leader was manipulated (low vs. high) along with a performance cue (good vs. bad). Following the proposition that the effect of performance should be moderated by leader–follower distance, Antonakis and Cacciatore (2003) did indeed find that participants weighted the performance cue heavily in forming judgments about leaders in low information conditions. Conversely, in high information conditions, participants used the individuating information about the leader in the vignette to make their judgments (cf. Eagly, Makhijani, & Klonsky, 1992, p. 17; Heilman, Martell, & Simon, 1988, p. 100; Tosi & Einbender, 1985). These results mirror the existence of both inferential and attributional processes for making judgments about leaders.

We will now present predictive models of voting which provide support for the existence of the two latter processes for leader emergence. Then we will discuss some of the traits which actually matter for leader outcomes and those which are often thought to matter but do not.

Voting for "Far-Out" Leaders

Economic models of voting suggest that (in situations of high leader–follower distance) individuals rely on attributional mechanisms to evaluate leaders (e.g., Fair, 1978, 2009). The central idea to economic models of voting is that of sociotropic retrospective voting; that is, voters considered the past national economic situation when they decided how to cast their vote. This theoretical approach has similar foundations as the attribution-romance perspectives of leadership. On the basis of their evaluation of the economy, voters decide either to punish or to reward the incumbent party to which they attribute responsibility for the economic situation (referred to as the reward–punishment hypothesis). Voters vote for the incumbent party if they judge the past national economic situation to be good; alternately, if they judge the economic situation to be bad, they vote for the challenging party (Lewis-Beck & Stegmaier, 2000).

A prominent example of economic models of voting is Ray Fair's presidential voting equation (Fair, 1978, 2009) which predicts the outcome of US presidential elections—and rather well we might add, given the parsimony of the model—based solely on incumbency and economic factors. What this model assumes is that voters consider the state of the economy and who has been in office for the past terms (the models also control for the effects both World Wars may have had on US elections).[3] The latest specification of this model was estimated using data covering all US presidential elections from 1916 to 2008 (Fair, 2010). We computed the data for the 2008 election, and found that Fair's presidential voting equation explained 91% of the variance of the two-party vote-share; this simple model also correctly predicts the winner in 20 of the 24 elections within the sample (Jacquart & Antonakis, 2012)! This result suggests that attributional mechanisms do indeed play an important role for leadership emergence in distant situations.

This model, however, does not account for the inferential processes we described earlier and which we suggested also play an important role in distant situations. For example, voters do not base their decision entirely on the macroeconomic factors and incumbency; they also care how leader-like the candidates are. We extended Fair's presidential voting equations by including individuating information (i.e., charisma) about the candidates, that is, information which voters may rely upon to determine which candidate overlaps more with a prototypical leader. Charisma is an implicit attribute of effective leadership which is endorsed across contexts and across cultures (Den Hartog, House, Hanges, & Ruiz-Quintanilla, 1999). Charisma should therefore play an important role when voters determine which candidate is best-suited for office. The literature on charismatic leadership has mostly focused on understanding outcomes of this influencing process. However, some researchers have also investigated the antecedents of charismatic leadership and particularly the strategies in which leaders engage in order to be attributed with charisma. For instance, Shamir, Arthur, and House (1994) hypothesized that charismatic leaders have an influence over their followers through their rhetoric. Broadly speaking, charismatic leaders differ from their non-charismatic counterparts both in the form (i.e., framing) and content (i.e., substantive statements) of their message.

In order to extend Fair's presidential voting equation in such a way that it would account not only for attributional mechanisms but also for inferential ones, we included a measure of candidates' charisma in the model (using the Antonakis et al., 2011 nonverbal markers of charisma). If political candidates are indeed more likely to be selected by voters the more they are charismatic (compared to their opponent) this would give support to the existence of the short-cut route that the actuality-ascription theory proposes. Furthermore, this would indicate that voters have developed valid stereotypes of efficient leaders. Indeed, charisma is strongly related to leader outcomes, as the results of several meta-analyses show (Judge & Piccolo, 2004; Lowe, Kroeck, & Sivasubramaniam, 1996). Consistent with the above theorizing, we found that our extended model outperforms the original Fair model. The extended model explains 96% of the variance of the two-party vote share and it correctly predicts the winner in all but one of the 24 elections in the sample period (Jacquart & Antonakis, 2012).

Of course, propositions regarding inferential and attributional mechanisms must consider other theoretical boundaries too (Dubin, 1976). Contextual factors beyond distance may affect which traits lead to leader effectiveness and leader emergence. For instance, national culture may affect the extent to which it is desirable for a leader to exert participative rather than directive leadership behaviors in order to be effective (Kanungo & Mendonca, 1996). An important contextual moderator should be crisis. Indeed, charismatic leaders are more likely to emerge and to be seen as effective in situations of crisis (House, 1977; Pillai, 1996). Michelle Bligh and colleagues (Bligh, Kohles, & Meindl, 2004) have conducted a very interesting study examining how crisis (the terrorist attacks of 9/11) affected the charismatic rhetoric of George W. Bush. The authors of this study propose that the events which unfolded on September 11, 2001 allowed George W. Bush to engage in more forceful behaviors and focus more on inspirational themes.[4]

NICE FROM AFAR, BUT FAR FROM NICE? WHAT *REALLY* MATTERS FOR LEADERSHIP

So far, we have discussed what traits matter for the emergence of leadership and have suggested certain traits that matter for actual effectiveness. To provide a complete account for actual and ascribed processes we briefly present current empirical evidence, which points out two main predictors of leadership emergence and effectiveness: ability (intelligence) and personality (Antonakis, 2012); ability is more associated with actual process and personality with ascribed process. We will discuss the links between these two domains of traits and leader outcomes. Regarding personality, we will discuss two major conceptualizations of personality, namely, the "big five" dimensions of personality and implicit motives. We will then turn the discussion toward those traits that do not seem to matter much for leader outcomes. Finally, we will finish off by discussing the impact of certain physical characteristics on leader outcomes (some of which actually matter for emergence and effectiveness, both directly and indirectly as the ascription-actuality theory suggests).

General Intelligence

As suggested previously, top-level leaders (e.g., US presidents) might not be selected for intelligence, though it appears that intelligence matters for leadership effectiveness. The previous discussion, however, was limited in that the intelligence was not directly measured. When measured directly, there is very strong evidence to show that general intelligence is the single most important predictor of work success (Schmidt & Hunter, 1998, 2004). Links between intelligence and effective leadership have been supported in several meta-analyses. For instance, Lord, De Vader, and Alliger (1986), who meta-analyzed the studies discussed by Mann (1959) in his review of leadership traits, report a correlation of $r = .52$ ($n = 1533$) between intelligence and leadership. Judge, Colbert, and Ilies (2004) report a correlation of $r = .33$ between objective measures of general intelligence and of leader effectiveness. Furthermore, the association between intelligence and job performance becomes stronger as the complexity of the job increases. Correlations between .50 and .59 for US samples (Hunter & Hunter, 1984) and between .51 and .62 for European samples have been reported for low and high complexity jobs, respectively (Salgado et al., 2003). Also, as indicated in Figure 6.3, the correlation between estimated intelligence of US presidents and job performance is very high ($r = .69$).

The Big Five Dimensions of Personality

Currently, the prevailing model of personality is organized around five traits (Goldberg, 1990): openness, conscientiousness, extraversion, agreeableness and neuroticism. It is noteworthy that the big five dimensions of personality are generally orthogonal to general intelligence, with the exception of openness which is modestly, albeit significantly, correlated with general intelligence (Goff & Ackerman, 1992) and that consequently, they may be used in combination with intelligence as predictors of leadership outcomes. We will briefly describe these five dimensions and note the meta-analytic correlations between them and leadership emergence and effectiveness, as reported by Judge, Ilies, Bono, & Gerhardt (2002). We report two coefficients—the first is with leader emergence, the second with leader effectiveness (coefficients which are underlined are significant at the alpha .05 level and within an 80% credibility intervals):

1. Openness ($r = \underline{.24}$ and $\underline{.24}$) includes having many interests, being curious, unconventional, imaginative, aesthetic, and open to emotions. Because leaders are expected to be visionary and think in novel ways, openness should theoretically be an important predictor of leadership.
2. Conscientiousness ($r = \underline{.33}$, and .16) includes being deliberative and dependable, being self-confident and self-disciplined, being orderly, and goal-orientated. Conscientiousness is most likely to be desirable for effective leadership.
3. Extraversion ($r = \underline{.33}$ and $\underline{.24}$) revolves around being assertive, active, adventurous, and gregarious. From a theoretical point of view, and given the fact that leadership must federate individuals and demonstrate constancy (i.e., by having a certain level of dominance), this factor is probably the most important personality predictor of leadership.
4. Agreeableness ($r = .05$, $.21$) includes being frank, compliant, softhearted, modest, having compassion, and being trustful of others. Whereas we would expect that leaders should be kind and show empathy, such qualities may make it hard for a leader to confront others or take a firm stand.
5. Neuroticism ($r = -.24$ and $\underline{-.22}$) refers to anxiety, displays of anger, depression, self-consciousness, and vulnerability. From a theoretical point of view, it is desirable for leaders to be low on neuroticism.

Of course, given that the personality factors are correlated, it is important to model their partial predictive effects. As reported by Judge, Bono,

Ilies, & Gerhardt (2002), the big five predict leadership emergence (multiple R = .53), with the following significant factors (standardized partial betas in parentheses): extraversion (.30), openness (.21), agreeableness (–.14), conscientiousness (.36). However, leadership effectiveness is also predicted (multiple R = . 39), though with a different set of factors: extraversion (.18), openness (.19). It appears that for effectiveness, only extraversion and openness matter; evidently, observers are not impressed with very agreeable individuals (i.e., who might not be forceful or assertive enough) or those who are conscientious (i.e., who might be too obsessed with achievement and organization, and who might be prone to micromanaging).

Implicit Motives

Although there is no meta-analytic evidence linking implicit motives to leadership, there is a rich body of research around implicit motives which seems to indicate that leader implicit motives significantly affect leader outcomes. It is noteworthy that implicit motives and explicitly measured traits (e.g., big five dimensions of personality) are fundamentally different aspects of personality that complement each other (Winter, John, Stewart, Klohnen, & Duncan, 1998). Whereas implicit motives elicit a specific category of behaviors, explicit traits determine how these behaviors will come into play. There are three main implicit motives, expressed as needs, which are thought to affect our behavior: The need for affiliation, achievement, and power (of which the last is often measured in conjunction with responsibility disposition, a psycho-social orientation which measures one's propensity to use power in a "responsible" way). Existing research linking implicit motives to leadership outcomes suggests that high levels of need for power, with low needs for affiliation and achievement are predictive of effective leadership (Antonakis & House, 2002; De Hoogh et al., 2005; House, Spangler, & Woycke, 1991; Spangler & House, 1991; Winter & Carlson, 1988; Winter et al., 1998), particularly for high-level (distant) leaders; however, achievement would seem to engender micromanagement and ineffective delegation (Antonakis & House, 2002; Jacquart, Antonakis, & Ramus, 2008). For low-level (close) leaders it appears that need for achievement is instrumental, given that success also depends on the result of the leader's individual efforts (McClelland & Boyatzis, 1982).

Emotional Intelligence

Although emotional intelligence has gained wide recognition amongst practitioners, there is, to date, no solid evidence indicating that emotional intelligence predicts leader outcomes. A recent meta-analysis showed that emotional intelligence correlated weakly with transformational leadership, that is, $r = .11$ (Harms & Credé, 2010a). In this study, the authors did not control for personality or general intelligence. When controlling for these two factors, this correlation becomes null (Harms & Credé, 2010b)—see also Antonakis (2009). Readers interested in hearing the arguments of proponents and opponents of emotional intelligence in leadership research can turn to a series of letters published in *The Leadership Quarterly* on this topic (Antonakis, Ashkanasy, & Dasborough, 2009). This construct has also been linked to distance (Antonakis, 2003, 2004); briefly, if in the unlikely event that emotional intelligence mattered for leader outcomes, emotional intelligence would probably work only from close situations, given that leaders would have the necessary social contact to react to followers' emotional states. However, at a distance, leaders cannot be overly "bogged down" by the emotional states of others and at times would need to take difficult decisions (which would be incompatible with being too emotionally intelligent).

Self-monitoring

A meta-analysis has shown that self-monitoring—measuring the extent to which individuals monitor their behavior in public (Snyder, 1979)—is positively associated with leader emergence with correlations varying between $r = .15$ and $r = .27$ depending on which criterion was employed (Day, Schleicher, Unckless, & Hiller, 2002). However, the exact unique contribution of this factor beyond the big five is unclear. Also—and in linking this factor to leader distance—Day et al. noted that self-monitoring might not predict leader outcomes for top-level leaders because high self-monitors "may be less likely than low self-monitors to adopt firm strategic positions or communicate a consistent vision on key issues" (p. 398).

Physical Characteristics: Height, Sex, and Age

As we discussed earlier, in distant situations individuals are prone to rely on specious factors to make judgments about leaders. The physical characteristics of leaders form readily available information that affects leadership emergence even though it may not (directly) matter for leadership effectiveness. Among the physical characteristics which affect leader outcomes are height, sex, and age. Indeed, Judge and Cable (2004) report significant meta-analytic correlations between height and performance ($r = .18$), height and income ($r = .24$), and height and leader emergence ($r = .24$). Although height correlates (weakly) with intelligence (Sundet, Tambs, Harris, Magnus, & Torjussen, 2005), which could indicate that taller leaders are actually smarter (due to a common genetic cause), it is more probable that the above meta-analytic correlations illustrate how the ascription route can lead back to the actuality route. Indeed, because taller individuals have a higher status, this probably affects their esteem (the correlation between esteem and height is .41), which thus makes taller leaders feel more efficacious and ultimately they become better leaders (possibly also because followers may believe that taller leaders are more self-efficacious, and may thus provide more currency and support for taller leaders).

Sex also affects leader outcomes. Indeed, leadership is stereotypically defined by masculine attributes which has a doubly binding effect on women seeking leadership roles (Eagly & Johannesen-Schmidt, 2001). Indeed, if women behave as women (i.e., they do not act agentic) they will be perceived as not possessing the attributes of a leader, and if women behave as men to match the leader prototype, they are perceived as displaying gender-incongruent behaviors and are thus disliked. Research also shows that in distance situations (where information uncertainty is high) women are evaluated in stereotypical ways; however, as more individuating information is provided to the observer, ratings of observers become more accurate (Heilman & Haynes, 2005).

Finally, age also affects leader outcomes. Indeed, age is a good proxy for experience (Antonakis, 2012). However, the implicit and often fallacious assumption is that individuals learn from their experience and thus that older individuals are more competent (given that age does indeed correlate with managerial experience, r = .53; Ostroff, Atwater, & Feinberg, 2004). Existing empirical evidence actually points toward a *negative* relationship between experience and leader effectiveness (Fiedler, 1970; Ostroff et al., 2004)! It is actually very difficult to learn in performance environments that do not provide direct and immediate feedback (Summers, Williamson, & Read, 2004). Thus, where individuating information is lacking, individuals reason by representativeness (Tversky & Kahneman, 1974, by stereotyping) and may select an older person for a leadership position, even though that person might not have the right characteristics to be successful.

CONCLUSION

We presented a theoretical explanation, as well as reviewing empirical papers, about how distance affects leadership influence processes. We trust that readers found our explanations interesting. One aspect that we did not cover, however, is the following: *Why* do observers rely on seemingly "Neanderthal-type" factors to make leadership judgments (e.g., having a proclivity to choose those who are tall, male, older, etc. for leadership roles)? We may have given it away by how we posed the question! We conclude with a very short explanation from evolutionary psychology which may provide some interesting answers to this question. Specifically, we think that the *mismatch hypothesis* provides the best explanation (Van Vugt, 2010; Van Vugt, Hogan, & Kaiser, 2008).

Mark van Vugt and colleagues (Van Vugt, 2010; Van Vugt, Johnson, Kaiser, & O'Gorman, 2008) suggest that over millions of years of living in small, egalitarian tribes with our kin, humans' genes adapted to the then prevailing form of leadership (Van Vugt, 2012). However, humans are now confronted with a mismatch between our evolutionary leadership psychology and what is required by modern leadership. Such a mismatch may come in the form of our preference for characteristics that are readily observable in leaders: that is, leaders are men, who are taller, who are better looking, and who are older. Apparently, these characteristics were well adapted for our ancestors, where mostly brawn and not much brains were needed for survival. Nowadays though, these characteristics are irrelevant for leadership; these traits do not actually (i.e., objectively) matter for leader outcomes, though others, which are not easily observable (e.g., intelligence) do.

As our review of the literature shows, it is highly likely that in the absence of individuating information about potential leaders, individuals choose leaders who have qualities that would have been valuable in ancestral times but do not matter today. Thus, it is imperative that we develop accurate selection systems and processes to ensure that evaluations downplay "outside" characteristics and focus on "inside" characteristics; the stakes are just too high nowadays. Although the stereotypical qualities sought may have had some adaptive function for our ancestors, for example, having domain-specific expertise (which would have correlated with age), or being physically dominant (which would have correlated with height and strength) they are simply irrelevant today in the vast majority of leadership situations. However, our genes have not yet caught up with the current milieu. Given the propensity of individuals to still be biased by our genetic baggage, the consequence of the mismatch hypothesis should thus be particularly evident in high-distance situations (where observers have very little individuating information about leaders, which could allow them to correct initial classifications).

To conclude, we have explored how distance in leader–follower relationships affects leader outcomes by reviewing current research investigating the links between exposure to politicians' faces and electoral outcomes, among other research. We suggested that in distant situations such as political elections, followers are particularly susceptible to irrelevant markers of leadership that are simply unrelated to leader outcomes. We then explained the actuality-ascription trait theory of leadership, showing the routes stemming from leader traits to leader outcomes, and discussing two processes (attributional and inferential processes) that bias observer evaluations of leaders. We also discussed some of the traits that matter and some that do not matter for leadership. Finally, we discussed an evolutionary explanation regarding observer's propensity to rely on seemingly spurious factors when selecting leaders. We trust that our "far side" explanations were not too far off!

NOTES

1   It is noteworthy that the effect of competence on election outcomes remained significant even when controlling for an array of other factors which could theoretically have been driving the results (i.e., familiarity with, or age and attractiveness of the candidate).

2   *Pair no. 1*: Stéphane Alaize (left) lost to Jean-Claude Flory (right) in the Ardèche electoral district, with 42.77% versus 57.23% of the vote. Of the children who rated this pair, 90% chose Flory.
Pair no. 2: Jean Vila (left) lost to Daniel Mach (right) in the Pyrenees-Orientales electoral district, with 44.26% versus 55.74% of the vote. Of the children who rated this pair, 79% chose Mach.
Pair no. 3: Claudine Ledoux (right) lost to Bérangère Poletti (left) in the Ardennes electoral district, with 46.02% versus 53.89% of the vote. Of the children who rated this pair, 77% chose Poletti.

Pair no. 4: Jean-Jacques Denis (left) lost to Laurent Hénart (right) in the Meurthe-et-Moselle electoral district, with 45.69% versus 54.31% of the vote. Of the children who rated this pair, 77% chose Denis.

Pair no. 5: Nicole Feidt (right) lost to Nadine Morano (left) in the Meurthe-et-Moselle electoral district, with 43.74% versus 56.26% of the vote. Of the children who rated this pair, 73% of children chose Morano.

3   The model captures the state of the economy using three different measures: (a) the growth rate of real per capita GDP in the first three quarters of the on-term election year (annual rate); (b) the absolute value of the growth rate of the GDP deflator in the first 15 quarters of the administration (annual rate) except for 1920, 1944, and 1948, where the values are zero; and (c) the number of quarters in the first 15 quarters of the administration in which the growth rate of real per capita GDP is greater than 3.2% at an annual rate, except for 1920, 1944, and 1948, where the values are zero. The effects of incumbency are captured by considering whether the current president is running again and by accounting for the number of consecutive terms the party in power has been in office up to the present day.

4   Bligh and colleagues (Bligh et al., 2004) do indeed find significant changes in the rhetoric of George W. Bush. We are currently reanalyzing this data to test for the causal effect of 9/11 on the rhetoric of George W. Bush.

REFERENCES

Ambady, N. & Rosenthal, R. (1992). Thin slices of expressive behavior as predictors of interpersonal consequences: A metaanalysis. [Review]. *Psychological Bulletin,* 111(2), 256–274.

Antonakis, J. (2003). Why "emotional intelligence" does not predict leadership effectiveness: A comment on Prati, Douglas, Ferris, Ammeter, and Buckley. *International Journal of Organizational Analysis,* 11(4), 355–361.

Antonakis, J. (2004). On why "emotional intelligence" will not predict leadership effectiveness beyond IQ or the "big five": An extension and rejoinder. *Organizational Analysis,* 12(2), 171–182.

Antonakis, J. (2009). "Emotional intelligence": What does it measure and does it matter for leadership? In G. B. Graen (Ed.), *LMX leadership: Game-changing designs: Research-based tools* (Vol. VII, pp. 163–192). Greenwich, CT: Information Age Publishing.

Antonakis, J. (2011). Predictors of leadership: The usual suspects and the suspect traits. In A. Bryman, D. Collinson, K. Grint, B. Jackson & M. Uhl-Bien (Eds.), *Sage Handbook of Leadership* (pp. 269–285). Thousand Oaks, CA: Sage.

Antonakis, J., Ashkanasy, N. M., & Dasborough, M. T. (2009). Does leadership need emotional intelligence? *Leadership Quarterly,* 20(2), 247–261.

Antonakis, J. & Atwater, L. (2002). Leader distance: A review and a proposed theory. *Leadership Quarterly,* 13, 673–704.

Antonakis, J., Bendahan, S., Jacquart, P., & Lalive, R. (2010). On making causal claims: A review and recommendations. *Leadership Quarterly,* 21(6), 1086–1120.

Antonakis, J. & Cacciatore, S. (2003). Heuristics and biases in evaluations of leaders: The effects of uncertainty. *University of Lausanne Working Paper.*

Antonakis, J., Cianciolo, A. T., & Sternberg, R. J. (2004). Leadership: Past, present, future.

In J. Antonakis, A. T. Cianciolo, & R. J. Sternberg (Eds.), *The Nature of Leadership* (pp. 3–15). Thousand Oaks, CA: Sage.

Antonakis, J. & Dalgas, O. (2009). Predicting elections: Child's play! *Science,* 323(5918), 1183.

Antonakis, J., Fenley, M., & Liechti, S. (2011). Can charisma be taught? Tests of two interventions. *Academy of Management Learning and Education,* 10(3), 374–396.

Antonakis, J. & Hooijberg, R. (2007). Cascading vision for real commitment. In R. Hooijberg, J. G. Hunt, J. Antonakis, K. B. Boal, & N. Lane (Eds.), *Being there even when you are not: Leading through strategy, structures, and systems* (Vol. 4, pp. 235–249). Amsterdam: Elsevier Science.

Antonakis, J. & House, R. J. (2002). An analysis of the full-range leadership theory: The way forward. In B. J. Avolio & F. J. Yammarino (Eds.), *Transformational and charismatic leadership: The road ahead* (pp. 3–34). Amsterdam: JAI.

Antonakis, J. & House, R. J. (2012). A fuller full-range leadership theory: Instrumental, transformational, and transactional leadership. *Submitted for publication.*

Barrick, M. R. & Mount, M. K. (1993). Autonomy as a moderator of the relationships between the big 5 personality dimensions and job-performance. *Journal of Applied Psychology,* 78(1), 111–118.

Bass, B. M., Avolio, B. J., Jung, D. I., & Berson, Y. (2003). Predicting unit performance by assessing transformational and transactional leadership. *Journal of Applied Psychology,* 88(2), 207–218.

Bertrand, M. & Schoar, A. (2003). Managing with style: The effect of managers on firm policies. *Quarterly Journal of Economics,* 118(4), 1169–1208.

Bligh, M. C., Kohles, J. C., & Meindl, J. R. (2004). Charisma under crisis: Presidential leadership, rhetoric, and media responses before and after the September 11th terrorist attacks. *Leadership Quarterly,* 2(15), 211–239.

Bogardus, E. S. (1927). Leadership and social distance. *Sociology and Social Research,* 12, 173–178.

Bogardus, E. S. (1928). Occupational distance. *Sociology and Social Research,* 13, 73–81.

Calder, B. J. (1977). An attribution theory of leadership. In B. M. Straw & G. R. Salancik (Eds.), *New directions in OB* (pp. 179–204). Chicago: St Clair.

Cantor, N. & Mischel, W. (1977). Traits as prototypes: Effects on recognition memory. *Journal of Personality and Social Psychology,* 35(1), 38–48.

Carré, J. M., McCormick, C. M., & Mondloch, C. J. (2009). Facial structure is a reliable cue of aggressive behavior. *Psychological Science,* 20(10), 1194–1198.

Chen, C. C. & Meindl, J. R. (1991). The construction of leadership images in the popular press: The case of Donald Burr and People Express. *Administrative Science Quarterly,* 36(4), 521–551.

Chen, G., Kirkman, B. L., & Kanfer, R. (2007). A multilevel study of leadership, empowerment, and performance in teams. *Journal of Applied Psychology,* 92, 331–346.

Day, D. V. & Antonakis, J. (2012). Leadership: Past, present, future. In D. V. Day & J. Antonakis (Eds.), *The Nature of Leadership* (2nd ed.). Thousand Oaks, CA: Sage.

Day, D. V., Schleicher, D. J., Unckless, A. L., & Hiller, N. J. (2002). Self-monitoring personality at work: A meta-analytic investigation of construct validity. *Journal of Applied Psychology,* 89(2), 390–401.

De Hoogh, A. H. B., Den Hartog, D. N., Koopman, P. L., Thierry, H., Van den Berg, P. T., Van der Weide, J. G., et al. (2005). Leader motives, charismatic leadership, and subordinates' work attitude in the profit and voluntary sector. *Leadership Quarterly,* 16(1), 17–38.

Den Hartog, D. N., House, R. J., Hanges, P. J., & Ruiz-Quintanilla, S. A. (1999). Culture specific and cross-culturally generalizable implicit leadership theories: Are attributes of charismatic/transformational leadership universally endorsed? *Leadership Quarterly*, 10(2), 219–256.

Dionne, S. D., Yammarino, F. J., Atwater, L. E., & James, L. R. (2002). Neutralizing substitutes for leadership theory: Leadership effects and common-source bias. *Journal of Applied Psychology*, 87(3), 454–464.

Draper, N. R. & Smith, H. (1998). *Applied regression analysis* (3rd ed.). New York: Wiley.

Dubin, R. (1976). Theory building in applied areas. In M. D. Dunnette (Ed.), *Handbook of industrial and organizational psychology* (pp. 17–40). Chicago: Rand McNally.

Eagly, A. H. & Johannesen-Schmidt, M. C. (2001). The leadership styles of women and men. *Journal of Social Issues*, 57(4).

Eagly, A. H., Makhijani, M. G., & Klonsky, B. G. (1992). Gender and the evaluation of leaders: A metaanalysis. *Psychological Bulletin*, 111(1), 3–22.

Erickson, D. J. & Krull, D. S. (1999). Distinguishing judgements about what from judgments about why: Effects of behaviour extremity on correspondant inferences and causal attributions. *Basic and Applied Social Psychology*, 21(1), 1–11.

Fair, R. C. (1978). The effect of economic events on votes for President. *Review of Economics and Statistics*, 60(2), 159–173.

Fair, R. C. (2009). Presidential and Congressional vote-share equations. *American Journal of Political Science*, 53(1), 55–72.

Fair, R. C. (2010). Presidential and congressional vote-share equations: November 2010 update. Working Paper, Yale University. http://fairmodel.econ.yale.edu/RAYFAIR/PDF/2010C.pdf (accessed January 19, 2012).

Fiedler, F. E. (1970). Leadership experience and leader performance: Another hypothesis shot to hell. *Organizational Behavior and Human Performance*, 5(1), 1–14.

Finkelstein, S. & Hambrick, D. C. (1990). Top-management-team tenure and organizational outcomes: The moderating role of managerial discretion. *Administrative Science Quarterly*, 35, 484–503.

Fiske, S. T. (1995). Social cognition. In A. Tesser (Ed.), *Advanced social psychology* (pp. 149–193). Boston: McGraw-Hill.

Fiske, S. T. & Taylor, S. E. (1991). *Social cognition* (second ed.). New York: McGraw-Hill.

Flynn, F. J. & Staw, B. M. (2004). Lend me your wallets: The effect of charismatic leadership on external support for an organization. *Strategic Management Journal*, 25, 309–330.

Gelman, A. & King, G. (1990). Estimating Incumbency advantage without bias. *American Journal of Political Science*, 34(4), 1142–1164.

Gemmill, G. & Oakley, J. (1992). Leadership: An alienating social myth? *Human Relations*, 45(2), 113–129.

Gilbert, D. T., Pelham, B. W., & Krull, D. S. (1988). On cognitive busyness: When person perceivers meet persons perceived. *Journal of Personality and Social Psychology*, 54(5), 733–740.

Goff, M. & Ackerman, P. L. (1992). Personality-intelligence relations: Assessment of typical intellectual engagement. *Journal of Educational Psychology*, 84(4), 537–552.

Goldberg, L. R. (1990). An alternative "description of personality": The big-five factor structure. *Journal of Personality and Social Psychology*, 59(6), 1216–1229.

Hambrick, D. C. & Finkelstein, S. (1987). Managerial discretion: A bridge between polar views of organizational outcomes. *Research in Organizational Behavior*, 9, 369–406.

Hambrick, D. C. & Mason, P. A. (1984). Upper echelons: The organization as a reflection of its top managers. *Academy of Management Review*, 9(2), 193–206.

Harms, P. D. & Credé, M. (2010a). Emotional intelligence and transformational and transactional leadership: A meta-analysis. *Journal of Leadership & Organizational Studies*, 17(1), 5–17.

Harms, P. D. & Credé, M. (2010b). Remaining issues in emotional intelligence research: Construct overlap, method artifacts, and lack of incremental validity. *Industrial and Organizational Psychology*, 3(2), 154–158.

Heilman, M. E. & Haynes, M. C. (2005). No credit where credit is due: Attributional rationalization of women's success in male-female teams. *Journal of Applied Psychology*, 90(5), 905–916.

Heilman, M. E., Martell, R. F., & Simon, M. C. (1988). The vagaries of sex bias: Conditions regulating the undervaluation, equivaluation, and overvaluation of female job applicants. *Organizational Behavior and Human Decision Processes*, 41(1), 98–110.

Hooijberg, R., Hunt, J. G., Antonakis, J., Boal, K. B., & Lane, N. (Eds.). (2007). *Being there even when you are not: Leading through strategy, structures, and systems.* Amsterdam: Elsevier Science.

House, R. J. (1977). A 1976 theory of charismatic leadership. In J. G. Hunt & L. L. Larson (Eds.), *The cutting edge*. Carbondale: Southern Illinois University Press.

House, R. J., Spangler, W. D., & Woycke, J. (1991). Personality and charisma and the U.S. presidency: A psychological theory of leader effectiveness. *Administrative Science Quarterly*, 36, 364–396.

Hunt, J. G. (1991). *Leadership: A new synthesis*. Newbury Park, CA: Sage.

Hunter, J. E. & Hunter, R. F. (1984). Validity and utility of alternative predictors of job-performance. *Psychological Bulletin*, 96(1), 72–98.

Jacquart, P. & Antonakis, J. (2012). "It's the economy stupid," but charisma matters too: A dual-process model of presidential election outcomes. *Submitted for publication.*

Jacquart, P., Antonakis, J., & Ramus, C. (2008). Does CEO personality matter? Implications for financial performance and corporate social responsibility. *International Journal of Psychology*, 43(3/4), 596–596.

Jones, B. F. & Olken, B. A. (2005). Do leaders matter? National leadership and growth since World War II. *Quarterly Journal of Economics*, 835–864.

Jones, E. E. & Harris, V. A. (1967). The attribution of attitudes. *Journal of Experimental Social Psychology*, 3, 1–24.

Judge, T. A., Bono, J. E., Ilies, R., & Gerhardt, M. W. (2002). Personality and leadership: A qualitative and quantitative review. *Journal of Applied Psychology*, 87(4), 765–780.

Judge, T. A. & Cable, D. M. (2004). The effect of physical height on workplace success and income: Preliminary test of a theoretical model. *Journal of Applied Psychology*, 89(3), 428–441.

Judge, T. A., Colbert, A. E., & Ilies, R. (2004). Intelligence and leadership: A quantitative review and test of theoretical propositions. *Journal of Applied Psychology*, 89(3), 542–552.

Judge, T. A., Ilies, R., Bono, J. E., & Gerhardt, M. W. (2002). Personality and leadership: A qualitative and quantitative review. *Journal of Applied Psychology*, 87(4).

Judge, T. A. & Piccolo, R. F. (2004). Transformational and transactional leadership: A meta-analytic test of their relative validity. *Journal of Applied Psychology*, 89(5), 755–768.

Kanungo, R. N. & Mendonca, M. (1996). Cultural contingencies and leadership in developing countries. *Sociology of Organizations*, 14, 263–295.

Katz, D. & Kahn, R. L. (1978). *The social psychology of organizations*. New York: John Wiley & Sons.

Lawson, C., Lenz, G. S., Baker, A., & Myers, M. (2010). Looking like a winner: Candidate appearance and electoral success in new democracies. *World Politics*, 62(4), 561–593.

Lenz, G. S. & Lawson, C. (2009). Looking the part: Television leads less informed citizens to vote based on candidates' appearance. Paper presented at the annual meeting of the Midwest Political Science Association 67th Annual National Conference.

Lewis-Beck, M. S. & Stegmaier, M. (2000). Economic determinants of electoral outcomes. *Annual Review of Political Science,* 3(1), 183–219.

Lieberson, S. & O'Connor, J. F. (1972). Leadership and organizational performance: A study of large corporations. *American Sociological Review,* 37(2), 117–130.

Longman, R. S., Saklofske, D. H., & Fung, T. S. (2007). WAIS-III percentile scores by education and sex for US and Canadian populations. *Assessment,* 14(4), 426–432.

Lord, R. G., Binning, J. F., Rush, M. C., & Thomas, J. C. (1978). The effect of performance cues and leader behavior on questionnaire ratings of leadership behavior. *Organizational Behavior and Human Performance,* 21(1), 27–39.

Lord, R. G., De Vader, C. L., & Alliger, G. M. (1986). A meta-analysis of the relation between personality traits and leadership perceptions: An application of validity generalization procedures. *Journal of Applied Psychology,* 71(3), 402–410.

Lord, R. G., Foti, R. J., & De Vader, C. L. (1984). A test of leadership categorization theory: Internal structure, information processing, and leadership perceptions. *Organizational Behavior and Human Performance,* 34, 343–378.

Lowe, K. B. & Gardner, W. L. (2001). Ten years of the leadership quarterly: Contributions and challenges for the future. *Leadership Quarterly,* 11(4), 459–514.

Lowe, K. B., Kroeck, K. G., & Sivasubramaniam, N. (1996). Effectiveness correlates of transformational and transactional leadership: A meta-analytic review of the MLQ literature. *Leadership Quarterly,* 7(3), 385–425.

Mann, R. D. (1959). A review of the relationship between personality and performance in small groups. *Psychological Bulletin,* 56(4), 241–270.

McClelland, D. C., & Boyatzis, R. E. (1982). Leadership motive pattern and long-term success in management. *Journal of Applied Psychology,* 67(6), 737–743.

Meindl, J. R. & Ehrlich, S. B. (1987). The romance of leadership and the evaluation of organizational performance. *Academy of Management Journal,* 30(1), 91–109.

Minkes, A. L., Small, M. W., & Chatterjee, S. R. (1999). Leadership and business ethics: Does it matter? Implications for management. *Journal of Business Ethics,* 20, 327–335.

Napier, B. J. & Ferris, G. R. (1993). Distance in organizations. *Human Resource Management Review,* 3(4), 321–357.

Nickerson, R. S. (1998). Confirmation bias: A ubiquitous phenomenon in many guises. *Review of General Psychology,* 2(2), 175–220.

Oliphant, J. (2008, April 9). '08 campaign costs nearing $2 billion. Is it worth it? *Los Angeles Times.* Retrieved from http://latimesblogs.latimes.com/washington/2008/04/campaign expense.html.

Olivola, C. Y. & Todorov, A. (2010). Elected in 100 milliseconds: Appearance-based trait inferences and voting. *Journal of Nonverbal Behavior,* 34(2), 83–110.

Ostroff, C., Atwater, L. E., & Feinberg, B. J. (2004). Understanding self-other agreement: A look at rater and ratee characteristics, context, and outcomes. *Personnel Psychology,* 57(2), 333–375.

Park, C. W. & Lessig, V. P. (1981). Familiarity and its impact on consumer decision biases and heuristics. *Journal of Consumer Research,* 8(2), 223–230.

Park, R. E. (1924). The concept of social distance as applied to the study of racial attitudes and racial relations. *Journal of Applied Sociology,* 8(5), 339–344.

Pfeffer, J. (1977). The ambiguity of leadership. *Academy of Management Review,* 1, 104–112.

Pillai, R. (1996). Crisis and the emergence of charismatic leadership in groups: An experimental investigation. *Journal of Applied Social Psychology,* 26(6), 543–562.

Plato & Jowett, B. (1901). *The republic of Plato; an ideal commonwealth* (Rev. ed.). New York: Colonial Press.

Poutvaara, P., Jordahl, H., & Berggren, N. (2009). Faces of politicians: Babyfacedness predicts inferred competence but not electoral success. *Journal of Experimental Social Psychology,* 45(5), 1132–1135.

Rosenzweig, P. M. (2007). *The halo effect—and the eight other business delusions that deceive managers.* New York: Free Press.

Rule, N. O., Ambady, N., Adams, R. B., Ozono, H., Nakashima, S., Yoshikawa, S., et al. (2010a). Polling the face: Prediction and consensus across cultures. *Journal of Personality and Social Psychology,* 98(1), 1–15.

Rule, N. O., Freeman, J. B., Moran, J. M., Gabrieli, J. D. E., Adams, R. B., & Ambady, N. (2010b). Voting behavior is reflected in amygdala response across cultures. *Social Cognitive and Affective Neuroscience,* 5(2/3), 349–355.

Salancik, G. R. & Pfeffer, J. (1977). Constraints on administrator discretion: The limited influence of mayors on city budgets. *Urban Affairs Quarterly,* 12, 475–498.

Salgado, J. F., Anderson, N., Moscoso, S., Bertua, C., & de Fruyt, F. (2003). International validity generalization of GMA and cognitive abilities: A European Community meta-analysis. *Personnel Psychology,* 56, 573–605.

Salgado, J. F., Anderson, N., Moscoso, S., Bertua, C., de Fruyt, F., & Rolland, J. P. (2003). A meta-analytic study of general mental ability validity for different occupations in the European Community. *Journal of Applied Psychology,* 88(6), 1068–1081.

Sashkin, M. (2004). Transformational leadership approaches: A review and synthesis. In J. Antonakis, A. T. Cianciolo, & R. J. Sternberg (Eds.), *The nature of leadership* (pp. 171–196). Thousand Oaks, CA: Sage.

Schein, E. H. (1990). Organizational culture. *American Psychologist,* 45(2), 109–119.

Schmidt, F. L. & Hunter, J. E. (1996, June 11). *The validity and utility of selection methods in personnel psychology: Practical and theoretical implications of 85 years of research findings.* Paper presented at the Meeting of the Korean Human Resource Managers, Seoul, South Korea.

Schmidt, F. L. & Hunter, J. E. (1998). The validity and utility of selection methods in personnel psychology: Practical and theoretical implications of 85 years of research findings. *Psychological Bulletin,* 124(2), 262–274.

Schmidt, F. L. & Hunter, J. E. (2004). General mental ability in the world of work: Occupational attainment and job performance. *Journal of Personality and Social Psychology,* 86(1), 162–173.

Schneider, B. (1987). The people make the place. *Personnel Psychology,* 40, 437–453.

Shamir, B. (1995). Social distance and charisma: Theoretical notes and an exploratory-study. *Leadership Quarterly,* 6(1), 19–47.

Shamir, B., Arthur, M. B., & House, R. J. (1994). The rhetoric of charismatic leadership: A theoretical extenson, a case study, and implications for research. *Leadership Quarterly,* 5(1), 25–42.

Simonton, D. K. (1988). Presidential style: Personality, biography, and performance. *Journal of Personality and Social Psychology,* 55(6), 928–936.

Simonton, D. K. (2002). Intelligence and presidential greatness: Equation replication using updated IQ estimates. *Advances in Psychology Research,* 13, 163–174.

Simonton, D. K. (2006). Presidential IQ, openness, intellectual brilliance, and leadership:

Estimates and correlations for 42 US chief executives. *Political Psychology*, 27(4), 511–526.

Slater, A. & Quinn, P. C. (2001). Face recognition in the newborn infant. *Infant and Child Development*, 10(1/2), 21–24.

Snyder, M. (1979). Self-monitoring process. In L. Berkowitz (Ed.), *Advances in experimental social psychology* (pp. 85–128). New York: Academic Press.

Spangler, W. D. & House, R. J. (1991). Presidential effectiveness and the leadership motive profile. *Journal of Personality and Social Psychology*, 60(3).

Summers, B., Williamson, T., & Read, D. (2004). Does method of acquisition affect the quality of expert judgment? A comparison of education with on-the-job learning. *Journal of Occupational & Organizational Psychology*, 77, 237–258.

Sundet, J. M., Tambs, K., Harris, J. R., Magnus, P., & Torjussen, T. M. (2005). Resolving the genetic and environmental sources of the correlation between height and intelligence: A study of nearly 2600 Norwegian male twin pairs. *Twin Research and Human Genetics*, 8(4), 307–311.

Todorov, A., Mandisodza, A. N., Goren, A., & Hall, C. C. (2005). Inferences of competence from faces predict election outcomes. *Science*, 308(5728), 1623–1626.

Tosi, H. L. & Einbender, S. W. (1985). The effects of the type and amount of information in sex-discrimination research: A meta-analysis. *Academy of Management Journal*, 28(3), 712–723.

Tversky, A. & Kahneman, D. (1974). Judgment under uncertainty: Heuristics and biases. *Science*, 185(4157), 1124–1131.

Van Vugt, M. (2010). *Selected: Why some people lead, why others follows, and why it matters.* London: Profile Books.

Van Vugt, M. (2012). The nature in leadership: Evolutionary, biological, and social neuroscience perspectives. In D. V. Day & J. Antonakis (Eds.), *The nature of leadership* (2nd ed.) (pp. 141–175). Thousand Oaks, CA: Sage.

Van Vugt, M., Hogan, R., & Kaiser, R. B. (2008). Leadership, followership, and evolution: Some lessons from the past. *American Psychologist*, 63(3), 182–196.

Van Vugt, M., Johnson, D., Kaiser, R., & O'Gorman, R. (2008). Evolution and the social psychology of leadership: The mismatch hypothesis. In C. Hoyt, D. Forsyth & A. Goethals (Eds.), *The social psychology of leadership*. London: Praeger.

Waldman, D. A. & Yammarino, B. J. (1999). CEO charismatic leadership: Levels-of-management and levels-of-analysis effects. *Academy of Management Review*, 24(2), 266–285.

Weber, R., Camerer, C., Rottenstreich, Y., & Knez, M. (2001). The illusion of leadership: Misattribution of cause in coordination games. *Organization Science*, 12(5).

Willis, J. & Todorov, A. (2006). First impressions: Making up your mind after a 100-ms exposure to a face. *Psychological Science*, 17(7), 592–598.

Winter, D. G. & Carlson, L. A. (1988). Using motive scores in the psychobiographical study of an individual: The case of Richard Nixon. *Journal of Personality*, 56(1), 75–103.

Winter, D. G., John, O. P., Stewart, A. J., Klohnen, E. C., & Duncan, L. E. (1998). Traits and motives: Toward an integration of two traditions in personality research. *Psychological Review*, 105, 230–250.

Yagil, D. (1998). Charismatic leadership and organizational hierarchy: Attribution of charisma to close and distant leaders. *Leadership Quarterly*, 9(2), 161–176.

Zebrowitz, L. A. & Montepare, J. M. (2005). Appearance DOES matter. *Science*, 308(5728), 1565–1566.

Section III

Moving Forward: Emerging Concepts and Extensions of Leader–Follower Distance

7

Women as Leaders: Paths Through the Labyrinth

Alice H. Eagly

In an *Atlantic Monthly* article titled "The End of Men," Rozin (2010) described a new type of "alpha woman" and announced the decline of dominant men. Women, she argued, are smarter and more resourceful than men. Although women are not now as well represented as men in top leadership positions, Rozin acknowledged, they are climbing rapidly and doing extremely well as leaders. This prominently published article is a recent instance of a trend that has been out there on the cultural edge since the beginning of the twenty-first century: the depiction of women as powerful and competent leaders. As an earlier example, consider the following statement appearing in *Business Week*: "After years of analyzing what makes leaders most effective and figuring out who's got the Right Stuff, management gurus now know how to boost the odds of getting a great executive: Hire a female" (Sharpe, 2000, p. 74). *Business Week* followed along with a cover story on the new gender gap, stating, "Men could become losers in a global economy that values mental power over might" (Conlin, 2003, p. 78).

This upbeat journalistic view of women's rise is not consistent with commonly observed reactions to women in high places. Consider, for example, the disrespectful treatment that Hilary Clinton received during the 2008 presidential campaign. Especially in broadcast media and internet postings, she was often described as a "bitch" and as "castrating" (Falk, 2010). Speaker of the House Nancy Pelosi was similarly vilified, despite her many legislative successes. On the political right, Sarah Palin elicits passionately negative reactions, with the conjunction of "Sarah Palin" and "hate" generating 40,700,000 hits on Google. Genuinely powerful women, it appears, aren't just distrusted but are feared and loathed by at least a portion of the US population.

The enthusiasm often expressed about women's accomplishments is not easily reconciled with the extremely negative reactions to women who do achieve high positions. The intensity of these reactions to powerful women suggests that gender equality is an elusive goal if it is defined in terms of equality of authority and influence. On the one hand, most Americans prize the equality of opportunity that allows ambitious women to rise, but on the other hand, many do not want to have a woman in authority over them (e.g., Carroll, 2006). The reservations that many people have about female leaders mean that women have a longer and more difficult route to travel to reach positions of power and authority than men do. Even in female-dominated organizations and professions, men ascend to leadership faster than women—a phenomenon known as the "glass escalator" (e.g., Maume, 1999; Williams, 1995).

Women also have a tougher time being successful in leadership roles because of the necessity of overcoming other people's beliefs that being female is a leadership liability. Therefore, if a woman realistically con-templated the distance between the beginning point of her career and the goal that she may have of occupying a high-level leadership position, that distance should be greater than what her male counterparts are likely to encounter, even though she may attain such a position. Moreover, this greater distance should not be symbolized as a highway leading straight to her goal. Rather, to recognize the often obstructed and circuitous paths traversed by women leaders and aspiring leaders, Eagly and Carli (2007a, 2007b) offered the metaphor of the *labyrinth*. Thus, compared with the relatively straight path taken by men, women's progress requires more forethought and careful maneuvering. This chapter considers aspects of this labyrinth—specifically, it considers the sources of prejudice and discrimination against women as leaders as well as the realities of women's leadership styles and effectiveness in leader roles.

ROLE INCONGRUITY THEORY

Prejudice against women as leaders does not emerge from a general dislike of women or a negative stereotype about them. Classic analyses of prejudice would suggest that people disparage women and therefore believe them unqualified to lead. Conventionally prejudice has been defined as a negative attitude toward a social group, which unfavorably biases judgments of individuals and produces inequitable treatment (e.g., Allport, 1954). The error in this type of analysis is apparent in research findings that women are evaluated on the whole quite positively, often more favorably than men. Cultural stereotypes thus portray women as the nicer, kinder, friendlier sex. Even though both positive and negative attributes are ascribed to both sexes, summing up all of these attributes from studies of stereotypes of women and men shows that women are somewhat more favorably evaluated in most tests (Langford & MacKinnon, 2000; Rudman & Goodwin, 2004). This "women-are-wonderful" effect (Eagly & Mladinic, 1994) belies the understanding of prejudice as an overall negative attitude toward a target group. Instead, prejudice must be understood as contextual. It arises at the intersection of social groups and social roles (Eagly & Diekman, 2005). Prejudice thus emerges in relation to certain groups of people occupying certain types of roles, regardless of groups' overall evaluation.

Gender stereotypes undergird people's skepticism about women as leaders. The pervasiveness of gender stereotypes comes from the fact that merely classifying persons as male or female automatically evokes masculine or feminine qualities (e.g., Banaji & Hardin, 1996; Ito & Urland, 2003). According to research in the United States and many other nations, people expect men to be agentic—assertive, dominant, competent, competitive, and authoritative. In contrast, people expect women to be communal—warm, supportive, kind, socially sensitive, and helpful (Diekman & Eagly, 2000; Newport, 2001; Williams & Best, 1990). These mental associations, or stereotypes, can be influential even when people are unaware of them (e.g., Sczesny & Kühnen, 2004).

The tendency to regard women as the nicer, kinder sex qualifies them for social roles that are thought to favor such qualities—particularly for the homemaker role and paid employment in service occupations and other jobs that especially reward cooperative social interaction (e.g., secretaries and administrative assistants, store clerks, nurses, teachers). The positive attributes that are ascribed more to women than men are not regarded as the most important qualifications for leadership roles. Instead, assertive, agentic qualities stereotypical of men are more strongly associated with leaders (Koenig, Eagly, Mitchell, & Ristikaari, 2011).

These widely shared ideas about men and women do not imply superficial or unimportant masculine and feminine traits. Rather, people essentialize gender by believing that behavioral sex differences reflect deep underlying essences that are inherent but different in women and men (Prentice & Miller, 2006). Demonstrating this gender essentialism, research on 40 social categories found that female and male categories were judged as among the most natural, necessary, immutable, discrete, and stable, with female the most essentialized of all categories. Gender is thus the prime example of human *natural kind* categories (Haslam, Rothschild, & Ernst, 2000). Therefore, for many observers, a woman as president of the United States or CEO of a large corporation seems not just unexpected but unnatural. Moreover, this idea that gender has an underlying essence that makes men and women different emerges early in childhood (Gelman, 2003). The implications of these differences for leadership are apparent early in development, with children commonly expressing serious doubts about women's interest in and competence for leadership (e.g., Bigler, Arthur, Hughes, & Patterson, 2008).

Prejudice against women as leaders follows from the incongruity that people often perceive between the characteristics typically ascribed to women and the typical requirements of leader roles (Eagly & Karau, 2002; see also Burgess & Borgida, 1999; Heilman, 2001). Role incongruity for women as leaders follows from the disjunction between those communal qualities believed to be intrinsic to the female sex and the mainly agentic qualities that people believe are required to succeed as a leader. This incongruity takes the form of *cultural distance* between consensually defined concepts of women and leadership, whereas cultural closeness exists between men and leadership. Thus, to the many distance concepts invoked in the chapters of this volume, I propose the concept of cultural distance, defined as the distance between cultural stereotypes that are applied to the same person, in the manner that concepts of women and leaders are applied to women who occupy or attempt to occupy a leader role.

Consistent with this idea that prejudice resides at the intersection of a group's stereotype and the requirements of roles that group members attempt to occupy, Eagly and Karau (2002) proposed a *role incongruity theory* of prejudice toward female leaders, which is an extension of the social role theory of sex differences and similarities (Eagly, 1987). In this analysis, the beliefs commonly held about the characteristics of women and men comprise two types of expectations: *descriptive norms* (or *descriptive stereotypes*), which are consensual expectations about what members of a social group actually do, and *injunctive norms* (or *prescriptive stereotypes*), which are consensual expectations about what group members ought to do or ideally would do (Cialdini & Trost, 1998). The term *gender role* refers to both the descriptive and the injunctive expectations associated with women and men.

Stereotypes based on race, ethnicity, and other group memberships can further complicate women's leadership (Eagly & Chin, 2010). For example, Black women are stereotyped as assertive and independent and are seen as more masculine in general than White women (Goff, Thomas, & Jackson, 2008). This finding suggests that Black women should experience less role incongruity in relation to leadership positions than White women do. Alternatively, Black women may experience discrimination based on race and gender, creating a more complex form of discrimination (Bowleg, 2008; Sanchez-Hucles & Davis, 2010). In particular, Black women may encounter backlash from Whites, perhaps especially from White men, because they are perceived as *too* masculine.

Evidence for Role Incongruity

The claim of role incongruity theory that the female gender is inconsistent with leader roles enjoys abundant empirical support (Koenig et al., 2011). Specifically, beliefs about leaders are more similar to beliefs about men than women, as Schein (1973, 2001) demonstrated in studies in her *think manager, think male paradigm.* In Schein's studies, participants rated men, women, or successful middle managers on a large list of gender-stereo-typical traits. A correlational analysis was then conducted on the ratings to determine whether leaders' traits are more similar to—that is, more highly correlated with—the traits of men or women. In a related *agency-communion paradigm* (Powell & Butterfield, 1979), participants rated leaders on agentic and communal traits. These ratings were analyzed to determine whether leaders were viewed as relatively more communal or agentic. Similarly, other researchers have assessed gender stereotypes about leaders by having participants rate various types of leader and managerial occupations on bipolar scales measuring masculinity versus femininity (Shinar, 1975).

A meta-analysis has examined the findings of the studies that implemented these three methods of investigating the perceived masculinity of leaders—that is, the studies in the think-manager, think-male paradigm, the agency–community paradigm, and the masculinity–femininity paradigm (Koenig et al., 2011). This project established that leadership is decidedly masculine in its cultural construal. Depending on the research paradigm, leaders were viewed as more similar to men than women (e.g., Schein, 1973), more agentic than communal (e.g., Powell & Butterfield, 1979), and more masculine than feminine (e.g., Shinar, 1975). These effects were large and robust across multiple studies.

Implications of Role Incongruity

The implications for women of this large cultural distance between women and leaders are profound: As exemplified by the negative reactions that powerful women often receive, women do not typically impress others as especially qualified for leadership. Even those women who possess objectively excellent qualifications generally have to overcome preconceptions that they are not well equipped to lead. Moreover, the descriptive aspects of gender roles can act as self-fulfilling prophecies that compromise women's leadership. Knowing that others hold particular expectations about one's behavior can elicit confirmation of these expectations (see review by Geis, 1993). For example, if a friend or colleague thinks that a woman is too shy and unassertive to be an effective manager, these expectations can undermine her self-confidence and influence her behavior in a stereotype-confirming direction. One form of this undermining is that women can lose interest in putting themselves forward as potential leaders. Such an effect appeared in experiments on *stereotype threat* in which presenting participants with gender stereotypical portrayals of women prior to a group task caused the women (but not the men) to express less interest in becoming the group leader and more interest in taking a follower role (Davies, Spencer, & Steele, 2005). Although sometimes women show reactance rather than vulnerability when stereotypes of women's inferior leadership ability are blatantly activated, resisting stereotype threat appears to be unlikely when a woman is in an all-male or mixed-sex group (compared with an all-female group; see Hoyt, Johnson, Murphy, & Skinnell, 2010).

Descriptive stereotypes also limit the kinds of leadership positions that women are likely to achieve. In particular, women attain fewer line-management positions than their male counterparts, thus giving women less access to positions that yield responsibility for profit and loss (Catalyst, 2004; Galinsky et al., 2003). Women more often hold staff management positions, which confer less authority than those of men even when controlling for job status, education, and experience (Smith, 2002). Women managers also are less likely than men to gain appropriately demanding assignments, known as *developmental job experience* (e.g., Lyness & Thompson, 2000; Ohlott, Ruderman, & McCauley, 1994). Experimental evidence has shown that women often end up doing work that is simpler than what men do and therefore more boring, repetitive, and less likely to yield recognition for outstanding accomplishment (e.g., De Pater et al., 2009).

Despite women's difficulties in achieving interesting assignments, they are *more* likely than men to be given highly risky assignments that often produce failures, a phenomenon known as the *glass cliff* (Ryan & Haslam, 2007). Based on archival research on firms in the United Kingdom (Ryan & Haslam, 2005), women were more likely than men to be appointed to leadership positions for companies experiencing downturns in stock market performance (see also Haslam, Ryan, Kulich, Trojanowski, & Atkins, 2010). These riskier assignments—for example, in companies in crisis—are less likely to advance their careers because good outcomes are relatively uncommon (Bruckmüller & Branscombe, 2010). Also, in the political area, the electoral opportunities of women (vs. men) more often emerge in relation to seats or offices that are more difficult to win because of the strength of the opposition party (see Ryan, Haslam, & Kulich, 2010). Moreover, even though women managers may receive credit for their successful performance by gaining increased charisma and ascription of leadership ability, their successes seem not to have as direct implications for increased pay as the successes of men (Kulich, Ryan, & Haslam, 2007).

Although the descriptive aspects of gender roles can cause women to retreat from leadership and produce difficulty in attaining career-enhancing assignments, their prescriptive aspects place competing demands on women who do occupy leader roles. Such women often face a double bind (Eagly & Carli, 2007a, 2007b), given that the cultural prescriptions for women emphasize being especially communal while the prescriptions for most leadership roles emphasize being especially agentic. The resulting dilemma is that communal female leaders may be criticized for not being tough enough and not taking charge, and agentic female leaders may be criticized for not being nice or considerate enough. In many people's perceptions, if a woman confirms her gender stereotype, she is not acting as a proper leader, but if she confirms the leader stereotype, she is not acting as a good woman. Violating either of these culturally distant stereotypes can produce dislike of women leaders and lower evaluations of their performance (e.g., Eagly &

Karau, 2002; Heilman, Wallen, Fuchs, & Tamkins, 2004). Female leaders can alleviate this dilemma to some extent by exhibiting both agentic and communal behavior, but finding the right androgynous mix of behaviors is not an easy task (Johnson, Murphy, Zewdie, & Reichard, 2008; see also Eagly & Carli, 2007a).

Demonstrating the devaluation of especially assertive women, a meta-analysis of experiments that varied the sex of leaders while holding their other attributes constant found that the women were evaluated less favorably than the men, despite their objective equivalence. This devaluation of women leaders was particularly pronounced when their behaviors were stereotypically masculine, especially when they were autocratic or directive (mean $d = 0.30$; Eagly, Makhijani, & Klonsky, 1992). Thus, a male manager who takes charge in a forceful, assertive manner is generally regarded as behaving appropriately and merely displaying leadership, whereas a female manager who behaves in exactly the same way is vulnerable to being regarded as pushy and unpleasant. For example, women receive more negative reactions than men do when they discipline subordinates (Atwater, Carey, & Waldman, 2001). Paradoxically, male managers appear to suffer no penalty when they manifest culturally feminine collaborative and democratic leader behavior (Eagly et al., 1992).

Because women can be criticized for being both like and unlike leaders, they can find leadership challenging. These difficulties emerge very clearly when women attempt to exert influence (see Carli, 2001). Influence, or the ability to affect the beliefs or behaviors of others, is essential to effective leadership, but the double bind can produce resistance to women's influence, especially in masculine settings. People can resist a woman manager because she just doesn't seem all that nice or likable, or they can resist her because she seems insufficiently forceful, so she is not respected as a leader. Yet people have greater influence if they are both respected and liked. Overcoming this double bind to become an influential and effective leader thus requires a skillful balancing act (Eagly & Carli, 2007a).

In sum, the descriptive aspects of cultural stereotyping make it more difficult for women than men to obtain leader roles in the first place. Once a woman has successfully met this challenge, the prescriptive aspects of stereotyping become critical by producing conflicting expectations concerning how she should behave. The challenge for women is thus to be agentic enough to fulfill expectations about the leader role but communal enough to fulfill expectations about women (Eagly & Karau, 2002).

CONTEMPORARY MODELS OF GOOD LEADERSHIP: DOES GENDER MATTER?

Given the considerable cultural distance between leadership roles and the female gender role, the scientific and popular focus on women's leadership styles is not surprising. Women leaders themselves report that it is a definite challenge to achieve an appropriate and effective leadership style, especially one that is acceptable to their male colleagues. Demonstrating this concern, a study of women executives in the *Fortune* 1000 found that 96% rated as *critical* or *fairly important* that they develop a style with which male managers are comfortable, with comparable percentages emerging in similar surveys in Canada (90%) and the United Kingdom (94%; Catalyst, 2000).

Democratic, Participative Versus Autocratic, Directive Leadership

What are the attributes of the leadership styles that women commonly display? To answer this question, meta-analyses have compared female and male leadership styles in studies of women and men in the same or similar leadership roles. The studies are generally based on behavioral ratings of leaders, often by leaders' subordinates but sometimes by their superiors, peers or by leaders themselves or researchers. The first of these meta-analyses reviewed the classic leadership-style research, which featured measures of style that distinguished between task-oriented and relationship-oriented styles as well as between autocratic and democratic styles (Eagly & Johnson, 1990; see also follow-up meta-analysis by Van Engen & Willemsen, 2004). Except for college students serving as leaders in laboratory experiments, the findings did not support gender stereotypes by showing that women lead in an interpersonally oriented style and men in a task-oriented style. The major difference between female and male leaders was that the women tended on the average to adopt a somewhat more democratic or participative style and a less autocratic or directive style than the men (mean $d = 0.22$). However, this difference became smaller in more male-dominated leadership roles, in which the women and men were very similar. Apparently, without a critical mass of women to affirm the legitimacy of a more culturally feminine, collaborative style, women leaders tend to opt for styles typical of their male colleagues.

One reason that a sex difference did emerge on autocratic versus democratic styles may be that women gain more acceptance as leaders when they share power with subordinates and colleagues by being at least somewhat participative and collaborative. Because an autocratic, directive style violates prescriptive norms about how women should act, female managers may learn that resistance to their leadership lessens if they adopt a more collaborative style. However, it is not clear that such a style is necessarily more effective in general than a more autocratic and directive style. Research has shown that the effectiveness of autocratic and democratic styles is contingent on various features of group and organizational environments (see meta-analyses by Foels, Driskell, Mullen, & Salas, 2000; Gastil, 1994). Although in some situations autocratic and directive styles tend to be effective, this effectiveness may be curtailed for women because the constraints of the double bind produce resentment and dislike of autocratic women. Relevant to this issue are cultural differences in expectations for more autocratic versus participative leadership styles (Ayman & Korabik, 2010). In cultures favoring autocratic leadership, women may find leadership especially challenging because they are not allowed to enact this style.

Transformational, Transactional, and Laissez-Faire Leadership

Interest in women's styles of leadership in recent years has centered on *transformational leadership* as a contemporary and valued mode of exercising authority (see Avolio, 1999; Bass, 1998;). In the past twenty years, leadership in the United States and perhaps other nations appears to have undergone a shift toward more complex models that emphasize the importance of leaders' multiple interconnections with individuals and groups within and outside their own organization (e.g., Lipman-Blumen, 2000). Researchers' interest in transformational leadership reflects this shift, and this mode of leadership has become quite widely accepted as a model of good managerial practices. Moreover, research has shown that transformational leadership is correlated with leaders' effectiveness (see meta-analysis by Judge & Piccolo, 2004).

Transformational leadership involves functioning as a role model by gaining followers' trust and confidence (see Table 7.1). Such leaders state future goals, develop plans to attain them, and consider new solu-

TABLE 7.1

Definitions of Transformational, Transactional, and Laissez-Faire Leadership Styles in the MLQ

Type of MLQ Scale and Subscale	Description of Leadership Style
Transformational	
Idealized influence (attribute)	Demonstrates qualities that motivate respect and pride from association with him or her
Idealized influence (behavior)	Communicates values, purpose, and importance of organization's mission
Inspirational motivation	Exhibits optimism and excitement about goals and future states
Intellectual stimulation	Examines new perspectives for solving problems and completing tasks
Individualized consideration	Focuses on development and mentoring of followers and attends to their individual needs
Transactional	
Contingent reward	Provides rewards for satisfactory performance by followers
Active management-by-exception	Attends to followers' mistakes and failures to meet standards
Passive management-by-exception	Waits until problems become severe before attending to them and intervening
Laissez-faire	Exhibits frequent absence and lack of involvement during critical junctures

Source: A. H. Eagly, M. C. Johannesen-Schmidt, & M. van Engen, Transformational, transactional, and laissez-faire leadership styles: A meta-analysis comparing women and men. *Psychological Bulletin*, 129 (2003): 571.

tions to problems, even when their organization is generally successful. Transformational leaders mentor and empower followers by encouraging them to develop their full potential. Consistent with this description of transformational leadership, the style is neither masculine nor feminine when considered in its entirety but instead culturally androgynous (Ayman & Korabik, 2010). Yet, because one of its elements, the mentoring and empowering of subordinates, is culturally feminine (Hackman, Furniss, Hills, & Paterson, 1992), transformational leadership appears to be slightly more aligned with the female than the male gender role (Duehr & Bono, 2006; Kark, 2004).

Transformational leadership is generally contrasted with *transactional leadership*, which emphasizes give-and-take relationships that appeal to subordinates' self-interest. One aspect of transactional leadership that is quite effective is rewarding good performance by followers (Judge & Piccolo, 2004). In contrast, elements of transactional leadership involving reprimanding or otherwise sanctioning followers for their mistakes and failures are not as effective. Yet another potential leadership style, labeled *laissez-faire*, entails a general failure to take responsibility for managing. This approach is quite ineffective (Judge & Piccolo, 2004).

A meta-analysis of 45 studies examined all available published and unpublished research that had assessed transformational, transactional, and laissez faire leadership styles (Eagly, Johannesen-Schmidt, & van Engen, 2003). This project found small sex differences, such that women were generally more transformational in leadership style than men (mean $d = -0.10$) and also more transactional in terms of providing rewards for satisfactory performance (mean $d = -0.13$). Women's transformational leadership was especially evident in their focus on developing and mentoring followers and attending to their individual needs (mean $d = -0.19$). In contrast, men were more likely than women to emphasize followers' mistakes and failures (mean $d = 0.12$). In addition, men were more likely than women to wait until problems become severe before intervening (mean $d = 0.12$) and to avoid taking responsibility for leading (mean $d = 0.16$). Although these more negative and ineffective aspects of transactional and laissez faire leadership were more common among men than women, they were not typical of leaders of either sex. These meta-analytic findings comparing female and male leadership were replicated in a large-scale study of leadership by Antonakis, Avolio, and Sivasubramaniam (2003).

Given men's greater access to leadership, it is surprising that these particular meta-analytic findings emerged, even though they are only small average differences. One way of describing these findings is thus that women received higher ratings than men on the aspects of leadership style that relate positively to effectiveness, and men received higher rating than women on the aspects that do not enhance effectiveness. The implications of these findings for effectiveness were corroborated by the somewhat better performance of female than male managers on the effectiveness measures used in the studies included in the meta-analysis (Eagly et al., 2003).

The causes of these differences in female and male leadership style may lie in several factors (Eagly et al., 2003). One possibility is that the transformational repertoire (and the rewarding aspect of transactional leadership) can resolve some of the incongruity between leadership roles and the female gender role because most of these leader behaviors are not distinctively masculine. Another possibility is that gender roles influence female leaders by means of their internalization of gender-specific norms, thereby facilitating the somewhat feminine aspects of transformational leadership. A third possibility is that a double standard for entering into managerial roles results in female leaders being more qualified and skilled than male leaders. Additional primary research is needed to resolve these causal issues.

Whatever the causes of women's more transformational style and greater use of reward to motivate subordinates, these tendencies would seem to advantage women because of their positive correlations with effectiveness. However, confidence in this generalization is moderated somewhat by Ayman, Korabik, and Morris's (2009) finding that the greater was women's tendency to lead transformationally (in terms of intellectual stimulation and individualized consideration), the less effectiveness they were accorded by male (but not female) subordinates. Thus, men may have reservations about women's leadership ability even when they manifest a generally valued style. Additional complexities arise because transformational leadership may be less effective in more hierarchical, less egalitarian cultures (Kirkman, Chen, Farh, Chen, & Lowe, 2009), making such cultures less favorable environments for women's somewhat more transformational, less masculine styles.

Yet another issue related to women's leadership styles is whether people's expectations about the transformational, transactional, and laissez-faire leadership styles of women and men are accurate and constitute an advantage or a disadvantage for women's access to leadership positions in organizations. Research by Vinkenburg, Van Engen, Eagly, and Johannesen-Schmidt (2011) on stereotypes of female and male managers showed that participants correctly estimated the sex differences that had appeared in the meta-analysis of studies comparing these styles in individual male and female managers (Eagly et al., 2003). People's descriptive gender stereotypes of leader behavior thus appeared to be at least roughly accurate in this domain. Although this accuracy might seem to advantage women, a second study by these researchers introduced a further consideration by investigating *prescriptive* stereotypes about the importance of transformational and transactional leadership styles for the promotion of women and men to different levels in organizations. One especially agentic aspect of transformational style, inspirational motivation, was perceived as more important for men than women and especially important for promotion to CEO. In contrast, another, more communal aspect, individualized consideration, was perceived as more important for women than men and especially important for promotion from middle to senior management. These findings on prescriptive stereotyping revealed conventional gender norms whereby women are especially encouraged to enact more communal behaviors—that is, individualized consideration as leaders—but thereby would manifest behaviors that are only somewhat helpful for achieving the highest, or CEO, level of corporate success. Evidently it is only men who are especially encouraged to enact the more charismatic behaviors that particularly speed progress to the very top of organizations. These subtleties of transformational leadership thus complicate women's path to high positions.

THE EFFECTIVENESS OF FEMALE AND MALE LEADERS

It is possible that, despite the complexities I have described, women who do attain high positions are effective and perhaps more generally skilled as leaders than male leaders are. In fact, experimental research suggests that women who do attain success in very high-status roles can be perceived as highly competent because people assume that such women encountered a double standard whereby they had to be more qualified than their male counterparts (Rosette & Tost, 2010).

But how about the performance of women and men as leaders? Providing one answer, researchers have examined the relation between the percentages of women in executive positions and how well their organizations perform financially. Such studies have been conducted examining *Fortune* 1000 and other large US companies. Results show that the higher the percentage of women in executive roles or on boards of directors, the better are companies' financial outcomes (e.g., Carter, Simkins, & Simpson, 2003; Erhardt, Werbel, & Shrader, 2003; Krishnan & Park, 2005). Also, a study of European-based companies compared the financial performance of organizations having the greatest gender diversity in top management with the average performance of companies in their economic sector. This analysis also showed that gender diversity was correlated with better financial outcomes (Desvaux, Devillard-Hoellinger, & Baumgarten, 2007). Yet, in terms of corporate reputation, a British study found that the presence of more women on corporate boards was associated with a more positive corporate reputation only in companies operating close to final consumers—that is, in consumer services companies (Brammer, Millington, & Pavelin, 2009), perhaps because of the belief that women are particularly well equipped to take account of customers' gender diversity. Introducing another complexity, Lee and James (2007) found that unfavorable stock market returns were associated with the appointment of a female CEO in US companies from 1990 to 2000. There is of course considerable ambiguity associated with all correlational associations between gender diversity and measures of corporate success. Yet, research suggests that women executives can be a corporate asset, despite the investor caution that can follow the appointment of women to leadership positions (see Haslam et al., 2010, for discussion).

Other studies have examined leaders' effectiveness by having research participants rate how effective individual managers are. Such ratings may be contaminated by gender bias and other biases but nevertheless would be at least somewhat valid because managers can be successful only if their leadership is generally accepted by subordinates and colleagues. In a meta-analysis of 96 such studies comparing the effectiveness of male and female leaders holding comparable leadership roles, no overall difference was found between these women and men (Eagly, Karau, & Makhijani, 1995). However, this result was overwhelmed by findings showing that some contexts clearly favored male leaders, and some favored female leaders: In masculine settings, particularly the military, men received higher effectiveness ratings than women, whereas in less masculine settings, such as in education, women received somewhat higher effectiveness ratings than men (Eagly et al., 1995). This pattern of findings may well reflect gender stereotyping. In male-dominated settings, people are most likely to equate good leadership with stereotypically masculine behaviors, creating doubt about women's effectiveness as leaders and thereby compromising their effectiveness. Therefore, the meta-analysis's overall finding of no effectiveness difference between male and female managers was an arbitrary result of the types of contexts investigated in the individual studies that were included: The masculine settings and the feminine settings balanced one another to produce the overall finding of no sex differences in effectiveness.

In summary, in terms of research on the effectiveness of women versus men as leaders, there are hints in corporate studies that, on balance, the inclusion of women is advantageous. However, studies of individual managers suggest that masculine settings and highly male-dominated roles remain very challenging environments for female leaders, whereas women's achievements are more apparent in less masculine settings and leadership roles that are not very male-dominated.

HOW CAN WOMEN MAKE THEIR WAY THROUGH THE LABYRINTH?

Even though women's access to leadership is currently limited by multiple factors, some of which are discussed in this chapter, women have gained considerable access in recent decades. Women no longer face barriers that completely obstruct their access to powerful leadership positions. In evidence, across all organizations in the US, women now constitute 51% of those in professional and managerial positions, and 25% of chief executives (US Bureau of Labor Statistics, 2010, Table 11). However, in the *Fortune* 500, only 14% of all corporate officers, 16% of board members, and 3% of Chief Executive Officers are women (Catalyst, 2012). And less than 3% of Chief Executive Officers of the Global Fortune 500 are women (*Fortune*, 2010). Also, women's political leadership has increased in the US and other nations, despite their continuing underrepresentation in the more powerful elected positions. In the US, women are 17% of Senators, 17% of Congressional Representatives, 12% of state governors, and 25% of state legislators (Center for American Woman and Politics, 2010). Women also comprise 28% of the Senior Executive Service of the federal government (US Office of Personnel Management, 2007). In addition, the under-representation of women from some minority groups in leadership roles, relative to their numbers in the population, is generally even greater than that of White women. Specifically, among US managers, White and Asian women are better represented than Black and Hispanic/Latina women are in relation to their numbers in the population (US Bureau of Labor Statistics, 2010).

Corresponding to women's increasing access to powerful positions is cultural change in how people think about leadership. The meta-analysis on the masculinity of leader stereotypes thus found that, in all three of the research paradigms that have investigated this stereotype, it has changed to become less masculine (Koenig et al., 2011). This shift toward androgyny is consistent with leadership roles becoming generally more hospitable to women. Nevertheless, women have a long way to go before their power and authority are equal to those of men. The changes that have occurred in women's representation as leaders can be viewed as encouraging because they represent progress for women or as discouraging because of their slow pace, depending on one's perspective. One reason that impressions of the speed of change differ is that change is uneven, faster in some organizations and sectors of the economy than in others, and faster in some nations than other nations.

Evidence of change raises questions about how some women, the trail-blazers of change, make their way through the labyrinth and how organizations and societies progressively move toward the inclusion of women in positions of authority. Eagly and Carli (2007a) argued that individual women generally gain from a blended leadership style that incorporates both agentic and communal workplace behaviors. As explained earlier, transformational leadership provides one type of blending of agency and communion. In this or other androgynous modes, women can address both sides of the double bind: They show that they are directive and assertive enough to be leaders but that this agency does not undermine the warmth and sociability that is expected of women. Mixing masculine and feminine behavior can help women build workplace social capital. Given that career success requires being welcomed in networks and included in relationships that foster advancement, it is not surprising that women managers worry so much about having an acceptable leadership style. The pressure on women to tailor their leadership behavior to satisfy various audiences can create some authenticity challenges for women in their day-to-day enacting of leader roles. Therefore, the advice to just "be yourself" is misleading for women who exercise authority (see Eagly, 2005). Yet, "being oneself" in a leader role is a luxury that men often enjoy in view of the closeness between cultural concepts of men and leadership.

Negotiating the labyrinth of career challenges is often regarded as a problem for women to solve by themselves, but it is also a problem that should be addressed by the organizations that present impediments that are damaging to women's, but not men's, career progress (e.g., Acker, 1990). Although this many-sided issue is beyond the scope of this chapter, there are many sensible organizational innovations that foster progressive change (Eagly & Carli, 2007a, 2007b). For example, reforming gender-biased per-formance evaluations is essential. Also, given the very long hours often expected in managerial roles (Brett & Stroh, 2003; Hewlett & Luce, 2006), allowing some flexibility in the timing and mode of meeting workplace demands is helpful to employees, especially if they have family care responsibilities. On-site childcare can be additionally supportive for parents of young children. To accommodate employees' family care responsibilities, some organizations have implemented multiple changes in their personnel policies that have improved their retention of talented women (see Benko & Weisberg, 2007). Tempering features of some organizations' cultures such as widespread sexual or appearance-related bantering can also be helpful. Another effort involves legitimating and validating women's effectiveness as leaders by, for example, making their task-relevant competence salient and explaining that women are generally effective in similar leadership roles (e.g., Hogue, Yoder, & Ludwig, 2002; Lucas, 2003). Because managerial roles are in flux because of broader changes in the economy and society, building in innovations that can make organizations as welcoming to women as to men should become a priority. In favorable circumstances, demanding managerial roles can be compatible with women's family roles (Greenhaus & Powell, 2006), as research on female leaders has shown (e.g., Cheung & Halpern, 2010).

Sociopolitical changes, including moving toward gender equality, require individual commitment and collective struggle. As women gain greater equality, some people resent these changes, producing backlash. Ideologically traditional individuals often wish for a return to familiar arrangements in which men provided for their families and women tended to domestic matters sometimes supplemented by part-time or volunteer work. With the near-disappearance of the activism once inspired by the feminist movement and a degree of backlash against the changes that have occurred, the collective march toward gender equality appears to have paused on many fronts (see Blau, Brinton, & Grusky, 2006), despite the decrease in the cultural distance between women and leaders (Koenig et al., 2011). Without the clear guideposts of feminist ideology and advocacy, individual women are under pressure to find their own way through the labyrinth.

Social science research can help fill this void by illuminating the causes and consequences of gender inequality. In offering this research, researchers should be careful not to offer simplistic single-idea theories and insights as solutions that will eliminate discrimination against women as leaders. The causes of this discrimination are complex, consistent with the labyrinth metaphor. Yet, sharing the insights that research has yielded can help guide women who are thoughtfully and persistently making their way through this labyrinth.

BIBLIOGRAPHY

Acker, J. (1990). Hierarchies, jobs, bodies: A theory of gendered organizations. *Gender & Society*, 4, 139–158. doi:10.1177/089124390004002002.

Allport, G. W. (1954). *The nature of prejudice.* Cambridge, MA: Perseus Books.

Atwater, L. E., Carey, J. A., & Waldman, D. A. (2001). Gender and discipline in the workplace: Wait until your father gets home. *Journal of Management*, 27, 537–561. doi:10.1177/014920630102700503.

Antonakis, J., Avolio, B. J., & Sivasubramaniam, N. (2003). Context and leadership: An examination of the nine-factor full-range leadership theory using the Multifactor Leadership Questionnaire. *Leadership Quarterly*, 14, 261–295. doi:10.1016/S1048-9843(03)00030-4.

Avolio, B. J. (1999). *Full leadership development: Building the vital forces in organizations.* Thousand Oaks, CA: Sage.

Ayman, R. & Korabik, K. (2010). Leadership: Why gender and culture matter. *American Psychologist*, 65, 157–170. doi:10.1037/a0018806.

Ayman, R., Korabik, K., & Morris, S. (2009). Is transformational leadership always perceived as effective? Male subordinates' devaluation of female transformational leaders. *Journal of Applied Social Psychology*, 39, 852–879. doi:10.1111/j.1559-1816.2009.00463.x.

Banaji, M. & Hardin, C. (1996). Automatic stereotyping. *Psychological Science*, 7, 136–141. doi:10.1111/j.1467-9280.1996.tb00346.x.

Bass, B. M. (1998). *Transformational leadership: Industry, military, and educational impact.* Mahwah, NJ: Erlbaum.

Bigler, R. S., Arthur, A. E., Hughes, J. M., & Patterson, M. M. (2008). The politics of race and gender: Children's perceptions of discrimination and the U.S. presidency. *Analyses of Social Issues and Public Policy*, 8, 83–112. doi:10.1111/j.1530-2415.2008.00161.x.

Blau, F. D., Brinton, M. C., & Grusky, D. B. (Eds.) (2006). *The declining significance of gender?* New York: Russell Sage Foundation.

Bowleg, L. (2008). When Black + lesbian + woman ≠ Black lesbian woman: The methodological challenges of qualitative and quantitative intersectionality research. *Sex Roles*, 59, 312–325. doi:10.1007/s11199-008-9400-z.

Brammer, S., Millington, A., & Pavelin, S. (2009). Corporate reputation and women on the board. *British Journal of Management*, 20, 17–29. doi:10.1111/j.1467-8551.2008.00600.x.

Benko, C. & Weisberg, A. C. (2007). *Mass career customization: Aligning the workplace with today's nontraditional workforce.* Boston: Harvard Business School Press.

Brett, J. M. & Stroh, L. K. (2003). Working 61 hours a week: Why do managers do it? *Journal of Applied Psychology*, 88, 67–78. doi:10.1037/0021-9010.88.1.67.

Bruckmüller, S. & Branscombe, N. R. (2010). The glass cliff: When and why women are selected as leaders in crisis contexts. *British Journal of Social Psychology*, 49, 433–451. doi:10.1348/014466609X466594.

Burgess, D. & Borgida, E. (1999). Who women are, who women should be: Descriptive and prescriptive gender stereotyping in sex discrimination. *Psychology, Public Policy, and Law*, 5, 665–692. doi:10.1037/1076-8971.5.3.665.

Carli, L. L. (2001). Gender and social influence. *Journal of Social Issues*, 57, 725–741. doi:10.1111/0022-4537.00238.

Carroll, J. (2006, September 1). *Americans prefer male boss to a female boss.* Retrieved from http://www.gallup.com/poll/24346/americans-prefer-male-boss-female-boss.aspx.

Carter, D. A., Simkins, B. J., & Simpson, W. G. (2003). Corporate governance, board diversity, and firm value. *Financial Review*, 38, 33–53. doi:10.1111/1540-6288.00034.

Catalyst. (2000). *Across three cultures: Catalyst finds top barriers to women's professional advancement.* Retrieved September 20, 2008 from https://www.catalyst.org/press-release/29/across-three-cultures-catalyst-finds-top-barriers-to-womens-professional-advancement.

Catalyst. (2004). *Women and men in U.S. corporate leadership: Same workplace, different realities?* Retrieved from http://catalyst.org/file/74/women%20and%20men%20in%20u.s.%20corporate%20leadership%20same%20workplace,%20different%20realities.pdf.

Catalyst. (2012). *Pyramids: U.S. women in business.* Retrieved from http://www.catalyst.org/publication/132/us-women-in-business.

Center for American Woman and Politics. (2010). *Women in elective office 2010.* Retrieved from http://www.cawp.rutgers.edu/fast_facts/levels_of_office/documents/elective.pdf.

Cheung, F. M. & Halpern, D. F. (2010). Women at the top: Powerful leaders define success as work + family in a culture of gender. *American Psychologist*, 65, 182–193. doi:10.1037/A0017309.

Cialdini, R. B. & Trost, M. R. (1998). Social influence: Social norms, conformity and compliance. In D. T. Gilbert, S. T. Fiske, & G. Lindzey (Eds.), *The handbook of social psychology* (4th ed., Vol. 2, pp. 151–192). Boston: McGraw-Hill.

Conlin, M. (2003, May 26). The new gender gap: From kindergarten to grad school, boys are becoming the second sex. *Business Week.* Retrieved from http://www.businessweek.com/magazine/content/0321/b3834001mz001.htm?chan=search.

Davies, P. G., Spencer, S. J., & Steele, C. M. (2005). Clearing the air: Identity safety moderates the effects of stereotype threat on women's leadership aspirations. *Journal of Personality and Social Psychology* 88, 276–287. doi:10.1037/0022-3514.88.2.276.

De Pater, I., Van Vianen, A., Humphrey, R., Sleeth, R., Hartman, N., & Fischer, A. (2009). Individual task choice and the division of challenging tasks between men and women. *Group & Organization Management*, 34, 563–589. doi:10.1177/1059601108331240.

Desvaux, G., Devillard-Hoellinger, S., & Baumgarten, P. (2007). *Women matter: Gender diversity, a corporate performance driver.* Paris: McKinsey & Company.

Diekman, A. B. & Eagly, A. H. (2000). Stereotypes as dynamic constructs: Women and men of the past, present, and future. *Personality and Social Psychology Bulletin*, 26, 1171–1188. doi:10.1177/0146167200262001.

Duehr, E. E. & Bono, J. E. (2006). Men, women, and managers: Are stereotypes finally changing? *Personnel Psychology*, 59, 815–846. doi:10.1111/j.1744-6570.2006.00055.x.

Eagly, A. H. (1987). *Sex differences in social behavior: A social-role interpretation.* Hillsdale, NJ: Erlbaum.

Eagly, A. H. (2005). Achieving relational authenticity in leadership: Does gender matter? *Leadership Quarterly*, 16, 459–474. doi:10.1016/j.leaqua.2005.03.007.

Eagly, A. H. & Carli, L. L. (2007a). *Through the labyrinth: The truth about how women become leaders.* Cambridge, MA: Harvard Business School Press.

Eagly, A. H. & Carli, L. L. (2007b). Women and the labyrinth of leadership. *Harvard Business Review*, 85(9), 62–71.

Eagly, A. H. & Chin, J. L. (2010). Diversity and leadership in a changing world. *American Psychologist*, 65, 216–224. doi:10.1037/a0018957.

Eagly, A. H. & Diekman, A. B. (2005). What is the problem? Prejudice as an attitude-in-context. In J. F. Dovidio, P. Glick, & L. Rudman (Eds.), *On the nature of prejudice: Fifty years after Allport* (pp. 19–35). Malden, MA: Blackwell.

Eagly, A. H., Johannesen-Schmidt, M. C., & van Engen, M. (2003). Transformational, transactional, and laissez-faire leadership styles: A meta-analysis comparing women and men. *Psychological Bulletin,* 129, 569–591. doi:10.1037/0033-2909.129.4.569.

Eagly, A. H. & Johnson, B. T. (1990). Gender and leadership style: A meta-analysis. *Psychological Bulletin,* 108, 233–256. doi:10.1037/0033-2909.108.2.233.

Eagly, A. H. & Karau, S. J. (2002). Role congruity theory of prejudice toward female leaders. *Psychological Review,* 109, 573–598. doi:10.1037/0033-295X.109.3.573.

Eagly, A. H., Karau, S. J., & Makhijani, M. G. (1995). Gender and the effectiveness of leaders: A meta-analysis. *Psychological Bulletin,* 117, 125–145. doi:10.1037/0033-2909.117.1.125.

Eagly, A. H., Karau, S. J., Miner, J. B., & Johnson, B. T. (1994). Gender and motivation to manage in hierarchic organizations: A meta-analysis. *Leadership Quarterly,* 5, 135–159. doi:10.1016/1048-9843(94)90025-6.

Eagly, A. H., Makhijani, M. G., & Klonsky, B. G. (1992). Gender and the evaluation of leaders: A meta-analysis. *Psychological Bulletin,* 111, 3–22. doi:10.1037/0033-2909.111.1.3.

Eagly, A. H. & Mladinic, A. (1994). Are people prejudiced against women? Some answers from research on attitudes, gender stereotypes, and judgments of competence. In W. Stroebe & M. Hewstone (Eds.), *European Review of Social Psychology* (Vol. 5, pp. 1–35). New York: Wiley.

Erhardt, M. L., Werbel, J. D., & Shrader, C. B. (2003). Board of director diversity and firm financial performance. *Corporate Governance,* 11, 102–111. doi:10.1111/1467-8683.00011.

Falk, E. (2010). *Women for president: Media bias in nine campaigns.* Urbana: University of Illinois Press.

Foels, R., Driskell, J. E., Mullen, B., & Salas, E. (2000). The effects of democratic leadership on group member satisfaction: Integration. *Small Group Research,* 31, 676–701. doi:10.1177/104649640003100603.

Fortune. (2010). *Global 500: Women CEOs.* Retrieved from http://money.cnn.com/magazines/fortune/global500/2010/womenceos/.

Galinsky, E., Salmond, K., Bond, J. T., Kropf, M. B., Moore, M., & Harrington, B. (2003). *Leaders in a global economy: A study of executive women and men.* New York: Families and Work Institute.

Gastil, J. (1994). A meta-analytic review of the productivity and satisfaction of democratic and autocratic leadership. *Small Group Research,* 25, 384–410. doi:10.1177/1046496494253003.

Geis, F. L. (1993). Self-fulfilling prophecies: A social psychological view of gender. In A. E. Beall & R. J. Sternberg (Eds.), *The psychology of gender* (pp. 9–54). New York: Guilford Press.

Gelman, S. A. (2003). *The essential child: Origins of essentialism in everyday thought.* New York: Oxford University Press.

Goff, P., Thomas, M., & Jackson, M. (2008). "Ain't I a woman?": Towards an intersectional approach to person perception and group-based harms. *Sex Roles,* 59, 392–403. doi:10.1007/s11199-008-9505-4.

Greenhaus, J. H. & Powell, G. N. (2006). When work and family are allies: A theory of work-family enrichment. *Academy of Management Review,* 31, 72–92. doi:10.2307/20159186.

Hackman, M. Z., Furniss, A. H., Hills, M. J., & Paterson, T. J. (1992). Perceptions of gender-role characteristics and transformational and transactional leadership behaviours. *Perceptual and Motor Skills*, 75, 311–319. doi:10.2466/PMS.75.4.311-319.

Haslam, N., Rothschild, L., & Ernst, D. (2000). Essentialist beliefs about social categories. *British Journal of Social Psychology*, 39, 113–127. doi: 10.1348/014466600164363.

Haslam, S. A., Ryan, M. K., Kulich, C., Trojanowski, G., & Atkins, C. (2010). Investing with prejudice: The relationship between women's presence on company boards and objective and subjective measures of company performance. *British Journal of Management*, 21, 484–497.

Heilman, M. E. (2001). Description and prescription: How gender stereotypes prevent women's ascent up the organizational ladder. *Journal of Social Issues*, 57, 657–674. doi:10.1111/0022-4537.00234.

Heilman, M. E., Wallen, A. S., Fuchs, D., & Tamkins, M. M. (2004). Penalties for success: Reactions to women who succeed in male gender-typed tasks. *Journal of Applied Psychology*, 89, 416–427. doi:10.1037/0021-9010.89.3.416.

Hewlett, S. A. & Luce, C. B. (2006). Extreme jobs: The dangerous allure of the 70-hour workweek. *Harvard Business Review*, 84(12), 49–59.

Hogue, M. B., Yoder, J. D., & Ludwig, J. (2002). Increasing initial leadership effectiveness: Assisting both women and men. *Sex Roles*, 46, 377–384. doi:10.1023/A:1020457312806.

Hoyt, C. L., Johnson, S. K., Murphy, S. E., & Skinnell, K. H. (2010). The impact of blatant stereotype activation and group sex-composition on female leaders. *Leadership Quarterly*, 21, 716–732. doi:10.1016/j.leaqua.2010.07.003.

Ito, T. A. & Urland, G. R. (2003). Race and gender on the brain: Electrocortical measures of attention to the race and gender of multiply categorizable individuals. *Journal of Personality and Social Psychology*, 85, 616–626. doi:10.1037/0022-3514.85.4.616.

Johnson, S., Murphy, S., Zewdie, S., & Reichard, R. (2008). The strong, sensitive type: Effects of gender stereotypes and leadership prototypes on the evaluation of male and female leaders. *Organizational Behavior and Human Decision Processes*, 106, 39–60. doi:10.1016/j.obhdp.2007.12.002.

Judge, T. A. & Piccolo. R. F. (2004). Transformational and transactional leadership: A meta-analytic test of their relative validity. *Journal of Applied Psychology*, 89, 901–910. doi:10.1037/0021-9010.89.5.755.

Kark, R. (2004). The transformational leader: Who is (s)he? A feminist perspective. *Journal of Organizational Change Management*, 17, 160–176. doi:10.1108/09534810410530593.

Kirkman, B. L., Chen, G., Farh, J.-L., Chen, Z. X., & Lowe, K. B. (2009). Individual power distance orientation and follower reactions to transformational leaders: A cross-level, cross-cultural examination. *Academy of Management Journal*, 52, 744–764.

Koenig, A. M., Eagly, A. H., Mitchell, A. A., Ristikaari, T. (2011). Are leader stereotypes masculine? A meta-analysis of three research paradigms. *Psychological Bulletin*, 137(4), 616–642.

Krishnan, H. A. & Park, D. (2005). A few good women—on top management teams. *Journal of Business Research*, 58, 1712–1720. doi:10.1016/j.jbusres.2004.09.003.

Kulich, C., Ryan, M. K., & Haslam, S. A. (2007). Where is the romance for women leaders? The effects of gender on leadership attributions and performance-based pay. *Applied Psychology: An International Review*, 56, 582–601. doi:10.1111/j.1464-0597.2007.00305.x.

Langford, T. & MacKinnon, N. J. (2000). The affective bases for the gendering of traits: Comparing the United States and Canada. *Social Psychology Quarterly*, 63, 34–48. doi:10.2307/2695879.

Lee, P. M. & James, E. H. (2007). She'-e-os: Gender effects and investor reactions to the announcements of top executive appointments. *Strategic Management Journal*, 28(3), 227–241. doi:10.1002/smj.575.

Lipman-Blumen, J. (2000). *Connective leadership: Managing in a changing world.* New York: Oxford University Press.

Lucas, J. W. (2003). Status processes and the institutionalization of women as leaders. *American Sociological Review*, 68, 464–480. doi:10.2307/1519733.

Lyness, K. S. & Thompson, D. E. (2000). Climbing the corporate ladder: Do female and male executives follow the same route? *Journal of Applied Psychology*, 85, 86–101. doi:10.1037/0021-9010.85.1.86.

Maume, D. J., Jr. (1999). Occupational segregation and the career mobility of White men and women. *Social Forces*, 77, 1433–1459.

Newport, F. (2001, February 21). *Americans see women as emotional and affectionate, men as more aggressive.* Gallup Poll News Service. Retrieved from http://www.gallup.com/poll/1978/Americans-See-Women-Emotional-Affectionate-Men-More-Aggressive.aspx.

Ohlott, P. J., Ruderman, M. N., & McCauley, C. D. (1994). Gender differences in managers' developmental job experiences. *Academy of Management Journal*, 37, 46–67. doi:10.2307/256769.

Powell, G. N. & Butterfield, D. A. (1979). The "good manager": Masculine or androgynous? *Academy of Management Journal*, 22, 395-403. doi:10.2307/255597.

Prentice, D. A. & Miller, D. T. (2006). Essentializing differences between women and men. *Psychological Science*, 17, 129–135. doi:10.1111/j.1467-9280.2006.01675.x.

Propp, K. M. (1995). An experimental examination of biological sex as a status cue in decision-making groups and its influence on information use. *Small Group Research*, 26, 451–474. doi:10.1177/1046496495264001.

Rosette, A. S. & Tost, L. P. (2010). Agentic women and communal leadership: How role prescriptions confer advantage to top women leaders. *Journal of Applied Psychology*, 95, 221-235. doi:10.1037/a0018204.

Rozin, H. (2010, July/August). The end of men. *Atlantic Monthly.* Retrieved from http://www.theatlantic.com/magazine/archive/2010/07/the-end-of-men/8135/.

Rudman, L. A. & Goodwin, S. A. (2004). Gender differences in automatic in-group bias: Why do women like women more than men like men? *Journal of Personality and Social Psychology*, 87, 494–509. doi:10.1037/0022-3514.87.4.494.

Ryan, M. K. & Haslam, S. A. (2005). The glass cliff: Evidence that women are over-represented in precarious leadership positions. *British Journal of Management*, 16, 81–90.

Ryan, M. K. & Haslam, S. A. (2007). The glass cliff: Exploring the dynamics surrounding women's appointment to precarious leadership positions. *Academy of Management Review*, 32, 549–572. doi:10.1111/j.1467-8551.2005.00433.x.

Ryan, M. K., Haslam, S. A., & Kulich, C. (2010). Politics and the glass cliff: Evidence that women are preferentially selected to contest hard-to-win seats. *Psychology of Women Quarterly*, 34, 56–64. doi:10.1111/j.1471-6402.2009.01541.x.

Sanchez-Hucles, J. V. & Davis, D. D. (2010). Women and women of color in leadership: Complexity, identity, and intersectionality. *American Psychologist*, 65, 171–181. doi:10.1037/a0017459.

Schein, V. E. (1973). The relationship between sex role stereotypes and requisite management characteristics. *Journal of Applied Psychology*, 57, 95–100. doi:10.1037/h0037128.

Schein, V. E. (2001). A global look at psychological barriers to women's progress in management. *Journal of Social Issues*, 57, 675–688. doi:10.1111/0022-4537.00235.

Sczesny, S. & Kühnen, U. (2004). Meta-cognition about biological sex and gender-stereotypic physical appearance: Consequences for the assessment of leadership competence. *Personality and Social Psychology Bulletin,* 30, 13–21. doi:10.1177/0146167203258831.

Sharpe, R. (2000, November 20). As leaders, women rule: New studies find that female managers outshine their male counterparts in almost every measure. *BusinessWeek,* p. 74. Retrieved from http://www.businessweek.com/common frames/ca.htm?/2000/00 47/b3708145.htm.

Shinar, E. H. (1975). Sexual stereotypes of occupations. *Journal of Vocational Behavior,* 7, 99–111. doi:10.1016/0001-8791(75)90037-8.

Smith, R. A. (2002). Race, gender, and authority in the workplace: Theory and research. *Annual Review of Sociology,* 28, 509–542. doi:10.1146/annurev.soc.28.110601.141048

US Bureau of Labor Statistics. (2010). *Labor force statistics from the current population survey.* Retrieved from http://www.bls.gov/cps/tables.htm.

US Office of Personnel Management. (2007). *Senior executive service: Facts and figures.* Retrieved from http://www.opm.gov/ses/facts_and_figures/demographics.asp.

Van Engen, M. L. & Willemsen, T. M. (2004). Sex and leadership styles: A meta-analysis of research published in the 1990s. *Psychological Reports,* 94, 3–18. doi: 10.2466/PR0. 94.1.3-18.

Vinkenburg, C. J., Van Engen, M. L., Eagly, A. H., & Johannesen-Schmidt, M. C. (2011). An exploration of stereotypical beliefs about leadership styles: Is transformational leadership a route to women's promotion? *Leadership Quarterly,* 22(1), 10–21.

Williams, C. L. (1995). *Still a man's world: Men who do "women's" work.* Berkeley, CA: University of California Press.

Williams, J. E. & Best, D. L. (1990). *Measuring sex stereotypes: A multination study.* Newbury Park, CA: Sage.

8

The Tyranny of Normative Distance: A Social Identity Account of the Exercise of Power by Remote Leaders

David E. Rast, III, Amber M. Gaffney,
and Michael A. Hogg

Describing a person as "distant" may bring to mind an image of someone who is aloof and uncaring (i.e., socially distant), or perhaps physically removed from the current situation. In either case, the perception of this "distance" has important ramifications for the quality of the relationship between the distant other and the perceiver of the distance. For example, we often hear of the difficulties of *long-distance* relationships (e.g., they never last, they are difficult to maintain) and in addition, when romantic partners "grow apart" or become *distant* from one another, the implication is that the relationship is characterized by poor quality and that it may indeed end. Leader–follower relations, though arguably less interpersonal (Hogg & van Knippenberg, 2003; cf. Schyns, this volume), are nonetheless impacted by perceptions of both physical and psychological distance (see Antonakis & Atwater, 2002), where less distance between the leader and his or her followers generally implies better and more effective leadership and thus group output (although not always, see Shamir, this volume). While leaders vary in their social, psychological, and interactional distance from followers at an interpersonal level, on the intragroup level leaders also strive to close the gap between themselves and what is normative for their group and its members. This second type of distance, which we term "normative distance" is also a key component in understanding the leader–follower relationship, as well as perceptions of a leader's effectiveness.

Effective leader–follower relations are crucial to the survival and success of groups and organizations. With rapidly evolving advances in technology and an increasingly globalized world, leaders continually face the challenge of maintaining close relationships with their followers in the absence of traditional face-to-face interaction. Today, it is not uncommon for leaders to guide their followers from remote locations such as telecommuting from home, conference calling while working in different states or countries, or more often via email communications. As such, there often exists great physical distance between leaders and followers; yet a leader's ability to influence followers or exert authority over them is greatly diminished when the leader is absent or removed from the setting (e.g., Milgram, 1963, 1974). Other forms of distance—such as perceptions of a leader's emotional distance, a lack of a strong interpersonal relationship between leader and follower, the perception of a psychologically distant leader, and the normative distance between a leader and the group's psychological representation—also impact the quality of leader–follower relations and the leader's effectiveness.

Traditionally, leadership research focused on the personality traits or specific leader behaviors that make for good or bad leadership (e.g., Stogdill, 1974; Katz, 1955) and situational factors that encourage certain leadership styles (e.g., Fiedler, 1964; House, 1971). More recently, however, theoretical approaches, such as leader–member exchange (LMX) and transactional leadership, emphasize how the dyadic relationship between leaders and followers can impact leader effectiveness and support (see Hogg, 2010, for recent overview). The assumption of these approaches is that certain leader behaviors (e.g., social skills, goal setting) or personality characteristics (e.g., extraversion, charisma) promote a positive, close relationship between leaders and followers and thus produce effective leadership, which promotes group cohesion, positive group outcomes, and group productivity. Some approaches even suggest that leadership is a talent that only a few charismatic individuals possess and these "special" individuals are capable of inciting innovative change and motivating their followers to work together toward common goals (Avolio & Bass, 1987; Northouse, 2010).

Such approaches often overlook a fundamental part of the leader–follower relationship—leadership at its very core is a group process. Overlooking this point means that these theories may not pay sufficient attention to how leaders normatively fit (or do not) within their group or the role of followers' perceptions of the leader in their examination of leader–follower relations. As a member of the group, a leader's agenda may be close to the normative group position or far from it. The leader may hold a position that embodies the thoughts, feelings, and actions of most of the group, or alternatively, the leader may choose to advocate a position that is somewhat or markedly disparate from the majority of the group to incite important changes within the group or organization. As such, many leaders must strategically manipulate their own distance from the normative group position to maintain the group's cohesion, while promoting change and innovation.

In this chapter we explore how normative distance between leaders and followers influences leadership evaluations and effectiveness. Our analysis draws extensively on the social identity framework (Tajfel & Turner, 1979; Abrams & Hogg, 2010) with an emphasis on the social identity theory of leadership (Hogg, 2001a, 2010). Our focus is ultimately on the leader's group prototypical position as a form of normative "distance." We define normative distance as the extent to which the leader approximates the group's prototype. In general, a leader close to the group's prototypical position will wield more influence, while a leader remote from the proto-type will be less influential (for exceptions see Abrams, Randsley de Moura, Marques, & Hutchison, 2008; Rast, Gaffney, Hogg, & Crisp, 2012). We begin with a brief overview of social identity theory, and then provide a detailed account of the social identity theory of leadership. We subsequently describe how the extent to which leaders and followers occupy normative positions within a group affects both the perception of leader–follower distance and the amount of support given to the leader. The final part of the chapter explores the influences of intergroup leadership and uncertainty on perceptions of leader–follower distance.

<hr>

SOCIAL IDENTITY

The social world is complex and multifaceted. To render this milieu meaningful, people cognitively represent social stimuli in terms of social categories such as men and women, black and white, leader and follower. Most people belong to many categories and categorize the self and others into groups quickly and automatically. The process of social categorization depersonalizes the self and others, such that both the self and others are no longer viewed as distinct, unique individuals but rather as embodiments of the in- or outgroup's prototype (Abrams & Hogg, 2010; Hogg, 2006). Group prototypes are fuzzy interrelated properties that define and delineate who belongs to one's ingroup and who does not by describing and prescribing the ingroup's values, attitudes, and behaviors. Prototypes are configured in such a way that they adhere to the metacontrast principle: maximizing the ratio of perceived inter-category to intra-category differences and accentuating between group differences and within group similarities (Tajfel, 1959). As such, prototypes maximize perceptions of entitativity where one's ingroup is perceived as being internally homogeneous with clear boundaries and social structure, hierarchical leadership, and so forth (e.g., Campbell, 1958; Hamilton & Sherman, 1996). Particularly relevant to the social identity analysis of leadership is that members pay close attention to how well they and others conform to or deviate from the group's prototype. Members within a group are contrasted against their "fit" to the group's prototype so they can be more or less prototypical compared to other category members. Hence, "group members conform to, and thus are influenced by, the prototype" (Hogg, 2001a, p. 189).

As people identify more strongly with a particular group they come to internalize the group's prototype, as well as the associated attitudes and behaviors, as their own. This represents true internalization and private acceptance of group prototypical attitudes and opinions, not just mere compliance to group norms (see Abrams & Hogg 1990; Hogg & Turner, 1987). Furthermore, once the group's prototype is internalized, attitude–behavior correspondence is likely to be high if the attitudes are prototypical of people's important and relevant social identifications (Hogg & Smith, 2007; Terry & Hogg, 1996, 2001a). Consequently, when social identity is salient the prototype becomes the basis of social influence within and between groups (Hogg & Turner, 1987). A key implication of this analysis for leadership is that as social identity becomes salient, feelings of liking, respect, admiration, popularity, and trust for ingroup members transform from personal to depersonalized social attraction (Hogg, 1993). This suggests that when social identity is salient, prototypical group members are more trusted, liked, and popular than non-prototypical members, even when they are physically distant or absent altogether.

The social identity framework provides a metatheoretical approach to help understand a multitude of group processes and intergroup phenomena, including conformity, normative deviance, stereotyping, prejudice, discrimination, intergroup conflict, group decision making, minority influence, extremism and, particularly relevant to the current chapter, leadership (for recent overviews see Abrams & Hogg, 2010; Gaffney & Hogg, in press; Hogg, 2006).

SOCIAL IDENTITY THEORY OF LEADERSHIP

Leaders who personify both the ideal and normative attributes of their group and provide a clear group vision have successfully united and mobilized their followers in both large social movements (e.g., Equal Rights Movement) and small-group activities (e.g., team building) for centuries. Groups provide their members with a social identity and leaders are often liaisons between group norms and group members. Moreover, leaders are the most immediate source of group-relevant information for their followers. In this respect, followers not only look to their leaders to provide stability, security, and direction, but also depend on leaders to furnish and exemplify, as well as to create and transform their social identity. Leaders play a key role in defining social identity by telling followers who they are, how they should behave, and what attitude they hold. Thus followers attend to and provide constraints for the identity the leader promotes. Because leadership is inextricably a group process and leaders are group members who hold a disproportionate amount of influence over their group and followers (Gaffney & Hogg, in press; Hogg, 2010), the social identity framework is directly relevant to the social psychology of leadership. These implications have been formalized into the social identity theory of leadership (Hogg, 2001a; Hogg & van Knippenberg, 2003).

The key premise of the social identity theory of leadership is that as members identify more strongly with their group, followers' support for their leader and the leader's effectiveness become reliant on the extent to which followers consider their leader to be prototypical of the group. In this analysis, followers define and create the group's leadership—members follow leaders who construct a group identity that is in accordance with the normative constraints followers place upon leaders (Hogg, 2008). When members identify strongly with a group, they attend to the group's prototype, as well as to those close to the prototype. As previously noted however, members are influenced by the group's prototype and therefore are also influenced by those occupying positions that are prototypical, thus members close to the prototype are typically cast into leadership positions.

Group members often believe that prototypical group members act in their group's best interest, and indeed, prototypical members identify more strongly with the group than non-prototypical members. Indeed, research supports this idea and demonstrates that followers believe that prototypical leaders (in comparison to non-prototypical leaders) act in the best interest of their groups over their own self-interest (Platow, van Knippenberg, Haslam, Spears, & van Knippenberg, 2006) and self-sacrifice on behalf of the group (van Knippenberg & van Knippenberg, 2005). As such, prototypical leaders tend to favor fellow ingroup members (Cheng, Fielding, Hogg, & Terry, 2009) and pursue depersonalized, opposed to differentiated leader–follower relationships (Hogg, Martin, Epitropaki, Mankad, Svensson, & Weeden, 2005; Hogg, Martin, & Weeden, 2004). Such beliefs about prototypical leaders substantiate their membership credentials of being prototypically "one of us." According to Hogg (2010), "the key factor is that the [prototypical] leader behaves in ways that build trust based on shared identity and the perception that the leader is centrally invested in the group" (p. 1196). Conversely, engaging in group-oriented behaviors is required for non-prototypical leaders to bolster their membership credentials (Abrams, Randsley de Moura, Marques, & Hutchison, 2008; Platow & van Knippenberg, 2001). Leaders who express behaviors consistent with group goals (e.g., self-sacrificing behaviors) can use such behaviors to be perceived as close to the prototypical group position, bestowing them with influence to lead followers; while leaders who pursue their own self-interests will be perceived as distant from the group's prototype, resulting in reduced influence over followers.

The social identity theory of leadership has received robust empirical support for its general ideas, as well as its application to a wide range of leadership phenomena (Ellemers, de Gilder, & Haslam, 2004; Hogg & van Knippenberg, 2003; van Knippenberg, van Knippenberg, DeCremer, & Hogg, 2004). This research consistently demonstrates that followers perceive prototypical leaders as more effective, charismatic, trustworthy, attractive, and group-oriented than non-prototypical leaders. Furthermore, this research reveals that these positive evaluations of prototypical leaders also affect follower behaviors: followers are more likely to support, endorse, and vote for prototypical than non-prototypical leaders, irrespective of physical, interactional, and social distance (Platow, van Knippenberg,

Haslam, van Knippenberg, & Spears, 2006; van Knippenberg & van Knippenberg, 2005; Giessner, van Knippenberg, & Sleebos, 2009).

ENTREPRENEURS OF IDENTITY

Social identity processes specify that prototypical leaders have considerable power to maintain their leadership position. Prototypical leaders take an active role in constructing, transforming, and managing category definitions such that they are able to establish or redefine what the group stands for, as well as group members' social identities. That is to say, prototypical leaders are "entrepreneurs of identity" (Reicher & Hopkins, 1996, 2003). Because of their ability to exert influence over the group, prototypical leaders have the ability to incite change within groups by effectively influencing the group's prototype. Such leaders not only represent a source of information to which followers can turn to determine their own place within the group and their own group identity, but these leaders can also actively change what it means to be prototypical of the group, creating new group norms and reconstructing the identity of the group.

There are several strategies leaders use to enhance perceptions of their own prototypicality to gain influence within their groups or to deviate from the very prototypical position that brought them into power. Leaders can employ group-related rhetoric to enhance perceptions of their own prototypicality, vilify other members or leaders as deviants, making their non-prototypicality salient, or they can change relevant outgroups for social comparisons in a manner that best positions them as prototypical (Hogg, 2001a, 2008). If the leader is relatively prototypical, raising ingroup salience or engaging in relevant outgroup comparisons is beneficial, while lowering ingroup salience or changing comparison outgroups benefits non-prototypical leaders. For instance, GOP leaders have convincingly argued that their opponents (the Democrats) are out of touch with the "American" people and plagued Obama's healthcare reform as a non-prototypical American position, to gain political support and votes in the 2010 midterm election.

The social identity theory of leadership treats leaders and followers as active participants in the leader–follower relationship (Reicher, Haslam, &

Hopkins, 2005). Although leaders are essential in crafting category definitions (Seyranian & Bligh, 2008), leaders and followers are mutually dependent on one another to define and create common sense of "we-ness" and provide a shared vision for the group. However, followers can reject leaders who are too distanced from the group's prototype or those who lack the group-based credentials to instigate innovation and change. Sarah Palin is a current real-world example of a leader who may have become too distanced from her group's prototype. She vehemently stresses that she is a Washington outsider, highlights her lack of government experience at the federal level, has published a book titled *Going Rogue,* and is one of the unofficial leaders of the extremely conservative Tea Party. These issues have made Palin a very polarizing figure, and have led many high-ranking Republicans to argue that she is unelectable in the 2012 presidential election (Siegel, 2010). Indeed recent ABC News/Washington Post polls (2010a, 2010b) indicate that only 8% of those surveyed would support Palin for president, while 60% reported they definitely would not support her and almost 70% indicated she is unqualified to run for president. Without the support and trust of their followers, leaders such as Palin would be unable to wield any influence over the group.

PROTOTYPE-BASED LEADER–FOLLOWER DISTANCE

Group members are sensitive to cues about the group's prototype and notice subtle differences regarding how close they or others are to the prototype (see Hogg, 2010). Highly prototypical members receive more attention than less prototypical members as prototypical members provide more information about the group's prototype and subsequently, one's own relative distance from the prototype (e.g., Hogg & Gaffney, in press). Because highly prototypical leaders stand out in their groups and have a disproportionate amount of influence, other group members are likely to assign personality attributes to their leader that help make sense of his or her behavior—that is, why their leader is able to influence others, why he or she is so popular, liked, or trusted, and why he or she can be innovative. In this context, followers are more likely to perceive prototypical leaders as more charismatic and transformational than non-prototypical leaders

(Giessner, van Knippenberg, & Sleebos, 2009; van Knippenberg & van Knippenberg, 2005). This is because when group membership is salient, followers pay particular attention to those members occupying the central prototypical group positions. Because they stand out in the group, prototypical leaders are more distinctive and their group-oriented behavior is (mis)attributed to dispositional characteristics (Fiske & Taylor, 2008). As a consequence, charisma is not something possessed by the leader, but rather an attribution ascribed to the leader by his or her followers (Conger & Kanungo, 1988; Haslam & Platow, 2001). Thus, prototypical leaders reap the benefits associated with charismatic and transformational leadership (Avolio & Yammarino, 2003) such as greater organizational performance and job satisfaction when followers identify strongly with the organization or group (Cicero, Bonaiuto, Pierro, & van Knippenberg, 2008; Cicero, Pierro, & van Knippenberg, 2007). Indeed van Knippenberg and Hogg (2003) explicitly discuss the overlap between charismatic or transformational leadership and the social identity theory of leadership. They argue that the social identity analysis of leadership provides a framework to better understand the social and cognitive psychological processes underlying perceptions of charismatic/transformational leaders.

For group members who identify strongly with their group, perceiving a leader as prototypical, regardless of their physical distance to or from the leader, provides the group members with a great deal of group- and self-relevant information and they are therefore perceived as charismatic, compared to those remote from the group's prototype. Thus attributions of charisma and evaluations of effectiveness for a non-prototypical leader may hinge on how physically close the leader is, because followers can directly evaluate the non-prototypical leader's behaviors and characteristics; whereas a prototypical leader will be perceived as charismatic regardless of physical distance because they occupy a central group position and are therefore normatively close to their followers (cf. Yagil, 1998). Thus, we agree with Antonakis and Atwater (2002) that physical and social (including normative) distances are distinct and independent constructs. That is, both normatively close (i.e., prototypical) or normatively distant (i.e., non-prototypical) leaders can be either physically near to or far from followers. However, we believe there is an additional consideration for examining the effect of leader–follower distance: strength of follower identification with the group. Our reasoning suggests that evaluations of the same leader will vary with situational or contextual changes among followers who strongly identify with their group. That is, a leader might be prototypical in one context but not another, and leader support and evaluations will hinge on the extent to which the leader is perceived as group prototypical. For example, Obama may be perceived as prototypical of the US when he engages in international relations with Russia; however, with respect to the Republican-controlled House, he may be perceived as more distanced from the American prototype depending on the GOP's rhetoric. When followers do not identify or weakly identify with their group, leader evaluations will be based on the leader–follower relationship (e.g., exchange vs. communal) or the leader's personality, behavior, or performance (Hogg, Martin, Epitropaki, Mankad, Svensson, & Weeden, 2005).

Group prototypicality also influences the amount of trust and legitimacy that followers bestow on their leader. Followers believe that prototypical leaders are trustworthy and that they act in group-serving ways. Indeed, prototypical group members tend to identify strongly with their groups (more so than non-prototypical members) and act in ways that promote the group's interests (Hogg, 2001b). Prototypical leaders favor and provide fairer treatment toward ingroup followers compared to outgroup followers, and ingroup followers evaluate the leader more favorably when doing so (Cheng, Fielding, Hogg, & Terry, 2009). This creates a paradox: prototypical leaders are trusted to act in the group's best interest even when the leader is actually not acting in the group's best interest.

For instance, Jim Jones, founder of the infamous 1960s religious cult called the People's Temple, was believed by his followers to be acting in their best interest when he moved the cult from Indiana to San Francisco, and finally to Jonestown, Guyana (Reiterman & Jacobs, 1982). The first move to San Francisco allowed Jones to recruit more people to promote his own political agenda, through which Jones was later appointed as Chairman of the San Francisco Housing Authority Commission. The move from California to Jonestown was a result of an IRS tax investigation and investigations of abuse within the cult, although Jones claimed to his followers the move was to save the cult from the oppressive American government. Jones's final act of self-indulgence also came at the group's expense. After Congressman Leo Ryan was murdered during a visit to Jonestown, Jones knew his arrest was imminent. Rather than facing jail time and losing his followers, Jones ordered the congregation to drink poisoned flavored water, which resulted in the infamous Jonestown mass suicide. This example demonstrates the considerable influence prototypical leaders are afforded, simply due to their group prototypicality. Furthermore, because leaders are trusted and their leadership credentials are perceived as legitimate, they have leeway to distance themselves from the group prototype to promote change and innovation. When leaders are perceived to be prototypical they can deviate from the prototype and because of their influential position and their ability to effectively modify the prototype, remain in a prototypical position, this allows leaders to enact change and innovation (Abrams, Randsley de Moura, Marques, & Hutchison, 2008). For example, prototypical leaders might employ rhetoric to promote a non-normative group change. Because the leader is centrally located within the group, this rhetoric, over time, might make the advocated change appear to be in the group's best interest. A non-prototypical leader who is remote from the group's central position will encounter more difficulty advocating a non-normative position, and may even see polarization away from the very non-normative position they support. Indeed, Jones was trusted and supported unconditionally by his followers even though his most important decisions regarding the People's Temple were for his own benefit, not the group's benefit.

PERCEIVED SIMILARITY

People like and are attracted to similar others (Newcomb, 1961), and leaders are no exception. Shamir (1995) and Yagil (1998) suggest that perceptions of leader–follower similarity rest on how physically close or distant the leader is: physically close leaders are perceived as more similar to followers than physically distant ones. Further, closeness leads followers to identify with the leader but this relationship is mediated by perceived similarity. Recent research extends this perspective, demonstrating that shared group membership enhances perceptions of leader–follower similarity. Drawing primarily on the social identity theory of leadership, Alabastro, Rast, Lac, Hogg, and Crano (2012) examined how attitudinally similar followers perceived themselves to Barack Obama and John McCain before and after the 2008 US presidential election. Before the election, both Obama and McCain—neither of whom is physically close to their followers—were perceived as attitudinally similar to their respective followers. That is, liberals perceived Obama as attitudinally similar and

McCain as dissimilar to themselves, and the opposite was true for conservatives.

After the election ended, a different story emerged: conservatives attitudinally distanced themselves from McCain following his loss, but accentuated similarity to Obama following his win. Thus, we can conclude that physical closeness (or distance) does not necessarily result in enhanced (or diminished) perceptions of leader–follower similarity; instead leader–follower similarity is dependent on social identification, and not identification with the leader. From our perspective, identification with the group results in perceived leader–follower similarity. Before the election, Obama and McCain were leaders of groups locked in an intergroup competition for control of the United States. After the election, however, only Obama became the leader of both subgroups—the superordinate group's leader—the leader of the United States (e.g., Brewer, 1991). In addition, the increase in similarity that conservatives experienced toward Obama may also have been impacted by the new status that Obama attained as president. Obama's presidential status enhanced followers' perceptions of his prototypicality, which in turn positively impacted his influence, legitimacy, and power over them (Ridgeway, 2003).

REMOTE PROTOTYPICAL LEADERS

While prototypical leaders are perceived as "one of us," their leadership role by definition requires some amount of distance from followers. Leaders close to the group prototype are conferred with status, charisma, and legitimacy that distances them from the rest of the group. Over time, this distance may create the perceptions of "us followers" versus "them leaders" and accentuate status and power imbalance within the group—leaders have the power and status, followers have neither (Hogg, 2001a). Recent research indicates that leaders are perceived as being "higher in the hierarchy" and distanced from followers, and that this perceived normative distance enhances the perception of greater status and power (Giessner & Schubert, 2007). While increased psychological distance and status are not in and of themselves negative, there are certain conditions when this combination has the potential to have very negative consequences.

From a social identity perspective, this condition comes into play with a prototypical leader who operates very remotely from his or her followers. Examples would include a CEO who is often viewed as out of touch with the rank and file (e.g., Tony Hayward, former CEO of BP) or a national leader who has drifted far from the normative goals and identity prescriptions of the nation (e.g., Sarah Palin and the Republican Party). Under these conditions, prototypical leaders, even when physically removed from their followers, still exert significant influence over their followers. However, when prototypical leaders are very remote from followers, this normally benign prototype-based leadership can easily transform into hierarchical power-based leadership where leaders have excessive power to influence followers (Hogg, 2001a, 2007b). In this situation, leaders fail to yield to constraints that followers place on them and leadership literally becomes absolute; the leader does whatever he or she wants with little regard for group norms.

Equally problematic for the group's welfare, followers have been known to endorse prototypical leaders even when the leader is not acting in the best interests of the group. Social identity research has gone so far as to demonstrate this effect in laboratory settings, even when groups are created on a trivial basis. For example, Duck and Fielding (2003) employed a minimal group paradigm to examine follower (the participants) evaluations of an in- or outgroup leader who favored the in- or outgroup members. Outgroup leaders were evaluated negatively unless they favored the participant's ingroup over the outgroup. Ingroup leaders were evaluated the most positively when they favored the ingroup; however, they were still positively evaluated even when favoring the participant's outgroup. History is also rife with naturally occurring examples, such as David "Moses David" Berg, who founded and led the Children of God (COG) for nearly thirty years (Kent, 2000). Berg lived in secrecy and completely separated from his followers, only communicating with them through his publications known as the "Mo Letters" (these letters can be found on the cult's public database at http://pubs. xfamily.org/). As the founder of the COG, Berg was able to create, maintain, and rebuild the group's prototype whenever he desired. Being prototypical, his followers looked to him to provide a clear vision about how they should behave, what attitudes to hold, and most importantly, how to reduce their feelings of uncertainty. He remained prototypical of the group even though he lived completely removed from them, yet still wielded significant influence over his followers' attitudes and behaviors through his letters.

As previously discussed, with increased normative distance between leaders and followers, a schism can occur where leaders are no longer viewed as "one of us" but rather as "one of them." This creates an intergroup, rather than an intragroup relationship between leaders and followers (see Hogg, van Knippenberg, & Rast, 2012, for an overview of intergroup leadership). This effect can readily be seen in both corporate and military contexts. Corporate officers and military generals have considerably more communication within the leadership elite than they do with those outside of it, even when their offices are located on the same floor or in the same building as their followers (Treviño, 2005). Therefore, leaders become increasingly out of touch with the rank-and-file followers. If the leader does not realize he or she is out of touch with the group and its members, the members may distance themselves from the leader—the leader is essentially rejected and isolated from the group. Once this occurs the leader's influence over followers is markedly reduced, causing the leader to exercise his or her power over others to gain compliance (Hogg, 2010; Turner, 2005). Thus prototype-based leadership is again transformed into hierarchical power-based leadership where the leader "leads" through compliance and coercion rather than commitment and internalization. If, however, the leader recognizes his or her isolation from the group soon enough he or she can re-establish their prototypical group position by engaging in group-oriented behaviors or otherwise purposefully reducing normative distance (Platow & van Knippenberg, 2001; see also Shamir, this volume).

Group members may ultimately decide to loosen their ties from a group whose leader is perceived to be remote and out of touch with the group's norms, or they may get behind a different leader. However, disidentification is not a viable option if people's identity is heavily invested in one specific group, such as religious zealots or cult members (Hogg, Adelman, & Blagg, 2010; Festinger, Riecken, & Schachter, 1956). Luckily most people's social identities are tied to several group memberships rather than just one, and they are thus free to change allegiance. For example, employees may shift their loyalties to a different leader that more closely aligns with their interests and seems more likely to look out for the group's welfare.

UNCERTAINTY-IDENTITY THEORY

Under some circumstances, a leader can use the social context to gain followers' support, even if the leader holds a non-prototypical position within the group. It is possible that leaders can strategically evoke uncertainty among their followers or leverage their followers' existing uncertainties to their own advantage, especially when there is greater normative distance between leaders and followers (Rast, Gaffney, Hogg, & Crisp, 2012). While effective leaders are supposed to provide a sense of belonging and security for followers, paradoxically they might be seen as more effective by first evoking uncertainty among followers then exercising their own power to resolve such uncertainties (Seyranian, 2010). For instance, uncertainty surrounding how the 2010 Gulf of Mexico oil spill would affect day-to-day lives presented President Obama with a situation where Americans turned to him to reduce their uncertainty—looking to him to execute a clear plan to deal with the appalling disaster. Those who did not feel that Obama responded quickly enough or did not respond with decisiveness or passion very likely reduced their support for Obama as their leader. Further, a leader who does not reduce his or her followers' uncertainty is not likely to be perceived as effective. Indeed, a 2010 Gallup Poll found that 53% of Americans disapproved of how Obama dealt with the oil spill, while another Gallop Poll suggested that at this same time, approval ratings of Obama as president dropped to a low in his presidency (only 46% of those polled approved of Obama's job as president; Morales, 2010). As such, managing uncertainty is one of the most important challenges leaders face.

Indeed, perceptions of leader–follower distance are strongly affected by uncertainty. The impact of uncertainty on leadership processes can readily be explored in terms of uncertainty-identity theory (Hogg, 2000, 2007, 2012). Uncertainty-identity theory argues that people are motivated to reduce feelings of uncertainty, especially those related to oneself and one's social context. This motivation to reduce uncertainty is directly related to social identity processes. Group memberships provide people with a shared sense of self built around the group prototype: groups tell us how to behave, what to think, and what to feel. One of the most effective means to reduce uncertainty is therefore to identify or more strongly identify with groups. The basic hypothesis of uncertainty-identity theory is that as people feel more uncertain they are more likely to identify or more strongly identify with groups. In addition, groups with a clear, consensual prototype are more attractive and more effective at reducing uncertainty than those with a vague prototype, or low in entitativity. These general hypotheses have received much empirical support (for overview see Hogg, in press). Similarly, in times of uncertainty followers yearn for leaders who can reduce their self-uncertainty.

Recently research has applied uncertainty-identity theory to the social identity theory of leadership (Hohman, Hogg, & Bligh, 2010; Rast, Gaffney, Hogg, & Crisp, 2012). Consistent with previous research, these studies demonstrate that prototypical leaders receive greater support and endorsement compared to non-prototypical leaders. Additionally, when people feel low levels of uncertainty about themselves, their place in the world, and their future, they prefer prototypical leaders to non-prototypical leaders. However, when they feel highly uncertain, people increase their support for non-prototypical leaders, while still demonstrating a preference for prototypical leaders (Rast et al., 2012). These findings suggest that heightened self-uncertainty alters the perceived normative distance of leaders to their group's prototype and that increasing uncertainty may benefit non-prototypical leaders. That is, under uncertainty people may prefer a normatively close leader but, in the absence of other alternatives, one will support a normatively distanced leader. It is possible that when uncertainty is heightened people simply desire a group-oriented leader (e.g., Rast, Hogg, & Giessner, 2010), or that feelings of uncertainty alter the perceived normative distance of leaders to their group's prototype.

Heightened uncertainty may thus allow leaders to distance themselves, even slightly, from the group's prototype, while still maintaining power over the group. While followers yearn for a group prototypical leader, when uncertainty is high, they are more willing to support and endorse a leader who either is close to or remote from the group's prototype. Furthermore, this shift in preference extends beyond distance from the group's prototype. Times of uncertainty also promote the transformation from prototype-based to hierarchical power-based leadership (Hogg, 2007a, 2007b; see also Rast, Hogg, & Giessner, 2010). For instance, in the classic leadership study by Lippitt and White (1943), they found that compared to autocratic and laissez-faire leadership style, democratic leadership was the most effective. The group with the democratic leader had a friendly, group-oriented atmosphere and it was relatively productive. Noteworthy, however, these outcomes were not affected by whether the leader was physically close or remote for groups with the democratic leader, but distance did affect consequences for the group with the autocratic leader.

Recently Rast, Hogg, and Giessner (2010) conducted a similar series of studies but also manipulated or measured followers' feelings of uncertainty, along with their strength of identification. In addition to replicating Lippitt and White, they found that both students and real-world organizational employees who strongly identified with their group trusted and supported autocratic leaders more but democratic leaders less when uncertainty was heightened. Interestingly, this result was not affected by physical or temporal distance: it did not matter if followers worked alongside their leader or worked with the same leader for a week or 15 years. These results do suggest, however, that in times of uncertainty followers who strongly identify with the group are more likely to endorse a normatively distant, power-hungry leader rather than a normatively close, group-centric leader. This is because the former leadership style is better suited than the latter for the important uncertainty-reduction function that high identifiers seek under uncertainty.

As previous research demonstrates, effective leaders must be able to successfully reduce and manage their followers' uncertainty. Followers look to their leaders to reduce their uncertainty and are thus more likely to support a distant, non-prototypical leader when uncertainty is high rather than low. Furthermore, strong and directive (i.e., autocratic) leaders are better suited than democratic to reduce their followers' uncertainty; however, this effect is weakened when followers weakly identify with their group—that is, when followers are distant from the group. Consistent with the social identity framework, these findings are independent of the leader's physical and temporal distance. Although these findings provide a rather dark picture of leadership under uncertainty, they also provide a warning about blind followership in times of uncertainty and crises, such as directly after a terrorist attack or an economic collapse. Future research would benefit from elucidating how uncertainty and leader support affect percep-tions of the leader's normative distance.

INTERGROUP LEADERSHIP

The social identity theory of leadership has an intragroup focus on prototype-based leadership. Yet, many leadership situations often call for intergroup leadership where leaders must effectively transcend conflict-charged intergroup relations to bridge divisions and transcend boundaries between groups to build an integrative social identity. This leadership is often better conceptualized as intergroup leadership (e.g., Hogg, van Knippenberg, & Rast, 2012; Pittinsky, 2009). Intergroup leaders face the difficult challenge of constructing a shared social identity in a manner such that intergroup distinctiveness is not threatened or infringed. Intergroup leadership occurs when a leader is categorized as an outgroup member by one or more of the formal groups or organizations being led. These same processes that lead to increased influence in an intragroup setting (e.g., trust, liking, self-sacrificing) diminish their effectiveness if leadership is between groups. In fact, perceiving a leader as a prototypical member of one of the groups being led is problematic because the leader will be viewed as nepotistic if she favors her ingroup, or viewed as "selling out" if she favors the outgroup, both of which result in decreased trust in and support for the leader (e.g., Cheng, Fielding, Hogg, & Terry, 2009; Tyler & Blader, 2003).

Recently, researchers and theorists have begun to examine leadership across cultural and group divides (Hogg, van Knippenberg, & Rast, 2012; Pittinksy, 2009; Smith & Peterson, 2002). Hogg, van Knippenberg, and Rast (2012) proposed a theory of *intergroup leadership* in which they delineated how leaders can successfully bridge group boundaries. Intergroup leadership refers to leading one or more formal groups toward a collaborative goal, where the presence of these groups is the basis for the collaboration. For example, how can President Obama successfully lead the US out of the current economic depression without the collaborative efforts of both Democrats and Republicans? One of the key issues regarding effective intergroup leadership relates to distance: intergroup leaders may be close to their fellow ingroup members but distanced from outgroup members as there is no unified intergroup prototype. From a social identity theory of leadership perspective, for instance, Obama cannot simultaneously be prototypical of both Democrats and Republicans. Intuitively, it might seem that Obama should emphasize his prototypical position with the overarching, superordinate group (i.e., the United States); however, research demonstrates that this is not effective and may backfire because it threatens the identities of both Democrats and Republicans (e.g., Hohman, Hogg, & Bligh, 2010; Hornsey & Hogg, 2000; van Leeuwen & van Knippenberg, 2003). Counter-intuitively then, in an intergroup-leadership context Obama should emphasize the interdependence between Democrats and

Republicans. By strengthening the extent to which Democrats and Republicans identify with the collaborative intergroup relational identity, Obama's perceived normative distance should decrease while his support increases. Future leadership and organizational research would benefit greatly from examining leadership in an intergroup context, and directly examine the processes through which intergroup leaders may communicate their closeness to their fellow ingroup members but distance from outgroup members.

SUMMARY AND CONCLUSIONS

Distance is an important concern for leader–follower relations within and between groups, and it has recently garnered much attention from leadership researchers (e.g., Antonakis & Atwater, 2002). While leader–follower distance has traditionally been defined in terms of physical or geographical distance, this chapter shows that other conceptualizations of distance, such as psychological or normative distance are important factors in leader–follower relations. Our analysis draws on the social identity theory of leadership, which emphasizes the identity function of leadership, to address normative distance between leaders and followers. The theory suggests that a leader's distance from a prototype and thus his or her psychological distance from the group will impact followers' willingness to support their leader and thus the power they bestow upon their leader. Followers are more likely to support and trust leaders who more closely approximate the group's prototype; they are also more likely to be perceived as charismatic and effective.

A leader's ability to appear close to the group's prototype allows the leader greater influence to incite change within the group, while a leader who is distant from the group's prototype will have less power to enact change within the group. Our analysis suggests that leaders may be able to utilize their followers' uncertainty as a means to counteract the negative impact of being distant from the group's prototype, and thus gain some influence within the group. As we write this chapter, election season is in full force in the US, and both Democrats and Republicans have tried to paint their opponents as "distant" and "out of touch" with the American prototype. In addition, both parties work to gain support and votes by capitalizing on their followers' uncertainties regarding the economy and the direction of the country. For undecided voters, the prospective leader with the best ability to reduce such uncertainty, and who paints the clearest vision of the future and offers the best plan to enact said vision, will get the vote. Importantly, this vote will hinge upon how normatively distant the prospective leader is from the American prototype—we do not elect political leaders who we think are out of touch with what it means to be an American.

Our theoretical perspective has several implications for leader–follower relations as our environments are becoming increasingly geographically and technologically diverse. For instance, when leaders and followers within an organization are geographically dispersed, from our perspective, leaders can be more effective by increasing followers' commitment to and identification with the organization, which will allow the leader to enhance or maintain his or her influence if he or she can be seen as group prototypical. Leaders can alter their prototypicality in several ways; for example, leaders can actually strive to embody the central position of their group, they can engage in rhetoric that highlights their own prototypical position or effectively highlight their rivals' non-prototypical positions, they can evoke feelings of uncertainty or crisis in the absence of a more prototypical leader, and they can engage in group-oriented behaviors rather than striving for their own self-interests. As leader prototypicality becomes increasingly significant, the mode through which leaders influence (e.g., face-to-face, electronically) becomes much less important.

Although our analysis dealt primarily with normative distance to an ingroup prototype, future research will doubtlessly elucidate the relationship between physically close or distant leaders and perceptions of that leader's normative distance from the group. For example, future research might consider whether a physically remote leader can be perceived as psychologically close to the group, or if physical distance implies a lack of group cohesiveness and out-of-touchness that does not allow the leader to be perceived as prototypical. Are the relationships different among work groups as opposed to large-scale social categories (e.g., team leaders vs. leaders of multinational organizations)? We hope that the social identity analysis of leadership can provide a foundation from which leadership scholars can extend leader–follower distance beyond a physical and geographic sense, and continue to incorporate aspects of psychological and normative distance.

BIBLIOGRAPHY

ABC News/Washington Post Poll. (Sept. 30–Oct. 3, 2010a). GOP Advantage Eases, but Still Large as Economic Optimism Shows a Pulse. Retrieved December 18, 2010 from Langer Research Associates.

ABC News/Washington Post Poll. (Dec. 9–12, 2010b). Six in 10 Rule Out Palin in the Hunt for 2012. Retrieved December 18, 2010 from Langer Research Associates.

Abrams, D. & Hogg, M. A. (Eds.). (1990). *Social identity theory: Constructive and critical advances.* Hemel Hempstead, UK: Harvester Wheatsheaf, and New York: Springer-Verlag.

Abrams, D. & Hogg, M. A. (2010). Social identity and self-categorization. In J. F. Dovidio, M. Hewstone, P. Glick, & V. M. Esses (Eds.), *The SAGE handbook of prejudice, stereotyping and discrimination* (pp. 179–193). London: SAGE.

Abrams, D., Randsley de Moura, G., Marques, J. M., & Hutchison, P. (2008). Innovation credit: When can leaders oppose their group's norms? *Journal of Personality and Social Psychology, 95,* 662–678.

Alabastro, A. B., Rast, D. E., III, Lac, A., Hogg, M. A., & Crano. W. D. (2012). Intergroup bias and perceived similarity: The effects of successes and failures on support for in- and outgroup political leaders. *Group Processes and Intergroup Relations,* 136843021243 7212, first published on March 1, 2012.

Antonakis J. & Atwater L. (2002). Leader distance: A review and a proposed theory. *Leadership Quarterly, 13,* 673–704.

Avolio, B. J. & Bass, B. M. (1987). Transformational leadership, charisma and beyond. In J. G. Hunt, B. R. Balaga, H. P. Dachler, & C. A. Schriesheim (Eds.), *Emerging leadership vistas* (pp. 29–50). Elmsford, NY: Pergamon Press.

Avolio, B. J. & Yammarino, F. J. (Eds.). (2003). *Transformational and charismatic leadership: The road ahead.* New York: Elsevier.

Brewer, M. B. (1991). The social self: On being the same and different at the same time. *Personality and Social Psychology Bulletin, 17,* 475–482.

Campbell, D. T. (1958). Common fate, similarity, and other indices of the status of aggregates of persons as social entities. *Behavioral Science, 3,* 14–25.

Cheng, G. H.-L., Fielding, K. S., Hogg, M. A., & Terry, D. J. (2009). Reactions to procedural discrimination in an intergroup context: The role of social identity of the authority. *Group Processes and Intergroup Relations, 12,* 463–478.

Cicero, L., Bonaiuto, M., Pierro, A., & van Knippenberg, D. (2008). Employees work effort as a function of leader group prototypicality: The moderating role of team identification. *European Review of Applied Psychology, 58,* 117–124.

Cicero, L., Pierro, A., & van Knippenberg, D. (2007). Leader group prototypicality and job satisfaction: The moderating role of job stress and team identification. *Group Dynamics, 11,* 165–175.

Conger, J. A. & Kanungo, R. N. (1988). *Charismatic leadership: The elusive factor in organizational effectiveness.* San Francisco: Jossey-Bass.

Dovidio, J. F., Gaertner, S. L., & Lamoreaux, M. J. (2009). Leadership across group divides: The challenges and potential of a common group identity. In T. Pittinsky (Ed.), *Crossing the divide: Intergroup leadership in a world of difference* (pp. 3–16). Cambridge, MA: Harvard Business Publishing.

Duck, J. M. & Fielding, K. S. (2003). Leaders and their treatment of subgroups: Implications for evaluations of the leader and the superordinate group. *European Journal of Social Psychology, 33,* 387–401.

Eagly, A. H. & Karau, S. J. (2002). Role congruity theory of prejudice toward female leaders. *Psychological Review*, 109, 573–598.

Ellemers, N., De Gilder, D., & Haslam, S. A. (2004). Motivating individuals and groups at work: A social identity perspective on leadership and group performance. *Academy of Management Review*, 29, 459–478.

Festinger, L.., Riecken, H. W., & Schachter, S. (1956). *When prophecy fails: A social and psychological study of a modern group that predicted the end of the world*. Minneapolis: University of Minnesota Press.

Fiedler, F. E. (1964). A contingency model of leadership effectiveness. In L. Berkowitz (Ed.), *Advances in experimental social psychology* (Vol. 1, pp. 149–190). New York: Academic Press.

Fiske, S. T. & Taylor, S. E. (2008). *Social cognition: From brains to culture*. New York: McGraw-Hill.

Gaffney, A. M. & Hogg, M. A. (in press). Group processes. In W. S. Bainbridge (Ed.), *Leadership in science and technology: A reference handbook*. Thousand Oaks, CA: Sage.

Giessner, S . R. & Schubert, T. W. (2007). High in the hierarchy: How vertical location and judgments of leaders' power are interrelated. *Organizational Behavior and Human Decision Processes*, 104, 30–44.

Giessner, S. R., van Knippenberg, D., & Sleebos, E. (2009). License to fail? How leader group prototypicality moderates the effects of leader performance on perceptions of leadership effectiveness. *Leadership Quarterly*, 20, 434–451.

Hamilton, D. L. & Sherman, S. J. (1996). Perceiving persons and groups. *Psychological Review*, 103, 336–335.

Haslam, S. A. & Platow, M. J. (2001). Your wish is our command: The role of shared social identity in translating a leader's vision into followers' action. In M. A. Hogg & D. J. Terry (Eds.), *Social identity processes in organizational contexts* (pp. 213–228). Philadelphia: Psychology Press.

Hogg, M. A. (1993). Group cohesiveness: A critical review and some new directions. *European Review of Social Psychology*, 4, 85–111.

Hogg, M. A. (2001a). A social identity theory of leadership. *Personality and Social Psychology Review*, 5, 184–200.

Hogg, M. A. (2001b). From prototypicality to power: A social identity analysis of leadership. In S. R. Thye, E. J. Lawler, M. W. Macy, & H. A. Walker (Eds.), *Advances in group processes* (Vol. 18, pp. 1–30). Oxford: Elsevier.

Hogg, M. A. (2004). Uncertainty and extremism: Identification with high entitativity groups under conditions of uncertainty. In V. Yzerbyt, C. M. Judd, & O. Corneille (Eds.), *The psychology of group perception: Perceived variability, entitativity, and essentialism* (pp. 401–418). New York: Psychology Press.

Hogg, M. A. (2005). Uncertainty, social identity, and ideology. In S. R. Thye & E. J. Lawler (Eds.), *Advances in group processes* (Vol. 22, pp. 203–229). San Diego, CA: Elsevier.

Hogg, M. A. (2006). Social identity theory. In P. J. Burke (Ed.), *Contemporary social psychological theories* (pp. 111–136). Palo Alto, CA: Stanford University Press.

Hogg, M. A. (2007a). Uncertainty-identity theory. In M. P. Zanna (Ed.), *Advances in experimental social psychology* (Vol. 39, pp. 69–126). San Diego, CA: Academic Press.

Hogg, M. A. (2007b). Organizational orthodoxy and corporate autocrats: Some nasty consequences of organizational identification in uncertain times. In C. A. Bartel, S. Blader, & A. Wrzesniewski (Eds.), *Identity and the modern organization* (pp. 35–59). Mahwah, NJ: Erlbaum.

Hogg, M. A. (2008). Social identity theory of leadership. In C. L. Hoyt, G. R. Goethals, &

D. R. Forsyth (Eds.), *Leadership at the crossroads. Volume 1: Leadership and psychology* (pp. 62–77). Westport, CT: Praeger.

Hogg, M. A. (2009). From group conflict to social harmony: Leading across diverse and conflicting social identities. In T. Pittinsky (Ed.), *Crossing the divide: Intergroup leadership in a world of difference* (pp. 17–30). Cambridge, MA: Harvard Business Publishing.

Hogg, M. A. (2010). Influence and leadership. In S. T. Fiske, D. T. Gilbert, & G. Lindzey (Eds.), *Handbook of social psychology* (5th ed., Vol. 2, pp. 1166–1207). New York: Wiley.

Hogg. M. A. (in press). Leadership. In J. M. Levine (Ed.), *Group processes.* New York: Psychology Press.

Hogg, M. A. (2012). Uncertainty-identity theory. In P. A. M. Van Lange, A. W. Kruglanski, & E. T. Higgins (Eds.), *Handbook of theories of social psychology* (Vol. 2, pp. 62–80). Thousand Oaks, CA: Sage.

Hogg, M. A. & Abrams, D. (1988). *Social identifications: A social psychology of intergroup relations and group processes.* London & New York: Routledge.

Hogg, M. A. & Abrams, D. (1993). Towards a single-process uncertainty-reduction model of social motivation in groups. In M. A. Hogg & D. Abrams, (Eds.), *Group motivation: Social psychological perspectives* (pp. 173–190). Hemel Hempstead, UK: Harvester Wheatsheaf, and New York: Prentice Hall.

Hogg, M. A., Adelman, J. R., & Blagg, R. D. (2010). Religion in the face of uncertainty: An uncertainty-identity theory account of religiousness. *Personality and Social Psychology Review,* 14, 72–83.

Hogg, M. A. & Gaffney, A. M. (in press). Prototype-based social comparison within groups: Constructing social identity to reduce self-uncertainty. In Z. Krizan & F. Gibbons (Eds.), *Communal Functions of Social Comparisons.* New York: Cambridge University Press.

Hogg, M. A., Hains, S. C., & Mason, I. (1998). Identification and leadership in small groups: Salience, frame of reference, and leader stereotypicality effects on leader evaluations. *Journal of Personality and Social Psychology,* 75, 1248–1263.

Hogg, M. A., Hardie, E. A., & Reynolds, K. (1995). Prototypical similarity, self-categorization, and depersonalized attraction: A perspective on group cohesiveness. *European Journal of Social Psychology,* 25, 159–177.

Hogg, M. A., Martin, R., Epitropaki, O., Mankad, A., Svensson, A., & Weeden, K. (2005). Effective leadership in salient groups: Revisiting leader-member exchange theory from the perspective of the social identity theory of leadership. *Personality and Social Psychology Bulletin,* 31, 991–1004.

Hogg, M. A., Martin, R., & Weeden, K. (2004). Leader–member relations and social identity. In D. van Knippenberg & M. A. Hogg (Eds.), *Leadership and power: Identity processes in groups and organizations* (pp. 18–33). London: Sage.

Hogg, M. A., Sherman, D. K., Dierselhuis, J., Maitner, A. T., & Moffitt, G. (2007). Uncertainty, entitativity, and group identification. *Journal of Experimental Social Psychology,* 43, 135–142.

Hogg, M. A. & Smith, J. R. (2007). Attitudes in social context: A social identity perspective. *European Review of Social Psychology,* 18, 89–131.

Hogg, M. A. & Terry, D. J. (2000). Social identity and self-categorization processes in organizational contexts. *Academy of Management Review,* 25, 121–140.

Hogg, M. A. & Turner, J. C. (1985a). Interpersonal attraction, social identification and psychological group formation. *European Journal of Social Psychology,* 15, 51–66.

Hogg, M. A. & Turner, J. C. (1985b). When liking begets solidarity: An experiment on the role of interpersonal attraction in psychological group formation. *British Journal of Social Psychology*, 24, 267–281.

Hogg, M. A. & Turner, J. C. (1987). Social identity and conformity: A theory of referent informational influence. In W. Doise & S. Moscovici (Eds.), *Current issues in European social psychology* (Vol. 2, pp. 139–182). Cambridge: Cambridge University Press.

Hogg, M. A., Turner, J. C., & Davidson, B. (1990). Polarized norms and social frames of reference: A test of the self-categorization theory of group polarization. *Basic and Applied Social Psychology*, 11, 77–100.

Hogg, M. A. & van Knippenberg, D. (2003). Social identity and leadership processes in groups. In M. P. Zanna (Ed.), *Advances in experimental social psychology* (Vol. 35, pp. 1–52). San Diego, CA: Academic Press.

Hogg, M. A., van Knippenberg, D., & Rast, D. E., III (2012). Intergroup leadership in organizations: Leading across group and organizational boundaries. *Academy of Management Review*, 37, 232–255.

Hohman, Z. P., Hogg, M. A., & Bligh, M. C. (2010). Identity and intergroup leadership: Asymmetrical political and national identification in response to uncertainty. *Self and Identity*, 9, 113–128.

House, R. J. (1971). A path-goal theory of leadership effectiveness. *Administrative Science Quarterly*, 16, 321–338.

Hornsey, M. J. & Hogg, M. A. (2000). Assimilation and diversity: An integrative model of subgroup relations. *Personality and Social Psychology Review*, 4, 143–156.

Katz, R. L. (1955). Skills of an effective administrator. *Harvard Business Review*, 33, 33–42.

Kent, S. A. (2000). Brainwashing and re-indoctrination programs in the Children of God/The Family. *Cultic Studies Journal*, 17, 56–78.

Lippitt, R. & White, R. (1943). The "social climate" of children's groups. In R. G. Barker, J. Kounin, & H. Wright (Eds.), *Child behavior and development* (pp. 485–508). New York: McGraw-Hill.

Morales, L. (2010, Jan 7). Americans rate Obama 7 points worse on spill than overall. *Gallup Daily*. Retrieved August 27, 2010, from: http://www.gallup.com/poll/139406/americans-rate-obama-points-worse-spill-overall.aspx.

Milgram, S. (1963). Behavioral study of obedience. *Journal of Abnormal and Social Psychology*, 67, 371–378.

Milgram, S. (1974). *Obedience to authority*. London: Tavistock.

Moscovici, S. (1980). Toward a theory of conversion behavior. In L. Berkowitz (Ed.), *Advances in experimental social psychology* (Vol. 13, pp. 202–239). New York: Academic Press.

Newcomb, T. M. (1961). *The acquaintance process*. New York: Rinehart & Winston.

Northouse, P. G. (2010). *Leadership: Theory and practice* (5th ed.). Thousand Oaks, CA: Sage.

Pittinsky, T. (Ed.). (2009). *Crossing the divide: Intergroup leadership in a world of difference*. Cambridge, MA: Harvard Business Publishing.

Platow, M.J. & van Knippenberg, D. (2001). A social identity analysis of leadership endorsement: The effects of leader ingroup prototypicality and distributive intergroup fairness. *Personality and Social Psychology Bulletin*, 27, 1508–1519.

Platow, M. J., van Knippenberg, D., Haslam, S. A., van Knippenberg, B., & Spears, R. (2006). A special gift we bestow on you for being representative of us: Considering leader charisma from a self-categorization perspective. *The British Journal of Social Psychology*, 45, 303–320.

Rast, D. E., III, Gaffney, A. M., Hogg, M. A., & Crisp, R. J. (2012). Leadership under uncertainty: When leaders who are non-prototypical group members can gain support. *Journal of Experimental Social Psychology*, 48, 646–653.

Reicher S. D. & Hopkins, N. (1996). Seeking influence through characterizing self-categories: An analysis of anti-abortionist rhetoric. *British Journal of Social Psychology*, 35, 297–311.

Reicher, S. D. & Hopkins, N. (2003). On the science of the art of leadership. In D. van Knippenberg and M. A. Hogg, (Eds.), *Leadership and power: Identity processes in groups and organizations* (pp. 197–209). London: Sage.

Reicher, S., Haslam, S. A., & Hopkins, N. (2005). Social identity and the dynamics of leadership: Leaders and followers as collaborative agents in the transformation of social reality. *Leadership Quarterly*, 16, 547–568.

Reiterman, T. & Jacobs, J. (1982). *Raven: The Untold Story of Reverend Jim Jones and His People*. New York: Dutton.

Ridgeway, C. L. (2003). Status characteristics and leadership. In D. van Knippenberg and M. A. Hogg, (Eds.), *Leadership and power: Identity processes in groups and organizations* (pp. 65–78). London: Sage.

Seyranian, V. (2010). Constructing extremism: Uncertainty provocation and reduction by extremist leaders. In M. A. Hogg & D. Blaylock (Eds.), *The Psychology of Uncertainty and Extremism*. Oxford: Blackwell.

Seyranian, V. & Bligh, M. C. (2008). Presidential charismatic leadership: Exploring the rhetoric of social change. *Leadership Quarterly*, 19, 54–76.

Shamir, B. (1995). Social distance and charisma: Theoretical notes and an exploratory study. *Leadership Quarterly*, 6, 19–47.

Sherif, M. (1966). *In common predicament: Social psychology of intergroup conflict and cooperation*. Boston: Houghton Mifflin.

Siegel, E. (2010, December 14). Sarah Palin not 'electable for presidency,' says GOP operative who helped reelect Ronald Reagan. *The Huffington Post*. Retrieved December 18, 2010, from http://www.huffingtonpost.com/2010/12/14/sarah-palin-sigrogich_n_796267.html.

Smith, P. B. & Peterson, M. F. (2002). Cross-cultural leadership. In M. J Gannon & K. L. Newman (Eds.), *The Blackwell handbook of cross-cultural management* (pp. 217–235). Oxford: Blackwell.

Stogdill, R. (1974). *Handbook of leadership*. New York: Free Press.

Tajfel, H. (1959). Quantitative judgement in social perception. *British Journal of Psychology*, 50, 16–29.

Tajfel, H. & Turner, J. C. (1979). An integrative theory of intergroup conflict. In W. G. Austin & S. Worchel (Eds.), *The social psychology of intergroup relations* (pp. 33–47). Monterey, CA: Brooks/Cole.

Terry, D. J. & Hogg, M. A. (1996). Group norms and the attitude-behavior relationship: A role for group identification. *Personality and Social Psychology Bulletin*, 22, 776–793.

Terry, D. J. & Hogg, M. A. (Eds.). (2000). *Attitudes, behavior, and social context: The role of norms and group membership*. Mahwah, NJ: Erlbaum.

Treviño, L. K. (2005). Out of touch: The CEO's role in corporate misbehavior. *Brooklyn Law Review*, 70, 1195–1197.

Turner, J. C. (2005) Explaining the nature of power: A three-process theory. *European Journal of Social Psychology*, 35, 1–22.

Turner, J. C., Hogg, M. A., Oakes, P. J., Reicher, S. D., & Wetherell, M. S. (1987). *Rediscovering the social group: A self-categorization theory*. Oxford: Blackwell.

Tyler, T. R. (1997). The psychology of legitimacy: A relational perspective on voluntary deference to authorities. *Personality and Social Psychology Review,* 1, 323–345.

Tyler, T. R. & Blader, S. L. (2003). The Group Engagement Model: Procedural justice social identity and cooperative behavior. *Personality and Social Psychology Review,* 7, 349–361.

van Knippenberg, D. & Hogg, M. A. (2003). A social identity model of leadership in organizations. In R. M. Kramer & B. M. Staw (Eds.), *Research in organizational behavior,* 25: 243–295.

van Knippenberg, B. & van Knippenberg, D. (2005). Leader self-sacrifice and leadership effectiveness: The moderating role of leader prototypicality. *Journal of Applied Psychology,* 90, 25–37.

van Knippenberg, D., van Knippenberg, B., De Cremer, D., & Hogg, M. A. (2004). Leadership, self, and identity: A review and research agenda. *Leadership Quarterly,* 15, 825–856.

van Leeuwen, E. & van Knippenberg, D. (2003). Organizational identification following a merger: The importance of agreeing to differ. In S. A. Haslam, D. van Knippenberg, M. J. Platow & N. Ellemers (Eds.), *Social identity at work: Developing theory for organizational practice* (pp. 205–221). New York and Hove, UK: Psychology Press.

Yagil, D. (1998). Charismatic leadership and organizational hierarchy: Attribution of charisma to close and distant leaders. *Leadership Quarterly,* 9, 161–176.

Yukl, G. (2010). *Leadership in organizations* (7th ed.). Upper Saddle River, NJ: Prentice Hall.

9

The Apple does not Fall Far from the Tree: Steve Jobs's Leadership as Simultaneously Distant and Close

Moran Anisman Razin and Ronit Kark

> I think it's [technology] brought the world a lot closer together, and will continue to do that.
>
> **Steve Jobs, *Rolling Stone* (Goodwell, 2003)**

This quotation, taken from Jobs's interview with *Rolling Stone* magazine in 2003, describes Jobs's view of technology. In his mind, technology was about bringing people closer. This was his purpose and his guide for creating new technologies, both inside and outside Apple. His leadership style also reflected the issue of distance and closeness from his customers (followers).[1] Steve Jobs was the Chief Executive Officer (CEO) of Apple for 14 years, and was described as a genius. He was an extraordinary person and was greatly admired by Apple fans and many others, not only those in the field of technology but by millions of people whose lives were influenced by his products. Typically, large company CEOs are thought to be distant from their employees and even more so from their customers. However, we argue that Steve Jobs managed to shape people's perceptions of him as a charismatic leader who was simultaneously close and distant. According to leadership theory, close charismatic leaders and distant charismatic leaders are perceived differently by followers. This has been suggested to result in different types of effects and outcomes. Close leaders usually influence their followers through their observable behaviors and their personal relationships with them, whereas distant leaders influence followers through image-building techniques. Leaders who can capitalize on a dual perception of both closeness and distance may benefit from being able to influence followers from both near and afar.

Our goal here is to draw from theories of leadership and distance (e.g., Antonakis & Atwater, 2002; Napier & Ferris, 1993; Shamir, 1995; Waldman & Yammarino, 1999; Yagil, 1998) and use the case study of Steve Jobs to develop a conceptual framework to advance further theoretical thinking and empirical studies on the underlying mechanisms that enable leaders to influence their followers' perceptions of their distance from the leader and, ultimately, affect their behaviors and organizational-related outcomes. Thus, our aim here is threefold. First, we aim to present the idea that leaders can enact distance and create perceptions of distance and proximity, which are independent, to some extent, of their predetermined formal organizational distance (such as hierarchy, social distance and physical distance). Second, we aim to understand different mechanisms used by leaders to shape followers' perception of distance and proximity from them. Last, we aim to explore possible outcomes of leaders' distance and proximity. We use the case study of Steve Jobs to uncover the ways in which leaders are able to actively increase and decrease distance from their followers. By focusing on the case study of Steve Jobs, we will present the notion of leaders "doing distance and proximity," by exploring different ways in which leaders actively shape the way they are perceived by followers as near or far from them. We suggest that Steve Jobs's dual-distance strategy (of eliciting both a sense of distance and a sense of proximity among followers) was a leadership strategy which distinguished Jobs from other business leaders (CEOs) and helped to create the myth of Jobs as an extraordinary and legendary leader. By being both close and distant, he stood out as a charismatic and unique leader, eliciting strong emotions and attachment between the customers and his products, as well as between the customers and himself as a leader. In the following, we start by presenting a short biography of the life of Steve Jobs. Then, drawing on behaviors and effects of close and distant leaders we demonstrate how he made use of both distant charisma and close charisma. We then focus on the notion of "doing distance" and attempt to reveal and understand the enactment of leadership distance. Finally, we investigate four different mechanisms used by Steve Jobs to shape distance. We conclude with the implications of doing distance and consider future directions for research.

THE LIFE OF STEVE JOBS

Steven Paul Jobs was born on February 24th, 1955, to two unmarried graduate students who decided to give him up for adoption. During his high school years, he spent his free time at Hewlett-Packard in Silicon Valley California, where he met a fellow computer fan—Steve Wozniak (known as Woz). After graduating from high school, Jobs enrolled at Reed College in Portland, Oregon. However, soon after, he stopped going to the classes he was enrolled in and started attending the classes he found interesting and he officially dropped out after one semester. He spent the next 18 months attending classes he found interesting, such as calligraphy, which influenced the way he later designed typefaces and space between fonts for the Mac. After dropping out he worked for Atari, Inc. for some time. In 1976, at the age of 21, together with Wozniak he founded Apple Computers in his parents' garage in Los Altos, California. For the next nine years, Apple grew and Jobs and Wozniak invented different computers that changed the face of the computer industry—Apple I, Apple II (known as one of the first personal computers—PC—in the world) and the Macintosh (named after the McIntosh apple and intentionally misspelled). In 1985 Jobs was forced out of the company, after a power struggle with Apple's CEO at the time—John Sculley. He then founded another computer company called NeXT, bought the then failing Pixar Studios (named The Graphics Group at the time), which under his management became one of the leading animation studios in the world.

The next chapter in Jobs's life started in 1996, when Apple was unprofitable and was facing possible bankruptcy. Apple decided to buy Jobs's company NeXT, and brought him back as interim chief executive (iCEO). In 2000 Jobs became the company's permanent CEO. In the years that followed Apple not only got back on track, but also became one of the most profitable companies in the world.[2] Jobs led Apple to success by focusing the company on a few core products (desktop computers and laptops) as opposed to many different ones and by creating groundbreaking products like the MacBook Air. Apple prided itself in its sleek, elegant and easy-to-use computers like the iMac, MacBook, and MacBook Air. The creation of new digital devices such as the iPod, iPhone, and iPad made Apple a household name around the world.

In 2003 Jobs discovered he had pancreatic cancer. After a struggle of eight years, he passed away on October 5, 2011. His death was mourned by many around the world, and major TV networks in the United States and across the world interrupted scheduled programming to broadcast the news. Several key figures, including the President of the United States Barack Obama, British Prime Minister David Cameron and Microsoft founder Bill Gates commented on his death. Many Apple enthusiasts and Jobs's fans gathered in Apple stores around the world to pay their respects to Jobs.

Below we explore the complex dynamic in which Steve Jobs enacted distance and proximity from Apple customers and wider audiences, in an attempt to uncover one of the processes that contributed to the strong bond that developed between Steve Jobs and Apple clients/fans.

LEADERSHIP AND CEO DISTANCE

Leadership distance can be defined as an aspect of the organizational context (Cole, Bruch, & Shamir, 2009; Porter & McLaughlin, 2006) that influences leadership processes in organizations. Leadership distance has been described as resulting from leaders' hierarchical level, their physical location with regard to followers, psychological distance (perceived and actual similarity), the frequency of interactions with followers, and the quality of their relationship in general (Antonakis & Atwater, 2002; Napier & Ferris, 1993; Shamir, 1995; Yagil, 1998). The majority of previous theories and typologies presented distance as a stable facet of leadership context, which is an integral part of the position and role of the leader and is therefore under minimal control by the leader. We approach leadership distance in a somewhat different manner by conceptualizing leadership distance as a characteristic that can to some extent be defined, constructed, molded, and influenced by leaders themselves. We draw on earlier work on "sense-making" and "sense-giving," arguing that leaders are able to influence aspects of their distance and the ways followers interpret it, by creating a perception of distance or proximity through manipulation of their messages and personal image. Through the transcendence of inherent dimensions of distance, leaders can influence and shape followers' perceptions of their distance. In this chapter we explore the ways in which Steve Jobs attempted to influence his followers' perception of him as a leader and their behavior toward Apple as a company, through his manipulation of leader distance. In our analyses of the followers we focus only on Apple customers, and do not refer to Apple employees.

As Apple's CEO, Jobs was at the top of the hierarchy and was likely to be perceived as distant by followers. Companies' CEOs are distant from their followers on different dimensions. They are physically distant, as their employees and customers are usually scattered across the country or are located in other countries, and their offices are usually some distance from their employees. CEOs are also socially and psychologically distant. They differ from their followers in many ways including their job profiles, status, power, and demographic characteristics. They might also be perceived as dissimilar to followers on other characteristics such as values and general personality (e.g., being achievement-oriented, very successful, and rich). Since CEOs lead a large number of followers, they rarely interact directly with their followers, and when they do, it is at best a unilateral interaction, in which the leader presents his or her strategy or vision. This is rarely a reciprocal conversation between two equals. According to Waldman and Yammarino (1999), CEOs can be close to their followers; however, these followers are those with whom they have direct working relationships; namely the top management team. With the majority of their followers they have a "distant relationship" that includes symbolic behaviors and a presentation of their vision (Waldman & Yammarino, 1999). Therefore, CEO leadership is seen as a distant form of leadership, one that is not a part of the followers' everyday life and one that is characterized by leaders' use of impression-management strategies and followers' attributions processes toward the leader.

In this chapter we explore a different case, a CEO whose unusual and unique behavior created a different type of leadership and perception of distance that is simultaneously distant and close.

DUAL-DISTANCE STRATEGIES: THE PERCEPTION OF STEVE JOBS AS A CLOSE AND DISTANT LEADER

Close and distant leaders have been conceptualized as possessing and demonstrating different characteristics and behaviors and as having different influences on their subordinates (Antonakis & Atwater, 2002; Cole et al., 2009; Shamir, 1995; Yagil, 1998). Distant charismatic leaders are perceived as having extraordinary qualities and are perceived in general as more heroic figures (Antonakis & Atwater, 2002; Shamir, 1995; Yagil, 1998), as having more courage and as being more persistent (Shamir, 1995). Attributions they elicit are based upon their presentation of their ideas (Yagil, 1998), their articulation of a vision and their rhetorical skills (Shamir, 1995), as well as on organizational performance cues and image-building techniques, which create an ideal image of the leader (Antonakis & Atwater, 2002). On the other hand, close charismatic leaders are often described in a more realistic and less ideal manner than distant leaders. Close charismatic leaders are usually described in terms of their personal qualities and behaviors (Antonakis & Atwater, 2002; Shamir, 1995) and serve as behavioral role model for their followers (Yagil, 1998; Shamir, 1995). Thus, the literature suggests that close and distant charismatic leaders are portrayed and perceived as two different prototypes of leadership who demonstrate different traits, behaviors, and characteristics. Distant charismatic leaders are perceived as more heroic figures, whereas close charismatic leaders are perceived as more humane.

We contend that Steve Jobs represented a unique leader in that he was able to incorporate both aspects as a leader. He actively shaped a sense of distance, in that he was perceived as "larger than life" and a sense of proximity, in that he could also be perceived as a "close friend." Jobs as a leader clearly enacted both closeness and distance. Below we analyze and illustrate this effect. We first discuss Steve Jobs as a distant charismatic leader and then show how he was perceived as a close leader. To do so we make use of a variety of supplementary material including daily newspapers and magazine articles, popular press articles, online "blog" posting, YouTube videos, Apple advertisements, books on the life of Steve Jobs and documentary movies about Jobs's life and Apple "fans."

Jobs as Characterized by Distant Charisma

One of the key characteristics of distant charismatic leaders is their presentation of a vision (Shamir, 1995; Waldman & Yammarino, 1999; Yagil, 1998), which is an idealized image of the future (Conger & Kanungo, 1998; Shamir, 1995). Among Jobs's most renowned characteristics was his vision for the technology industry. *Fortune's* technology reporter Miguel Helft wrote in Jobs's obituary that "On Wednesday, America lost its most successful chief executive, the technology industry lost its greatest visionary, and Silicon Valley lost a giant whose influence will be felt for years to come" (2011). In a movie by the Discovery Channel broadcast after his death, Michio Kaku, a physicist from the City College of New York, said "Steve Jobs had a great vision" (Halpin, 2011). He is also described in the movie as "the guy who envisioned a computer in every desk, an ear-bud in every ear and a device that will take multitasking to a whole new level. He didn't just envision. He made it happen" (Halpin, 2011). In the press, Jobs was presented as " a man who changed the way we live. The word used most often is 'visionary'" (Claburn, 2011). Also metaphorically he was portrayed as a person who "reached for the stars and pulled a few down to earth for the rest of us to enjoy" (Lappin, 2011). Almost every description of Jobs in the media included presenting him as a visionary. By presenting a vision and pursuing it throughout his life, Jobs exemplified a major characteristic of distant leaders. However, his vision presentations would not have been complete without his famed rhetoric skill, which has been described as an ability to mold reality and make others perceive it as he wished—his "reality distortion field" (Isaacson, 2011a).

Rhetorical skills have also been defined as a key characteristic of distant charismatic leaders (Shamir, 1995; Waldman & Yammarino, 1999; Yagil, 1998). As the front man of Apple, Steve Jobs was in charge of the company's unveiling of new products and services in the form of the Apple keynote speeches at major Apple events. The keynote speeches were very popular and well known all around the world: people would arrive a day early to the Macworld and Apple Expo conferences and camp out near the entrance to get a good seat for the keynote speech (Shely, 2009). In these keynotes Jobs demonstrated his unique rhetoric skill, often eliciting great applause from the excited audience. Internet bloggers and Apple fans dubbed these speeches "Stevenote" (Cult of Mac, 2011; "Stevenote," n.d.), to reflect their special nature and appeal. Whenever he was presenting to the crowds, Jobs was welcomed with great applause by the audience and managed to elicit enthusiasm and acceptance from them. One example is the audience's reaction to Jobs's announcement at the 1997 Macworld Expo, that Microsoft was investing $150 million in Apple in order to help the company during its financial crisis. The audience was not happy with the news and expressed it, as they booed at Jobs's announcement. As a reaction, Jobs delivered an unexpected sermon emphasizing the importance of the relationship with Microsoft, resulting in the audience's approval of the step. This event demonstrates Jobs's ability to shape and influence public opinion through his well-calculated and elaborate rhetorical skill.

Many times Jobs's exceptional rhetorical skill was compared to that of other CEOs as can be seen in articles that appeared in the *Guardian*:

> If the chief executive of Cadbury-Schweppes speaks at a conference, or Nike's boss introduces a new kind of trainer, you might expect to see it covered in specialist magazines, then quickly forgotten. But on Tuesday a chief executive will stand up and announce something, and within minutes it will be scrutinized across the web and on stockbrokers' computers. It will be in newspapers. They'll talk about it for months. That chief executive is Steve Jobs, and I know why that speech makes an impact. To a casual observer it is just a guy in a black shirt and jeans talking about some new technology products. But it is in fact an incredibly complex and sophisticated blend of sales pitch, product demonstration and corporate cheerleading, with a dash of religious revival thrown in for good measure. It represents weeks of work, precise orchestration and intense pressure for the scores of people who collectively make up the "man behind the curtain" . . . When Apple announces something new, people pay attention. This is due, in large measure, to Steve and the way he delivers Apple's messages.
>
> (Evangelist, 2006)

These examples demonstrate Jobs's rhetorical skill, one of his unique characteristics that differentiated him from other executives in the business world, which reinforced his image as a distant charismatic leader.

Perceptions of distant leaders are also influenced by organizational performance cues. Starting in 1996, when Jobs returned to Apple, and especially during the 2000s, Apple garnered vast success and popularity among customers all around the world. This success and customer loyalty was mainly attributed to Jobs. For example, *Forbes* contributor Scott Goodson was asked why Apple's customers are forgiving and loyal to the company, even when there are issues and problems with the product. His answer was "Well, it's mainly because of the late, great Steve Jobs. Apple is Steve Jobs. Steve Jobs is Apple. People feel like they have a personal relationship with Apple because they're essentially thinking of Steve" (Goodson, 2011). Apple's success thus served as a basis for the evaluation of Jobs as a leader. Apple is Steve Jobs, and hence its success is his. This quotation demonstrates another aspect of Jobs's distant leadership style— the heroic perception of the leader. Distant leaders are usually perceived as heroic and extraordinary individuals, who have special characteristics that make them the successful leaders they are (Antonakis & Atwater, 2002; Shamir, 1995). Jobs was presented many times as the "hero that saved Apple" when he returned to the company in 1997 (Macworld, 2011; Shinal, 2011). The extraordinary attributions, were also reflected in the financial markets' response to his medical leaves throughout his illness. Every one of his medical leaves or news about his health influenced Apple's stock, with the deterioration in Jobs's health leading to a decline in Apple stock.

All the above demonstrate the perceptions of Jobs as a distant charismatic leader. He was seen as extraordinary and heroic, able to articulate a vision and highly capable of presenting it in a manner that excited followers. However, as shown in Goodson's comment (2011), Steve Jobs was not the usual CEO or distant leader. In Jobs's case people felt that they had a personal relationship with Apple, because they felt as though they had a personal relationship with Jobs himself. Thus, Jobs's image as a leader also encompassed characteristics, personality traits, behaviors and relationships with followers that have been found in previous research to be attributed to close charismatic leaders (Shamir, 1995; Waldman & Yammarino, 1999; Yagil, 1998).

Jobs as Characterized by Close Charisma

Close charismatic leaders tend to be described in terms of their expertise, competence and intelligence (Shamir, 1995). These traits were frequently used to describe Jobs (Isaacson, 2011b; *The Economist*, 2011). Jobs was also known for setting very high standards, another trait ascribed to close charismatic leaders (Shamir, 1995). Google's engineer, Vic Gundotra worked with Jobs for a while. One Sunday he received a phone call from Jobs, who had "something urgent to discuss" with him (Gundotra, 2011). The urgent matter was the yellow gradient of the letter O in the Google logo when browsing on the iPhone. This is one of many examples demonstrating Jobs's concern that even the smallest details had to be perfect in his products, thus setting high standards for those with whom he worked.

Close charismatic leaders are also defined in terms of their effects on followers, which also characterized Jobs. Role modeling was suggested as one of the effects attributed to close charismatic leaders. Steve Jobs was referred to as a role model for hard work and success:

Jobs may be a multibillionaire, but that hasn't cut into his work ethic. He brings an entrepreneur's energy to tasks many CEOs would see as beneath them, whether it's personally checking the fine print on partnership agreements or calling reporters late in the evening to talk over a story he thinks is important.

(Burrows, Grover, & Green, 2006)

During his life and after his death there was much debate about whether Jobs was a good or a bad role model, but many times he was referred to as role model (e.g. Hepp, 2011; Subramaniya, 2009).

In his commencement speech at Stanford University in 2005, Jobs advised the graduates that "your time is limited so don't waste it living someone else's life," advice which resonated with Kamael Ann Sugrim, a graduate of the class. She says she was inspired by Jobs to carve her own path, just as he did for himself (Halpin, 2011). On the memorial webpage to Jobs, an Apple customer wrote "I just wanted to say Steve jobs was and still is my idol. He made me want to chase MY dreams and not the world's."

Role modeling was also found to be related to general attribution of charisma to close leaders, but not to distant leaders (Yagil, 1998). As Steve Jobs was frequently referred to as a role model, this characteristic is a good indication of a leadership style that increased proximity. Identification with the leader is described as a fundamental characteristic of charismatic leadership (Conger & Kanungo, 1988; Shamir, 1995), which also serves as a power source for the leader. In writings on Steve Jobs, the sense of identification from a stance of closeness is evident. When describing Jobs one interviewee said "If you ask me what my three major influences were, they've got to be, you know—my dad, John Lennon and Steve Jobs" (Shely, 2009). Many messages on Steve Jobs's memorial webpage reflected a similar sense of personal identification and close attachment (http://www.apple.com/stevejobs/).

Nevertheless, the most interesting thing about Jobs's leadership was the way people all over the world felt close to him and felt they had a personal relationship with him. Individuals did not know Steve Jobs personally but felt a connection to him, were inspired by him and were emotionally attached to him, something that became very noticeable after his death. One of the interviewees in the movie *MacHeads* (Shely, 2009) said "I'm willing to follow him; I think that whatever he says is fine with me. You're great Steve I will always love you." After his death, the Apple headquarters and Apple stores around the world became pilgrimage sites where people left flowers, notes, greeting cards and apples. Apple created a webpage called "Remembering Steve," where people could write messages to and about Jobs (http://www.apple.com/stevejobs/). Over a million people wrote messages on the webpage, expressing their sadness and thoughts. While admiration is related to both close and distant charismatic leadership, positive affect has mainly been ascribed to close charismatic leaders (Napier & Ferris, 1993; Shamir, 1995). Individuals felt very strong emotions toward Jobs as can be seen from their messages at the memorial page. For example, Zach wrote "I can't believe the person I have looked up for many years is now gone . . . I am deeply saddened by it"; Amanda wrote "You will truly be missed and we'll never forget! . . . steve UR [you are] always in our heart no matter what"; Chuck wrote "you'll never know how you changed my life. you've touched every person on this earth with a smile. thank you"; and John wrote "I feel as if I've lost a close friend. One that I've never met, but was part of my life every day." Many of these messages are phrased as personal letters to Jobs himself, reflecting the deep personal connection his customers/admirers felt for him.

Thus, Steve Jobs was perceived and experienced by his customers simultaneously as a distant heroic charismatic leader, as well as a close and humane charismatic leader. These perceptions were partially shaped and molded by Jobs himself through his intentional and unintentional actions, which we define as actions of "doing distance."

DOING DISTANCE: THE ENACTMENT OF LEADERSHIP DISTANCE

As human beings we shape and construct our physical and social environment, and to some extent the environment can be seen as a product of our creation. Through this process individuals also influence others' perceptions of themselves and various aspects of reality (Reicher, Haslam, & Hopkins, 2005). Thus leadership distance can be conceptualized not only as a predetermined characteristic of leadership or the context, but also as an attribute that can be crafted and controlled to some extent by the individual (i.e., the leader). Hence individuals can actively influence their perceived distance from others by enacting distance or "doing distance." The notion of "doing distance" encompasses a perception of leadership distance as a flexible and dynamic construct that can be influenced, shaped, re-shaped and transformed in the process of leaders' interactions with their followers. The enactment of "doing distance" is one way in which leaders take part in the process of "meaning making" and "sense making" (for meaning making see: Ashforth, Harrison, & Corley, 2008; Bartunek, Krim, Necochea, & Humphries, 1999; Sharma & Grant, 2011). While being novel to the field of leadership and distance, various streams of the leadership literature have presented leaders as creators of meaning (Ashforth et al., 2008; Bartunek et al., 1999; Conger, 1989). One such theoretical direction can be found in the work of Gardner and Avolio (1998), who make use of the dramaturgical perspective to understand charismatic leaders as carriers and constructors of meanings. According to their approach, charismatic leaders create meanings in social situations by engaging in "performances" of impression management and expressing themselves in different ways that are designed to shape the situation, events and the leaders' image according to their perceptions (Gardner & Avolio, 1998).

The impression management process includes four behaviors derived from the dramaturgical perspective: framing, scripting, staging and performing (Gardner & Avolio, 1998). Framing is defined as "a quality of communication that causes others to accept one meaning over another" (Fairhurst & Sarr, 1996, p. xi). Fairhurst and Sarr's (1996) definition of framing defines leaders as construing social reality for themselves and their followers. It is about explaining and presenting people and the world as the leader sees it. The second is scripting, which is defined as "the development of a set of directions that define the scene, identify actors and outline expected behavior" (Benford & Hunt, 1992, p. 38). The third element is staging, which refers to the development and manipulation of symbols such as physical appearance, settings props and other artifacts (Gardner & Avolio, 1998). Goffman (1959) includes wardrobe and grooming as an extension of one's personality, and such elements of appearance are often used by leaders, for example when a commander wears medals on his uniform as symbols of his esteem and power (Gardner & Avolio, 1998). Staging also includes manipulating the mass media, for example when business leaders appear in the company's commercials (Bryman, 1992; Conger, 1989; Gardner & Avolio, 1998). Finally, performing is defined by

Gardner and Avolio (1998) as exemplification and self-promotion. This process is used by charismatic leaders.

We draw on the work of Gardner and Avolio (1998) and contend that one of the major ways in which leaders construct meanings and make use of framing, scripting, staging, and performing strategies is that of "doing distance." We suggest that the manipulation of distance and proximity by leaders is an active means that enables leaders to build their image, influence the relationship between the leader and his or her followers, and influence followers' performance in different work and organizational tasks. Thus 'doing distance,' by shaping followers' perspectives of the leader as near and far, both physically and psychologically, includes the use of different mechanisms such as different leader behaviors, use of language, construction of artifacts and symbols, and different forms of relating to followers. Below we explore several such mechanisms of "doing distance" used by Steve Jobs.

MECHANISMS FOR CREATING DISTANCE AND PROXIMITY

As the CEO of a large company, Steve Jobs was first and foremost a distant leader. He ran a multibillion dollar company and was in charge of tens of thousands of employees. The company interacted with millions of customers around the globe. Thus, "objectively" he was physically and socially distant from his customers and did not interact directly with most of them. However, he managed to transcend the inherent distance of his position from Apple's customers by acting in different ways that made his customers feel close to him. We identified four mechanisms that were used by Steve Jobs to construct and transform his followers' sense of distance into a sense of proximity. These are the use of artifacts, youth and playfulness, intimacy with the product and the leader, and visibility and close interaction with customers. These different forms of "doing distance" are discussed below.

Artifacts

Artifacts are defined as "artificial products, something made by human beings and thus any element of a working environment" (Hornby, 1974, p. 43). In the literature, artifacts are defined as "the phenomena that you would see, hear and feel" (Schein, 2004, p. 23), they are intentionally made products perceived by individuals (Gagliardi, 1992). These definitions include not only physical objects, but also social constructs such as language, logos and symbols (Baruch, 2006; Cappetta & Gioia, 2006). It was argued that artifacts are the most superficial aspect of culture (Schein, 1990); however, more recent work considers them as influential factors that have a vast significance for individuals and organizations (Cappetta & Gioia, 2006; Rafaeli & Pratt, 2006). Through the use of artifacts, individuals communicate to others who they are (Pratt & Rafaeli, 2001). This suggests that artifacts are powerful symbols used by individuals and organizations to convey deep meanings about themselves and their desired image (Cappetta & Gioia, 2006). Two important types of artifacts were used by Steve Jobs to construct his figure as that of a close leader—his attire, and the Apple logo and name.

Jobs's Attire

Clothing is an artifact which communicates powerful messages about the person (Rafaeli & Pratt, 1993) and serves as "sensegivers" to influence others' perceptions and understanding of reality (Cappetta & Gioia, 2006). Different aspects of attire that were discussed as relevant to this symbolic process are colors of dress, dress style and the material of the items (Rafaeli & Pratt, 1993). Clothing, as symbols, can reflect relationships, since it reveals the nature of the connection between two individuals by communicating the difference and similarities between the individuals involved (Pratt & Rafaeli, 2001). Rafaeli and Pratt (1993) proposed that dress style elicits attributions of power and status, since there are dress styles that symbolize higher status. Rollman (1977; in Rafaeli & Pratt, 1993) found that professors who dressed more casually (jeans, sneakers) were seen as having less status than their counterparts who dressed more formally.

One of the major ways in which Steve Jobs shaped the perception of distance from his customers was his dress code. Jobs's dress style was unique, especially when compared to other executives, even in the less formal high tech industry. Steve Jobs was known for his informal attire, and his trademark black turtleneck shirt, jeans and a pair of sneakers were the clothes he wore at every keynote presentation. These were his "uniform," his "signature style." Jobs explained that he wanted to have a uniform for all of Apple's employees to create a bond between them and the company.

When they refused, he decided to create his own personal uniform which would be identified with him (Isaacson, 2011a).

It has been claimed that in the workplace men tend to have less freedom with regard to the choice of attire, and are expected to wear a suit or a professional looking shirt and pants (Burgoon, Guerrero, & Floyd, 2010). However, unlike other CEOs, or even the image of a typical executive, Jobs did not wear suits or other formal garments. He wore casual clothing, the kind one would not expect from a person in such a position of power and wealth. Thus, Jobs's dress style did not communicate power or status. His style defined him less as a high-powered high tech executive, but more as a closer figure with less power distance.

In addition, the informality and youth of his dress was suggestive of similarities between Jobs's dress style and that of his customers. As clothes are used to point to similarities and differences (Pratt & Rafaeli, 2001), using clothes to enhance or create such similarities can help create perceptions of proximity. By dressing like his customers, rather than in an expensive and formal manner, Jobs created a perception of similarity between himself and his customers, conveying a message of proximity and closeness with them. Thus, through his carefully chosen attire, Steve Jobs manipulated his perceived social distance and created a sense of social closeness between himself and his customers. Furthermore, clothes can be used to distinguish people (Cappetta & Gioia, 2006), and Jobs's attire set him apart from other CEOs, such as Bill Gates. Jobs and Gates were a part of similar circles as of the 1970s when both took part in the Homebrew Computer Club, to the 2000s when they were the heads of the two largest computer companies in the world. Unlike Gates, who was usually seen wearing suits and button-down shirts, as most CEOs do, Jobs's dress style fit the "cool kid" image. In a parody animation movie portraying a cartoon figure of Jobs versus a cartoon figure of Gates in a competition scene, Gates is portrayed as the computer nerd and Jobs as the "cool" guy (e.g., spiky hairstyle, jeans, informal outfit, sneakers) (Faure-Brac, 2007). This "cool" image of Jobs allowed him to overcome the image of the "geek"[3] and the possibly remote genius and weirdo profile. This perhaps made him less of an outsider to the general public (perhaps creating a positive image to his fellow geek customers).

The Apple Name and Logo

Logos and names are artifacts that represent and symbolize companies, and represent the organization (Baruch, 2006; Schultz, Hatch, & Ciccolella, 2006). They are graphic images that are used to create an image of an organization, communicate a message and to create certain impressions of the organization (Baruch, 2006). Logos influence individuals both on a logical conscious level and a more emotional unconscious level, since they elicit a deep intuitive experience of meaning (Baruch, 2006). Thus the Apple name and logo are artifacts that communicate messages defining Apple and Steve Jobs.

In 1975 when Steve Jobs and Steve Wozniak decided to turn their computer building hobby into a business, Jobs suggested the name Apple Computer Inc. He explained that "It sounded fun, spirited and not intimidating. Apple took the edge off the word computers" (Isaacson, 2011a, p. 63). Isaacson explained that the choice to name it "Apple" was a smart choice: "the word instantly signaled friendliness and simplicity" (2011a, p. 63). In 1979 Apple started working on a new computer model (which Jobs took charge of in late 1980), named Macintosh (after the McIntosh apple cultivar). It was nicknamed—and has been ever since—the Mac, continuing Apple's attempts to portray computers as friendly.

Another aspect of the Apple logo is that it is an image of an apple with a bite taken out of it. The actual figure of the apple makes it seem concrete and familiar (Trope & Liberman, 2010), something that customers can easily touch and hold.[4] The bite also makes the logo seem more tangible, making it easy for the customers to imagine that they had actually taken a bite.[5]

In contrast, the IBM, Intel or Microsoft's logos are their names. Rather than images that represent them, they represent themselves through abbreviations that reflect computers. For example Intel stands for the Integrated Electronics Corporation. Jobs and Apple chose to enhance their image by using a fun colorful image to symbolize their company (later it would turn into a sleek image). Thus, through the manipulation of the logo and firm name Apple and Jobs portrayed themselves as "friends" with their public and as part of the same social group as their followers. This enabled Jobs to create a sense of closeness with the customers.

A logo is also used to distinguish a company from others, to represent its distinctive identity and heritage, and convey a central idea or a vision (Schultz et al., 2006). By using an image that communicates friendliness, simplicity and fun, Jobs and Apple differentiated themselves from other computer companies which were then depicted as formal and rigid. An example of this depiction of other companies can be seen in Apple's famous "Big Brother" commercial for the first Macintosh that aired during the SuperBowl in 1984. The commercial hinted at an Orwellian "1984" scenario—men marching while listening to the "Big Brother" presented on a large screen. Then a young woman holding a large hammer runs in and throws it at the screen: the narrator explains that Apple will be introducing the Macintosh, saying: "And you'll see why 1984 won't be like '1984'" (miniroll32, 2008).

Jobs and Apple used the name and logo of the company to portray a different image to their customers, as a friendly company that poses an alternative to the big computer giants. This young and rebellious image created closeness between Jobs and his customers. He was "on their side" in the battle against "Big Brother." Jobs and his customers are one social group fighting the 'mean companies.' This image suggests some similarity in values and characteristics between Jobs and his customers, thus creating a sense of closeness between them.

Youth and Playfulness

Creating a Youthful Image

CEOs and the majority of their customers are socially and psychologically distant due to the gap in status, power, and (often) their seniority. A second mechanism that Jobs used to decrease this social distance was to use images and concepts of youth. Youth refers to a certain mindset, an attitude of freshness, vigor or spirit one holds, regardless of their actual age. Therefore, youth brings to mind informality and fun, images which are quite the opposite of the common image of a CEO (someone serious and distant who works hard and does not play). When Jobs described and referred to himself as young, this framing implied he was psychologically closer to his customers. He also took advantage of Gardner and Avolio's other processes of scripting, staging, and performing (1998).

Jobs presented himself as young in several ways. He was portrayed, or casted as a "cool," young, rebellious genius. This notion is emphasized in different stages of his life story. For example, in all the historical articles and movies on the beginning of Apple, Jobs is presented as the young guy who started his own computer company out of his parents' garage. This image is related to kids playing with electronics. Later on Jobs focused on animation movies and became the co-founder and chief executive of Pixar Animation Studios, and eventually became a member of the board of directors of the Walt Disney Company in 2006. In these capacities he developed technologies for animation movies for children (e.g., *Toy Story*, *Bugs' Life*, *Finding Nemo*) and is credited in *Toy Story* (1995) as an executive producer. These roles and the type of movies he produced helped maintain an aura of fun and youth. Even at later stages in his life, after he became ill and looked older, he still highlighted the notion of youth. In his talk in 2011, after months of media absence due to his illness, he said in a formal speech to customers: "Five months ago I had a liver transplant, so I now have the liver of a mid-twenties person, who died in a car crash." Even at this stage he portrayed himself as having an organ of a young person willing to take risks (KLGCooperation, 2011). The perception of Steve Jobs as youthful was further supported by his informal dress style. A reporter described Jobs as follows: "Boyish is probably the word that best describes our first impression. He was wearing jeans and a turtleneck as he bounded up the stairs" (Gendron & Burlingham, 1989).

Another means to reinforce Jobs's youthful image and to elicit closeness with his customers, was the use he made of language and slang. Jobs often spoke in a very informal colloquial way, which characterized a youthful attitude to life and business. Jobs received personal emails from customers, and in his responses the language stands out. For example, when asked by a customer named Ricky if it was really him reading his emails, Steve's answer was "Yep. I do" (Milian, 2011, p. 264). As a response to an international customer complaining to Jobs about iPad stock in Europe, Jobs replied, "Are you nuts? We are doing the best we can" (Subramony, 2011). In his famous keynote presentations that were broadcast worldwide, he often used informal language to describe the products. When presenting the first iPad in 2010, Jobs describe it as "An awesome way to enjoy your music collection" (Apple, 2010) and frequently talked about the products as being "cool." Jobs and the firm also applied shorter words, resembling nicknames, to their products (Apps for applications, Mac for Macintosh, etc.).

Using formal and polite language is related to greater social distance while informal colloquial language is related to social proximity (Holtgraves & Yang, 1992; Stephan, Liberman, & Trope, 2010). By using an informal language combined with slang, Jobs created a youthful perception of himself and constructed a sense of proximity.

Playing and Having Fun

Jobs also manipulated distance by framing the use of the products, as well as the company and Jobs himself, as "playful" and "fun." To reinforce these concepts Jobs used various playtime metaphors to describe the company's products. For example, in one talk he referred to computers by saying that "computers are like bicycles to our mind" (Michael Lawrence Films, 2006). The scripting and staging of these concepts are evident in Apple commercials. For example, Apple's 2011 iPod commercial starts with an image of someone sending a text message saying: "wanna play?" and then it shows young people playing together on their iPods, smiling and having fun. At the end of the commercial a slide appears which reads "Share the fun" (Apple, 2011c). In one of the "I'm a Mac, I'm a PC" Apple ads, the person representing the Mac says "I am into doing a lot of fun stuff like movies, music, podcasts and stuff like that," while the guy representing the PC responds "I also do fun stuff like time sheets and spreadsheets and pie charts" (iMediaTube, 2008). This ad further emphasized Apple's fun and playfulness as opposed to the PC's serious focus on work.

Play is usually attributed to children — "kids play, adults work" (Kark, 2011a). While the work sphere is thought of as a formal environment, where one is expected to strive toward achieving defined goals and ends (Glynn, 1994), framing tasks as play leads to different outcomes, such as enjoyment and the focus on the means rather than goals and efficiency (Kark, 2011a). By promoting a playful image of Apple and its products, Jobs promoted a similar image of himself. He was described as "the ultimate end-user, the guy who is on our side" by writer Dan Lyons (as cited by Nouchi, 2010). Being the ultimate end-user does not only emphasize the similarity between Jobs and his customers but also exemplifies his playful nature as a person who enjoys "playing" with his recent inventions.

Jobs's final message at the commencement speech at Stanford University in 2005 was: "stay hungry, stay foolish" (a phrase he took from the "Whole Earth Catalog" (Stanford University, 2008)).[6] This message further reinforces the image of "young" and "playful." Thus, using images, metaphors, language and attire, Jobs framed, scripted, staged and enacted the notion of youth. Using this mechanism skillfully, he was able to craft and transform his image from a distant, leading and senior CEO, to a youthful and playful 'guy' who was perceived by people as psychologically close.

Intimacy with the Product and the Leader

"I have an iPhone which is the extension of me"—Cindy Gallop, Founder and CEO, IfWeRanTheWorld (Halpin, 2011). This quotation reflects the deep connection Apple's customers have with their products. Creating a sense of intimacy with the product and the leader is the third mechanism used by Steve Jobs to decrease his perceived distance. He created products that people felt were a part of their identity and signified who they are as individuals. Through the deep connection people developed with their iMacs, iPhones, iPods and iPads, they experienced a strong bond with Jobs himself, who was perceived as a representation of the computer devices. This strong connection between the technology and Jobs was achieved by the presentation of computers as human, by designing them to have specific characteristics, and by connecting the customers' identities to the products.

Bonding through the Humanization of Technology

Steve Jobs saw technology in a different way than other people; he talked about technology and computers as if they were living things with whom he had an intimate relationship. Intimacy is "a form of close relatedness in which an individual shares his or her innermost emotions, experiences, and thoughts with the other and experiences empathic responsiveness, a depth of understanding and a sense of shared meaning" (Kark, 2011b, p. 424). Although this definition focuses on interactions between human beings, an emotional connection can also develop toward objects. This type of connection is evident in the relationships of Apple users with their computers and other gadgets. Guy Kawasaki (Apple's former chief evangelist) said: "no one has fallen in love with their Taurus" (a computer brand), implying that people can fall in love with their Macs (Shely, 2009).[7] This attitude toward Apple products is a result of a scripting process that humanizes and personifies technology. This process involves ascribing a human role, characteristics and even abilities to the computer. In an interview in *Inc.* magazine, Jobs's tendency to humanize technology is expressed in the way he talks about it, as though he were talking about an actual person with an independent will: "Sometimes the technology just doesn't want to show you what it can do" (Gendron & Burlingham, 1989).

Another example of this perception of computers as somewhat human can be seen in the presentation of the first Macintosh computer in 1984. Jobs said: "we've done a lot of talking about Macintosh recently. But today, for the first time ever, I'd like to let Macintosh speak for itself." Then the computer presented itself and said: "Hello. I'm Macintosh. It sure is great to get out of that bag . . . obviously I can talk. But right now I'd like to sit back and listen. So it is with considerable pride that I introduce a man who's been like a father to me, Steve Jobs" (Isaacson, 2011a, p. 170). This presents the computer as a human being: it talks, it jokes, it sits back and listens, and it has a father.

Apple's strategy of humanizing its technology was developed further in the twenty-first century, when it revealed its new iPhone in October 2011. Its newest feature is called "Siri," a personal assistant which will help its owner perform different tasks on their phone. It was described as "this amazing assistant, that listens to you, understands you, can answer your questions, it can even accomplish tasks for you . . . [it has] the ability to understand what you mean, and act on it" (Apple, 2011a). This human relationship is also present in the ads for the new iPhone. In these ads people are presented talking to "Siri" as they would to a real person. For example, a woman is filmed asking her phone "What's my day look like?" and Siri answers "Not bad . . . only two meetings today" (Apple, 2011b). Talking about technology as human transforms the device from an object made of circuits, metal and plastic to a living creature, one that shares a relationship with you. Thus, Jobs, who is highly identified with the Apple products, reduced distance between his humanized products and his customers. This inevitably leads to a sense of proximity of the customers with Jobs himself.

Connecting through Physical Contact with the Product

Individuals' relationships with their Apple products and with Jobs are further elicited through the design of the products. When designing the first Macintosh, Jobs insisted that it should look "friendly" and it was designed to look like a human face (Isaacson, 2011a). Apple's products are not only friendly looking, but they also encourage their owners to interact with them in ways that create perceived relationships, for example through touch. Apple did not invent the touch screen, but its iPod Touch and especially the iPhone have made the touch device very popular. Touch symbolizes closeness; touch is the aspect of relationships that reflects and influences the nature and quality of the relationship. Above all, touch immediately enhances intimacy (Thayer, 1986). This is demonstrated in the movie *MacHeads*, showing a young woman waiting at a repair shop to get her computer fixed, sitting on a bench, hugging her iMac computer and petting it like an animal (a computer which weighs about 22 pounds). She appears very concerned and upset (Shely, 2009).

Another feature of these electronic devices that contributes to creating this bond is their portability. Mobile devices such as iPods, iPhones, and iPads are devices that people carry in their pockets or their hands. They touch their devices, and through this constant contact they develop an intimate relationship with them. This relationship is extended to Jobs himself. People feel that when they carry their iPhone in their pocket, they carry him, as expressed by actress Martha Plimpton: "Rest in Peace, Steve Jobs. Kinda can't believe he's gone. Carrying a little part of him in my pocket every day" (Allen, 2011).

Connecting through Identity

People use objects to communicate who they are to others (Cappetta & Gioia, 2006). According to Guy Kawasaki: "People have to consider a Mac as an extension of themselves, that's just the way it is" (Shely, 2009). Apple's customers see their electronic devices as reflecting who they are:

> I mean, only mac people really put stickers all over their laptops and I think it's indicative that this is kind of something that is close to me, like my clothing and it is an identification and it really shifts the computer from being just a business application to being something personal that is mine.
> (Deborah Schultz, Digital Media Strategist, cited in Halpin, 2011)

Individuals' self-identity is a multidimensional construct which is dynamic and changing and can therefore be influenced by leaders (Kark & Shamir, 2002; Lord & Brown, 2001, 2004). Jobs's leadership, actions and decisions regarding Apple and its products led customers to see the products as a means to communicate their self-identity. Steve Jobs constructed Apple's products as representative of who he and his customers are. Most of Apple's products names start with i— iMac, iPod, iPhone, as does some of its software— iTunes, iLife, iWork. The "i" originates from the first computer Apple made after Jobs's return to the company in the 1990s, the iMac. The "i" stands for internet, individual, instruct, inform, inspire (Zeusprp, 2011). But it is first of all "I"—the first person singular pronoun, the word people use when referring to themselves. This choice of the letter conveys a message to customers that individuals can express and represent themselves through their devices. As can be seen in this quote from an Apple fan in the movie *MacHeads*: "The great thing about the mac is that you can completely customize it . . . I can self-individuate my computer in a way that has meaning to me" (Shely, 2009).

Effective leadership tends to elicit personal identification with the leader. This identification is expressed when an individual's belief about a leader becomes self-defining (Kark & Shamir, 2002; Kark, Shamir, & Chen, 2003). When followers feel that their devices represent them, they feel that they share similar values with the leader, and they identify with him or her, thus creating personal identification. By eliciting customers' self-identity and presenting certain themes and values that they hold (individuality), Jobs prompted his customers to identify with Apple as a company and with him personally as a leader. This created a sense of oneness and proximity between the image of Jobs and the customers. Thus, through the personalization of computers, which are brought to life as "talking" and "listening" individuals that people can touch, carry close to the body (e.g. the pocket) and feel are part of their innermost identity, owners can form a sense of strong bond and personal relatedness to Steve Jobs, who is perceived as the "man behind" the devices.

Visibility and Close Interaction with Customers

Perhaps the most extraordinary and powerful mechanism used by Steve Jobs to reduce his distance from his customers was the way he skillfully constructed his visibility to the Apple customers and the way he structured direct interaction with them. First, as a CEO Jobs was very visible: he presented all of Apple's new products. Even when he was on medical leave in 2011, he took to the stage to present the iPad2, saying "we've been working on this product for a while and I did not want to miss today" (Apple, 2011d). His visibility was not only apparent in announcements and special events, but also when controversies and problems were encountered.

In April 2011, an issue regarding customer privacy with the iPhone 4 caught the public attention. People were worried and upset when they discovered that their iPhone was delivering location-based information to Apple. Although on a medical leave, Jobs came in person to participate in a rare television interview and addressed customers' complaints (Fried, 2011). This action demonstrates that although he was a distant indirect leader, he handled short-term, momentary events by being present and in view (Yammarino, 1994). This event was not rare, since Jobs was known to have dealt many times with customer service issues personally, while interacting directly with customers.

Similarly, when a customer emailed about a long wait to get his computer fixed, the Apple CEO called him personally on the phone to apologize for the wait, updated him that he had expedited the repair and thanked him for his support of Apple (Milian, 2011). This is quite an unusual act for a CEO of a company that has as many customers as Apple. This example does not only exemplify Jobs's tendency to get involved in such matters as customer service, but also demonstrates an important aspect of leader–follower relationships; namely, direct interaction between Jobs and the customers.

Another way in which Jobs interacted directly with his customers was through email. His Apple email address was publicly known and he received many emails from customers; some of them elicited a response from him and were documented by his enthusiastic fans in different blogs and websites. Some of his responses were short "yep" or "coming," but sometimes he engaged in longer email exchanges with customers, resembling actual conversations (Milian, 2011). These emails reflect the closeness Apple's customers felt toward him in another way. Most of these emails start with the familiar form of "Dear Steve" and not with the words "Dear Mr. Jobs" (Milian, 2011). Jobs's written interactions with customers encouraged them to feel they had an actual genuine close relationship with him.

Jobs's interactions with Apple customers were not only email-based. In 2007, shortly after the release of the iPhone, Jobs was invited by his friend Andy Grove (the co-founder of Intel), who was teaching a business class, to a student's presentation on the iPhone. He came and posed a challenge to the student by asking difficult questions and eventually taking the stage himself (Milian, 2011). Such interactions decreased the perceived distance between Jobs and his customers. By engaging in occasional dialog with his public, Jobs managed to influence their perceptions of him and position himself as much closer than he was.

DISCUSSION

The conceptualization of leadership distance presented here portrays leader distance as a malleable active process in which leaders can shape, re-shape, structure and transform their distance and proximity from their followers. We propose that one way in which leaders influence the processes of sense giving and meaning making is by the manipulation of distance between their figures and their followers and between the organization and its products and the followers (employees, customers, etc.). We present different ways in which leaders can actively "do distance," through their use of artifacts (e.g., attire and logos), the images they present of themselves and of the company (e.g., young and playful versus senior and settled), the design of their products, the type of interactions they have with their followers (e.g., intimate versus formal) and their level and type of visibility to their followers.

We used the case study of Steve Jobs to explore the different ways in which leaders enact distance, suggesting that he had a unique strategy of enacting distance by eliciting a perspective of himself as a leader who was simultaneously close and distant, near and far. In his role as CEO of Apple he was distant from his customers on many dimensions: geographically, physically, in terms of power distance, and other parameters. However, he was able to decrease the sense of distance and form a sense of closeness with many of his customers, as exemplified in the analyses above.

The ability of leaders to transform and affect followers' perception of their distance from them is of importance, since leader–follower distance and proximity have been suggested in the literature to result in different types of outcomes in terms of the ways the leader is perceived by the followers and in terms of their behavior. For example, distant charismatic leadership leads to an idealized image of the leader and followers' trust and confidence in him or her. It also better enables leaders to influence followers' political attitudes and behaviors (Antonakis & Atwater, 2002; Shamir, 1995; Waldman & Yammarino, 1999; Yagil, 1998). Close charismatic leadership, and close leadership in general, was found to create more positive affect toward the leader, and leads to identification with the leader and emulation of the leader's behavior. It was also conceptualized as leading to several follower-level outcomes, such as higher self-efficacy perceptions, greater motivation, higher performance evaluation, higher job satisfaction, and lower employee turnover (Napier & Ferris, 1993; Shamir, 1995; Yagil, 1998).

In the case study we explored how Jobs's ability to juggle the duality of distance and proximity enabled him to benefit from both the effect of a distant leader (followers' admiration, confidence, trust, and a sense of heroism and extraordinary personality) as well as from the effects of closeness (followers' positive affect, identification with the leader, and emulation of his behaviors). Thus, "doing distance" can contribute to leaders' ability to influence and affect different forms of followers' perceptions, beliefs, affect, and behaviors.

We presented a framework of leadership distance that may contribute to further research on leadership processes. In addition, we have raised some issues that merit attention in future studies. Four qualifications should be added at this point. First, while we maintain that leaders can affect the sense of distance and proximity of their followers, we do not imply that leaders can always control this influence. Various contextual characteristics, such as objective distance, the organizational structure and norms, the seniority of the leader, and the size of the organization, may limit leaders' ability to enact different forms of distance and proximity. Second, although we contend that leaders are able to consciously manipulate their distance from followers, it is possible that often this process may be difficult to manage consciously and may occur without the leader's awareness. Third, it is possible that the same leader may enact closeness toward one group of his or her followers and distance toward another group of followers. According to leader–member exchange theory (Graen & Uhl-Bien, 1995; Uhl-Bien & Arnaud, 2001) and notions put forward by Klein and House (1995) on heterogeneous charismatic effects, it is possible that the same leader may behave differently toward different followers who have different motivational needs. Thus, the leader can improve his or her influence and effectiveness by enhancing closeness with one group and enforcing distance with another. For example, in the case study of Steve Jobs we focused on his relationship with his customers. However it is more than likely that had we focused on his relationship with Apple employees we may have found a different form of enacting distance and proximity. It is also possible that the same leader will enhance distance in one channel and reduce distance in another channel of communication. For example, a leader may convey a message of distance in terms of the images he uses, but have very close daily interactions with his followers.

Fourth, we do not contend that one type of distance with its related outcomes is superior or more effective than another. Rather, we believe that the relative effectiveness of different distance strategies is contingent on the circumstances and the various attributes of the context (e.g., follower group composition, task characteristics, situation of the economic markets). Furthermore, culture may be an external factor influencing leaders' ability to enact distance and closeness. While Western cultures are in general lower on power distance, Eastern cultures are higher on that dimension and perceive leaders and authority figures as inherently more distant from their followers, and accept this as the desired situation (Hofstede, 1994). Some cultures are more democratic and open to different styles of leadership; however, others may not be so open to nontraditional forms of leadership. In some cultures seniority in the organization is important, and behaviors such as casual attire, using informal language, and being playful may be considered childish and inappropriate. Such cultural differences may be relevant not only to different countries, but also to different industries within a country. Technology companies like Apple have a more open and informal organizational culture which allows managers and employees to be less formal in their attire and conduct. However, other industries, such as manufacturing or more traditional workplaces such as banks, may wish to create a different perception of the organization and its leadership.

Finally, although the framework we offer explores the leader's role as the individual who enacts distance, it is more than likely that followers may play an important role in this process (Dvir & Shamir, 2003; Ehrhart & Klein, 2001; Howell & Shamir, 2005). A leader may wish to influence his perceived distance; however, followers may not be willing to accept the image he or she promotes, possibly rejecting the leader's attempts to become closer or more distant.

Although "doing distance" may be an important managerial instrument by assisting leaders in their daily work with employees, it may have a "dark side" which is important to address. "Doing distance" is a form of manipulating individuals' perceptions in order to accomplish goals of a different nature. In Apple's case, Steve Jobs's perceived proximity is possibly one of the things that made Apple more popular among customers, essentially resulting in larger revenues for the company. The use of closeness within the domain of work and business needs to also be viewed with some caution, since organizations may take advantage of followers' feelings of closeness as a means for achieving organizational goals. Thus, companies and leaders can set up proxy closeness relationships as a subtle form of attaining normative control over their employees and customers.

In conclusion, we do not know the extent to which leaders' enactment of distance affects the process of meaning making and followers' perceptions and behaviors. However, the case study of Steve Jobs gives us a strong basis to argue that leaders' distance and proximity can play an important role in their attempt to influence others. The lack of a sufficient understanding of the mechanisms by which these leadership strategies are used and the way they further affect leader–follower relationships and follower outcomes suggests that further theoretical development as well as empirical testing of the phenomenon of "doing distance" are crucial.

NOTES

1   In this paper we are interested in focusing on the theoretical concept of leadership and followership. Since our case study is focused on Apple and the leadership of Steve Jobs in the business and organizational arena, we refer to managers (CEOs) and employees, but mostly customers, when examining the leader–follower relationship. Although this may not represent all types of leader–follower relationships, it does portray various aspects of this relationship.

2   In July 2011, Apple reported a record quarterly revenue of $28.57 billion and a record quarterly net profit of $7.31 billion, or $7.79 per diluted share, for the fiscal 2011 third quarter. The gross margin was 41.7% compared to 39.1% in the previous year's quarter. The company sold 20.34 million iPhones, 9.25 million iPads and 3.95 million Macs. Taken from: http://www.apple.com/pr/library/2011/07/19Apple-Reports-Third-Quarter-Results.html.

3   Geek—The word geek is a slang term, with different meanings ranging from "a computer expert or enthusiast" to "A derogatory reference to a person obsessed with intellectual pursuits for their own sake, who is also deficient in most other human attributes so as to impair the person's smooth operation within society" (Geek, n.d.).

4   The apple with the bite also reminds people of the story of Adam and Eve, which exemplifies the commonalties and familiarity between all people. This can also be seen in a caricature from *USA Today*, depicting an angel welcoming Steve Jobs to heaven saying "To be honest, Mr. Jobs, the last time an apple caused so much excitement around here involved Adam, Eve and a snake."

5   An example of the impact of Apple's logo can be seen after Jobs's death. People brought actual apples to the memorial sites created by the public at Apple stores. This reflects the deep connection made between Jobs and Apple.

6   The Whole Earth Catalog was a counter-culture catalog, published in the 1960s and 1970s, that presented different products. It promoted an individualistic worldview, science, intellectual endeavor, blending new and old technologies (taken from: http://www.wholeearth.com/history-whole-earth-catalog.php).

7   We experienced such a feeling ourselves; as one of the authors of this paper described how she bought her laptop: "I went into the shop and fell in love with it [the computer] . . . I could not resist its charm. So I bought the MacbookAir."

REFERENCES

Allen, M. (2011, October 6). What Celebrities are Saying About Steve Jobs. Retrieved from http://www.opposingviews.com/i/technology/gadgets/what-celebrities-are-saying-about-steve-jobs.

Antonakis, J. & Atwater, L. (2002). Leader distance: A review and a proposed theory. *Leadership Quarterly*, 13(6), 673–704.

Apple (Producer). (2010, January 27) Apple announces iPad. Apple keynotes. Podcast retrieved from iTunes Store.

Apple. (2011a, October 6). Apple – Introducing iPhone 4S [Video file]. Retrieved from http://www.youtube.com/watch?v=f_JRZI9o49w&feature=relmfu.

Apple. (2011b, October 30). Apple – iPhone 4S – TV Ad – Siri, Snow Today [Video file]. Retrieved from http://www.youtube.com/user/Apple?feature=watch#p/u/4/5ba0tZ_P5cg.

Apple. (2011c, November 23). Apple – iPod touch – TV Ad – Share The Fun [Video file]. Retrieved from http://www.youtube.com/user/Apple?feature=watch#p/u/0/gGrDMV k2isc.

Apple (Producer). (2011d, March 2). Apple Special Event, March 2011. Podcast retrieved from http://www.apple.com/apple-events/.

Ashforth, B. E., Harrison, S. H., & Corley, K. G. (2008). Identification in organizations: An examination of four fundamental questions. *Journal of Management*, 34(3), 325–374.

Bartunek, J., Krim, R., Necochea, R., & Humphries, M. (1999). Sensemaking, sensegiving, and leadership in strategic organizational development. *Advances in qualitative organizational research*, 2, 37–71.

Baruch, Y. (2006). On logos, business cards: The case of UK universities. In A. Rafaeli & M. G. Pratt (Eds.), *Artifacts and organizations: Beyond mere symbolism* (pp. 181–198). Mahwah, NJ: Lawrence Erlbaum.

Benford, R. D. & Hunt, S. A. 1992. Dramaturgy and social movements: The social construction and communication of power. *Sociological Inquiry*, 62(1), 36–55.

Bryman, A. 1992. *Charisma and leadership in organizations*. London: Sage.

Burgoon, J. K., Guerrero, L. K., & Floyd, K. (2010). *Nonverbal Communication* Boston: Pearson Education.

Burrows, P., Grover, R., & Green, H. (2006, February 6). Steve Jobs' Magic Kingdom. *Bloomberg Businessweek*. Retrieved from http://www.businessweek.com/magazine/content/06_06/b3970001.htm.

Cappetta, R. & Gioia, D. (2006). Fine fashion: Using symbolic artifacts, sensemaking, and sensegiving to construct identity and image. In A. Rafaeli & M. G. Pratt (Eds.), *Artifacts and organizations: Beyond mere symbolism* (pp. 199–219). Mahwah, NJ: Lawrence Erlbaum.

Claburn, T. (2011, October 7). Steve Jobs: 11 Acts Of Vision. *InformationWeek*. Retrieved from http://www.informationweek.com/news/galleries/global-cio/interviews/231900299.

Cole, M. S., Bruch, H., & Shamir, B. (2009). Social distance as a moderator of the effects of transformational leadership: Both neutralizer and enhancer. *Human Relations*, 62(11), 1697–1733.

Conger, J. A. (1989). *The charismatic leader: Behind the mystique of exceptional leadership*. San Francisco: Jossey-Bass.

Conger, J. A. & Kanungo, R. N. (1988). The empowerment process: Integrating theory and practice. *Academy of Management Review*, 471–482.

Conger, J. A. & Kanungo, R. N. (1998). *Charismatic leadership in organizations*. Thousand Oaks, CA: Sage.

Cult of Mac. (2011, December 1). Check out Steve Note, All of his Best Public Appearances in One Place [Web log comment]. Retrieved from http://www.cultofmac.com/132700/ check-out-steve-note-all-of-his-best-public-appearances-in-one-place/.

Dvir, T. & Shamir, B. (2003). Follower developmental characteristics as predicting transformational leadership: A longitudinal field study. *Leadership Quarterly*, 14(3), 327–344.

Ehrhart, M. G. & Klein, K. J. (2001). Predicting followers' preferences for charismatic leadership: The influence of follower values and personality. *Leadership Quarterly*, 12(2), 153–179.

Evangelist, M. (2006, January 5). Behind the magic curtain. *Guardian*. Retrieved from http://www.guardian.co.uk/technology/2006/jan/05/newmedia.media1.

Fairhurst, G. T. & Sarr, R. A. (1996). *The art of framing: Managing the language of leadership*. San Francisco: Jossey-Bass.

Faure-Brac, J. (2007, February 13). Gates vs. Jobs: SuperNews! [Video file]. Retrieved from http://www.youtube.com/watch?v=qHO8l-Bd1O4.

Fried, I. (2011, April 27). Interview: Apple CEO Steve Jobs on How the iPhone Does and Doesn't Use Location Information [Web log comment]. Retrieved from http://all thingsd.com/20110427/exclusive-apple-ceo-steve-jobs-on-how-the-iphone-does-and-doesnt-use-location-information/.

Gagliardi, P. (1992). *Symbols and artifacts: Views of the corporate landscape*. New York: Aldine de Gruyter.

Gardner, W. L. & Avolio, B. J. (1998). The charismatic relationship: A dramaturgical perspective. *Academy of Management Review*, 32–58.

Geek. (n.d.). In Wikipedia. Retrieved December 11, 2011, from http://en.wikipedia.org/ wiki/Geek

Gendron, G. & Burlingham, B. (1989, April 1). The Entrepreneur of the Decade. *Inc.* Retrieved from http://www.inc.com/magazine/19890401/5602.html.

Glynn, M. A. (1994). Effects of work task cues and play task cues on information processing, judgment, and motivation. *Journal of Applied Psychology*, 79(1), 34–45.

Goffman, E. (1959). *The presentation of self in everyday life*. Garden City, NY: Doubleday Anchor.

Goodson, S. (2011, November 27). Is Brand Loyalty the Core to Apple's Success? [Web log comment]. Retrieved from http://www.forbes.com/sites/marketshare/2011/11/27/is-brand-loyalty-the-core-to-apples-success-2/.

Goodwell, J. (2003, December 3). Steve Jobs: The *Rolling Stone* Interview. Rolling Stone. Retrieved from http://www.keystonemac.com/pdfs/Steve_Jobs_Interview.pdf.

Graen, G. B. & Uhl-Bien, M. (1995). Relationship-based approach to leadership: Development of leader–member exchange (LMX) theory of leadership over 25 years: Applying a multi-level multi-domain perspective. *Leadership Quarterly*, 6, 219–247.

Gundotra, V. (2011, August 25). Icon Ambulance [Web log comment]. Retrieved from https://plus.google.com/107117483540235115863/posts/gcSStkKxXTw.

Halpin, C. (Executive Producer). (2011, October 16). iGenius: How Steve Jobs changed the world [Television broadcast]. New York, NY: Peacock Productions.

Helft, M. (2011, October 6). Steve Jobs, 1955–2011: Technology's greatest visionary. *Fortune Tech*. Retrieved from http://tech.fortune.cnn.com/2011/10/06/steve-jobs/.

Hepp, J. (2011, October 19). Steve Jobs—Role Model For All Entrepreneurs [Web log comment]. Retrieved from http://jaimehepp.wordpress.com/2011/10/19/job/.

Hofstede, G. (1994). Management scientists are human. *Management Science* (40), 4–13.

Holtgraves, T. & Yang, J. N. (1992). Interpersonal underpinnings of request strategies: General principles and differences due to culture and gender. *Journal of Personality and Social Psychology*, 62(2), 246.

Hornby, A. S. (Ed.) (1974) *Oxford Advanced Learner's Dictionary of Current English*. Oxford: Oxford University Press.

Howell, J. M. & Shamir, B. (2005). The role of followers in charismatic leadership: Relationships and their consequences. *Academy of Management Review*, 30, 96–112.

iMediaTube. (2008, April 5). Apple Inc. Get a Mac Ad: Work vs. Home [Video file]. Retrieved from http://www.youtube.com/watch?v=6lAgbR7JvUs.

Isaacson, W. (2011a). *Steve Jobs*. London: Little, Brown.

Isaacson, W. (2011b, October 29). The Genius of Jobs. *New York Times*. Retrieved from http://www.nytimes.com/2011/10/30/opinion/sunday/steve-jobss-genius.html?page wanted=all.

Kark, R. (2011a). Games managers play: Play as a form of leadership development. *The Academy of Management Learning and Education (AMLE)*, 10(3), 507–527.

Kark, R. (2011b). Workplace intimacy in leader–follower relationships. In K. S. Cameron & G. M. Spreitzer (Eds.), *The Oxford Handbook of Positive Organizational Scholarship* (pp. 423–438). New York: Oxford University Press.

Kark, R. & Shamir, B. (2002). The dual effect of transformational leadership: Priming relational and collective selves and further effects on followers. In B. J. Avolio & F. J. Yammarino (Eds.), *Transformational and charismatic leadership: The road ahead* (Vol. 2, pp. 67–91). Oxford: Elsevier Science.

Kark, R., Shamir, B. & Chen, G. (2003). The two faces of transformational leadership: Empowerment and dependency. *Journal of Applied Psychology*, 88(2), 246–255.

Klein, K. J. & House, R. J. (1995). On fire: Charismatic leadership and levels of analysis. *Leadership Quarterly*, 6, 183–198.

KLGCooperation. (2011, January 20). The health problem of Steve Jobs 2011! [Video file]. Retrieved from http://www.youtube.com/watch?feature=endscreen&v=THWsjxXVO kM&NR=1.

Lappin, J. (2011, October 6). Steve Jobs, Lifetime Visionary [Web log comment]. Retrieved frm http://www.forbes.com/sites/joanlappin/2011/10/06/steve-jobs-lifetime-visionary/.

Lord, R. G. & Brown, D. J. (2001). Leadership, values, and subordinate self-concepts. *Leadership Quarterly*, 12(2), 133–152.

Lord, R. G. & Brown, D. J. (2004). *Leadership processes and follower self-identity*. Mahwah, NJ: Lawrence Erlbaum.

Macworld. (2011, October 6). Remembering Steve Jobs, the man who saved Apple [Web log comment]. Retrieved from http://www.macworld.com/article/162763/2011/10 remembering_steve_jobs_the_man_who_saved_apple.html.

Milian, M. (2011). Letters to Steve: Inside the E-mail Inbox of Apple's Steve Jobs. Available from http://www.amazon.com/Letters-Steve-Inside—mail-ebook/dp/B006B16JLQ/ref=sr_1_1?ie=UTF8&qid=1323599947&sr=8-1.

miniroll32. (2008, August 27). "1984" Apple Macintosh Commercial [Video file]. Retrieved from http://www.youtube.com/watch?v=hHsWzJo2sN4.

Michael Lawrence Films. [mlfilms]. (2006, June 1). Steve Jobs, "Computers are like a bicycle for our minds." [Video file]. Retrieved from http://www.youtube.com/watch?v=ob_GX50Za6c.

Napier, B. J. & Ferris, G. R. (1993). Distance in organizations. *Human Resource Management Review*, 3(4), 321–357.

Nouchi, F. (2010, February 1). Steve Jobs, the ultimate end-user. *Le Monde*. Retrieved from http://watchingamerica.com/News/45994/steve-jobs-the-ultimate-end-user/.

Porter, L. W. & McLaughlin, G. B. (2006). Leadership and the organizational context: Like the weather? *Leadership Quarterly*, 17(6), 559–576.

Pratt, M. G. & Rafaeli, A. (2001). Symbols as a language of organizational relationships. *Research in Organizational Behavior*, 23, 93–132.

Rafaeli, A. & Pratt, M. G. (1993). Tailored meanings: On the meaning and impact of organizational dress. *Academy of Management Review*, 32–55.

Rafaeli, A. & Pratt, M. G. (2006). Introduction: Artifacts and organizations: More than the tip of the cultural iceberg. In A. Rafaeli & M. G. Pratt (Eds.), *Artifacts and organizations: Beyond mere symbolism* (pp. 1–8). Mahwah, NJ: Lawrence Erlbaum.

Reicher, S., Haslam, S. A., & Hopkins, N. (2005). Social identity and the dynamics of leadership: Leaders and followers as collaborative agents in the transformation of social reality. *Leadership Quarterly*, 16(4), 547–568.

Schein, E. H. (2004). *Organizational culture and leadership* (Vol. 2). San Francisco: Jossey-Bass.

Schein, E. H. (1990). Organizational culture. *American psychologist*, 45(2), 109–119.

Schultz, M., Hatch, M., & Ciccolella, F. (2006). Brand life in symbols and artifacts: the LEGO company. In A. Rafaeli & M. G. Pratt (Eds.), *Artifacts and organizations: Beyond mere symbolism* (pp. 141–160).

Shamir, B. (1995). Social distance and charisma: Theoretical notes and an exploratory study. *Leadership Quarterly*, 6(1), 19–47.

Sharma, A. & Grant, D. (2011). Narrative, drama and charismatic leadership: The case of Apple's Steve Jobs. *Leadership*, 7(1), 3–26.

Shely, K. (Producer & Director). (2009). *MacHeads* [Motion picture]. (Available from iTunes Store.)

Shinal, J. (2011, September 26). The Day Steve Jobs Saved Apple [Web log comment]. Retrieved from http://finance.yahoo.com/news/pf_article_113566.html.

StanfordUniversity. (2008, March 7). Steve Jobs' 2005 Stanford Commencement Address [Video file]. Retrieved from http://www.youtube.com/watch?v=UF8uR6Z6KLc.

Stephan, E., Liberman, N., & Trope, Y. (2010). Politeness and psychological distance: A construal level perspective. *Journal of Personality and Social Psychology*, 98(2), 268–280.

Stevenote. (n.d.). In Wikipedia. Retrieved November 30, 2011, from http://en.wikipedia.org/wiki/Stevenote.

Subramaniya, M. (2009, June 27). Steve Jobs—My role model and an icon [Web log comment]. Retrieved from http://ms.mymindleaks.com/steve-jobs-my-role-model-and-an-icon.

Subramony, A. (2011, June 20). 10 Best Steve Jobs Emails Ever [web log comments]. Retrieved from http://www.maclife.com/article/gallery/10_best_steve_jobs_emails_ever#slide-9.

Thayer, S. (1986). Touch: Frontier of intimacy. *Journal of Nonverbal Behavior,* 10(1), 7–11.

The Economist (2011, October 8). A genius departs. *The Economist.* Retrieved from http://www.economist.com/node/21531530?fsrc=scn/tw/te/ar/ageniusdeparts.

Trope, Y. & Liberman, N. (2010). Construal-level theory of psychological distance. *Psychological Review,* 117(2), 440–463.

Uhl-Bien, M. & Arnaud, A. (2001). Comparing and contrasting LMX with transformational and neo-charismatic leadership approaches: How might these literatures speak to one another? Paper presented at the Festschrift for Dr. Bernard M. Bass, Center for Leadership Studies, Binghamton, NY.

Waldman, D. & Yammarino, F. (1999). CEO charismatic leadership: Levels-of-management and levels-of-analysis effects. *Academy of Management Review,* 24(2), 266–285.

Yagil, D. (1998). Charismatic leadership and organizational hierarchy: Attribution of charisma to close and distant leaders. *Leadership Quarterly,* 9(2), 161–176.

Yammarino, F. J. (1994). Indirect leadership: Transformational leadership at a distance. In B. M. Bass & B. J. Avolio (Eds.), *Improving organizational effectiveness through transformational leadership* (pp. 26–47). Thousand Oaks, CA: Sage.

Zeusprp. (2011, October 7). The First iMac Introduction [Video file]. Retrieved from http://www.youtube.com/watch?v=GTdIAT8_cBk.

10

American Presidential Leadership: Leader Credit, Follower Inclusion, and Obama's Turn

Edwin P. Hollander

INTRODUCTION: POWER DISTANCE AND OTHER DIFFERENCES

The American president has been called the most personal of our elected officials (Barber, 1972), and yet is seen at a distance from the public, even when viewed on television at home. The "majesty" of the presidency also can make for perceived aloofness psychologically from citizens and their everyday concerns. This chapter is directed primarily at how a president, a powerful but distant leader, bridges the "power distance gap." His essential leadership task (and someday hers) is to reach followers, to gain and hold their support, by showing how he will fulfill their and national needs, because to be a leader depends importantly on followers.

Followers have expectations about what their leaders will provide. "Whether in a corporation . . . or an entire nation, constituents seek four things: meaning or direction, trust in and from the leader, a sense of hope and optimism, and results" (Bennis, 1999, p. 19). These benefits are basic to "leader–follower interdependence," and are rewarded by a leader *receiving credit from followers*, who identify with and support the leader (Hollander, 1958, 1992a, 1992b). Follower needs determine whether rewards, intangible as well as tangible, are satisfactory to motivate them to follow. Even when appointed, a leader benefits from a following. John Gardner, renowned psychologist-author (1961, 1963, 1990), served in Lyndon Johnson's Cabinet after heading a major foundation, and said, "Executives can be given subordinates, but a following must be earned" (1987, p. 4), making a vital point of a leader's legitimacy.

LEGITIMACY AND CREDITS FROM FOLLOWERS

The truism that there is no leadership without followers poses the inevitable questions of, "Who are they, and will they still follow?" This is very relevant in the case of President Obama, who is the first African-American elected US president, but with only 43% of the White vote, showing race still matters. Moreover, the denial of his legitimacy comes with the emotional residue of slavery, desegregation, and affirmative action (Kennedy, 2011). Yet, Shelby Steele (2011), a conservative critic of African-American heritage, has contended that Obama benefited by "a cultural charisma . . . because his presidency flatters Americans to a degree" (p. A17). But if so, this was with proportionally far less White than non-White votes, and does not fit his low favorability among Whites, hovering around 40%, well below the standing he has had with non-Whites. There also are sharply divergent attitudes about him regularly found between members of the two main political parties, as shown in Table 10.1. Such severe attitudinal differences can affect his ability to exert his authority from legitimacy by election, and to gain and use credits for action. Indeed, Obama has been a target of hostile media and congressional opponents dedicated from the outset to trying to stop his initiatives, so he fails.

For a president, legitimacy is obviously essential and usually decided by the results of an election. In President Obama's case, however, some detractors had posed immediate doubts about whether he was born in the United States, as a candidate must be to enter a presidential election. This accusation had the effect of "discrediting" him and delegitimizing him by denying his election was valid. The most prominent "delegitimizing" approach is the so-called "birther" movement, which was taken on opportunistically by Donald Trump in his brief appearances as a potential presidential candidate. After demanding it be shown, many birthers still denied that Obama's "long form" birth certificate was authentic, meaning to them that he has not proven he was born in Hawaii, therefore is not a citizen, so cannot have been elected president. Before he released it, early in 2011 a national survey of Republican primary voters found that 51% said he was not a citizen, 21% said they were not sure, and just 28% said he was (Rich, 2011). Psychologically, even if unsound, these attitudes need to be recognized in trying to reach the electorate.

TABLE 10.1

Comparative Democrats' and Republicans' Percentages Responses to President Obama on Several Issues, after a Year in Office.

	Democrats	Republicans	Difference
Approval of job Obama is doing as president	81	14	−67
Obama trying to reach out to change politics in Washington	72	18	−54
Think Obama blames Bush administration too much for the country's situation	11	79	+68
Think Obama is better described as a Washington insider rather than outsider	28	50	+22

Source: Adapted from Blow (2010a), *New York Times*, February 6, p. A-19.

Many of his detractors, including media commentators, also had proclaimed that Obama is a Muslim, seeking to extend the distance separating him from the "mainstream." He had asserted that he is and has been a Christian, never otherwise, and wrote about taking on Christianity long ago in his autobiographical book (Obama, 1995).

Obama's background, growing up in Hawaii and Indonesia, led to some suspicions about his education and values, but Sharma (2011) considered that this exposure influenced him in a multi-cultural, conciliatory way, as their norm. Expressions of dissatisfaction with this style were captured in Maureen Dowd's (2011) point that, "It's not enough to understand how everybody in the room thinks. You have to decide which ones . . . are right, and stand with them. A leader is not a mediator or an umpire . . . With each equivocation, the man in the Oval Office shields his identity and cloaks who the real Barak Obama is." But a pragmatic view is that he tries not being seen unfairly as an "Angry Black," because race matters (Hayden, 2011; Kennedy, 2011).

Whether to trust him, that these doubts raise, has also been sorely tied to his patriotism, often challenged by his detractors. However, he had a good response to his national healing address early in 2011, after the Tucson, Arizona shootings, with wide praise for his compassion. Six people were killed, including a Federal judge and a nine-year-old girl, and Congresswoman Gabrielle Giffords was severely wounded, among many others. Obama's remarks not only were well received, but his handling of the tragedy had a 74% approval rating in a national poll. Still, hostile sources ceaselessly directed accusations at him, mainly questioning his motives. They clearly were not giving him credit for this, or anything, which goes to a prominent theme here of "getting credit" and "achieving inclusion," or "nothing."

Obama had further modified his approach, and acted by some Executive Orders to show things he positively would fight for that most concerned the public, with his slogan, "We just can't wait any longer." These are economic issues, in general, and continuingly high long-term unemployment, in particular, made raw by home foreclosures at a historically high rate. These vexing national problems take precedence, especially in presidential election season. But an apt old political adage for him and his followers is that, "You'd better stand for something, or you're likely to fall for anything," as he was seen to do at the end of 2010 by going along, keeping the about-to-expire-Bush-era tax cuts for upper-income brackets. This concession to his congressional opponents set the stage for the summer 2011 battle by them not to raise the "Debt Ceiling" without further concessions by him, with no new taxes, only budget cuts. All of this was with his opposition clearly denying him any successes to ensure that he fails, at whatever national costs, and does not win a second term. He had needed a consistent, compelling message to counteract them.

A leader, whether Obama or someone else, nonetheless has to face the reality that, correctly or not, judgments about his or her qualities are made by others. Indeed, one focus of the study of leadership has shifted from assessing a leader's character to how the leader is seen by followers, and how they then respond to the leader (e.g., Hollander & Julian, 1969, 1970). The particular "discrediting" process used against Obama has aimed to nullify the legitimacy of his election. This created a barrier to his gaining support for his actions, because "he's not one of us." Also, this amplified and extended the usual differences between those who favor or reject a president, often based on party, with pro or anti responses to him, as shown in Table 10.1. Further fundamental splits also exist in reactions to appeals *for change or for keeping things the same,* seen when either is proposed. Resistance to change or demands for it are powerful motives, especially when socially supported, as seen, for example, in the "Tea Party" and more recent "Occupy Wall Street" movements. There also are issues, among others, about freedom vs. responsibility, and freedom vs. security.

As indicated, an approach here to understanding leader–follower relations is to think of followers giving credits to a leader when he or she is seen as belonging and performing well. However, credits that would be earned from the electorate by their perceptions of a president's competence and loyalty to the nation are not given to him if he has been branded a "foreigner." If believed not legitimately elected, he is likely also to be considered not trustworthy. Negative attitudes about his policies, seemingly based on economic, organizational, military, or moral concerns, have actually been fixed firmly by prior political tendencies (Westen, 2007). Important as a consequence is the potentially greater psychological distance Obama had to surmount in relating to others in constituencies such as another party and/or race.

In general, credits cannot be earned if there are limiting conditions such as these. A major lack is the absence of an "open system" less constrained by authority pressures, or in this case by opposition media campaigns and denial of whom and what a leader is and does. In politics, using negative attributions is a well-known device, but the content here has been unusually emotionally strident, with Obama at times portrayed as Hitler and referred to as the Anti-Christ.

For a president to accomplish the feat of keeping a following in the face of powerful antagonism requires trying, through the media, at a distance, to present facts about how he has been "attempting to get things done." These messages must fit the needs and expectations of a diverse electorate, by no means all of whom are his followers. Some will be skeptical and even hostile. The general evaluation of a president, pro or con, is usually based on his party initially, and underlies the attitudes about him, his policies, and his ability to "sell" them successfully to constituencies and to Congress. This explains the need for a "continuous campaign mode," so a president can keep up a following. He needs positive views of what he has done and tried to do, on a timely basis, despite negative opposition messages.

The physical and psychological distance between a president and his audience is bridged through media transmissions, not just from him but by many others about him, including on the internet. These messages are then interpreted by individuals' identification with or rejection of the president, filtered through their primary groups as social supports (Katz & Lazarsfeld, 1955). A president's loyal followers are likely to have positive perceptions of him and his policies, which carries over to turning out to vote for his party's candidates in presidential and midterm elections, and getting out other voters. This "loyalty effect" has long been seen (e.g., Campbell, Gurin, & Miller, 1954; Lazarsfeld, Berelson, & Gaudet, 1948).

INCLUSIVE LEADERSHIP: TRUST AND LOYALTY

"Inclusive leadership" is directed toward "doing things with people, rather than to people." As noted before, it stresses "respect, recognition, responsiveness, and responsibility, both ways," for loyalty to occur. As its name indicates, it involves *including others in the tasks of leadership, as seen by listening to them about their needs and interests, and keeping them informed* (Hollander, 2009, pp. 3–5). Follower perceptions of legitimacy and performance combine with evaluations of *how much the leader shows of these four inclusive elements* are vital in perpetuating the *trust and loyalty* found in positive leader–follower relationships. Followers may then be alert to check on a leader's behavior for inclusion in policies, and seek alterations in them, or a change of leaders. Former British Prime Minister Tony Blair (2010) concluded from his career, "not that the power of politics is needed to liberate the people . . . but that the power of people is needed to liberate the politics" (p. 687).

On this point, our midterm post-election surveys in different places and times showed that follower loyalty was associated with a president's signs of inclusive leadership. These practices in leader–follower relations are not the same as "stroking" constituents for their votes, because they encourage inclusion by openness to follower influence on leader behavior. This is aptly called "upward influence" (Hollander, 2004b). It is likely to prove the value of two-way communication in achieving productive outcomes, by listening as a respectful, important feature of inclusive leadership that maintains relationships.

IDENTIFICATION WITH A PRESIDENT: PERCEPTUAL AND ELECTORAL EFFECTS

As already indicated, identification with a president is significantly related to followers' perceptions of issues, voter preferences, and voter turn-out. This accords with Freud's (1921) conception of shared identification with a leader, who is an "ego-ideal" for followers, and also fits cognitive balance theory (Heider, 1958). Its effects are demonstrated in post-election surveys studying a president's "pull" in his first midterm election. These archival findings from surveys directed by this author in Pittsburgh in 1954 with Eisenhower, and in Buffalo in 1962 with Kennedy, showed that continued loyalty to the president of one's own party significantly influenced voting for congressional candidates of the same party and perceptions of economic conditions as good. Despite others who defected, *those still loyal to the president reported that economic conditions were good, even if their own income had dropped* (Seaman, Hollander, & Richer, 1975; Hollander, 1983). International issues had less effect, given that the United States was not at war, other than the "Cold War" with the Soviet Union, when these surveys were done in 1954 and 1962. Fighting in Korea had ended, and major American entry into Vietnam had not yet occurred. Also, few "independents" were in our samples then, compared with now.

A president is elected with a vice president for a four-year term by the national electorate, and is both head of state, like Britain's Queen, and head of government, like Britain's Prime Minister. These roles are separable enough for a president to be liked as head of the nation, but less for his policies and/or politics, as President Obama had found. As is often the case with a new president, Obama began on a "high" of percentage favorability calculated in the 70% range. Such numbers carry "great expectations" that can produce a significant drop when unmet. Obama fell below 50% after his first anniversary in office, even with legislative gains. Though these were painfully achieved, with long, much publicized deal-making, against strong and very vocal foes and media sources, he was back to no higher than 50% by his second anniversary in office.

A year before, in February 2010, President Obama had held a "health care summit" to speak with congressional leaders of both parties. David Axelrod, then a presidential advisor, had stated the case for it saying that the president couldn't just "snap his fingers or even twist arms and make change happen." He added that, "in this great democracy of ours, that's not the way it is" (Stolberg, 2010). Still, the president got crucial votes needed to pass the health reform bill by a great deal of persuasion, a president's major power in gathering support for what he wants done (Neustadt, 1990). Kellerman (1984) considered such political skill essential to an effective presidency. She explained that the president and his constituents have a relationship that evolves over time, and that presidential leadership must be accomplished within the "world of other people," a "base" whose needs are served.

Trade-offs soon became necessary. President Obama had announced he was allowing some coastal oil drilling, then the April 2010 oil disaster occurred in the Gulf of Mexico, and he called a six-month halt in deep-water drilling there to study ways to avoid a repetition, but in the face of profound opposition. James Carville, a major Democratic strategist, said some drilling was important if Congress was to pass his energy program, to keep him succeeding (Harwood, 2010). This attempt did not work, either in terms of passing an energy bill or broadening his base. He also received criticism from some of his supporters, along with a loss of credit. A key concern always has been to keep supporters, while seeking to include different others, to decrease the distance gap and incorporate a larger group into his camp.

President Obama faced another such unresolved conflict in the economic crisis dubbed "Main Street vs. Wall Street." He had hoped it would improve enough from the 2009 Recovery Act (the "stimulus bill") that provided funds to create jobs related to state and national needs, including those for teachers, police officers, and firefighters. The initial positive effect did not last, and the unemployed more widely in the recession had been unable to find work for a historically long time. This predicament was mainly blamed on Obama, as is usual for an incumbent. He had 59% expressing dissatisfaction with his economic policies in a June 2011 national survey. Many who had supported him were especially distressed, comparing huge governmental programs to the "bail out" of banks and other financial and industrial organizations, with insufficient actions to help get jobs for those needing them who could then rejoin and boost the lagging consumer economy. Former Labor Secretary for President Clinton, Robert Reich, lamented that "little has been done since 2008 to widen the circle of prosperity. Health-care reform is an important step forward but it is not nearly enough . . . Policies that generate more widely shared prosperity lead to stronger and more sustainable economic growth—and that is good for everyone" (Reich, 2010). In short, the inability to buy reduces demand and delays ending a recession until consumers get jobs and income.

A related crisis existed in housing foreclosures executed by mortgage lenders, especially banks assisted with taxpayer funds. Very few home-owners, many of whom lost jobs, had been enabled to save their homes from lender takeover, even with a major government program (Home Affordable Modification Program, or HAMP) designed to cut the great numbers of foreclosures. The banks and other mortgage-holders were under no obligation to take part, since participation was only voluntary. The despair this created fell on Obama as the incumbent president, even though the lending policies being criticized came about by policies of the previous administration. As another president, John F. Kennedy, famously said, "Life is not fair," so it became Obama's task to make constituents satisfied with what he had done and would do for them. Compared to many others, however, his administration had been seen as slow and diffuse in getting information to the media about his programs' intentions and benefits when proposed and after enacted.

An innovative CEO, the late Sidney Harman (2003), wrote, "Developing a reasoned analysis and evaluation that you can communicate to others is the mark of a true leader . . . able to exercise critical judgment . . . rather than force the facts to fit a predetermined conclusion" (p. 5). In good political leadership, Robert Tucker (1981) stipulated three phases are vital: *diagnosing the problem* facing the constituency; *prescribing a course of action,* that is, "policy formulation"; and *mobilizing action,* that is, "policy implementation." The latter also needs motivated followership (Hollander, 2007, 2009), able to be activated, especially for elections.

In that way, President Obama won in 2008 by activating supporters, notably new young voters, and others who saw him as a smart and effective communicator. They were energized by what he was expected to bring to his presidency. At times he had indeed done well, such as with his widely praised handling of the assault on Osama bin Laden. But at other times, such as the ongoing and increasing housing foreclosure crisis, his approach was a classic case of "anticipointment." The government program (HAMP) he promoted to save the homes of millions actually helped far less than even half a million homeowners. This deficiency was portrayed by Henninger (2011) in a June 2011 column in the *Wall Street Journal* (*WSJ*) saying Obama raised expectations about what he would do about the economy, then "dropped them over a cliff" (p. A-17). A month and a half before, the *New York Times* (2011) began its editorial about Obama's encouraging April 13, 2011 speech, stating, "The man America elected president has re-emerged" (p. A-26). But later views from that and other editorial pages presented a more sober assessment of what he had achieved, pointing to a lack of persistent focus, with limited results. After he signed the Health Care Act in March of 2010, eighteen months passed before he produced a comprehensive Jobs Bill, which was pulled apart by his congressional opponents, and largely unpassed.

Political leadership, particularly at a distance, needs to have *continuity of communication* in providing *information* and *memorable imagery*. These three elements of communication support each other on the basic foundational beliefs that "perception is reality," and "repetition creates truth," even if untrue. What has proven to be true is that appealing personal and policy narratives have more impact than mountains of facts. That is especially so when amplified with a compelling slogan conveying a theme, such as "New Deal," "Great Society," and "Morning in America" were for Presidents Roosevelt, Johnson, and Reagan, respectively. President Obama had lacked such a theme with appealing elements in presenting and drawing support for his programs. The "Winning the Future" theme, from his January 25, 2011, State of the Union Address, seemed headed into the 2012 election, but may have been replaced by "We can't wait any longer," late in the year.

CONTRADICTORY AND CONTRASTING POSITIONS

The public and politicians may want consistency of policies and programs, but adaptability is necessary when new conditions arise. Faced with the nation's ongoing economic crisis, including the national debt, Obama had been forced into contradictory positions by having to cut budgets. That almost inevitably boosted unemployment, and was opposite to what he proposed as necessary by spending on national investments in infrastructure, education, and science. Obama, therefore, continued to be in conflict about those expenditures, most often with the House of Representatives controlled by Republicans. Their position has been to limit the size and cost of government and not support additional spending until the national debt had been greatly reduced. Cuts in generally popular programs at the Environmental Protection Agency and Food and Drug Administration exemplified those passed.

This ongoing philosophical battle between a conception of government as necessary to do things for the general good that individuals and organizations in the private sector will not do, has sharply contrasted with a view that the marketplace will take care of those things. The latter argument is clearly faulty, in the face of the need for public safety, public health, public education, laws and criminal justice, armed forces, and more, all of which are paid for by taxes. Further, what government does and can provide is inevitably related in the political process to its leaders, notably the president. This connection brings out supporters to presidential rallies and speeches. On Election Day, these actions conclude a social contract of "leader–follower interdependence" when favorable votes come in, aided by inclusive practices such as listening to constituents, and explaining realities clearly. Presidents who achieve this, as with other leaders, are rewarded by *receiving credit from followers,* who will identify with and support them (Hollander, 1958, 1992a).

GAINING AND USING CREDITS FROM FOLLOWERS

The longstanding "leader-centric" focus on leader qualities viewed leaders separately from how they affected their followers. To help connect these, the concept of "idiosyncrasy credits" was put forward (Hollander, 1958, 1964, 1978, 2004a, 2006, 2007). Credits earned from followers' perceptions of his or her competence and loyalty to their group, even the whole nation, can be used to provide latitude for the acceptance of a leader's influence and other actions. How successful the leader is in effecting change then depends upon the perceptions followers have of the leader's activities and associated motivations. A leader seen to fail to produce results will be vulnerable to blame. It is as if followers said, "We expect good results from you. If you choose an unusual course of action, we will go along with you and give you some latitude. But you will be responsible if the outcome fails to achieve our goals."

An important related expectation is that, once accumulated, credits will be used to take needed actions. Failing to do so results in losing credits, because the leader who "sits" on his or her credits can be seen as not fulfilling his or her role obligations. What followers do about it depends on such actions as elections can provide. This is part of "transactional leadership," involving a social exchange in which the leader gives something and gets something (Homans, 1974, ch. 11). A president's distance gap may be bridged if a "fair exchange" is perceived, where the incumbent is considered doing well enough to deserve the advantages of his status (Jacobs, 1970). However, followers may feel an inequity if the leader fails because of an apparent lack of effort, or from a disregard for followers' interests, so that the leader is seen as a "out of touch" (Hollander, 1978, 1992a, 1992b). Followers may then lack enthusiasm, even feel despair, and shun the leader and process. In this way, poor leaders can create angry followers, alienated—and, if not protesting, then with loss of interest and of participation (cf. Kelley, 1992; Kellerman, 2008).

To avoid this dysfunctional state, inclusive leadership is useful. It offers an overarching conception and systematic process emphasizing relational factors to create and sustain loyalty as a form of leader–follower bond. It incorporates the credit concept to indicate the evaluative element in follower effects on leaders. Indeed, whether leaders are called transforming or transactional, the common element that unites them is attention to followers' needs, and evidence of care, when asked, "What have you done for us lately?" In the political arena, Burns stated, "only the followers themselves can ultimately define their own true needs. And they can do so only when they ... can make an informed choice among competing 'prescriptions'" (1978, p. 36).

THE PRESIDENT'S ROLES AND TASKS

The big picture of the multiple roles filled by a president, and the tasks they relate to, is shown in Table 10.2. Presented there are a large part of what political scientists, historians, journalists, and others have listed as the responsibilities of this immense position, even characterized as "Leader of the Free World." All belong on any list, but they are not independent. Overlapping and merging of them occurs, and in carrying out these functions many forces can intrude. Among them are inevitable sudden crises, an uprising abroad in a strategic place, an increase in unemployment, a physical disaster at home or elsewhere, all needing to be addressed, and often all at once. Altogether, this has led to calling the presidency, the "most impossible job in the whole world ... even though Obama projects a demeanor of unruffled cool" (Stone, 2010, pp. 29–30). Different voices of contending constituencies want attention and prompt action in their sector of concern, instead of in others.

TABLE 10.2

Presidential Roles and Tasks—Dynamic, Overlapping, Interrelated

Roles

- Head of State, Chief Executive, Head of Party
- Commander-in-Chief of the Armed Forces
- Chief diplomat, chief spokesperson of government
- "National healer," "The decider," "Definer of reality"

Tasks

- Identify issues, offer solutions, press legislation
- Appoint personnel, assign and monitor functions
- Provide information, conduct international relations
- Set Budget, relate to legislative and judicial branches
- Oversee and coordinate Departments and Agencies
- Conciliate among contending constituencies
- Attain and maintain an active following by "continuous campaign mode"

FURTHER CHALLENGES TO LEGITIMACY

As stated earlier, as an elected leader a president generally benefits from legitimization by followers committed to his four-year term of office. Two traditional sayings reflect this: "We only have one president at a time," and "The president is president of all the people." Both are contradicted by the use of untruths and abusive terms about a president, more evident now in the mass media and on the internet than ever before.

Once in office a new president fills what journalist Lou Cannon called "the role of a lifetime," in the title of his book about Ronald Reagan. However, having an inauguration makes every president play a special set of roles, shown in Table 10.2. A new president usually has had a "honeymoon period," in which the public would "rally around" if the president initially had difficulties. In his first year, John F. Kennedy, as an example, gained substantially in the polls after taking responsibility for the failed invasion of Cuba at the Bay of Pigs in 1961. The next year, he was more decisive, questioning the institutional positions and advice of senior officials, and then showing restraint in the 1962 Cuban Missile Crisis. Again Kennedy gained in ratings with the public. These linked events can be confused with each other, but reveal a president's progress as a leader in international diplomatic-military crises.

The degree of a follower's closeness, and identification with a president, is usually affected by party identity, and whether or not that person voted for the incumbent. The sense of his legitimacy is based also in respect for the integrity of the electoral process and the nature of the election victory. It was severely tested in the 2000 Bush/Gore election, in which Al Gore won the popular vote but the Supreme Court decided for George W. Bush, after it stopped the recount of votes in Florida, giving its Electoral College votes to Bush. Rancor over this process still remains alive.

Regarding an earlier time, George Reedy (1973), who had been a press spokesman for Lyndon Johnson during the 1960s, asserted that "a man might have only 51 percent of the votes, or even less, and still be able to make some rather sweeping changes . . . Many Presidents have found their following has increased enormously the day after election" (p. 26). The pronounced partisan split in the public's attitudes revealed in Table 10.1 makes this view seem quaint now, given Barack Obama's 53% of all votes, with the highest total number ever. Yet, even thwarted, he had notable bills passed: pay equity, child health, recovery act/stimulus, college student loan reform, and financial and credit card reform, among them.

Legitimacy is not seen, therefore, just in taking on but also in performing in the presidential role, especially in the public's response to laws passed, political stands taken, and a host of other issues, such as the president's appointments. Obama at times has seemed outdistanced in political battles, his credit limited and deflating. As presidential scholar Sean Wilentz (2010) considered it, "Obama looks less like a political messiah and more a victim of unrealistic expectations raised . . . by his election campaign" (p. 34), with opponents determined he should fail.

A frank statement of the intent of his political opponents was given by the Republican Leader of the Senate, Mitch McConnell, in the fall of 2010, saying that his first priority was to stop President Obama from having a second term. That seemed evident well before, as the so-called "Party of No" had blocked Obama's initiatives and used unprecedented numbers of Senate "filibusters," preventing bills from being voted on, to achieve that end. Given this context, it was notable that Republican Senator John McCain of Arizona, whom he defeated in the 2008 election and with whom he had cool relations after, praised Obama's address—approved 71% nationally—following the shootings in Tucson. Writing in the *Washington Post*, Senator McCain stated, with one condition, "I disagree with many of the president's policies, but I believe he is a patriot sincerely intent on using his time in office to advance our country's cause. I reject accusations that his policies and beliefs make him unworthy to lead America or opposed to its founding ideals. And I reject accusations that Americans who vigorously oppose his policies are less intelligent, compassionate or just than those who support them" (McCain, 2011).

Bill Clinton won office in 1992 with just 43% of the vote, although it was in a three-way race. That contributed to the difficulties he had instituting his programs at the outset, particularly a health care bill that had not gained enough support in Congress. But President Obama, even with 53% of the vote, has faced the "birther" legitimacy hurdle already noted, assertions that he is a Muslim, and reactions to his race, which Susan Fiske and her colleagues (2009) found to be positive in the 2008 election campaign for both non-Blacks and Blacks, who fit him into the "moderately warm, highly competent Black-professional" social subtype. This fit with what he put in *The Audacity of Hope* (Obama, 2006, pp. 234–40), about his acceptance racially, campaigning in Illinois for the US Senate. However, his 49% overall favorability after 18 months as president had declined most among Whites to 41%.

Though a ratings drop is usual in a president's second year, these global evaluations needed further analyses to reveal particular publics' attitudes about a president's politics and policies. President Obama's initiatives for change exposed a basic split that exists when those who are comfortable with the way things are feel threatened. Rather than credit him for such initiatives as health care reform, they had criticized it, often based on opponents' distortions, and shown a feeling of distrust. Indeed, just a year after his inauguration, even with his eloquence about change, the public's trust in him fell into the 40% range across the board for his handling of the economy, health care, the budget deficit, and terrorism. After his first year, therefore, Obama had about the same percentages as did Republican leaders (Blow, 2010b). Hopes can inspire, but followers need clarity about programs' values.

CHARISMA AND ITS LIMITS

Though charisma has been imputed to President Obama, if he does have it with some supporters, for his opponents it seems more like its polar opposite, "derisma," coined from "derision" or "derisive." Had charisma helped with his programs and counteracted the criticism he receives? The answer in general is "No, or at best only for a while." Can charisma help in bridging the power distance gap? Possibly, but usually the charismatic appeal of emotional arousal and identification has limited permanence, and may be accompanied by negative features such as narcissism (Howell & Avolio, 1992; Howell & Shamir, 2005). Its proponent, Max Weber (1947), said that charisma depends upon perceptions by followers who can withdraw it, "if the leader is long unsuccessful" (p. 360). Peter Drucker (1988) said that charisma should not be confused with performance. "Doing, not dash" is what matters, he said. In fact, much of what constitutes charisma is in the "eye of the beholder" (Simonton, 2008).

Charisma can be thought of as having a big credit balance from your supporters, initially usable for getting things done. Detractors do not want that to happen. Even for supporters, reality enters along with obstacles that make it harder to have things go your way. Major ones for a president are opposition politicians, congressional leaders such as dominant committee chairs, even of one's own party, and interest group lobbies. At the other end of the scale is discontent among citizens with the "power distance gap" and income disparities. Responding by "inclusion" is shown as satisfaction by such phrases as "he cares about people like me," when a president goes to speak and hear from citizens, helpful to getting action in Congress.

IDIOSYNCRASY CREDIT (IC), AND TRANSFORMING (TF) AND TRANSACTIONAL (TA) LEADERSHIP

A link can be made between credit and Burns's (1978) concept of "transformational (aka 'transforming') leadership." Such leaders, wishing to create change, provide benefits to followers that facilitate reaching that goal. These are rewards, which are more likely to earn credit from followers and be directly oriented to a change process, by *defining a situation* and *giving direction to activity* (Hollander & Julian, 1969).

Burns said that TF leaders bring people together for higher purposes, more than garnering votes. They want to create change institutionally and systemically, "to achieve broad human purposes and moral aspirations . . . among potential followers, bringing them to fuller consciousness of their needs . . . The secret of transforming leadership is the capacity of leaders to have their goals clearly and firmly in mind" (Burns, 1984, p. 103). Two presidential examples Burns gives are Franklin Roosevelt and Ronald Reagan. Though having very different political views in office, it is noteworthy that Reagan said he admired Roosevelt, and he had voted for and supported him when he, Reagan, was a Democrat and served as head of the Screen Actors Guild, a union, in Hollywood.

In his extension of work on TF leadership, Bass (1997) had identified and measured "*intellectual stimulation*" and "*inspiration*" as two of its major qualities. These are clearly appropriate for a successful presidency, among others that characterize TF leadership (see Bass & Riggio, 2006). Regarding the first, a president needs to communicate a credible "social reality" that becomes a shared understanding. His "definition of the situation" is necessary for a president's standing with constituents, persuaded by explanations of what is needed and why. An inspirational appeal may be adequate for campaigning, but not governing, that is, trying to be the leader versus successfully doing the tasks required of the leader.

Also noteworthy, these evident rewards associated with what the leader provides to followers has led Burns to state:

> I think my book (1978) is overly dichotomized. There is a stronger connection between transforming and transactional leadership than I led readers to believe. I think we have a spectrum. A few leaders operate wholly on the transforming side, but most work on both sides of that spectrum and combine transforming and transactional leadership.
>
> (Burns, 2007, p. viii)

RESPONSIBILITY IN LEADERSHIP

A quotation attributed to the French philosopher Jean-Paul Sartre, "To be a leader is to be responsible," conveys an essential feature of leadership, certainly in a president. However, in Obama's handling of a health reform bill even his friendliest supporters said he had neither inspired nor informed the electorate enough, as he did to get elected. He was faulted in particular for not specifying what he wanted, though he had eventually, in reaching a deal. But he had left the bill's features to the bargaining with congressional opponents that played out on TV for most of a year.

Obama allies had said he wished to avoid President Clinton's mistake of having his health bill resented by a Congress that then let it die. In 2009, two versions of the bill, as usual one from each congressional chamber, eventually passed. In that year, though, opposition voices gave frequent misinformation about the bills' provisions. Fear-provoking allegations, such as "government death panels," were not refuted soon and strongly, but left largely unchallenged, after damage was done. The refutations were not in time to be effective. This lapse was in the face of opposition in Congress that was uniformly arrayed against any votes that would let the Obama programs pass. The goal was clear even before one opponent, Senator Jim DeMint, Republican of South Carolina, said that failing to pass the health reform bill would be "Obama's Waterloo." The historian Garry Wills (2010) added that in this situation a president must exercise power, or at least have it "be feared," rather than signal weakness. This was Machiavelli's basic advice to his prince centuries ago. Nevertheless, Obama's approach has been conciliatory, continually trying persuasion (Nagourney, 2009). Major issues he had wanted to have passed, such as immigration, energy policy (particularly regarding climate change), and tax reform, have not been addressed, but opposed by foes in Congress. Tax reform has been especially urgent, because it is needed to fund other bills.

Responsibility in leadership has applied also to those called the "loyal opposition," referring to their presumed obligation to the interests of the nation and its citizens. Shirking that responsibility had run the risk, among others, of further alienating the public from politicians, to no one's benefit. When a former, newly elected Republican majority under House Speaker Newt Gingrich in 1995 closed down the government in a budget battle with President Clinton, the immense effects and related outrage made it seem a never-to-do-again maneuver, but in a replay of that battle, it had been threatened in 2011, and resurfaced again over finances.

Maintaining communication with the citizenry, speaking about national problems, and dealing with grief after a great tragedy have been significant presidential tasks (Baker, 2010). This outspokenness has become routine in the politics of a "continuous campaign mode," related to what President Theodore Roosevelt called the "Bully Pulpit." Recent Presidents—Carter, Reagan, on through the second Bush, and Obama—tried to serve as the Voice of the People in "cheerleading" aimed at the "public" and "players" in

Congress, acting both as Chief Legislator and Chief of Party. Even with their different positions on the political spectrum, all of these presidents at some point tried using "running against Washington" as a theme. During the 1980 campaign, the political humorist Mark Russell noted that in 1976 Jimmy Carter said, "Washington is rotten, and I want to go there." "Now," said Russell, "four years later, he's the guy he warned us about."

Ronald Reagan's defeat of Carter in 1980 marked a seismic shift for twelve years back to Republican presidents, until Bill Clinton was elected in 1992 and reelected in 1996. Reagan's policies were predicated on his slogan that "Government is the problem, not the solution." He had considerable appeal, including with so-called "Reagan Democrats," who favored his early tax cuts—though he raised taxes later, and his anti-Soviet Union stand—though he eventually negotiated well with its leaders. He detached himself from government by referring to it in the third person as "they" or "them" in statements criticizing public employees, and said to listeners, "Send a message to Washington." His approach did illustrate how a president can create distance from Congress and the federal establishment, at the same time that he shows closer identification with ordinary citizens and their reasons for discontent. Reagan's reach extended to the second Bush presidency, and beyond, in that "Bush championed the policies of Reagan's that his father had abandoned, including supply-side tax cuts and missile defense" (Weisberg, 2008, p. 229). Republicans, including many of the 2012 presidential candidates, still spoke reverently of Reagan and his policies.

LEADERSHIP AS A PROCESS: MICRO AND MACRO

Leadership clearly is critical to the health of a group, organization, or nation. Because of its vital function, especially in the presidency, there is the potential for a so-called "leadership crisis" to occur and take on great significance. A major one is revealed in the expression about a "lack of leadership," suggesting aimless drift and purposelessness. Two helpful "inclusive leadership" remedies are *listening to concerns* and *clarifying intentions of what is proposed*. Having such open communication with followers makes possible inclusion to reduce the effects of psychological distance. Oftentimes, a crisis produces a call for "strong leadership," meaning an opposite approach, tending toward dominance by a leader. At best, what is desired is a balance that comes from authentic follower involvement in the leadership process. That is far more challenging to achieve at the macro level, given the distance from a president and intervening media voices.

In micro-leadership research, face-to face discussion groups predominate, concerned with topics such as influence, supervision of production groups, and group decision making (Kent, 1996). It does not translate particularly well to the macro-leadership of presidential leadership on a national, indeed global, scale because many things are different going from micro- to macro-leadership activities. Important among them are *the intensity and consequences of exercising power widely.* However, a basic process both in small groups and in society is that *an elected leader has a commitment from constituents who expect more from them.* Leader legitimacy, by election or appointment, has been found to create differing effects on American subjects in relating to leaders, with more expected of elected leaders by followers who voted for them (Hollander & Julian, 1970).

Study of the relationship of leaders and followers has increased in recent decades (e.g., Hollander & Offermann, 1990; Kelley, 1988, 1992). An early contributor to it was Chester Barnard (1938), with his "Acceptance Theory of Authority," centered on the follower's role in judging if an order is authoritative. Mary Parker Follett (1949; see also Graham, 1995) raised a similar point, putting forth her concept of "power with." Followership has now become more prominent as a field of study (e.g., Riggio, Chaleff, & Lipman-Blumen, 2008; Kellerman, 2008; Chaleff, 2003; Van Vugt, Hogan, & Kaiser, 2008). Price (2008) has done a philosophically based analysis to explain leader initiatives, especially as they are seen to be rule-breaking. Using the study of ethics and moral theories, he considered that leaders have special latitude from followers to behave in different ways, what he called "leader exceptionalism," which he had built on the idiosyncrasy credit model.

PERSONAL QUALITIES OF A PRESIDENT

Perceived competence is widely recognized as a major variable in evaluating performance, and it is especially essential in believing in a president's success. However, it can be highly affected by situational factors such as institutional structures and culture, as well as changed circumstances over which the leader has no control. But one is still held responsible by the attributions of followers (Calder, 1977). Among the examples, world oil cost more under Carter and less under Reagan (Hogan, Curphy, & Hogan, 1994), so a president is often credited or faulted for externalities, or a policy or situation left by his predecessor (Simonton, 2008).

Certain individual differences may not be recognized as significant until presidents deal with and show themselves to constituents, governmental officials, and institutions. The ability to reduce the distance gap by inclusion is worth attention by analyzing personal qualities such as empathy that are basic to character. When such "psychological" factors have been considered, they are seen mostly as the personality qualities of a particular president, as in "psycho-history," essentially a psychoanalytic biography (e.g., Betty Glad, 1980, on Jimmy Carter). Another approach is the character typology, i.e., active–passive crossed with positive–negative, contributed by Barber (1972). In that system, Franklin Roosevelt was an active-positive, and Richard Nixon, an active-negative. Obama has been repeatedly characterized as seeking conciliation, and not combat. However, what a leader takes to be a strength may be a weakness in the eyes and reactions of others. Kaplan and Kaiser (2006) present the case for a leader needing to know when to moderate a strength, so that it has not been relied on excessively. Otherwise, they say, there may be a descent into weakness, not recognized until losses have been felt. Wills (2010) has gone further and stated that a president must use or have others perceive the threat of his willingness to use power when needed to achieve his goals.

One of those often considered a great president is Abraham Lincoln, who was controversial at a bitter time leading up to and during the Civil War (1861–65). Yet he is recognized now for his ability to rally support for great attainments, not least ending slavery in the nation. Three qualities Lincoln possessed made him stand out among his followers, according to a Lincoln biographer, historian James Oakes (2009), namely: "capacity for growth," "political skill," and a "way with words" to communicate and persuade. Oakes concluded that in a responsive way great leaders invite themselves to be "forced into glory" by followers (pp. 3–5), thus saying that a leader's achievements come from others' strong identification with him.

Clearly, these individual differences among presidents affect the way they deal with power distance in relating to constituents and governmental institutions. Harold Laski (1940) emphasized at the outset of his classic work, *The American Presidency,* that political institutions "change with changes in the environment within which they operate, and . . . differ, from one moment to the other, in terms of [those] who operate them" (p. 1). David McClelland (1964) emphasized motives of achievement, power, and affiliation as a leadership needs system. His colleague, David Winter (1973), did content analyses of twentieth-century presidential inaugural addresses to assess these needs, and found that the need for power was mainly associated with presidents involved in the onset of wars. Usually, presidents seen as "great" in history were wartime ones. Is confidence inspired, then, by being "a wartime president," even if made distant from constituents who oppose the war? Does calling such critics "unpatriotic" protect a president from them?

Though it would seem not to benefit a president to preside over an unpopular war, a state of war does allow a president so inclined to extend his powers to the level of those of an absolute monarch. This had begun to be a criticism of President Obama, as he ordered action jointly in NATO against Libya, while waging two wars inherited from his predecessor, the second President Bush. George Washington rejected having the president be like a king, but concern had been expressed ever since over the "Imperial Presidency" (Schlesinger, 1973). The late Senator William Fulbright, whose name is on international teaching and study awards, deplored the "arrogance of power" in a 1966 book. He saw it in the presidency of a fellow Democrat, Lyndon Johnson, in conducting the war in Vietnam. These tendencies again were criticized when aggressive initiatives were recently taken abroad by various secret assertions of presidential power (Dean, 2003). The Gallup Poll (Newport, 2007) reported that the intensity of this issue explained President Bush's low approval rate of just 37% on the sixth anniversary of his inauguration—the lowest of all his prior polls.

Respondents had disapproved of President Bush's assertion of his role as "the decider," to do whatever he wanted without regard to the expectations and roles of constituents and Congress. An explanation for such behavior has been put forth by Lord David Owen (2007), a British Foreign Secretary in the 1970s, who is a psychiatrist. He contended that this was a sign of "hubris," as a clinical condition that had afflicted officials holding positions of power. Hubris's main symptoms are reckless overconfidence in their own judgment and contempt for advice, evidenced for example by Lyndon Johnson. A so-called "credibility gap" had arisen under him after he had escalated US Forces in Vietnam in 1964. His actions followed passage by

Congress of the Gulf of Tonkin Resolution that August, when he had given members the unverified story that an American destroyer had been attacked by Vietnamese gunboats. Jack Valenti (2007), then a major Johnson aide, reported that Johnson had been willing to try listening to criticism of the recommended military escalation. But after doing so, he then dismissed all alternative courses of action. A large and powerful persuader, Johnson was successful as Senate Majority Leader and as president in getting civil rights and voting rights legislation passed in 1965–66. Thanks to his great persuasive skills, he was also able to have many more "Great Society" social and economic programs passed in Congress. However, the Vietnam War, and his loss of credibility and credit with the public, led to his giving up another presidential run in 1968, in a surprising and memorable TV speech. A tragic figure, he had self-inflicted wounds to his presidency from a divisive war in which he said, "Our national honor is at stake," though he achieved major domestic social advances.

In the US–UK Iraq War, begun in 2003, President Bush and Prime Minister Blair also had these hubris effects. Part of the evidence Owen had cited in his book (2007) was that there were no plans for who or what would replace Saddam Hussein, or whether, and/or how, to handle the disbanding of his vast army. These two allied leaders had believed the invasion troops would be welcomed warmly. They had relied heavily on advice from expatriate Iraqi dissidents, who wanted "regime change," but not on other views, even from experts in Iraq history and culture.

Actually, though it is Congress that the Constitution mandates as the body to declare war, no president had requested it since Franklin Roosevelt when Pearl Harbor was attacked by the Japanese in December 1941. Garry Wills (2010) said this showed that the intent of the recent Bush administration to have a "unitary executive" had been to keep control, often by secret security programs. Tom Ricks (2006) noted that candidate Bush, in an October 2000 debate with candidate Gore, had said "I will be very careful about using our troops as nation builders. I believe the role of the military is to fight and win wars and to prevent war from happening in the first place" (p. 24). Subsequent events were clearly adverse, from the unpopular Iraq War, and a "change election" in November 2006 had put a Democratic majority in both the House of Representatives and the Senate. His high power distance, with a non-inclusive stance, had not been popular.

━━━━━━━

PRESIDENTIAL PROMISES AND "THE MANDATE"

In campaigning, a candidate makes "promises" that will not be fulfilled and inevitably disappoints many or at least some supporters once the president is in office. Beginning with primary contests, and even leaving aside the prior record, a candidate makes a host of statements in set speeches, responses to press questions, interviews, and off-the-cuff remarks. These will have highly variable applications to coherent and workable administration programs, and may even be contradictory.

An obvious fact of political life, therefore, is that what is promised to get elected may bear little relationship to what is delivered eventually. In an oft-cited, classic example, President Nixon pledged for a long time that he was opposed to wage and price controls to hold down inflation, though he later introduced them to a surprised public and party, when thought necessary. He supported national health insurance, which failed to pass in Congress, but did establish the Environmental Protection Agency, among his domestic legacies. Greatest public concern was directed, though, to the costs in casualties and treasure of his continued pursuit of the unpopular Vietnam War that he took over from President Johnson and promised to end. Secret military operations in adjacent Cambodia, the existence of which he had denied, led to many public protests in spring 1970, with four students shot dead at Kent State University, by Ohio National Guardsmen, tragically.

Among the most venerable of political beliefs is the notion that, once elected, a president has a "mandate" to put new or different programs into effect. This poses some troublesome problems of definition, insofar as supporters may have highly discrepant conceptions of what was promised. Also, constituencies usually brought together for the election have varying interests and may feel differently on major issues after the election, requiring further dealings to settle on programs.

President George W. Bush took his reelection in 2004 as a certain sign of a continuing mandate to do what he wanted in the Iraq War, and in such domestic matters as changing Social Security, mainly a government-run retirement insurance program, passed over Republican opposition in the 1930s under President Franklin Roosevelt's New Deal. Soon after reelection, President Bush said he had "political capital" and "intended to spend it" (cf. Verba, 1961), to "privatize" social security. However, this and other domestic intentions of his were not fulfilled. Changed circumstances may allow the bending or reinterpretation of a mandate. Further, determining what part of a president's program was supported by voters is made difficult by what may be the diversity of targeted appeals to "special interest constituencies." The relevant questions therefore may be: "What was promised? When? To which intended constituency?" At best, what can be assessed are statements about policies that a candidate puts forward as major campaign themes.

PARTY, PROGRAM, AND PERSONALITY

Three important factors that are most mentioned as sources of support for a candidate are party, program, and personality, not always in that order. The first of these, the national political party, is essential to a president's election, and he is bound to it. This may be troubling to the opposition, but as Rossiter (1956) said, " if he is to persuade Congress . . . achieve a loyal and cohesive administration . . . and [be] re-elected . . . he must put his hand firmly to the plow of politics" (p. 29). Kellerman used this theme in her *The Political Presidency* (1984), as noted earlier.

The party "platform" on which a candidate runs is a broad statement representing varying degrees of compromise between the candidate and factions of the national party. Beyond a general ideology, there is an imperfect basis for knowing what the candidate will do as president. This perplexity was stated by Julian Bond, a Carter supporter and Black leader, who said in the 1976 campaign that he was bothered by not being able to predict "what Jimmy Carter would do."

Carter did have a program, or pieces of a program, some of which were part of his promise. But he established one basis for his own demise when, in the 1976 campaign against Gerald Ford, he calculated a "misery index" that showed an inflation and unemployment rate each over 6%, thus yielding 12% for Ford, which Carter said was unacceptable. After Carter won and served a term, his *power distance gap* was already wide when he was challenged in 1980 by Reagan, who pointed to the current over 20% misery index. Carter came out badly from this contrast. A year before, Carter also had faced the burden of dealing with the Iranian government holding diplomats taken prisoner at the American Embassy. They were held hostage 444 days until the day he left office, in January 1981, as Reagan was inaugurated, despite Carter's failed attempt by a helicopter expedition to rescue them. A former Kennedy aide, historian Arthur Schlesinger, Jr., said in the 1980 campaign he could not forgive Carter for having made Ford look like a great president in retrospect. Ford was adversely affected by initially pardoning Nixon in 1975 for his role in the Watergate break-in of the Democratic Party's headquarters in 1972. Denying a possible arrangement beforehand, to circumvent justice and keep the public from learning the truth, Ford allies insisted that he had wished only to "heal the nation," thinking Nixon had agreed to make a statement on the matter, but Nixon never did.

Once in office, all presidents are evaluated for their performance, but they also are its executive producer with a formidable apparatus, uniquely capable of gaining the airwaves and headlines as a super mass-media voice. Some presidents, even with this enormous communication facility at hand, have suffered from lapses, gaffes, and distance gaps in reaching their audience. The public can and does assign meanings to events that are not the intended ones offered by politicians, including the president. Still, there is often an inclination for the public generally to want to believe in and depend on the image projected by the nation's leader. Richard Nixon, well before his resignation, said, "The American people want to believe that their president is not a crook. Well, I am not a crook." Oddly, in the coverage before he said it, the "crook" term was not used. This conception was his, not the public's.

As many observers have commented, a president usually is insulated from everyday concerns. In large part, this is due to his physical and likely psychological distance from the populace. On the other hand, the portrayals of presidents in settings with ordinary people—as "just like other folks"—often are seen as manipulative, however sincerely motivated. When the first President Bush was shown at a supermarket checkout counter, confronting a price-scanner whose workings he appeared not to know about, it showed him distinctly out of touch. Earlier, President Carter tried to appeal to the public by such populist gestures as walking down Pennsylvania Avenue with his wife Rosalind after his inauguration, and wearing a cardigan sweater on a TV "fireside chat" on energy savings. Some saw both presentations as too contrived.

POLICY MAKING

A president cannot lead entirely from a distance without grave risk of failure. In making policy, there are hazards from deferential staff members. They may keep a president continually at a distance from the give and take of informed, frank appraisals of alternative policies. Problem solving has been altered or at least affected in the president's presence. Usually, Reedy (1970) said, "White House councils are not debating matches in which ideas emerge from the heated exchanges of participants. The council centers around the President himself [and] the first strong observations to attract the favor of the President became subconsciously the thoughts of everyone in the room" (p. 12).

Being in a president's presence can be quite intimidating to all but a few. Encountering any prominent person can be stunning, but suddenly speaking to a president is especially so. President Obama had made a point of countering this potential failing by encouraging greater participation and allowing more time for discussion. However, he had been faulted by opposition criticism for so-called "diddling" when he had repeated meetings in 2009 with top military and other officials about the decision he had made to send more troops to Afghanistan. The tendency for "acceptable" views to converge toward the leader's, as a show of loyalty, is a major basis for Janis's (1972) "groupthink" phenomenon. It underlies many cases he cites of catastrophically bad group decisions by otherwise capable advisors, who fell into a "groupthink" effect. President Obama had said he wanted "to hear from everyone in the room," to listen to a range of alternate views. Still, the power distance gap may not be easily surmounted without a strong and persisting commitment to do so. A major obstacle has been that "the presidency is about as close to total estrangement as one can get in the modern world. The only time he ever meets a peer is during the rare visit of some foreign potentate, and . . . most of the potentates who visit . . . feel a bit diffident" (Reedy, 1970, p. 20). "Politicians need peers and without them they become remote from reality." An elder statesman Democratic senator, who had been a Johnson ally since his senatorial days, was asked by Reedy why he didn't go over and have a "heart-to-heart talk" with President Johnson about some national problems they agreed were bad. The senator said, "I can't talk to a President the way I can to a Senator" (Reedy, 1970, p. 30).

IMAGES VS. PERFORMANCE

Taking account of such insularity, it is no wonder that in the White House images may easily come to represent reality in assessing presidential performance. When President Nixon said he was "not a crook," as mentioned earlier, and President Carter promised, "I will never lie to you," they underscored a gap in image by begging the question of why they believed some people might think that. A statement by President Reagan that he was "not a bigot" seems comparable, though not entirely parallel. Reagan handled this problem of alleged bigotry by attributing it to misperception due to the media, since his intentions were good. He told his story of a "welfare queen driving a Cadillac," but not that she was Black.

President Reagan continually had more people reportedly liking his personality than supporting his policies on many issues. This kind of popularity of a president may give him credits to bounce back, as Reagan did after a 1982 congressional veto override, and later the Iran-Contra scandal, in which he initially denied giving weapons to Iran. At the time, the *Washington Post*'s Robert Kaiser (1983) said on the air that President Reagan "seems to lead a charmed life, getting away with things." His long, earlier movie career doubtless helped bolster his popularity, and gave him so-called "residual credits" in the IC model. His movie work yielded an Oscar nomination for *King's Row* in 1942, and in 1951 he credibly played a psychology professor who in real life had raised a chimpanzee for an heredity experiment, in *Bedtime for Bonzo*. Maltin (2006, p. 99) rated it good as a comedy, and rejected "absurdity" notions about it he said dogged Reagan later.

As is evident, presidents have used the mass media to reach and influence the public, and to do what they can to shape their own images. However, the statement that "an ounce of image is worth a pound of performance" is limited, because as followers gain experience with a leader they come to know whether their needs and expectations have been addressed and met. If so, there will likely be trust and loyalty, with solidarity of purpose, but the reverse is also true, with the loss of both.

Cognitive psychology findings bolster the point that "labeling" can effectively "deal" with a problem or can "kill" a policy, such as renaming the "estate tax" the "death tax" during the second Bush presidency. This calls to mind the subtitle, "Words that Succeed and Policies that Fail," from

Edelman's book *Political Language* (1977). Lakoff (2004) dealt with these points too in his *Don't Think of an Elephant,* regarding how issues are framed. He has advised not to argue by using the words of the other side that convey their frame. His further point about politicians' speech was the warning to "Watch what we do, not what we say."

In evaluating presidential performance, the atmosphere created by an administration is important. Before this age of terrorism, government leadership was said to have two main functions: to *reduce provocation* and to *act positively to increase opportunities for participation* (Lasswell, 1948). These are achieved through goal clarification, consultation, and other signs of evident *respect for individuals* up through *power sharing.* Both are desirable aspects of inclusion. Though they are expressions of ideal-type values, often unattainable, it has been *worthwhile to consider these two aspects as basic and to be aware of their absence.*

Regarding provocation, there is a reasonably clear issue of the degree to which political appeals embody threats or avoid them. In his analysis of the rioting by African-Americans in 1960s Los Angeles, the UCLA sociologist Ralph Turner (1969) defined the balance needed between trying to make a statement about injustice and avoiding an excessive load of threat in doing so, thereby producing "backlash." Riots, of course, are not calculated so rationally, as Turner indicated.

The basic point of *arousing without excessively threatening* fits psychological findings regarding moderate arousal, through limited fear appeals, to gain desired actions. Fear appeals can be used for political ends by raising concerns about the greater likelihood of terrorist attacks, voiced by the opposition as a criticism of presidential performance. The consequences of these tactics have been negative attitudes and a loss of trust in politicians and in government as a whole.

DEALING WITH FOLLOWER NEEDS AND AVOIDING "ANTICIPOINTMENT"

A president is the recipient of the people's votes that placed him in that high position. To attain and retain their support, attention to their interests and needs is essential. Programs must be seen at least to be trying to meet these. Raising hopes, which then are unfulfilled, obviously must be avoided.

Called "anticipointment," it has the potential of rapidly reversing positive feelings toward a leader to negative ones. This means a leader needs to be open about reality factors as much as possible.

"Followers judge leaders," said Wills (1994, p. 21), and the credit concept presented here emphasizes how follower perceptions affect leader emergence and latitude for action. The concept of inclusive leadership provides a further alternative for follower involvement through two-way communication and influence, to bridge the physical and psychological power distance gaps. Since only followers themselves can ultimately define their own true needs (Burns, 1978, p. 36, quoted earlier), then the basic point is that a president must be responsive to major constituent needs.

The public's top domestic concerns in 2011 had been unemployment, which also still threatened those who are employed but feared they might be next to lose a job; health coverage, specifically its rules and costs, even for those who have had it or had intended to get it under the new law; and foreclosure, with loss of one's home and the inability to take any equity value from it. Consternation had been expressed with government programs that only made loan modifications an option for lenders, not a requirement to provide some relief for borrowers. As a result, this and other issues remain priorities, especially for those who believed that the president, whom they supported enthusiastically, would deliver on these matters. They reviewed his record, compared to what he had promised, to see if enough relief was underway.

Disappointment had been evident too with President Obama's negotiating with his opponents. Employing a procedure often seen to be fruitless, he had spent a great deal of time meeting with those in Congress, trying persuasion, but some critics said giving too much too soon (Stolberg, 2010). Distressed allies would rather he had been "fighting for things he knows are right," as a major discouraged supporter, Cornel West, a leading Black Studies professor, said in a 2009 radio interview. Typical of such discontent, he lamented that the president "seemed to care more for bailing out the bankers than helping a lot of ordinary people who are hurting." Unmentioned was the fact that the "TARP" (Troubled Asset Relief Program) bill actually had been passed under President Bush, at the urging of his Treasury Secretary, Henry Paulson, former CEO of Goldman Sachs, who had said it would save the financial system and avoid a depression. Though TARP's results seemed positive, there still had been criticism of its lack of accountability. In September 2011, the acute need and dissatisfaction with the "remedy" were put bluntly as, "Three years ago, the federal government used tens of billions in taxpayer dollars to save the banking system. Now, at this dire economic moment, the country needs the banks to return the favor" (Nocera, 2011).

Without conditions placed on the banks for the benefits they received, many had just held back in fulfilling the ultimate intent of having them make loans for businesses and others to be on the way to recovery. Banks further continued to pay large bonuses to their top officers after getting public tax funds. Seen as "losses are public, but profits are private," this was another "heads I win, and tails you lose" game, yielding public outrage. Bankers then were offended when called "fat cats" by Obama, with many switching to support his opposition in the 2010 and 2012 elections. He said he was quoting a commentator's use of the term. They repeatedly claimed he was "anti-business," despite record corporate profits and surging stocks.

The concept of "anticipointment" better describes what occurred when high expectations were raised but not met from giving billions of taxpayer dollars to banks, since they were not required to do the much-needed lending in return. Though President Obama's Finance Reform bill passed Congress in the spring of 2010, it lacked key restraints to prevent the financial crisis from recurring. Yet he urged action in line with the discontent expressed about the banks in polls showing that more regulation of finance was favored 2 to 1 in national surveys, with big banks and their leaders particularly distrusted. But a reform bill that was described as a "loophole-ridden compromise" (Rich, 2010) became law, and was further diminished by Republican legislators' opposition to regulation, energized after their victory in the 2010 elections. That change-over in the lower house of Congress was facilitated by bitter resistance and antagonism from the financial sector itself. As noted above, many of its major leaders who had supported Obama in 2008 switched their funding to his opponents in 2010. Furthermore, the ruling by the Supreme Court in the 2010 Citizens United case made it possible for historically huge sums to come into Congressional and next presidential races without revealing their sources.

Remarkably, Obama's great personal effort to save the American automobile industry proved a big success on the basis of a loan program that had paid back or soon will virtually all the funds lent to General Motors and Chrysler. Ford had not needed nor asked for loans, and had done very well on its own. Hundreds of thousands of jobs were saved, not just in these firms but also in the hundreds of suppliers to the auto industry nationwide.

Obama's program, with admitted risks, was boldly pushed by him and his party, though denounced as a "giveaway" and "bail out" by opponents in and outside of Congress. Not a single Republican there had voted for its passage. Yet a drumbeat continued about the "anti-business president," neither crediting this major success against great opposition nor such other benefits as his small business tax credits.

Even in foreign affairs, opposition voices berated him for what he did or did not do about such uprisings as occurred in Egypt, and in supporting the Libyan rebels who ended Colonel Qaddafi and his 42-year rule. The report of Obama's speech at Cairo University in June 2009 (Cohen, 2011) indicated that he received a very favorable response when he said, "You must place the interests of your people and the legitimate workings of the political process above your party. Without these elements, elections alone do not make true democracy." It struck a chord regarding issues that can readily be seen as urgent here at home.

Seen in the fourth year of his term, President Obama appeared to have lost credit with many in his 2008 base of support, including independents that voted for him before, but were only "rented," as one observer had put it. President Obama was still dealing with the poor economy he found on entering office, which was still far from recovered and was only coming back slowly. Obama had much to do to restore credits with his base, some of whom were openly critical. "Main Street" concerns still demanded attention, even as he pointed out that company profits and stock prices had been climbing. An early jobs act did not meet needs sufficiently, and a second jobs act was seemingly stopped by congressional Republicans. Also, it will take years, if ever, before the health care act's key provisions take effect, in the face of ongoing congressional Republican opposition, and battles still in the courts.

A Democratic pollster praised the health care bill soon after it was signed in March 2010 as a victory, in a column entitled "A win is a win" (Greenberg, 2010). However, in addition to court cases, the bill was the object of repeal votes in 2011 in Congress, when Republicans took over the House by an overwhelming majority. Repeal was, however, stopped by the Democrats' slim majority in the Senate. Health care both raised expectations and disappointed followers, especially for not having a government-sponsored "public option." That would have allowed competition with private insurers, which they helped squelch. President Obama evidently did not fight for it, likely because he knew it was unattainable, given deals he took part in. Moreover, as noted earlier, the Health Act's signing was followed by a year and a half pause before he proposed his comprehensive Jobs Bill. Thus far, it had been stopped by congressional opposition, though portions might survive to be enacted.

This is a distinct setback, because a president has to continue to be perceived as getting needed things done, or he loses credits. An implicit question is, "Have you made or will you make my life better?" President Obama may still have modified his approach even more, and possibly have shown some favorable trends with conditions that most concern the public. Among them, the economic issues of unemployment and home foreclosures remained critical. Pointedly, the *New York Times* editorialized on the Labor Day Weekend of 2010, "Despite occasional signs of movement ... general paralysis in the housing market ... coupled with high unemployment [indicate] a slowing economy" (September 3, 2010).

In that regard, Blow (2011) several months later called attention to the fact that poverty went unmentioned in the president's 2011 State of the Union address; moreover, this was only the second time since Harry Truman's 1948 address that a Democratic president had failed to mention the problem on that occasion, the other being Jimmy Carter in 1980. Blow said that was very troubling to the estimated sixth of the US population under the poverty line, even heavier proportionally in the 18-years-of-age-and-under cohort. What accounted for this absence generally was attributed to Obama having projected a picture of optimism. He had trumpeted unprecedented corporate profits, and noted that, "The stock market has come roaring back," both points aimed at boosting his reelection in 2012. Blow reported that 73% of the poor, with incomes of $15,000 or less voted for him in 2008, so the inference was that Obama counted on those among the poor who are old enough to vote to vote for him again, and not for his opponent, whoever that turned out to be.

WHERE ARE TRUST AND LOYALTY?

Trust and loyalty had been seen as fraying, because government, spotlighted as leadership needed from the president, had seemed to let these economic tragedies fester, with weak action and less success. Two-way communication, including listening so as to do action-based inclusion, was needed to restore confidence. But, important as communication is to effective leadership, and fidelity to a cause or mission, its absence is serious, too. As one politician had put it, "Just because you ignore it, doesn't mean it will go away." Not uniquely, leveling with the electorate was vital to Obama's presidency, wrote Evan Thomas (2010) in *Newsweek*, in the wake of decisive election defeats in 2010.

For his supporters to stay with him, alienated ones to return, and new ones to join him, strong positive communications from Obama were required, showing how, as president, he had listened and furthered their interests by his policies. That task was made especially acute after the 2010 midterm elections, when his party lost the House of Representatives. Obama was then put in further contention with his opposition there, and some continuingly hostile media providing disinformation about him.

His inclination to keep trying conciliation, reaffirmed in the Remnick (2010) biography of him, had been challenged by persisting opposition. Other modes of engagement were needed to counter the assault and revitalize his support. Peggy Noonan (2011), who had served as a skilled speechwriter for Republican presidents, diagnosed Obama's style in her *Wall Street Journal* column as a matter of coolness and lack of a disarming touch in his relationship with adversaries. She said Reagan masterfully used such "outreach" to them, and that Obama's interpersonal lack had "made worse" the challenging economic and international situations he had faced. Her view was opposite to criticism of Obama as too pragmatic and unwilling to fight for what he felt needed to be done. Another example, the same week as Noonan's column, was that a Nobel Prize-winning MIT economist, nominated to the Federal Reserve Board, had withdrawn after a 14-months wait for a Senate vote. The president's image as weak in this responsibility was evident in editorial criticism in the *New York Times* (June 14, 2011) for his failure to appoint and, when doing so, to stand up for his nominees.

Seen to settle for whatever the other side wanted, Obama infuriated supporters who saw him as a poor negotiator (Andersen, 2011). Soon after the debt ceiling agreement, he seemed to cave in to anti-environmental and anti-regulation forces, by delaying air-quality control of ozone for two years, distressing them further. A major supporter said, in a much publicized comment, "Somehow we need to get back the president we thought we elected in 2008" (McKibben, 2011), a too familiar cry of despair. President Obama appeared to continue bowing to threats after clear signs that his opponents would still deny him credit for any successes, even saving the auto industry, or eliminating Osama bin Laden, and helping free Libya from Colonel Qaddafi and his regime.

The patriotic pride of Obama's opponents seemed absent, and much more being held back by them, including national economic recovery, rebuilding infrastructure, reforming health care, and serving other needs, to gain their stated aim of not allowing him to win a second term. Among Obama's strengths was the enthusiasm he showed in his 2008 campaign, still coming through in his speeches, such as "We can't wait any longer," and issuing Executive Orders. However, to get away from the disdained "leading from the rear" image, a paramount task for him was to be more inclusive. He must "show the way" by fighting for vital constituent economic needs, as the cause with which he had to be strongly identified. His passion here was likeliest to earn support from followers, and credit if he was seen to be producing results on what he promised.

With economic distress and persisting unemployment, time for remedies had been lost, and Obama seemed less effective and even more distant as a leader. To bridge the power distance gap, it was essential that the concern he showed in winning the presidency come back, as it did in his speeches and other appearances. Another overriding requirement had been to communicate more openness to inclusion. He had a start in this direction by a series of regional bus tours in the fall of 2011, reaching out to hear and respond to constituents' concerns, and maybe earn their trust and loyalty by showing when and where there had been positive results.

Perhaps President Obama's restored enthusiasm had come in time as a feature of his reelection campaign. The effects of this evident change were summed up by one commentator saying, "Americans who feel, rightly, that the world's order has shifted . . . want a leader whose emotional temperature validates their own sense of urgency. Obama has obviously concluded as much" (Bruni, 2011).

Three years after his election, Obama did adopt more populist rhetoric about fighting for economic fairness. In a Kansas town where President Theodore Roosevelt gave his "fair deal" speech a century before, he aligned himself with the Republican reformer to deplore and correct the growing income inequality. In Obama's speech, among his economic policies he proposed a slight tax increase of less than 2% on dollars earned above a million a year. He received an approving but nonetheless critical editorial in the *New York Times* (2011), concluding that he "was late to Roosevelt's level of passion and action on behalf of the middle class and the poor, having missed several opportunities to make the tax burden more fair and demand real action on the housing crisis from the big banks" (December 7, 2011).

An ironic, semi-prophetic story ran on Obama's election in 2008, in the humor publication, *The Onion,* beginning, "African-American man Barack Obama, 47, was given the least-desirable job in the entire country Tuesday when he was elected president of the United States of America. In his new high-stress, low-reward position, Obama will be charged with such tasks as overhauling the nation's broken-down economy, repairing the crumbling infrastructure, and generally having to please more than 300 million Americans . . . on a daily basis . . . spending four to eight years cleaning up the messes other people left behind" (November 5, 2008).

Some other perilous tasks for Obama included continuing to grapple with the determined partisan opposition his programs received in Congress, even when originally conceived by his opponents, such as the "health insurance mandate" and "cap and trade on energy pollution." If he came to favor a policy initiative, they stopped favoring it, and were now against it. Even with passage of the vital two-month extension of the payroll tax cut and unemployment payments for early 2012, opposition remained implacable, so the fate of the originally intended one-year passage stayed contentious, with "poison-pill riders" to kill it from the outset. This raised the question of what will be the counter-effects of moving away from his long-attempted and faulted conciliatory bipartisan stands?

Finally, abroad there are European financial issues creating risks here, plus trade deficits and loans from a surging China. A war was still being fought in Afghanistan, adjacent to restless Iran and Pakistan, related to many crises in a dangerous, unstable international scene. These presented Obama with a vast array of challenges, fired up further in the hotbed of presidential election-year campaigning. Furthermore, its expenditures will far exceed past election spending, with accountability greatly reduced and allowed to be hidden. Faced with all of this, a prevailing need still was for the president to break through the power distance gap to reach and show attention to constituents' basic concerns.

BIBLIOGRAPHY

Andersen, K. (2011). The madman theory. *New York Times*, Aug. 6, p. A17.

Avolio, B. J., Bass, B. M., & Jung, D. I. (1999). Reexamining the components of transformational and transactional leadership using the Multifactor Leadership Questionnaire. *Journal of Occupational and Organizational Psychology*, 72: 441–462.

Baker, P. (2010). Few news conferences, but still taking questions. *New York Times*, Feb. 4, p. A-20.

Barber, J. D. (1972). *The presidential character: Predicting performance in the White House.* Englewood Cliffs, NJ: Prentice-Hall.

Barnard, C. I. (1938). *The functions of the executive.* Cambridge, MA: Harvard University Press.

Bass, B. M. (1997). Does the transactional-transformational leadership paradigm transcend organizational and national boundaries? *American Psychologist*, 52 (2): 130–139.

Bass, B. M. & Riggio, R. E. (2006). *Transformational leadership*, (2nd ed.). Mahwah, NJ: Erlbaum.

Bennis, W. G. (1999). The leadership advantage. *Leader to Leader*, 12 (Spring): 18–23.

Blair, T. (2010). *A journey: My political life.* New York: Knopf.

Blow. C. (2010a, b). Obama gets his groove back. Republicans and Democrats differ. *New York Times*, Feb. 6 & 13, p. A19.

Blow, C. M. (2011). Hard-knock (hardly acknowledged) life. *New York Times*, Jan. 29, p. A23.

Bruni, F. (2011). Nice guy finishing last. *New York Times*, Oct. 16, p. SR3.

Burns, J. M. (1978). *Leadership.* New York: Harper & Row.

Burns, J. M. (1984). *The power to lead: The crisis of the American presidency.* New York: Simon & Schuster.

Burns, J. M. (2007). Foreword to R. A. Couto (Ed.), *Reflections on leadership* (pp. v–viii). New York: University Press of America.

Calder, B. J. (1977). An attribution theory of leadership. In B. M. Staw & G. R. Salancik (Eds.), *New directions in organizational behavior* (pp. 179–204). Chicago: St. Clair Press.

Campbell, A., Gurin, G., & Miller, W. E. (1954). *The voter decides.* New York: Harper & Row.

Chaleff, I. (2003). *The courageous follower* (2nd ed.). San Francisco: Berrett-Koehler.

Cohen, R. (2011). Mubarak Agonistes. *New York Times*, Feb. 4, p. A23.

Dean, J. (2003). *Worse than Watergate.* Boston: Houghton-Mifflin.

Dowd, M. (2011). Why is he bi? (Sigh). *New York Times*, June 26, p. SR 5.

Dowd, M. (2011). Tempest in a tea party. *New York Times*, July 31, p. SR 11.

Dowd, M. (2011). One and done? *New York Times*, Sept. 4. p. SR 11.

Dowd, M. (2011). Man in the mirror. *New York Times*, Oct. 5, p. A 25.

Drucker, P. F. (1988). Leadership: More doing than dash. *Wall Street Journal*, Jan. 6, p. 14.

Edelman, M. (1977). *Political language: Words that succeed and policies that fail.* New York: Academic Press.

Fiske, S. T., Bergsieker, H. B., Russell, A.M., & Williams, L. (2009). Images of Black Americans: Then, "Them." And Now, "Obama!" *DuBois Review*, 6(1): 1–19.

Follett, M. P. (1949). The essentials of leadership. In L. Urwick (Ed.), *Freedom and coordination* (pp. 47–60). London: Management Publication Trust.

Freud, S. (1921/1960). *Group psychology and the analysis of the ego.* New York: Bantam. (Originally published in German in 1921.)

Fulbright, J. W. (1966). *The arrogance of power.* New York: Random House.

Gardner, J. W. (1961). *Excellence.* New York: Harper & Row.

Gardner, J. W. (1963). *Self-Renewal: The individual and the innovative society.* New York: Harper & Row.

Gardner, J. W. (1987). Leaders and followers. *Liberal Education,* 73(2): 6–8.

Gardner, J. W. (1990). *On leadership.* New York: Free Press/Macmillan.

Glad, B. (1980). *Jimmy Carter: In search of the great White House.* New York: Norton.

Graham, P. (1995). *Mary Parker Follet: Prophet of management.* Boston: Harvard Business School Press.

Greenberg, S. B. (2010). For Democrats, a win is a win. *New York Times,* Mar. 23, p. A-29.

Harwood, J. (2010). The caucus. *New York Times,* Apr. 5, p. A10.

Harman, S. (2003). *Mind your own business.* New York: Doubleday Currency.

Hayden, T. (2011). In decrying Obama's centrism, Drew Westen ignores role of race. *The Nation,* August.

Heider, F. (1958). *The psychology of interpersonal relations.* New York: Wiley.

Henninger, D. (2011). Obama's cloud economy. *Wall Street Journal,* June 2, p. A-15.

Hogan, R., Curphy, G. J., & Hogan, J. (1994). What we know about leadership: Effectiveness and personality. *American Psychologist,* 49: 493–504.

Hollander, E. P. (1958). Conformity, status, and idiosyncrasy credit. *Psychological Review,* 65: 117–127.

Hollander, E. P. (1964). *Leaders, groups, and influence.* New York: Oxford University Press.

Hollander, E. P. (l978). *Leadership dynamics: A practical guide to effective relationships.* New York: Free Press/Macmillan.

Hollander, E.P. (1983). Paradoxes of presidential leadership: Party, popularity, promise, performance . . . and more. Invited Address to the APA Division of Personality and Social Psychology, Division 8, American Psychological Association Convention, August, Anaheim, CA.

Hollander, E. P. (1992a). The essential interdependence of leadership and followership. *Current Directions in Psychological Science, 1:* 71–75.

Hollander, E. P. (1992b). Leadership, followership, self, and others. *Leadership Quarterly,* 3(1): 43–54.

Hollander, E. P. (2004a, b) Idiosyncrasy credit; Upward influence. Two essays. In G. R. Goethals, G. J. Sorenson, & J. M. Burns (Eds.), *Encyclopedia of leadership* (pp. 695–700, 1605–1609). Thousand Oaks, CA: Sage.

Hollander, E. P. (2006). Influence processes in leadership–followership: Inclusion and the idiosyncrasy credit model. In D. Hantula (Ed.), *Advances in social and organizational psychology.* Mahwah, NJ: Erlbaum.

Hollander, E. P. (2007). Relating leadership to active followership. In R. A. Couto (Ed.), *Reflections on leadership.* Lanham, MD: University Press of America.

Hollander, E. P. (2009). *Inclusive leadership: The essential leader–follower relationship.* New York: Routledge/Psychology Press.

Hollander, E. P. & Julian, J. W. (1969). Contemporary trends in the analysis of leadership processes. *Psychological Bulletin,* 71: 387–397.

Hollander, E. P. & Julian, J. W. (1970). Studies in leader legitimacy, influence, and innovation. In L. Berkowitz (Ed.), *Advances in experimental social psychology,* Volume 5, pp. 33–69. New York: Academic Press.

Hollander, E. P. & Offermann, L. (1990). Power and leadership in organizations: Relationships in transition. *American Psychologist,* 45: 179–189.

Homans, G. C. (1974). *Social behavior: Its elementary forms* (Revised ed.). New York: Harcourt Brace Jovanovich.

Howell, J. M. & Avolio, B. J. (1992). The ethics of charismatic leadership: Submission or liberation? *Academy of Management Executive*, 6(2): 43–54.

Howell, J. M. & Shamir, B. (2005). The role of followers in the charismatic leadership process: Relationships and their consequences. *Academy of Review*, 30(1): 96–112.

Jacobs, T. O. (1970). *Leadership and exchange in formal organizations*. Alexandria, VA: Human Resources Research Organization.

Janis, I. (1972). *Victims of groupthink: A psychological study of foreign policy decisions and fiascos*. Boston: Houghton Mifflin.

Kaiser, R. (1983). *Commentary on "All Things Considered,"* National Public Radio, July 10.

Kaplan, B. & Kaiser, Rob. (2006). *The versatile leader*. San Francisco: Pfeiffer/Wiley.

Katz, E. & Lazarsfeld, P. F. (1955). *Personal influence*. Evanston, IL: Free Press.

Kellerman, B. (1984). *The political presidency*. New York: Oxford University Press.

Kellerman, B. (2008). *Followership: How followers are creating change*. Boston: Harvard Business School Press.

Kelley, R. E. (1988). In praise of followers. *Harvard Business Review* (Nov./Dec.), 88(6): 1–8.

Kelley, R. E. (1992). *The power of followership*. New York: Doubleday.

Kennedy, R. (2011). *The persistence of the color-line: Racial politics and the Obama presidency*. New York: Pantheon.

Kent, M. V. (1996). Leadership. In A. P. Hare, H. H. Blumberg, M. F. Davies, & M. V. Kent (Eds.), *Small groups: An introduction*. Westport, CT: Praeger.

Lakoff, G. (2004). *Don't think of an Elephant!* White River Junction, VT: Chelsea Green.

Laski, H. J. (1940). *The American Presidency: An interpretation*. New York: Grosset & Dunlap.

Lasswell, H. D. (1948). *Power and personality*. New York: W. W. Norton.

Lazarsfeld, P. F., Berelson, B., & Gaudet, H. (1948). *The people's choice* (2nd ed.). New York: Columbia University Press.

Maltin, L. (2006). *Leonard Maltin's 2007 movie guide*. New York: Signet.

McCain, J. (2011). After the shootings, Obama reminds the nation of the golden rule. *Washington Post*, Jan. 16, p. A-17.

McClelland, D. C. (1964). *The roots of consciousness*. New York: Van Nostrand.

McClelland, D. C. (1975). *Power: The inner experience*. New York: Irvington.

McKibben, B. (2011). Quotation of the day. *New York Times*, Sept. 3, p. A2.

Nagourney, A. (2009). A health care debate lesson: Obama plays by Washington's rules. *New York Times*, Dec.26, p. A-14.

Neustadt, R. (1990). *Presidential power and modern presidents* (Revised ed.). New York: Free Press. (Original 1960 from Wiley.)

New York Times. (2010). Editorial, Housing on the brink. Sept. 3, p. A20.

New York Times. (2011). Editorial, President Obama, Reinvigorated. April 14, p. A26.

New York Times. (2011). Editorial, Nearly a year since Dodd-Frank. June 14, p. A24.

New York Times. (2011). Editorial, Obama in Osawatomie. December 7, p. A30.

Newport, F. (2007). *Report on NPR of Gallup national poll results on President Bush* (January 20–21).

Nocera, J. (2011). Banker, can you spare a dime? *New York Times*, Sept. 10, p. A21.

Noonan, P. (2011). Obama and the debt crisis. *Wall Street Journal*, June 4, p. A-15.

Oakes, J. (2009). *Forty-fifth commencement address*. The Graduate Center, City University of New York, May 28. Avery Fisher Hall, Lincoln Center.

Obama, B. H. (1995). *Dreams from my father*. New York: Times Books.

Obama, B. H. (2006), *The Audacity of hope*. New York, NY: Three Rivers Press.

Owen, D. (2007). *The hubris syndrome: Bush, Blair and the intoxication of power*. London: Politico.

Price, T. L. (2008). *Leadership ethics.* New York: Cambridge University Press.

Reedy. G. E. (1970). *The twilight of the presidency.* New York: World Publishing.

Reedy, G. E. (1973). *The presidency in flux.* New York: Columbia University Press.

Reich, R. B. (2010). How to end the great recession. *New York Times*, Sept. 3, p. A- 21.

Remnick, D. (2010). *The bridge.* New York: Knopf.

Rich, F. (2010). Time for this big dog to bite back. *New York Times*, Sept. 12, Week in Review, p. 11.

Rich, F. (2011). The G.O.P.'s post-Tucson traumatic stress disorder. *New York Times*, Feb. 20, Week in Review, p. 12.

Ricks, T. E. (2006) *Fiasco.* New York: Penguin.

Riggio, R. E., Chaleff, I., & Lipman-Blumen, J. (Eds.). (2008). *The art of followership.* San Francisco: Jossey-Bass/Wiley.

Rossiter, C. (1956). *The American presidency.* New York: Harcourt, Brace & World.

Schlesinger, A. M. (1973). *The imperial presidency.* Boston: Houghton Mifflin.

Seaman, F. J., Hollander, E. P., & Richer, L. S. (1975). Candidate preference and economic attitudes in the 1972 presidential election. *American Psychological Association Convention*, September, 1975.

Sharma, D. (2011). Obama in Indonesia and Hawaii. Westport, CT: Praeger.

Simonton, D. K. (2008). Presidential greatness and its socio-psychological significance: Individual or situation? Performance or attribution? In C. Hoyt, G. R. Goethals, & D. Forsyth (Eds.), *Leadership at the crossroads: Vol. 1, Psychology and leadership* (pp. 132–148). Westport, CT: Praeger.

Steele, S. (2011). Obama's unspoken re-election edge. *Wall Street Journal*, May 25, p. A-17.

Stolberg, S. G. (2010). Gentle White House nudges test the power of persuasion. *New York Times*, Feb. 24, p. A-1.

Stolberg, S. G. (2011). And Now, the Cheerleader in Chief. *New York Times*, Jan. 30, p. 3.

Stone, D. (2010), Hail to the chiefs. *Newsweek*, Nov. 22, pp. 29–33.

The Onion. (2008). Black man gets nation's worst job, Nov. 5, p. 1.

Thomas, E. (2010).Truth or consequences. *Newsweek*, Nov. 22, pp. 34–37.

Tucker, R. C. (1981). *Politics as leadership.* Columbia, MO: University of Missouri Press.

Turner, R. H. (1969). The public perception of protest. *American Sociological Review*, 34: 815–831.

Valenti, J. (2007). *This time, this place.* New York: Harmony Books.

Van Vugt, M., Hogan, R., & Kaiser, R. B. (2008). Leadership, followership, and evolution. *American Psychologist*, 63(3): 1896.

Verba, S. (1961). *Small groups and political behavior: A study of leadership.* Princeton, NJ: Princeton University Press.

Weber, M. (1947). *The theory of social and economic organization* (Translated and edited by T. Parsons & A. M. Henderson). New York: Oxford University Press.

Weisberg, J. (2008). *The Bush tragedy.* New York: Random House.

Westen, D. (2007). *Political brain.* New York: Perseus.

Westen, D. (2011). What happened to Obama? *New York Times*, Aug, 7, p. SR-1.

Wilentz, S. (2010). Obama's fateful choice. *New York Daily News*, Jan. 17, pp. 34–35.

Wills, G. (1994). *Certain trumpets: The nature of leadership.* New York: Simon & Schuster.

Wills, G. (2010). *Bomb power: The modern presidency and the national security state.* New York: Penguin.

Winter, D. G. (1973). *The power motive.* New York: Free Press.

Zuckerman, M. (2011). Obama and the "competency crisis." *Wall Street Journal*, Aug. 25, p. A15.

Author Index

Subject Index